Asia Through the Back Door

Fourth Edition

**Rick Steves
and
Bob Effertz
with John Gottberg**

John Muir Publications
Santa Fe, New Mexico

John Muir Publications, P. O. Box 613, Santa Fe, NM 87504

Fourth edition. First printing June 1993

ISSN 1068-4352
ISBN 1-56261-109-7

Distributed to the book trade by
W. W. Norton & Company, Inc.
New York, New York

Maps: Dave Hoerlein and Janine Tejwaney
Photography: John Gottberg, Rick Steves, Bob Effertz, Rich Sorensen,
Risa Laib, Melinda Williams, Mark Smith, Nick Halpin, and Mike Barton
Other Writing Contributors: Melinda Williams (who wrote "The Woman
Traveling Alone," the Lombok and Sulawesi Back Doors, and revised
other Indonesian Back Doors), Nick Halpin (who wrote the "Dharamsala"
Back Door), and Risa Laib (much editing and travel savvy).
Research Assistance: Teresa Anderson, Dr. Stacy Globerman, Dr. Eric
Weiss, Claire McIntyre, Laurie Rich, Cathy Lanham, Bill and Jean
Chaplin, Diane Abeyta, Pramila Luthra of Asian Sky Travel Service, and
Luke Shepherd.
Editor: Sheila Berg
Cover: Jennifer Dewey and Peter Aschwanden
Typography: Ken Wilson, John Muir Publications
Printed by: Malloy Lithographing

All royalty payments earned from the sale of this book are given by the
authors to Bread for the World, Oxfam, and other nonprofit Third World
development and relief organizations.

Thanks to my parents for their encouragement, whatever I did, and to many for their support: Nick, Harry, Deb, Dave, among others, Mark and John for allowing time off from work, and Rick for his great encouragement.

—Bob Effertz

Thanks to my parents for dragging me out of the U.S.A. for the first time, to my wife, Anne, for making it possible to travel without leaving home, and to Emi Sato for genki-ness.

—Rick Steves

To
the People of Asia
and
to those who will
broaden their perspectives
through Asian
travel

Contents

Part Two: Thirty Asian Back Doors

Contents   179

Back Door Travel Philosophy

Spending money has very little to do with enjoying your trip. In fact, the more you spend, the farther you'll get from the real Asia. If you spend enough, you can surround yourself with other Westerners. You'll go through Asia's grand front entrance, receiving polite, formal—often stuffy—treatment. But going through the back door . . . well, that's a different story.

Traveling through the back door, we become temporary Asians. We approach Asia on its level, accepting its way of life, appreciating its different ways. A warm, relaxed, personable Asia welcomes us as intimate friends.

Most people enter Asia through the front door out of fear. It's a natural fear of the unknown—of the language, the alien culture, the risk of illness. To stay with the familiar, they sign onto a five-day Tokyo–Hong Kong tour or board a cruise ship to dance and dine from Bangkok to Bali. They buy themselves out of the risk, out of the difficulties, and sadly, out of the experience. From fear, they join a busload of tourists viewing Bangkok from a window, instead of sitting between a monk and a Thai businessman on a water taxi plying the brown Chao Phraya river.

This book will help you conquer the fears and apprehensions that inhibit travelers. Most people, with a little knowledge and some travel skills, can make their own way around Asia and actually enjoy it. You'll see a variety of people on the road: secretaries, teachers, students, factory workers, nurses, real estate agents, retired singles and couples. They are not Marco Polos but just extraordinary people like you who decided to break out of their routine.

You wonder, "But can I afford to travel?" Affording travel is a matter of priorities. Many people who "can't afford a trip" could sell their car and travel for two years. A friend who sits on $3,000 worth of living room furniture marvels at Rick's ability to come up with the money to travel. A relative who hasn't taken a vacation in twenty years wonders at Bob's occasional "disappearing acts." We feel we can't afford not to travel. We keep our overhead to a minimum and spend our free time and money roaming the world.

You can travel through most of Asia for $20 a day, excluding plane fares. A tight budget forces you to travel "close to the ground," meeting and communicating with the people, not relying on service with a purchased smile. We never sacrifice sleep, nutrition, safety, or cleanliness in the name of budget. We enjoy—and prefer—the local alternatives to expensive hotels and restaurants. We travel better because—not in spite of—our tight budget.

The first half of this book will teach you the skills you'll need to travel in Asia. You'll save time and money by learning from our mistakes rather than your own.

It's important to go slowly in Asia. Don't plan a whirlwind tour of all the Asian countries. You'll remember little, experience little, and get worn out. Ideally, if you have three weeks, spend it in one or two countries. Focus on a few areas and really get to know the people and the places. If you stay at least four or five days in one spot, you'll stop by your favorite restaurant and the owner will ask, "The usual?" You'll have a chance to deepen your relationships with the local people and other travelers. You'll have time to relax and feel the rhythm of the daily life.

We have found that if we don't enjoy a place, it's often because we don't know enough about it. Avoid tourist traps. Go to the small unknown shrines in Kyoto, and bicycle past thatch-roofed houses in the Indonesian countryside.

In the last half of the book, we'll give you the keys to some of Asia's most exciting back doors, our favorite discoveries, places where you can see Asia, not just other tourists.

A culture is legitimized by its existence. Give people the benefit of your open mind. We really have no right to ridicule a starving Hindu for not eating his fat cow. It's natural—but incorrect—to measure the world by America's yardstick of cultural values. We try to understand and accept without judging.

Of course, travel, like the world, is a series of hills and valleys. Be fanatically positive. Remember that a Bangkok traffic jam is so much more fun than those back home. Optimism is a mental discipline.

Travel is addictive. It can make you a happier American as well as a citizen of the world. Our Earth is home to five billion equally important people. That's wonderfully humbling. Globe-trotting destroys ethnocentricity and encourages the understanding and appreciation of various cultures. Travel changes people, and we like the results. Many travelers assimilate the best points of different cultures into their own character.

Let Asia welcome you. Be touched by its temples, moved by its mountains, romanced by its religions. So now we invite you to raise your travel dreams to their upright and locked position and travel with us . . . through the back door.

Part One
Basic Travel Skills

1
Planning and Preparation

The more you plan and prepare, the better your trip will be. An Asian adventure is a major investment of time and money. Those who invest wisely enjoy fabulous returns.

Tour versus Independent Travel

One of the first big decisions to make is whether to travel alone or with a group. Consider the pros and cons of each. The proper decision requires some introspection: Do you want the security of knowing that all your rooms are reserved and that a guide will take you smoothly from one hotel to the next? Do you require "normal" Western-style hotels and restaurant meals? Will you forgo adventure, independence, and the challenge of doing it on your own to take the worry and bother out of your travels? Is sitting on a bus (or boat or airplane) with the same group of tourists an acceptable way to spend your vacation? If the answer to these questions is "Yes," then you need a good tour company to show you Asia. Your travel agent can help you.

For people who like to go first class, tours can be the most economical way to see Asia. Without a tour, three restaurant meals a day and a big modern hotel are expensive. Large tour companies book thousands of rooms, meals, and flights year-round and can, with their tremendous economic clout, get prices that no individual tourist could even come close to. For instance, the 1993 price for a 14-day tour of the Orient offered by Maupintour, a well-known American company, is $2,968, or $214 a day (excluding airfare from the U.S.). While that price might at first glance seem absurdly high, don't forget that Asia is a vast continent, and distances between key destinations are measured in thousands of miles. This journey includes several international flights within Asia, 14 nights at five-star hotels, three hot meals a day, all land transportation, and the services of English-speaking Asian guides. Considering that each five-star hotel alone would have cost the tourist off the street between $100 and $150, the all-inclusive price is a bargain. Such comfort these days is far more expensive without a tour. (To get the most out of your tour, read Self-Defense on Guided Tours in chap. 10.)

But there are far cheaper ways to see Asia. The cheapest and, for us, the best is to travel independently. To the independent traveler, Asia can be a rewarding challenge and adventure as well as an enjoyable vacation at $20 per day ($50 in Japan) plus airfares. While the tour groups that unload on Asia's cities are treated as an entity—a profitable mob to be fed, shown around, and moved out—the individual traveler enjoys the personal side of international travel. From this point on, this book will focus mainly on the skills of do-it-yourself Asian travel.

But if you're destined for a tour, read on. Even on a bus with fifty other people, you can and should be in control—thinking as an independent tourist, not a prisoner in vagabondage.

Alone or with a Friend?

The independent traveler must weigh the advantages and disadvantages of traveling alone or with a friend. Traveling alone gives you complete freedom and independence. You never need to consider what your partner wants to see, where he wants to go, how fast he wants to travel, when he's tired, or how much he wants to spend. You go where you want to, when you want to. You will meet more people when you travel alone for two reasons: you are more accessible in the eyes of an Asian, and loneliness will drive you to reach out and make friends. When you're traveling with someone, it's just too easy to focus on your partner and forget about meeting the locals.

Solo travel is intensely personal. Without the comfortable crutch of a friend, you're more likely to know the joys of self-discovery and the pleasures found in the kindness of strangers. You'll be exploring yourself as well as a new city or country.

Traveling alone can be lonely. Hotel rooms become silent cells, and meals are served in a puddle of silence. Big cities can be cold and ugly when the only person you have to talk to is yourself. Being sick alone in a country where no one even knows you exist is an experience you'll try to forget.

However, Asia is full of solo travelers, and there are many natural meeting places. You're likely to find a partner in a guest house, a museum, a train or bus station. Budget travelers tend to follow a few well-worn paths through Asia, and your paths will converge.

There are some advantages to traveling with a partner. Shared experiences can be more fun: the highs are higher, and the lows are more tolerable.

India: You'll never walk alone

Traveling with a partner is cheaper. Rarely does a double room cost as much as two singles. In many countries, the rooms are so reasonable this may not amount to much unless you're on an extended trip. However, in places like Hong Kong, a single room may cost $30 and a double room $40—a savings of $10 a night per person. Those traveling in pairs are able to split the cost of travel guides, maps, magazines, taxis, storage lockers, and much more. Besides expenses, they can share the burden of time-consuming hassles. For example, only one person has to stand in ticket or bank lines.

Remember, traveling together greatly accelerates a relationship, especially a romantic one. You see each other constantly and make endless decisions. Niceties go out the window, and everything becomes very real. You are in an adventure—and a struggle—together. You can jam the experiences of years into one summer, for better or worse.

Both of us would have been scared to death to marry someone we hadn't traveled with. A mutual travel experience is unreasonably stressful on a relationship, revealing its ultimate course in a hurry. It's the greatest way to get to know somebody in every conceivable sense.

Your choice of a travel partner is crucial. It can make or break a trip. Traveling with the wrong partner can be like a two-month computer date. Before you go abroad with someone, analyze your travel styles and goals for compatibility. Consider a trial weekend together before merging your dream trips.

Rick once took a vacation to dive into as many cultures and adventures as possible. The trip was a challenge, and he planned to rest when he got home. His partner wanted to get away from it all, to relax and escape the pressures of the business world. Their ideas of acceptable hotels and good meals were quite different. The trip was a near-disaster.

Bob had a more successful experience. He left home with two friends with the understanding that they would split up when necessary to follow personal interests or just to have time apart. Several times, they branched off for a few days or a few weeks. They decided when and where they would meet up.

This "split and be independent" strategy can be valuable advice for anyone—even married couples. To minimize the stress of traveling together, it's important to recognize each other's individuality and need for independence. There's absolutely nothing dangerous, insulting, or wrong with taking time alone, but it's a freedom too few travel partners exercise. After you do your own thing for a few hours, or even days, your togetherness will be fun again.

Another way to minimize stress is to go communal with your money. Separate checks, double bank charges, and long lists of petty IOUs in six different currencies are a needless pain. Pool your resources, noting how much each person contributes, and just assume everything equals out in the long run. Keep track of major individual expenses, but don't worry about who got an extra postcard or sushi. Enjoy treating each other to taxis and dinner out of your kitty, and after the trip, divvy up what's left. If one person consumed $25 or $30 more, that's a small price to pay for the convenience of communal money.

Traveling in a threesome or foursome can be troublesome. Too many minds spell power struggles and petty jealousies. The "split and be independent" philosophy is particularly valuable here. Besides, when you're hitchhiking through Malaysia, you can't really expect the driver of that Mercedes to squeeze you all in the back seat.

Travel Styles and Purpose

You must consider your travel style before you plan your trip. Rick likes to fit a lot into his trips; thus, he spends time organizing and plans out every day. Bob, however, likes to go slow and has the philosophy, "I don't know if I want to stay until I get there." He often has a general idea of what he wants to do, buys a one-way ticket, and works out his plans as he goes. Either way is fine. But the former requires more advance research and planning.

"Purpose" is a loaded word. It means a lot of things to a lot of people. And it's something to consider before starting out. On the train from Delhi, every other person will ask you, "What is your purpose in coming to India?" And if you know, your trip to India and throughout Asia will be more focused and therefore richer.

The purpose of travel is as broad as life. Some people want to simply rest and relax after a stressful year. Others may want to pursue an interest, such as studying a religion or trekking in the mountains. Or it could be a combination of things. Understanding your purpose gives your planning a target.

Before Bob's last trip, he considered his purpose and set priorities. He wanted to get to know the locals as well as other travelers on a more personal level. He was also interested in Buddhism and Hinduism and in learning to play the Indian drums, the tabla. To get to know others more intimately, he decided to limit himself to a few places and stay a while. During three months in India, he spent a month meditating at a Buddhist temple in Bodhgaya, several weeks in Varanasi, and a month at a Hindu ashram in Rishikesh. While in Rishikesh, he studied the tabla. He stayed long enough in each place to develop some local friendships and also some strong connections with other travelers who had a similar purpose.

Before you start planning, consider that word—"purpose." If you prepare for the inevitable question from the Indian across the aisle on the train, you're more likely to have a satisfying journey.

Itinerary Planning

After you set your goals, make an itinerary. We never start a trip without a general plan. An itinerary forces you to consider your purpose and priorities. For instance, you have three weeks and want a leisurely trip to Thailand and Nepal. In planning, you find that once you fit in all your destinations, you have only two days on the beach to relax. You decide that hanging out on an island in Thailand is important and cut out Nepal. So you call your travel agent, get a round-trip ticket to Thailand, and put away the hiking gear.

Establish a logical travel plan. Your trip will better meet your needs if you consider potential problems with tourist crowds, culture shock, fatigue, weather, and inefficient transportation.

Here are ten points to consider in designing your itinerary.

1. Asian travel can be very time-consuming. For starters, compare distances in Asia to those in Europe or the United States. The air mileage from Tokyo to Singapore is about 3,700 miles, greater than the distance from Miami to Seattle or from London to Egypt. You'll quickly realize the importance of eliminating needless travel time and expense.

Few quick and efficient overland connections exist between Asian countries. In many cases, the only way to go is by air or sea. Fortunately, there are liberal and inexpensive stopover opportunities by air. (For more information, see chap. 2, Transportation.)

With the exception of Japan and its super Shinkansen, trains are much less reliable than in Europe. And in most less-developed countries, roads are one step above primitive and bus travel is slow. Allot extra time to cover the delays you're almost certain to encounter. For example, on the island of Flores in Indonesia, it took us five hours to get to our destination 35 miles away. This included the hunt for the bus as well as the slow, jarring ride on the chuckholed dirt road. Fortunately, this is not the norm, but allow time for problems and delays.

2. Make the most of the weather conditions you'll encounter. India and Southeast Asia are cooler and drier from October to March. China and Japan are best in the autumn and spring. Many islands in Indonesia are drier in the summer. These may be the best overall times to visit these places, but consider your purpose. Summer in India is monsoon season, but if you want to hike the Indian Himalayas, summer is the best time for your trip. For more about climates, see Nitty Gritty, Country by Country near the end of this book.

Careful climate planning is especially useful for long trips. For example, if you have six months in Asia, you might consider this. Start with a hike in Nepal during November when the air is cooler and clear for mountain views. Fly from Kathmandu to southern India in December when the weather is also cooler and dry. Head up to northern India during January as the chilly nights are warming. Fly to Thailand in February when the days are warm but not too hot. Travel in Southeast Asia until late March, then head to Japan to catch the cherry blossom season.

3. Save your good health. The Indian subcontinent has the worst track record for health disorders, notably, "Delhi Belly," so consider scheduling your stay in India near the end of your trip. If you get ill, you can recover at home missing work, not vacation.

No matter where you travel in Asia (with the exception of large Westernized cities like Singapore and those of Japan), you must take special care in your eating, drinking, and sanitation habits. (See chap. 7, Health.)

4. Consider your equipment. For hiking in many parts of Asia, you'll need to bring backpacking gear (except in Nepal where you can rent most items). If possible, do your hiking first. You not only take advantage of good health on arrival but you can also save yourself the hassle of hauling all that equipment around Asia. Once you've finished hiking, you can sell your gear, mail it home, or send it home as unaccompanied baggage on the plane.

If you decide to hike later in your trip, plan to leave your gear with the manager of your hotel or guest house. For example, on a recent trip, we left our hiking gear in the locked storage room of a guest house in Bangkok. We then explored Thailand and Malaysia with a light load. We returned to Bangkok to pick up our gear and flew to Nepal.

5. Punctuate a long trip with rest periods. Alternate between countryside and city. There are few things more grueling than extended travel through Asia—or any Third World region, for that matter—by local transport. Not only is the bus (or its alternative) exhausting but the brain is drained by trying to absorb a whole new set of unfamiliar cultural standards. We try to take one day off a week to do nothing in particular. If your trip is six weeks or longer, schedule a vacation from your vacation in the middle of it. Recharge your touristic battery by spending several days in a place where you couldn't see a museum or take a tour even if you wanted to. A stop on an island or in the mountains, on a lake or in a friendly rural town, or a visit with friends or relatives is a great way to revitalize your traveler's spirit.

6. Leave some slack in your itinerary. Everyday chores, small business matters, and transportation problems can add up to about a day a week.

Every Asian trip needs some slack time for just hanging around

7. Hit as many festivals and national holidays as you can. This takes some study. Ask the national tourist office of each country you'll visit for a calendar of events. (See our listing of festivals in the Appendix. National Tourist Offices are listed under each country in the Nitty Gritty section.) An effort to be in the right place at the right time is worth the trouble. Keep in mind that during holidays and festivals, businesses may be closed and transportation will be crowded. Do any business before the celebration starts, and try to plant yourself in one place until it's over.

· **8. Don't overestimate your powers of absorption.** Whether it's your first trip or your fiftieth, Asian travel is intense. Your senses are continually assailed by new sights, sounds, and smells. Each day is packed with incredible memories and experiences. It may be fantastic, but it can wear down your body. You have a saturation point. Rare is the tourist who doesn't become somewhat jaded after six or eight weeks of travel. Don't burn out on mediocre temples and museums. Be selective. Save your energy for the biggies.

9. See the countries first which are the least exotic culturally. For instance, if you plan to see Japan, Hong Kong, Thailand, and India, do it in that order so you'll ease into the more intense and difficult travel. If you make that trip in reverse order, you'll risk being bored by the orderliness of Hong Kong and Japan after the chaos of India.

10. Assume you will return. This Douglas MacArthur approach is a key to tourist happiness. You will never satisfy your thirst for Asia with one trip. Don't try to. Enjoy what you're seeing. Forget what you're missing. If you worry about things that are just out of reach, you won't appreciate what's at hand. Between the two of us, we've spent well over four years of our lives traveling in most of the countries of Asia, and we still need more time. It is a blessing that we can never see all of Asia.

Weigh and juggle these ten factors until you arrive at a plan that gives you the optimal mix. There are always trade-offs. Design the trip that best fits your needs.

Your Best Itinerary—In Ten Steps

1. Set goals. Decide what you want most out of your trip.

2. Study. Read up on Asia, and talk to travelers. What you want to see and do is determined by what you know.

3. List all the places you want to see, and then prioritize. Get as specific as possible.

4. List your sights in logical order. Consider the climate and your mode of transportation, and develop an efficient travel plan (minimizing miles).

5. Determine what is reasonable, and do no more. This is the hardest step. Assume you'll return.

6. Write in the number of days you'd like to stay in each place. So you get a feel for each stop, minimize one-night stands. Plan at least a week in each country. This is the bare minimum to get to know the culture. Allow for transportation time.

7. Minimize redundancy. Unless you're focusing on Hindu architecture, pick two ancient temple sites in India, not ten. Have a reason for every stop. Don't go to places just because they're famous.

8. Cut and trim. Adjust your itinerary to fit your time limit.

9. Fine tune. Ask your travel agent which flight departure days are cheapest. Be sure crucial sights are open the day you're in town. Maximize festival and market days. Fill out a day-by-day itinerary.

10. Resist the temptation to clutter your itinerary with additional sights. Be satisfied with your efficient plan and focus study and preparation on those places only.

Sample Itinerary Worksheet

Following is the process we suggest you go through in planning your trip (unless you want to just play it by ear).

Step 1. Set goals. You're interested in Southeast Asian culture. You want to relax. You like to hike and swim.

Step 2. Study. Read guidebooks on Southeast Asia.

Step 3. List places and prioritize. Your choices are:
1) Thailand: Bangkok, Ko Samui and Ko Phi Phi islands.
2) Indonesia: Yogyakarta and Mt. Bromo on Java island, Ubud and Kuta beach on Bali island.
3) Malaysia: Penang Island and Cameron Highlands.
4) Singapore.

Steps 4 to 6. List sights in logical order, and figure out what is reasonable considering the time you have available. You can get off work for 21 days. Consulting travel books and a travel agent, you come up with this outline:

1 day	Fly to Thailand
1 day	Bangkok
1 day	Travel to Ko Samui
2 days	Ko Samui—beach
1 day	Travel to Ko Phi Phi

1 day	Ko Phi Phi—beach
1 day	Travel to Penang Island, Malaysia
1 day	Penang Island—beach and city
1 day	Travel to Cameron Highlands
1 day	Cameron Highlands—hike
1 day	Travel to Singapore
1 day	Singapore
1 day	Travel to Yogyakarta, Java
1 day	Yogyakarta
1 day	Travel to Mt. Bromo
1 day	Mt. Bromo—hike
1 day	Travel to Bali
1 day	Kuta beach, Bali
1 day	Ubud, Bali
1 day	Fly home

———

21 days

It all fits, but out of 21 days, you'll spend 10 days on the road. You'll get only 3 days to relax at a beach. By the time you get home, you'll need two weeks to recover. One of your goals was to relax. Is this really what you want? Repeat steps 4 through 6.

Steps 7 and 8. Minimize redundancy, and cut and trim. Consider your goals and priorities. You decide to skip Java. It's tough, because it was a high priority, but you'd want at least a week there. With the efficiency of working stopovers into your flight plan, it's quick and easy to add a quick stopover in Bali.

1 day	Fly to Thailand (top priority)
3 days	Bangkok and vicinity
1 day	Travel to Ko Samui by bus
4 days	Ko Samui island (goal to relax and swim)
———	Drop Ko Phi Phi (redundant, another beach)
———	Drop Penang Island (redundant)
1 day	Travel to Cameron Highlands, Malaysia
3 days	Cameron Highlands—hike (goal to hike)
1 day	Travel to Singapore by bus
1 day	Singapore
1 day	Fly to Bali
4 days	Ubud and Kuta beach (goal to see Bali)
1 day	Fly home

———

21 days

Steps 9 and 10. Fine tune and focus. Check out the fine points of what you want to do at each destination. For example:

Day 1	Fly to Bangkok. Arrive late at night. Take taxi to town and stay at Shanti guest house.
Day 2	Enjoy a free morning settling in. See nearby Grand Palace and Wat Phra Keo temple in the afternoon.
Day 3	Get an early start. Take the water taxi along the river in Bangkok. Stop at the Wat Po and Wat Arun temples. Hire a boat to cruise the canals. Just wander and visit the markets. Go to a Thai dance performance at night.
Day 4	You timed the trip to spend the weekend in Bangkok. Visit weekend market.

Playing It by Ear

If you don't want to hassle with an itinerary, just pick the country or countries you want to visit. Consider the weather, especially if you're planning to hike. If you really want to leave things open for change, buy a one-way ticket. You can get reasonable fares for the return in many Asian cities. If you have a round-trip ticket, you are either forced to follow the routing or buy another ticket.

If you have several months, a loosely planned trip is ideal; you can respond to your mood. If you've had enough of the beach in Thailand, head for the mountains of Nepal. If you've met up with a traveler you like in Malaysia, you can drop your original plans for Indonesia, and head together to Sri Lanka.

Red Tape, Visas, and Other Bureaucratic Hassles

Nothing can foul up an itinerary faster than arriving at the immigration counter at an airport and discovering that your paperwork isn't in order.

For a short trip, get your visas ahead of time. Write to the embassy of the country you want to visit, requesting a visa application. After you receive the application, fill it out, and send it back with your passport, the fee, and required photographs via registered mail (don't even think of using ordinary first class). Remember to enclose an envelope—stamped, self-addressed, certified, with registered mail postage—for the return of your documents. Allow an average of two weeks turnaround time for each visa you intend to get.

On an extended trip, in which your flight plans are open-ended and you aren't 100 percent sure when you want to leave one country and head for the next, obtain visas as you travel. Almost every Asian country has an embassy in almost every Asian capital; call ahead to find out what hours the embassy is processing visa applications, then just drop by. But on a short trip, there's no point spending a full half-day chasing bureaucrats when you can get the visas in advance.

Throughout Asia, as far as quarantine regulations go, you must show proof of immunization against cholera, smallpox, or yellow fever if you are coming from an area infected with those diseases.

Valid passports are required for all countries. Visa requirements are given in Nitty Gritty, Country by Country near the end of this book. Political conditions can change requirements, so check current regulations with your travel agent, individual embassies, or the U.S. State Department.

Other documentation worth carrying includes an International Health Certificate (see chap. 7), a photocopy of your birth certificate, an International Driver's License (see chap. 2), an International Youth Hostel card (see chap. 3), and—if you qualify—an International Student Identification Card (ISIC). The student card doesn't earn the discounts it once did, since every petty counterfeiter from Hong Kong south runs them off his garage assembly line and sells them to over-aged tourists for $10 a shot. But if you can get the real McCoy from your school, it's worth the investment.

Life Left Behind

When we leave home, we don't plan to have problems on our trip, but we do plan ahead in case we do. Consider the following if you're going on a long trip.

Leave an itinerary and expected return date with a friend or relative. Leave photocopies of important documents such as the personal data page from your passport, traveler's check numbers, and airline ticket number. If you lose these items, this information will help speed up the reissue.

Consider assigning power of attorney to one of us or someone you trust. This will allow that person to look after your business and financial affairs and unexpected matters that might come up.

If you're storing your car at home during your trip, reduce your auto insurance to the minimum comprehensive coverage possible.

This is a small portion of the full coverage amount, and it is easy to reestablish full coverage on your return. Don't cancel the policy; once off the insurance company's records, it may be difficult to regain good and reasonable coverage, especially on older vehicles.

Jet Lag and the First Day of Your Trip

Start your trip on a happy note by leaving home rested and by minimizing the symptoms of jet lag. Flying halfway around the world is stressful. Having your days turned topsy-turvy by an international date line crossing doesn't help. If you leave frazzled after a hectic last night and wild bon voyage party, there's a good chance you won't be healthy for the first part of your trip. Just a hint of a cold, coupled with the stress of a long flight, will mean a sniffly first week. Once you're on the road, it's hard to slow down enough to fight that cold.

An early-trip cold was a regular part of our vacations until we learned an important trick. Plan as if you're leaving two days before you really are. Keep that last 48-hour period sacred, even if it means being hectic before your false departure date. Then, even if you still have to go to work, you have two orderly, peaceful days after you're packed and physically ready to fly. Mentally, you'll be comfortable about leaving home and starting this adventure. You'll fly away well rested and ready to enjoy the cultural bombardment that will follow.

Jet lag is the next hurdle to handle for a happy holiday. Anyone who flies through time zones has to grapple with this biorhythmic confusion. When you switch your wristwatch 16 to 18 hours forward—which it helps to do immediately on boarding your flight—your body says, "Hey, what's going on?" Body clocks don't reset so easily. All your life you've done things in a 24-hour cycle. Now, after crossing the Pacific, your body wants to eat when you tell it to sleep and sleep when you tell it to enjoy a temple or museum. You can't avoid jet lag, but with a few tips, you can minimize its symptoms.

Leave home well rested. You dehydrate during a long flight, so drink plenty of liquids. The flight attendants learn to keep us well supplied with orange juice. (Ask for two glasses, no ice.) Alcohol is stressful to your body and will aggravate jet lag. The in-flight movie is good for one thing—nap time. If you can't sleep, close your eyes and fake it. With a few hours of sleep during the transoceanic flight, you'll be functional the day you land. Get some exercise during the flight by hiking a few plane-laps. On arrival, make yourself stay awake until an early local bedtime. Your body may beg for sleep, but refuse. Jet lag hates exercise, bright daylight, and fresh air. Get out and walk. You must force your body's transition to the local time. After a solid night's sleep, you should wake up feeling, if not like super-tourist, at least functional.

Too many people assume their first day will be made worthless by jet lag. Don't prematurely condemn yourself to zombiedom. Many travelers can enjoy very productive, even hyper, first days. Jet lag is a joke to some and a major problem to others. It's hard to predict how serious your jet lag will be. Our personal experience is that it's tougher going west-to-east (losing hours) than traveling east-to-west (gaining hours). Those who keep strict 24-hour schedules will probably feel more jet lag than those who work swing shifts or keep crazy hours.

You'll read about many jet lag "cures." Most aren't worth the trouble. Just leave unfrazzled, minimize jet lag's symptoms, and give yourself a chance to enjoy your trip from the moment you step off the plane.

Packing Light to Avoid Vagabondage

The importance of packing light cannot be overemphasized. But for your own good, we'll try. It's heaven or hell, and the choice is yours. The measure of a good traveler is how light he or she travels. In Asia, there are two kinds of travelers—those who pack light, and those who wish they did.

Limit yourself to 20 pounds in a carryon-size bag (9" x 22" x 14" fits under the seat of an airplane or in the overhead luggage rack on a Japanese train). You're probably muttering, "Impossible," but believe us, it can be done. After you enjoy that sweet mobility and freedom, you'll never go any other way.

You'll walk with your luggage more than you think. Before leaving home, give yourself a test. Pack up completely, go into your hometown, and be a tourist for an hour. Fully loaded, you should enjoy window shopping. If you can't, go home and thin out.

When you carry your own luggage, it's less likely to get lost, damaged, or stolen. It sits on your lap or under your seat on the bus, taxi, and airplane. You don't have to worry about it, and when you arrive at an airport, you leave—immediately. It's a good feeling. When we land in Hong Kong, we are downtown before anyone else on the plane knows if their bags made it.

Too much luggage will dictate your style of travel. The "back door" is slammed shut, and changing locations becomes a major operation. Porters are a problem only to those who need them. One bag hanging on your back is nearly forgotten. Take this advice seriously. Don't be one of thousands of tourists who return home cursing their luggage and vowing never again to travel with so much stuff.

Packing light for a footloose and fancy-free trip

Backpackademia—What to Bring?

How do you fit a whole trip's worth of luggage into a small suitcase or rucksack? The answer is simple: bring very little.

Spread out everything you think you'll need on the living room floor. Pick up each item and scrutinize it critically. Ask yourself, "Will I really use this set of snorkel and fins enough to justify carrying it around all summer?" Not "Will I use it?" but "Will I use it enough?" We would rent a set in Bali before we would carry that extra weight through the Himalayas.

Think in terms of what you can do without, not what will be handy on your trip. The key rule is, "When in doubt, leave it out." We've seen people pack a whole summer's supply of deodorant, nylons, or razor blades, thinking they can't buy these overseas. Asians, especially city dwellers with a little money, have these American "necessities." The world is getting so small. You'll find Colgate toothpaste in Jakarta. You can get anything in urban Asia. Tourist shops in major international hotels are a sure bet whenever you have difficulty finding some personal item. Remember to experiment! Trying a strange brand of Pakistani toothpaste can be as memorable as a Chinese dim sum breakfast. Live off the land with relish.

With this "live off the land" approach, we pack exactly the same for a three-week or a three-month trip.

Rucksack or Suitcase?

Whether you take a small suitcase with a shoulder strap (wheels are silly) or a rucksack is up to you. This chapter applies equally to suitcase or rucksack travelers. Most young travelers go the rucksack route. If you are a "suitcase person" who would like the ease of a rucksack without forgoing the "respectability" of a suitcase, look into convertible suitcase/rucksacks with zip-away shoulder straps. These carryon-size bags give you the best of both worlds. (See the Back Door Catalog at the end of this book.)

We once carried frame packs because we had sleeping bags. Unless you plan to camp or sleep out a lot—something not very practical in most parts of Asia—a sleeping bag is a bulky security blanket. Even on a low budget, bedding will be provided. And sleeping bags can be rented in some hiking areas such as Nepal and Kashmir. We would rather risk being cold one or two nights out of the trip than carry our sleeping bags for 10 weeks.

Without a sleeping bag, a medium-size rucksack is plenty big. Start your trip with it only two-thirds full to leave room for picnic food and little souvenirs. And remember, bags never pack quite as nicely once you actually start living out of them. Sturdy stitching, front and side pouches, padded shoulder straps, and a low-profile color are rucksack virtues.

Clothing

The bulk of your luggage is clothing. Minimize by bringing less and washing more often. There is no need for a huge travel wardrobe (unless you enjoy carrying a bag full of dirty laundry). Every night you will spend five minutes doing a little washing in your hotel sink. This does not mean more washing; it just means doing a little washing as you go along.

It's worth starting out light so you can buy clothes along the way. And the type available is usually cheaper and in hot climates, more comfortable than what you'll find at home. Many countries now cater to tourist tastes. Bob stocks up on cotton Gucci pants in Bangkok (perfect imitations down to the counterfeit label). There are some wonderful batik-patterned clothes ready-made in Southeast Asia. And throughout Asia, you can find inexpensive tailors. Fabric shops have a fine array of cotton, silk, wool, and blends. If you want to blend in, wear the local-style clothes. In India, both men and women wear tunic tops and loose-fitting pajama pants—a cheap, comfortable, and respectable suit for travel.

Recommended Clothing

For summer travel (or year-round in the tropics), we recommend:

Two pairs of long pants—one lightweight pair and one extremely
lightweight pair, both made of cotton. Jeans are tight and too hot.
One pair of short pants.
Two T-shirts or short-sleeved shirts.
Long-sleeved shirt.
Dark, warm sweater—never looks wrinkled and is always dark, no
matter how dirty.
Light, waterproof windbreaker—folds quickly into a pocket. Under-
wear and socks—four sets, quick dry.
One pair of shoes—sturdy Vibram-type sole, good traction, well
broken in, light and cool.
Swimsuit for the beaches.
Teva-type sports sandals.
Wraparound skirt for women.

For travel in the mountains or winter travel in China and Japan,
you'll need warmer clothing. We suggest a down or synthetic coat,
medium- to heavy-weight pants, long johns, gloves, and an extra set of
socks and underwear (clothes dry slower in cold weather). If you're
trekking in the mountains, especially in late fall through early spring,
bring wool pants, shirt, and hat (see the Nepal Back Door on
trekking.) Pack with the help of our climate chart (see Appendix).

In many parts of Asia, shorts are considered improper or risque
(especially on women), though they are fine at the beach and touristy
areas and for lounging around the hotel.

Asia is casual. We have never felt out of place at Kabuki shows or
dance-dramas wearing clean pants and a good-looking sweater. Obviously, there are some situations where more formal attire would be in
order, but the casual tourist rarely encounters these. If you want to
dress up, throw in a tie or a scarf to wear with a sweater.

Bring dark clothes that wash and dry quickly and easily. Test your
clothes by hand-washing and wringing them dry at home before you
leave. You should have no trouble drying clothing overnight in your
hotel room. We know this sounds barbaric, but our bodies dry out a
damp pair of socks or a shirt in a jiffy. Most guest houses and hotels
will also do laundry for you. But remember, Marco Polo managed a
long trip with only a rare laundromat.

Other Things to Bring

Money belt (or neck pouch). Essential for the peace of mind it brings. You could lose everything except your money belt, and your trip could still go on. Pack it with your passport, traveler's checks, money, credit card, airline ticket, and other essential documents. Rick prefers a lightweight, water-resistant belt tucked under his pants like a shirttail (see Back Door Catalog). Bob finds that a belt gets uncomfortably sweaty in the tropics and opts instead for a lightweight pouch of cotton or nylon that hangs around his neck under his shirt. In either case, put your passport and checks inside a plastic zip-lock baggie first to protect them from sweat and rain. Carry a notecard in your money belt with emergency phone numbers and addresses, health insurance information, prescription for glasses, a tally of which traveler's checks you've yet to cash, and so on. Keep a duplicate in your rucksack, along with photocopies of your passport and airline ticket.

Cash. Bring American dollars for situations when you want to change only a few bucks and not a whole traveler's check, or when for some reason no one will cash your checks. Remember, it's risky to carry a lot of cash.

Foreign currency. Consider bringing about $20 worth of foreign currency for each country you'll visit. Your bank or AFEX (1-800-366-2339) can sell you foreign currency at reasonable rates.

Hostel sheet. Japan has lots of youth hostels, and they require sleeping sheets. You can bring your own or rent one there.

Combination lock. To secure your belongings inside your cut-rate hotel room when you don't trust the lock on your door (if your door has a lock; many hotels give you only a latch). Small padlocks with keys are sold all over Asia.

Day pack. These small nylon packs are great for carrying your sweater, camera, literature, and food while you leave most of your luggage in your larger rucksack or suitcase at the hotel.

Camera and film.

Knife. A good Swiss army knife has endless applications, from opening bottles to slicing open a lush pineapple. One with scissors, corkscrew, and tweezers is best.

First-aid kit. (See chap. 7, Health.)

Medicine. In original containers with legible prescriptions.

Sunglasses.

Extra glasses, contacts, and prescriptions. Contacts can be a hassle. Consider just wearing glasses.

Toiletries. Bring only the essentials. Toilet paper can be found almost everywhere. Tampons aren't always available (see chap. 8, The Woman Traveling Alone).

Small towel. Not all hotels provide a towel. Hand towel size is adequate.

Soap. Not all hotels provide soap, either. A plastic squeeze bottle of concentrated, multipurpose liquid soap is handy for laundry and much more. You can buy hand and laundry soap in small sizes locally.

Sewing kit. Clothes age rapidly while traveling.

Clothesline. For hanging up clothes to dry in your hotel room.

Zip-lock baggies. 1,001 uses. Great for leftover food, containing wetness, and bagging potential leaks before they occur.

Mini-notepad and pen. Carry in your back pocket as a great organizer, reminder, and communication aid.

Journal. If you fill an "empty book" with the experiences of your trip, it will prove to be your most treasured souvenir. We guarantee it. A hardbound type will last a lifetime; a spiral notebook may not make it through the trip.

Postcards from your hometown and family pictures. Always a great conversation piece with Asians you meet. Business cards make it easy to hand out your address. These are cheaply printed in Asian cities.

Address list. For sending postcards home and collecting new addresses. Taking a whole address book, unless very tiny, is not packing light.

Travel information. Rip out or copy appropriate chapters, staple them together, and store in a zip-lock baggie. When you are done, give the chapter to another traveler.

Asian map. A map best suited to your trip's needs. Ask your bookstore for Nelles's or Bartholomew's; they make the best regional maps. Get maps for specific local areas as you go.

A good paperback. There is plenty of empty time on a trip either to be bored or to enjoy some good reading. Ideally, the novel will relate to your travels (i.e., *Shogun* for Japan, *Dynasty* for Hong Kong, *A Far Pavilion* for India). When you finish, don't lug the paperweight; swap it for another traveler's book.

Earplugs. If night noises bother you, you'll grow to love a good set of plugs. Asia has more than its share of things that go bump in the night.

Alarm/calculator. If your watch doesn't have an alarm, bring along a small alarm clock or a calculator that includes one. A calculator is also useful for money conversions.

Nothing electrical. Every year some American plugs his universal adapter into our hotel and the whole place goes universally black.

Flashlight. If you bring other than a standard model, bring extra bulbs from home.

Poncho or parka. A plastic poncho protects you and your pack in a rainstorm and opens flat to serve as a tablecloth for picnicking and a ground cloth for sleeping on—ideal for hard-core vagabonds. Otherwise, a good weatherproof parka is the best bet. When it rains, it pours!

Hiking gear. If you plan a hike in the Himalayas, see the Nepal Back Door on trekking. For just an occasional hike, lightweight Vibram-sole shoes or just good running shoes will do.

Sleeping bag. Bring this bulky item only if you plan to sleep out in a colder climate. This would include fall through early spring in Japan, Korea, Taiwan, China, and northern India and any mountainous area almost any time of year. A light blanket or flannel sheet is a good compromise. We still have a sarong from our first trip to Indonesia which makes a wonderful sleeping sheet and beach blanket.

Information Sources

Books

Too many people spend their Asian vacations stranded on a Hong Kong street corner hemorrhaging money. They thought they could manage without a guidebook—or maybe they didn't think at all. You need a good directory-type guidebook. You can't fake it in Asia. Those who get the best trip for the least expense and with minimal headaches have a good guidebook, and they use it. We can step off a plane for our first time in Calcutta and travel like old pros by taking full advantage of a good guidebook.

Before buying a book, study it. How old is the information? The cheapest books are often the oldest—and no bargain. Who wrote it? What's the author's experience? Is it readable? Many guidebooks are useful only as powerful sedatives. Your book should be fun but not wordy. Don't believe everything you read. The power of the printed word is scary. Most books are peppered with information that is simply wrong. Incredibly enough, even this book may contain an error or two (but we could be wrong). Many writers succumb to the temptation to write guidebooks based on hearsay, travel brochures, and other books.

A comprehensive review of all the guides to Asia is beyond the scope of this book. We'll just mention a few books that we've found very helpful.

Lonely Planet Guides. You'd be hard pressed to find a knowledgeable budget traveler anywhere in Asia who isn't carrying at least one Lonely Planet guidebook. Their "Travel Survival Kits" cover individual countries, and their shoestring guides cover regions: Southeast Asia, Northeast Asia, and West Asia. They all give valuable specifics on transportation, budget hotels, and prices (which go out of date quickly). For a catalog, write to Embarcadero West, 112 Linden Street, Oakland, CA 94607 (tel. 510-893-8555).

Moon Publications. Some people prefer Moon's guidebooks because of their frank commentary on the politics and culture. They also offer valuable room, board, and transportation specifics. Their Indonesia and Japan handbooks are particularly good. For a catalog, write to P.O. Box 1696, Chico, CA 95927.

All-Asia Guide. Published and updated annually for over 80 years by the Far Eastern Economic Review (the Hong Kong-based equivalent of _Newsweek_ or _Time_), this book is useful if you want a general overview of each country within the entire vast continent.

Insight Guides. These are great books for advance planning and posttrip memories but not so practical for carrying along. The research is meticulous with regard to history and culture, and the photography and color reproductions are brilliant. But the books are intentionally geared toward an upper-income readership, the so-called sophisticated traveler. Some books are better than others; we particularly recommend Korea, Hong Kong, Taiwan, Burma, Indonesia, Sri Lanka, and Nepal.

Frommer, Fodor, Fisher, Baedeker, and others. Everybody has a finger in the tourist pie, and these are the Big Four. Each publisher has a slightly different approach, Frommer being the most budget oriented.

Frommer's comprehensive travel guides to Japan and Hong Kong are especially useful for identifying hotel and restaurant bargains. If you're headed for India, you might also take a look at *India on $40 a Day,* although we prefer the younger-at-heart Lonely Planet guides.

Of Fodor's eight books on this region, the most useful is his guide to Japan, specially slanted toward the low-rent districts. Its weakness is that it only covers major cities. Baedeker's books are especially helpful for their detailed maps and museum descriptions. Fisher guides are written for travelers with bucks to burn.

You'll find a variety of other English-language guidebooks on your arrival in Asia. Two of the most prevalent are the Papineau Guides from Singapore and the South China Morning Post books from Hong Kong. Both are sketchy. Save your cash.

There are many other handy books. Find a travel bookstore and just browse. For a great free catalog of guidebooks, call Book Passage, 1-800-321-9785. And don't forget magazines. Japan, Singapore, Thai International, and Cathay Pacific airlines all produce handsome in-flight magazines we're proud to place on our coffee tables. *Transitions Abroad,* a quarterly guide to overseas study, work, and budget travel, is an outstanding resource (Box 344, Amherst, MA 01004).

While adequate travel information is what keeps your ship afloat, be careful not to go overboard. You can always find good travel books in English in Asia.

To pack light, we rip our books up, bringing with us only the chapters we will need on our trip. There is no point carrying around 120 pages of information on the Philippines if we're not going there. When we finish seeing a country, we throw away our stapled-together chapter on that area or better yet, give it (with notes) to another traveler.

Both in Asia and at home, travelers love to share their mental souvenirs and the lessons they've learned. Tap the grapevine. Grab every opportunity you can to learn from others. Firsthand, fresh information is the best kind anywhere, and it just waits to be harvested. Keep in mind, though, that all assessments of a place's merit (including our own) are a product of the storyteller's biases, manufactured by his personality and the time he's spent there. It could have rained, he could have met the meanest people, or he may have been sick in "that lousy, overrated city." Or, he may have fallen in love in that "wonderful" village. All opinions are just that—opinions.

Some of the best guidebooks are not sold in the U.S.A., or, for that matter, in the English language. A few of the best guidebooks to Asian countries are published in French and German. Take advantage of every opportunity to swap information with fellow travelers from other parts of the Western world. This is particularly important when traveling in politically or economically unstable regions.

Classes

If you are now a student or can enroll part-time to prepare for your trip, there are plenty of worthwhile classes. While English is unquestionably the handiest language for traveling in Asia, knowledge of a foreign language—even a few phrases of Japanese, Chinese, or Malay—can only add to your enjoyment of Asia.

History makes Asia come alive. A basic Asian history course turns a 2,000-year-old ruin into a fascinating marvel. A class in Asian religions is probably the most valuable course for the prospective traveler. Almost all Asian art and architecture is religious in purpose, and with no background on the subject, it is difficult to appreciate. Please don't go to Asia without at least having read something on the Buddhist and Hindu religions. To whet your appetite, read chapter 5, Asia 101: A Cultural Primer.

National Tourist Offices

Tourism is an important part of most Asian countries' economies. Each country has a National Tourist Office to promote their attractions. As long as their budgets hold out (easier for some countries than others), they are happy to send you a free packet of information. Just send them a postcard. Mention your specific interests (e.g., trekking in Nepal, ancient ruins in Sri Lanka, maps, festivals, etc.) to get exactly what you need along with the general packet. You'll find a complete listing of National Tourist Offices in the Nitty Gritty section.

2
Transportation

Flying to Asia

Flying to Asia, while still a good value, is becoming more complicated and restrictive. Airline rules and regulations are confusing and always changing, but by understanding your options and using a good travel agent, you can make the right choice.

A key to budget flying is to find a travel agent who knows Asia and who will discount fares. An agent who discounts fares gives up part of his or her commission (which, on Asian flights, can be quite high) to sell you a ticket. Check the Sunday travel section of a big city newspaper for agents who discount tickets. Never buy directly from the airlines unless a great promotion is on. You'll invariably get a better deal through a good travel agent.

Put your energy into finding the right agent, not the cheapest flight, and you'll save money as well as headaches. While it's smart to understand your ticket, we can't (and don't want to) keep up with the ever-changing world of airfares. We rely on the experience of our agent, who specializes in budget travel, to work with us in coming up with the best combination of economy, flexibility, reliability, and convenience. These days, it's wise to research, and often book, your flight three to four months in advance.

There's really no way around it: getting to Asia will cost you a bundle—about $900 round-trip from the West Coast. Basically, you can get what you pay for—or less. Remember, a dollar saved may mean more restrictions, less flexibility, or more risk. There is no such thing as a free lunch (or, some would say, even a good lunch) in the airline industry. For instance, some of the very cheapest tickets are nonrefundable and nonendorsable. Nonendorsable means no other airline will honor it if, for some reason, the ticketing airline is unable to fly you as planned.

Your flight options include regular fare, various budget coach fares, round-the-world, circle-the-Pacific, and open jaws fares. An open jaws ticket allows you to fly into one city and leave another. You can ad-lib your transportation on the ground between segments of your flight.

Consider traveling off-season. You can save up to several hundred dollars on your ticket. High and low seasons vary from country to country in Asia, so check with your travel agent.

Short domestic flights are easy, cheap, and no more dangerous than surface options

Many tickets, even the discount ones, allow one free stopover. An extra stop usually costs $50 to $75. On the cheaper tickets, you're usually allowed one stop in each direction. You can save money by using these stops wisely. For example, going to Delhi, stop in Hong Kong on the way, and hit the beaches in Thailand on the way back. If you're going to Japan and onward, it's wiser to get a stopover in Tokyo than to purchase your onward ticket in Tokyo. Japan has expensive international fares.

For maximum flexibility, Bob often gets a one-way ticket to Asia and buys onward and return tickets from wherever he ends up. Although two one-way tickets cost more than a round-trip ticket, there is an advantage to one-way tickets. Many Asian airlines are not bound by International Air Transport Association (IATA) fare restrictions. Therefore you can often add many stopovers, sometimes at no additional cost. Not long ago, we could buy a Penang (Malaysia) to New York ticket for $620 with intermediate stops in Delhi, Bombay, and London. Or fly from Delhi to Europe via Moscow on Aeroflot for $350. Bombay to Nairobi, Kenya, was going for $280. But be warned that some Asian immigration officials can turn away anyone entering by air without a round-trip ticket, though within the last ten years, we've only heard of one incident—in Taipei, where they're very strict. (If you're worried about this, buy an open travel voucher from a travel agent, which can be applied toward purchase of a ticket. You can show this to immigration, and get a refund when you return to the U.S. We don't worry about it, though.)

Another option to keep in mind is the ITX fare. Some airlines offer cheap onward tickets in conjunction with their flights. Recently, for example, if you flew at least one way on Garuda Airlines to Bali, you could go onward to Singapore for $185. If purchased in Bali, the same ticket would cost almost $250.

Though no single airline circles the world today, most international carriers team up with other airlines to offer round-the-world (RTW) tickets. Fares are typically around $2,000 ($2,600 if Australia and the South Pacific are included, $600 extra for an extension to South America). The principal rules are that you must keep traveling in the same direction, and you must finish your trip in the same place you start it. Only the first leg must be reserved. Leave the rest of your ticket open-dated, and confirm your seat a few days ahead of departure for your next stop. Shop around a bit. Validity periods vary widely (from several months to a full year), and some airlines limit the number of stopovers. The best deals are from discount travel agents who piece a number of airlines together to make the whole ticket. Though more expensive, some of the airlines will put together a round-the-world package—for current prices and restrictions. Check with Korean (the cheapest), Cathay Pacific, Continental, CP Air, Japan, Northwest, Singapore, United, British Air, Delta, or Thai airlines.

Less expensive circle-the-Pacific fares follow the same criteria as RTW. For example, Garuda and Cathay Pacific offer a ticket for $1,500 (West Coast price) for a journey to Hong Kong, Bangkok, Singapore, and Jakarta with additional options of Yogyakarta, Bali, Irian Jaya, and Honolulu. Other airlines have similar circle-the-Pacific or round-the-world possibilities.

Scheduled airlines are very reliable. If for some reason they can't fly you home, they will find you a seat on another carrier. That is, if you have a reservation. If you don't, and the flights are booked for the next week, you'll have a long wait.

Here are a few important tips. On arrival, reconfirm your return ticket, and then check again three days before departure. This is especially important in less-developed countries such as India. In India, if you don't reconfirm at least three days in advance, you won't have a seat. Also be aware of high seasons if you decide to buy your onward tickets once you arrive. For example, October through November is the peak trekking season in Nepal, and Bangkok is the hub for flights to Nepal. You might not be able to book a ticket out of Bangkok to Kathmandu until December. However, in situations such as this, consider flying to a nearby place and going overland. For example, in the Nepal scenario, fly from Bangkok to Calcutta or Delhi and then go by train and bus to Kathmandu.

Flying within Asia

Asia is a big continent with a complicated bag of airfares. There are some great values, especially within countries. The real trick is knowing the ins and outs of the competition, economies, and regulations.

Some countries have much cheaper airfares than others. A lot of it has to do with the national tax structures and the country of departure. International airfares are generally less expensive in Delhi, Bangkok, Jakarta, Penang (Malaysia), and Hong Kong. Though these places are not the cheap ticket havens they once were, you can still get a one-way ticket from Bangkok to Kathmandu for about $200, or Bangkok to Calcutta for $180.

Singapore and Manila have more expensive airfares, and Sri Lanka and Korea are even worse. Japan is the most expensive.

While international flights can be expensive, domestic flights can be very cheap. For example, in Thailand, you can fly from Bangkok to Chiang Mai for $65; in Japan, from Tokyo to Sapporo for about $180; in Malaysia, from Kuala Lumpur across the South China Sea to Kota Kinabalu, Sabah (Borneo), for $175. Some of these fares will be lower if you go through a discount agent in the particular country. For example, you could save about $50 on the Kota Kinabalu flight.

Don't imagine that domestic carriers will offer you the creature comforts or taken-for-granted safety standards of international airlines. Lonely Planet travel writer Tony Wheeler says Zamrud, an Indonesian domestic carrier, is the world's most democratic airline. On a flight over the island of Timor, Tony's pilot took a poll to see whether his passengers preferred to fly along the coast or over the mountains; when the vote came out deadlocked, he offered to zigzag.

Whenever you're buying a ticket for a flight originating in Asia, shop around and find a good cut-rate travel agent. Check your guidebook and local newspaper ads. An agent can get you discounts that the airlines themselves are unable to offer. Although it's difficult, try to check into the reliability of an agent before buying from him. Ask your hotel clerk, the tourist information office, and other travelers for recommendations. If your U.S. travel agent has a travel agent "partner" or "ally" in Asia, be sure to get his or her card.

When buying a ticket in Asia, make sure the agent confirms a seat for you before you pay. The ticket may be a bargain, but you could end up on a month-long waiting list with hundreds of other travelers who jumped at the price.

By Boat to Asia

You're a sailor at heart, and that heart leaps at the thought of riding over the bounding main. Well, forget the Love Boat. You can't afford it. There are two viable alternatives.

One is freighter travel. The same freighter lines that abandoned passenger service a few years ago with the words, "Cargo doesn't eat and cargo doesn't complain," now are booking passengers again. Most of these boats can carry only 8 to 12 persons, and since their primary purpose is the transport of goods, they don't have the services or luxuries of cruise ships. And they're far more expensive than airline flights. But consider that you're traveling in a second-class hotel with full board for weeks on end, and you'll understand why the cost is roughly $100 a day. Your travel agent can recommend a line to meet your budget and itinerary.

The second way to get to Asia by sea is to find a private yacht headed that direction and sign on as crew. This isn't as off-the-wall as it may first sound. Many captains of 40- to 60-foot boats (and larger) are looking for cooks and deckhands, with or without experience. You'll have to ante up for your own share of food as well as boat maintenance, and so forth, but that's only fair. Your best bet is to check bulletin boards at local yacht clubs and marinas, or advertise yourself in the same place. If you're landlocked, find a southern California telephone directory and start writing letters to yacht clubs. In Asia, notices will sometimes be posted in popular guest houses on Bali, Penang, and other islands.

By Boat within Asia

Once you're in Asia, the possibilities of sea cargo routes that link countries and islands are almost unlimited. Prices are generally cheaper than air travel, and if you've got the time, these routes are a fascinating means of making lots of stops along the way and encountering a cross section of Asian society that you might not otherwise meet.

For example, you can island-hop through the Ryukyu chain from Kagoshima, Japan, to Keelung, Taiwan. You can travel by freighter from Singapore east to Java, Bali, and virtually the entire Indonesian archipelago. You can even cross the Bay of Bengal from Penang, Malaysia, to Madras, India, via the remote Andaman Islands.

Japan has some great ferry trips through the Inland Sea and between its major (and smaller) islands. A typical scene on a Japanese ferry is a crowd of people, many of them uniformed schoolchildren (who love to practice their Eng-goo-rish on foreigners), sitting cross-legged in stocking feet, munching oranges.

If you're island-hopping through Indonesia or the Philippines, you'll be traveling by land across the islands and by local ferry between them. There are often several connections a day, but you'll want to check ahead, especially if you're on a less-traveled route.

It is not a good idea to be caught in a small boat, least of all a private yacht, in the South China Sea. More than a couple of European crews have arrived in Singapore, Bangkok, or Manila with horror tales about their plunder and rape at the hands of Asian pirates. Other crews haven't returned at all. However, the larger cruise ships such as

the ones going from Hong Kong to Hainan Island in China are safe. And outside of the South China Sea, fair-weather boat travel is a breeze.

Speaking of Hainan Island, Bob recalls a particular two-day trip he took a few years ago from Guangzhou (Canton) to Hainan with his brother Steve. Deciding they didn't want to be in the hole below deck, they splurged for a $15 second-class cabin—four hard berths with a bare dim light bulb dangling from the ceiling. The old ship was clean, but the toilets down the hall were ripe. Bob and Steve had a few bread rolls from the tourist hotel in Guangzhou but would have stocked up had they known of the ship's fare. The main dish at each meal was soup, consisting of meatless bones drifting like bottomfish amid a rice mash topped with a grease slick. After the first day, most of the passengers were sick in their bunks.

Yes, we know. You're wondering, "Gee, how can I find out more about sea cargo routes?" While your travel agent may have information, your best bet is to inquire on your arrival. Steamship companies are often headquartered in most major port cities, and a simple phone call or drop-in visit will give you all the information you need about schedules and fares. Also check with the local tourist office.

If you're traveling between countries, be sure to confirm beforehand all visa arrangements for your port of arrival. Some countries have different regulations for sea arrivals than for air arrivals. We can think of few more miserable situations than to be turned away by Immigration and be forced back on a ship feeling filthy and seasick.

Trains

Most countries in Asia have good rail systems. The problem for international travelers is that few of them interconnect. The only three exceptions are India–Pakistan, Thailand–Malaysia–Singapore, and China–Mongolia. While you can travel extensively within a country by train, you'll often have to use other means—plane, boat, or local bus—to get between countries.

The quality and comfort of trains varies tremendously in Asia. Details on the train systems within each country are described in Nitty Gritty, Country by Country near the end of this book.

Off the Track Miscellany

Multistation Cities. Most large Asian cities and some small ones have more than one train station. Be sure you know which station your train leaves from, even if that means asking what may seem like a stupid question. Stations are easily connected by bus and other local transportation.

Train-splitting. Never assume the whole train is going where you are going, especially in India and China. Each car is labeled separately, because cars are usually added and dropped here and there all along the journey. Sometimes you'll be left sitting in your car on the track for 10 minutes, watching your train fade into the distance, until another train comes along and picks up your car. To survive all of this juggling easily, just check to be sure that your destination is listed on your car's nameplate. The nameplate lists the final stop and some (but not all) of the stops in between.

Baggage. Baggage has never been a problem for us on trains. Some people complain about porters (India) or the lack thereof (Japan). Frankly, we don't feel sorry for anyone who travels with more luggage than he or she can carry. Every train car has space allotted for luggage, so the average tourist never checks baggage through.

Using Train Time Wisely. Train travelers spend a lot of time on trains. Time well spent on the train frees up time spent off the train. It makes no sense to sit on the train bored, then arrive in Osaka only to sit in the station for an hour reading your information and deciding where to go for hotels and what to do next.

Spend train time studying, reading, writing postcards or journal entries, eating, organizing, cleaning, doing anything you can so you don't have to do it after you arrive. Talk to local people or other travelers. There is so much to be learned, including the language. Some Asians, especially Japanese, are initially less open and forward than Americans. You could sit across from a silent but fascinating and friendly Asian for an entire train ride, or you could break the ice by offering him some candy, showing him your Hometown, U.S.A., postcards, or asking him a question. This may start the conversation flowing and the friendship growing.

Station Facilities. Major Asian train stations can be one of the independent traveler's best and most helpful friends. Take advantage of the assistance they can offer. Many stations have a luggage checking service where, for a nominal fee, you can leave your luggage. (We'd feel very comfortable doing this in Japan, where honesty is the rule and security is nearly incorruptible. We might check bags—but never our valuables, which we'd keep in a day bag—in India, Indonesia, Thailand, or most other Third World countries.) People traveling light can usually fit two rucksacks into one storage locker, cutting their storage costs in half.

Most stations have comfortable waiting rooms. The bigger stations are equipped with, or are near, day hotels for those who want to shower, shave, and rest. And in India, you can stay overnight in the railway retiring rooms, which are run like hotel rooms.

Every station has a train information office that is ready to help you with scheduling. We usually consult the timetables ourselves first and write down our plan: for example, Tokyo (Ueno station)–Sendai 14:42, Track 6 (using the 24-hour clock). We then confirm this with the information desk. Written communication is easiest and safest. There is always someone working at the train station with enough English to help you.

A tourist information office can often be found either in the station (in the case of major tourist centers) or nearby. This is our first stop after leaving the station. We pick up a map and sightseeing information and, if we need advice and there is a room-booking service attached (you'll find this in Japan and sometimes elsewhere), we'll get suggestions on budget accommodations. Often at borders, the station's money-changing office is open long after banks and other offices have closed for the night. Train stations are major bus stops, so connections from train to bus are generally no more difficult than crossing the street. Buses fan out from stations to nearby towns that lack train service.

When reading the schedules posted in any station, remember that there are always two lists—trains arriving and trains departing. Concern yourself only with the departures. The assorted symbols on the schedule mean that particular trains are first class only, require surcharges or reservations, are sleeping cars only, leave only on certain days, and so forth. That is why, even after years of reading train schedules, we still confirm our plans at the information desk or with a conductor on the track.

A handy tool for planning Asian rail itineraries is the _Thomas Cook Overseas Timetable_. This book is published quarterly by Thomas Cook

Limited, P.O. Box 36, Peterborough PE3 6SB, England. It lists every significant train schedule on earth, divided by country and continent, and often lists connecting buses and ferries as well. If your travel agent is unable to lend you the timetable, you can send a check or money order for $21.95 to Cook's British publishing office, or order one through the Forsyth Travel Library (for their catalog, call 1-800-Forsyth). Practice using the timetable at home to learn how to read train schedules and to gauge the frequency and duration of the train trips you expect to take. Don't rely solely on the timetable for your specific route; always confirm your plans at the information desk of a train station.

Managing on the trains is largely a matter of asking questions, letting people help you, assuming things are logical, and using common sense. We always ask someone on the platform if the train is going where we think it is. (Unfortunately, this ploy does not always work in India, where people are conditioned to answer "Yes" to any question in English whether or not they know the answer.) Speak slowly, clearly, and with caveman simplicity. Be observant. If the loudspeaker comes on, gauge by the reaction of those around you if the announcement concerns you and if it's good or bad news. If, after the babble, everyone dashes across the station to Track 15, you should assume your train is no longer arriving on Track 2.

Luggage is never completely safe. There is a thief on every train (union rules) planning to grab a bag. Don't be careless. Before leaving our luggage in a compartment, we establish a relationship with surrounding passengers in the compartment. We're safer leaving our bag among mutual guards rather than a pack of vultures. However, we never leave behind our valuables, such as our passport, checks, and plane ticket. (For more information, read Theft and the Tourist, chap. 9.)

Which Class to Travel

We find second class reserved ("hard sleeper" in China) suits us in most countries. There may be a few extra family members crowded into the compartment, but you'll have a seat. In this class you'll meet the friendly locals, and it is comfortable enough for most people, though not up to Western standards (except in Japan).

First class ("soft seat" or "soft sleeper" in China) is almost double the price of second. For a bit more comfort, you're losing contact with the locals. You may end up with mostly foreign travelers, the wealthy and aloof, or sometimes no one at all. Occasionally, no one at all is what we want after an intense bus ride through India.

Third class or second class unreserved ("hard seat" in China) should be your choice only if you don't have one. In Asia (except Japan), unreserved means cattle car style—but with cows that smoke. We travel this class sometimes on trips less than five hours—and survive. Almost every trip we try to go this way once so we can remember what travel is like for 90 percent of Asians.

How to Sleep on the Train

The economy of night travel is tremendous. Sleeping while rolling down the tracks saves time and money, both of which, for most travelers, are limited resources. The economy of night travel applies to travel everywhere. The first concern after such a proposal is, "Aren't you missing a lot of beautiful scenery? You just slept through half of Thailand!" Well, there are very few train rides that will have you looking out the windows most of the time. (Hakodate to Sapporo in Japan, Taipei to Hwalien in Taiwan, and Kandy to Badulla in Sri Lanka are very scenic.) In other words, nearly every eight-hour train ride will be a bore unless you spend it sleeping. Obviously, you will miss a few beautiful sights, but you will be compensated by the whole extra day you gain in your itinerary.

The second concern usually voiced (which should be the first) is, "How do you sleep?" Sleeping on an overnight train ride can be a waking nightmare. One night of endless bouncing, sitting up straight in a dark eternity of steel wheels crashing along rails, trying doggedly—yet hopelessly—to get comfortable, will teach you the importance of finding a spot to stretch out for the night. Those with the greatest skill at this game sleep. Those not so talented will spend the night gnashing their teeth and cultivating sore necks and tailbones.

Happily though, many trains have seats that convert into recliners or berths. And on long-distance rides, we always ask for a sleeping car. Usually second class is good enough, but on occasion, we splurge for a first-class or air-conditioned car. Air-conditioned on Asian trains often means refrigeration. Cars that aren't air-conditioned have overhead fans. This is normally adequate, especially at night. On almost all sleeping cars you either get bedding for free or an attendant on board will supply some for a small fee. In the tropics, though, a sleeping sheet is often enough.

If you do end up on an overnight train without a berth, buy a cheap woven mat to throw out on the floor and then give away on arrival. A Therma-Rest or other kind of inflatable mattress can help, although it's not worth the extra bulk in your pack unless you plan to do some hiking.

For safety, never sleep without your valuables in a money belt or at least securely attached to your body. For good measure, clip and fasten your rucksack to the luggage rack. Some travelers use a lightweight bicycle cable with a lock. If one good tug doesn't take the bag, a thief will usually leave it alone rather than ask you how your luggage is attached.

Subways

Tokyo, Osaka, Kyoto, Sapporo, Hong Kong, and Singapore all have modern subway systems, reasonably priced and a delight to ride any time except rush hour. Route maps and fares are written in English as well as local languages, and if you have any questions about finding your way around, ticket window personnel are glad to help.

Buses

In many parts of Asia, buses are the only form of public transportation available. As your bus careens around a hairpin curve with only two wheels and your prayers keeping you from that river 5,000 feet below, you might feel that your life is in the hands of your driver. You're absolutely right.

Except for Japan, and sometimes Thailand, Taiwan, and Malaysia, public buses are always crowded, make every stop, and are excessively fast on curves and hills. A good sense of humor is prerequisite. A touch of masochism doesn't hurt.

Fortunately, most Asian countries now have private or government tour buses. These are often called Deluxe buses, and often the meaning of that word is stretched. In Southeast Asia, these buses can be very comfortable and are usually air-conditioned, but in Nepal and India, the buses are often run-down and the air-conditioning may not work. Video bus is another name for a Deluxe bus. Try to get a bus without a video. The videos are Kung Fu movies in Southeast Asia and typical Hindi song, drama, and romance films in India and Nepal. One is O.K., but eight hours of videos on one ride with the speakers blaring at top volume is no fun.

You'll always feel a lot more secure, regardless of what kind of bus you're riding in, if you have only one bag and carry it with you at all times. Many South Asian buses carry luggage on a rooftop rack, and it's not uncommon for a few items to fall off on those hairpin curves. Carry your bag on your lap or at least on an overhead rack inside the bus. If this isn't possible, go up on the roof yourself to secure your bag to the rack by its strap. With a bicycle cable, you can even lock your bag to the rack. In either case, keep all valuables in a small day bag with you.

If you really want to watch your bag on top, ride up on the roof. We do this in good weather and whenever the bus driver will let us. In India and Nepal, you'll find many others up there with you. Before going through police checkposts, the bus will stop and you'll have to crowd inside. On top you get great panoramas. And it's comforting to think you can jump if the bus misses the mountain curve.

Carry a small container of water (a plastic bicycle bottle is just the right size) and some food for snacking on bus rides. You won't have many opportunities to disembark in search of nourishment, and the

A good sense of humor is prerequisite

morsels that are pushed through the windows of the bus at local stops are interesting but rarely appetizing.

Tour and Deluxe buses usually have bathrooms in the rear, except in India and Nepal, where the buses will stop at restaurants along the way for you to use the toilet. Cleanliness levels range from medium-bad to bad. Public buses stop at either cheaper restaurants with bad toilets or just a village, and you'll need to find the public toilet. Just follow the locals off the bus.

Don't expect to sleep much on an overnight bus trip in Asia. Seats rarely recline, and there's no room to stretch out. The exceptions are on tour buses in Thailand, Malaysia, and Japan. Long, long bus trips are not advisable for the short-term traveler. If time isn't a factor but comfort is, you should consider breaking your journey halfway and finding a hotel room to stretch out in. The only good thing about riding Asian buses at night is that you can't see all the near misses.

Third World Ad-libbing

Bemos, becaks, samlors—they're all cultural manifestations of private entrepreneurial spirit alive and well in Asian society. In Indonesia, a bemo is a tiny pickup truck with benches built into each side of the back. A slightly larger minivan is called an *opelet*. A becak is a bicycle-driven pedicab. Its motorized counterpart is a *trishaw*, called a *helicak* in Java and a *samlor* or *tuktuk* in Thailand. Horse-driven carts are sometimes known as *dokar* or *andong*.

There are many other varieties of local transport in each Asian country. They make traveling in the Third World easy: they go when they're full, and they're never expensive.

Negotiate a price before you board. Listen first to locals, then bargain with confidence as if you knew exactly what the ride should cost. If the driver asks for more when you get there, just give him the agreed amount and walk away. With a couple, the driver may say the price was for one person. Make sure this point is clear at the start. If you think it was clear, and the driver still insists, again, just give the fair amount and walk away.

You may want to hire a becak or bemo for the whole day. This may be especially cost-effective if there are other travelers, perhaps in your guest house, who want to visit the same places.

Traveling by trishaw

Taxis and Hire Cars

If there are three or four of you to share the expense, this is an excellent way to cover a lot of ground in some nations and to see the countryside as well. We like this method in Malaysia and Thailand, where you can hire taxis and drivers for about $5 an hour, and in Sri Lanka, where you can travel for a week around the island republic, including your chauffeur-guide's expenses, for as little as $120. A jeep with a driver can be hired in Tibet as well as Burma (recently renamed Myanmar by its military dictatorship).

Driving

If you're seriously thinking about renting a car and driving it, either you're very naive about the hazards of driving in Asia (mainly maniac drivers) or you're very experienced and have no need for the advice in this book. Suffice to say that in Sri Lanka, it costs more to rent a car and drive yourself than it does to hire a driver with the car. Why? Insurance.

Some travelers may consider buying a car in Japan, driving it around the archipelago, and shipping it back to the U.S.A. at the end of their excursion. Fine and dandy, but consider that (1) with very few exceptions, all traffic signs (and most road maps) are in Japanese characters, and (2) Japanese drive on the left-hand side of the road, as in England and Australia. A left-hand drive car won't do you much good in the States. Rental prices are about $40 a day for the smallest compact. Consider renting a minivan for camping around Japan, and you'll save a lot on hotel costs.

Buying or renting motorcycles is another way to get around. In Japan, 50cc motorcycles don't need licensing or insurance. You will need an endorsement on your driver's license to rent motorcycles over 50cc. You can buy a jointly produced Indian/Japanese motorcycle in India. Bob met Mikkie and Freek, a Dutch couple, who bought a scooter in Delhi and drove thousands of miles around India, then resold it for nearly the same price. They found the trip dusty but enjoyed the freedom of travel the scooter provided. Indonesia and Thailand offer motor bike rentals at all the budget travel hangouts. You just need to show a regular driver's license and leave a deposit. Many travelers get around Bali this way. Some end up in the hospital this way. If you've never driven a motorcycle before, Asia might not be the place to start.

If you insist on driving, or if you think there's a chance you might wind up behind the wheel of a friend's car, go through the painless procedure of obtaining an International Driver's License before you leave home. You can get one for a small fee from any office of the American Automobile Association. It's basically a translation, in a spate of languages, of your U.S. driver's license—which makes it much easier for a foreign cop to write you a ticket.

Bicycling

More and more, travelers are touring Asia by bicycle. Bob still remembers the sight of a lone mountain biker on a rest break at the crest of a 16,000-foot pass in the Himalayas.

You can either bring your own bike or rent one in Asia. But renters beware! We know a traveler who rented a bike in China and in the middle of a busy intersection, discovered the bike had no brakes. She didn't get hurt, but she learned a valuable lesson. Check your rental bike before you take it out on the road.

Many popular budget guest houses throughout Asia rent bikes. These are often one-speed Indian or Chinese heavy-duty models, but now cheap Chinese/Taiwanese mountain bikes are available, especially in Kathmandu. These rental bikes are usually good enough for local touring. In some countries, such as Nepal, local companies offer mountain bike tours. Check with the national tourist office.

For a long tour, bring your own bike, tools, and spare parts. Many airlines will take your bike as part of your baggage allowance. Ask an airlines official about packing requirements.

Hitchhiking (Rules of Thumb)

Rules of the road vary widely with the diverse societies of Asia. You'll rarely see Asians actually hitchhiking, but a spirit of voluntarism thrives in the Third World, and if a vehicle has empty space, it often becomes filled with extra passengers—locals and creative travelers. If you need a ride, wave at anything that rolls.

In nations with good road systems (e.g., Japan and Malaysia), Westerners can ride their thumbs without a great deal of difficulty. In peninsular Malaysia, where the people with enough money to buy a car usually go whole hog, some hitchhikers have a motto: "If the car that stops for you isn't a Mercedes, wait for the next one." However, it's a sensual experience to ride from Penang to Batu Ferringhi in the back of a truck loaded down with durian fruit (more to come on durian).

Hitching around Japan is easy. The rare hitchhiker on the road is always a foreigner, and the Japanese feel obligated to stop. They can't let a guest to their country go without a ride. Bob hitched throughout Japan one summer. Each morning, he asked the manager of the guest house or hostel to print the Japanese for his next destination on poster board. He rarely waited more than a few minutes for a ride. On one ride, a businessman treated Bob to a meal on the way to the next town. He then drove him to an inn where they spoke English. The next day, the man took the day off to drive him to a remote mountain village and insisted on paying for his meals on the way. Stories like these are common travel talk in Japan.

In countries such as India and Indonesia, where cars are scarce and public transport is cheap, the risks and time involved in hitchhiking aren't worth the negligible savings. The same is true in China, where the few cars you'll see are owned by government officials. However, in China, you can sometimes hitch a ride on trucks. In India, if you flag down a truck, they'll expect you to pay, since this is the system the locals use.

Speed and safety are trade-offs when it comes to hitching. A single woman maximizes speed and risk. Two women travel safer and nearly as fast. A man and a woman together are the best combination. A single man with patience will do fine. Two men go slow, and three or more should split up and rendezvous later. Single men and women are better off traveling together; these alliances are easily made at accommodations frequented by travelers.

Your success as a hitchhiker will be determined by how well you follow several rules. The hitchhiking gesture is not always the outstretched thumb. In some countries, you make a downward wave with your hand. In others, you ring an imaginary bell. Observe and learn. Consider what the driver will want to let into his car. Look like the Cracker Jack boy or his sister—happy, wholesome, and a joy to have aboard. Arrange your luggage so it looks as small and desirable as possible. Those hitching with very little or no luggage enjoy a tremendous advantage.

To get the long ride, make a cardboard sign with your destination printed big and bold in the local language. Walk or take a local bus out of town to the open country. Pick a good spot on the road to give a driver plenty of time to see you and a safe spot to pull over. Look lonely. In many cases, the more sparse the traffic, the quicker we get a ride. On a busy road, people may assume that we can manage without them. On a quiet road, the driver senses that we might die of exposure if he doesn't stop. Establish eye contact. Charm the driver.

Discretion makes hitching less risky. Feel good about the situation before you commit yourself to it. Keep your luggage on your lap or at least out of the trunk so if things turn sour, you can excuse yourself quickly and easily. Women should not sit in the back seat of a two-door car. A fake wedding ring and modest dress are indications that you're interested only in transportation.

Trekking and Other Walks

The best way to experience a foreign culture is to walk. In Nepal, India, and other countries of the Himalayan region, the century-old highways are footpaths, and the accepted means of transportation is walking. In the past 25 years, many backpack-bred and oxygen-starved Westerners have discovered the joys of trudging 50 or 100 miles, up and down 15,000-foot ridges, to encounter high mountains, colorful tribes, and mystical religion on the roof of the world. See the Back Door, Himalayan Treks or Treats. The best book on the subject is Stephen Bezruschka's _Guide to Trekking in Nepal_, available at travel bookshops or through the Mountaineers in Seattle (you can write for their catalog at 300 3rd Ave. W., Seattle, WA 98119).

Don't think for a moment, however, that Nepal and the Himalayas are the only places where you can enjoy walking. Nearly every country in Asia offers fine opportunities. Walking in Asia is different from walking in North America or Europe, because in Asia you're never really far from people. Villages and other small communities are strung out in places where even the mapmakers can't find them.

John Gottberg, the original co-author of this book, recalls one wonderful walk that he took through Bali. While other travelers were zooming up and down the paved roads on motorcycles and in bemos, John and a friend found a little footpath leading directly away from the highways and just began walking. Well-meaning villagers tried to direct them back toward the towns, but they instead followed the behind-the-back laughter toward "Sawah"—which they eventually learned, after walking through enough of them, meant "rice field." They kept going for days, like Pied Pipers drawing throngs of curious youngsters in every community, staying overnight at village headmen's homes (where they were the object of interest of all local English students), and even being invited to participate in a rice harvest. They spoke no more than a dozen words of Indonesian and none of Balinese.

That kind of opportunity is always available. There are places where it's not wise to walk—such as the Thai border areas abutting strife-torn Cambodia and, at times, the heroin poppy-rich Golden Triangle area across the Thai border into Myanmar (formerly Burma) and Laos. (Less risky jungle treks can be arranged out of Pai, Chiang Mai, and Chiang Rai in Thailand.) The element of risk changes with the politics, so check with the locals and the local U.S. embassy for current conditions.

Consider the Cameron Highlands of Malaysia, interior China, Lammu and other outlying islands of the Hong Kong colony, and the Japanese Alps. Japan, in fact, has a string of youth hostels linking many communities, each an easy day's walk apart in the central mountains.

Dry humor: A mini-bus for 20 with a sun roof

3
The Budget—
Eating and Sleeping
on $20 (and Less) a Day

Spending only $20 a day for room, board, and local transportation in Asia is not farfetched, except in Japan. Civil people have a blast in Asia spending less than that. And the feedback we get from Back Door travelers bolsters our confidence. It can be done—by you.

In the 1990s, if you focus your Asian travels on a single region, you can travel comfortably for eight weeks on a surprisingly low sum. We estimate $1,900 for Southeast Asia ($900 for the round-trip plane ticket from the West Coast and $1,000 for room and board and ground/sea transportation); $2,100 for India ($1,200 for the plane ticket; $900 for room, board, and transportation); and $4,700 for Japan ($800 for the plane ticket; $3,900 for room, board, and transportation). This doesn't include souvenirs or personal incidentals. Admissions and sightseeing costs are minimal.

There are two halves to any budget—transportation and room and board. Transportation expenses are generally fixed and reasonable. Flying to Asia is more of a bargain now, with increasing trade and travel exchanges bringing more routes and more business, than it has ever been before. Getting a good deal on a ticket is not tricky. With adequate information, you'll pay no more than we do to fly to Asia. Ground and sea transportation are cheap in most Asian countries and affordable even in Japan if you take advantage of the Japan Rail Pass.

Room and board is more likely to make or break your budget than transportation. Transportation costs are about the same whether you are taking a $5,000 vacation or a $2,000 vacation. Thus, where you stay and eat can make a big difference in how long you can afford to travel. The following chart shows you these dramatic differences. It is also useful for planning your trip budget.

EXPENSE CHART (U.S. dollars/day, 1993 estimate)

Country	Accommodations			3 meals			Trans-portation	Daily Total	
	Med. Hotel	Guest House	Dorm	Med.	Low			High	Low
Japan	65	35	16	40	20	30		135	65
Singapore/Hong Kong	45	20	8	15	7	3		65	20
China	30	15	3	8	4	5		43	12
Southeast Asia	40	6	2	10	5	8		58	15
India/Nepal	25	6	1	8	4	4		37	10

Notes:

Accommodations: "Med. Hotel" is medium-priced, comparable to a low-grade Western hotel. "Guest House" stands for guest houses and cheap hotels. The costs are based on a single room. Add 25% for a double room. "Dorm" is for a bed in a shared room in a hotel or hostel.

Meals: "Med." is three meals at a medium-priced local restaurant. "Low" is three meals at a small cheap restaurant.

Transport: This is the average of what you would spend each day. (For example, Japan's total is based on the average daily cost of a Japan Rail Pass plus estimated use of subways and taxis.) The figures are for ground and sea transport only.

Daily Total: "High" is based on medium hotels, medium-priced restaurants, and transportation. "Low" is based on dormitory rooms, small budget restaurants, and transportation. These figures do not include airfare to or within the countries.

A budget is a tool, not a trap. We don't let our budget dictate how freely we travel in Asia. If we want to go somewhere, we will, taking advantage of whatever money-saving options we can. We came to travel.

Rick traveled every summer for years on a part-time piano teacher's income. Bob financed three years of Asian travel with odd jobs picked up along the way. Both ate and slept great by learning and using the skills that follow.

Sleeping Cheap

Hotels are the most expensive way to sleep and, of course, the most comfortable. But hotels can rip through a tight budget like a grenade in a dollhouse. We always hear people complaining about that "$200 double in Tokyo" or the "$120-a-night room in Singapore." They come back from their vacations with swollen, bruised, and pilfered pocketbooks telling stories that scare their friends out of international travel and back to Florida or Hawaii one more time. True, you can easily spend $200 for a room, but that's two weeks accommodations for us.

Hospitality, Nepal-style

As far as we're concerned, the more you spend for your hotel, the bigger wall you build between you and what you came to see. If you spend enough, you won't know where you are. Think about it. "In-ter-con-ti-nen-tal." What does that name imply? Uniform sterility, a lobby full of stay-pressed Americans with wheels on their suitcases, English menus, boiled water, lamps bolted to the tables, and all the warmth of a hospital room. It's just right for business travelers who wish they were still at home and for people who need a paper strip over their toilet seat assuring them that nobody's sat there yet.

Asia is full of other cheaper and more colorful and true-to-the-culture alternatives such as Asian-style business hotels, guest houses, hostels, temples, and houseboats, to name a few. You can also stay for free in people's homes through organizations such as Servas (more on that later).

Reservations

Reservations are a needless and expensive security blanket. They'll smother your spontaneity. Make reservations only if you require a specific hotel or location or if you're hitting a crowded festival or event.

There are three problems with reservations. First, you can't see what you're getting before accepting. Second, booking ahead destroys your flexibility. Nobody knows how long they'll enjoy Yogyakarta or what the weather will be like in the Himalayas. Being shackled to a rigid chain of hotel reservations all summer would be a crushing blow to the freedom and independence that make travel such good living. And finally, reservations are much more expensive than playing it by ear. Through our agent, it was impossible to book a room in Tokyo for less than $80. We're sure it would have been a fine room, but we didn't have $80 for a fine room. We went on our own and had no trouble landing a wonderfully adequate double for $50—$25 apiece.

Your agent is telling you the truth when he says there's nothing available or insists, "This is the cheapest room possible." But he's taught to think all of Tokyo is listed in his little book. Not so! Akiko's Ryokan never made it into any American travel agency's book of accommodations. You must have the courage and spirit to go there bedless and find it yourself.

Basic Bed-finding

In over 2,000 unreserved nights in Asia and Europe, we've been shut out three times. That's a 99.85 percent bedding average earned in peak season, very often in crowded, touristy, or festive places. (What's so traumatic about a night without a bed anyway? Our survey shows those who have the opportunity to be refugees for a night are a little more sensitive to people who make a life out of being bedless.)

We would rather know the basic bed-finding skills than have the best hotel listing in existence. With these tips, finding a room on arrival is rarely a problem.

1. Hotel lists. Have a good guidebook's basic listing of hotels and budget alternatives. These lists, while widely used, are reliable and work well (although prices normally will have risen). Tourist information services usually have a more complete list of local hotels and accommodations.

2. Room-finding services. Popular tourist cities sometimes have a room-finding service at the airport, train station, or tourist office. For a dollar or two, they'll get you a room in the price range and neighborhood of your choice. They have the complete listing of that city's available accommodations, and their service is usually well worth the price when you consider the time and money saved by avoiding the search on foot. Hong Kong's is especially good. Room-finding services aren't above pushing you into their "favored" hotels, and kickbacks are powerful motivators. Room-finding services only give hostel and dormitory information if you insist.

3. Use the telephone. If you're looking on your own, telephone the places on your list that sound best. Not only will it save the time and money involved in chasing down these places and possibly finding them full, but you're beating all the other tourists—with the same guidebook—who may be hoofing it as you dial. It's rewarding to arrive at a hotel when people are being turned away and see your name on the reservation list because you called first. If the room or price isn't what you were led to believe, you have every right to say, "No, thank you" and search on (See Telephoning in Asia, chap. 9.)

4. Hotel runners. They are ubiquitous at many Asian train and bus stations and smaller airports. Usually teenagers, they'll verbally assault you the moment you step into the fresh air. Our gut reaction is to steer clear, but these people are usually just hardworking entrepreneurs (or their children) who lack the location or write-up in a popular guidebook that can make life easy for a small hotel owner. If the guy seems O.K. and you like what he promises, follow him to his hotel. You are obliged only to inspect the hotel. If it's good, take it. If not, leave. You're probably near other budget hotels anyway.

5. The early bird gets the room. If you expect crowds, go to great lengths to arrive in the morning when the most (and best) rooms are available. If the rooms aren't ready until noon, take one anyway. Leave your luggage behind the desk, and they'll move you in when it's available. You're set up, free to relax and enjoy the city. One of the beauties of overnight train rides is that you arrive bright and early. (Your approach to room finding will be determined by the market situation—if it's a "buyer's market" or a "seller's market." Sometimes you'll grab anything with a pillow and a blanket. Other times you can arrive late, be selective, and have no problems.)

Kashmir houseboat

6. Leave the trouble zone. Often budget travelers follow the Lonely Planet guidebooks to the same spots. When these are packed, there's normally a pleasant hotel down the street that's not. And if the situation is really bad, thirty minutes by train or bus from the most miserable hotel situation anywhere in Asia is a town—Singabore or Zerokyo—that has the Singabore Hotel or the Zerokyo Inn just across the street from the station or right on the main drag. It's not full— never has been, never will be. There's a guy sleeping behind the reception desk. Drop in at 11:00 p.m., ask for 14 beds, and he'll say, "Take the second and third floors, the keys are in the doors." It always works. Chinese New Year, Sapporo Snow Festival, Kandy Perahera: your bed awaits in nearby Zerokyo.

7. Taxi tips. A great way to find a place in a tough situation is to let a cabbie, becak, or tuktuk driver take you to his favorite hotel. Even if he's getting a kickback, this can be helpful in a jam. These guys are also handy when you're wandering lost in a big city. Many times we've hired a cab, showed him that elusive address, and been driven directly to our hotel.

8. Let hotel managers help. Nobody knows the hotel scene better than local hotel managers. If a hotel is full or too expensive, ask that manager for help. Often he'll have a list of neighborhood accommodations or will even telephone a friend whose place just around the corner rarely fills up. If the hotel is too expensive, there's nothing wrong with asking where you could find a "not so good place." We've always found hotel clerks understanding and helpful. (Remember, our experience is based on budget Asian-style situations. People who specialize in accommodating soft, rich Americans are more interested in your money than your happiness. The staffs of Asia's small hotels, inns, and guest houses may offer only a pit toilet down the hall and a well with a bucket for bathing out back, but they are more interested in seeing pictures of your children than thinning out your wallet.)

Big-city hotels can be luxurious, but they are also most expensive

To Save Money, Remember . . .

Large hotels, government-owned hotels, international chains, and big-city hotels are expensive. Prices usually rise with demand during festival and holiday periods. Off-season, many hotel clerks will take an offer. If the place is too expensive, tell the clerk your limit. He may drop his price or come up with a simpler, cheaper room.

When going door to door, rarely is the first place you check the best. It's worth 10 minutes of shopping to find out the going rate before you accept a room. You'll be surprised how prices vary as you walk farther from the station or down a street strewn with small hotels. Never judge a hotel by its exterior or lobby.

Ask to see the room before accepting. Then the clerk knows the room must pass your inspection and he'll try to earn your business. Notice that the boy who shows you the room is given two keys. You only asked for one room. He's instructed to show the hard-to-sell room first. If you insist on seeing both rooms, you'll get the best. Check out the rooms, expressing displeasure at anything that deserves it. The price will come down, or they'll show you a better room. If you accept a room without seeing it first and complain to the clerk, he'll probably look at you, bob his head, and smile.

Think about heat. In northern Asia (Japan and the Beijing region of China), anytime but midsummer, confirm that the radiator is in operation and that you've got plenty of warm blankets. In tropical Asia (year-round) and subtropical Asia (in season), humidity can be a killer, so think about keeping cool. Few budget rooms come with air-conditioning, but they should definitely have a fan, preferably an oversized overhead model, in good working condition. One with variable speed is best. Also look for mosquito netting over the beds. Think about noise. It's worth climbing a few stairs to cheaper rooms higher off the noisy road. Some towns never shut up. A room in back may lack a view, but it will also lack night noise. A room with an attached toilet and bath costs more. Save money and fresh air by getting a room with a bathroom down the hall. The fragrance of an attached pit toilet is worth it only if you have diarrhea.

Room prices are determined not by room quality but by hotel features such as a 24-hour reception desk, an elevator (rare), a classy lobby, the shower-to-room ratio, and the age of the facilities. If you can climb stairs, ring the night bell, and find a small old hotel without a modern shower and TV in every room, your budget will smile.

A person staying only one night is bad news to a hotel. If, before telling you whether there's a vacancy, they ask you how long you're staying, be ambiguous. Some hotels offer a special price for a long stay . . . to those who ask for it.

Avoid doing business through your hotel. It's much better style to go to the arena and get the sumo wrestling ticket yourself. You'll learn more, you'll save money, and you won't sit with other tourists who drown your Banzai! cheers with Yankee-pankee. So often, tourists are herded together by a conspiracy of hotel managers and tour organizers and driven through touristy evenings—500 flash attachments in a gymnasium drinking cheap sake and watching samurai swordsmen on stage—and leave disappointed. You can't relive your precious Asian nights, so do them right, on your own.

Always, on arrival, pick up the hotel's business card or address. In the most confusing cities, the cards include a little map. In many countries, they come written in English as well as the local script. Even the best pathfinders get lost in a big city, and it's scary not knowing the location of your hotel. With the card, you can hop into a cab and be home in minutes.

Always establish the complete and final price of a hotel before accepting. Know what is included and what taxes and services will be added on. More than once we've been given a bill that was double what we expected.

Asian-style Hotels

Cheap Asian hotels are dingy, old-fashioned, a bit run-down, central, friendly, safe, and government regulated, offering good-enough-for-the-locals, good-enough-for-me beds for $5 to $15 a night ($35 in Japan). No matter what your favorite newspaper travel writer or travel agent says, these are hard-core Asia: fun, cheap, and easy to find.

"Roughing it" in your own thatched hut

Guest Houses—Minshuku, Losmen, and Asian B&Bs

Guest houses are usually a notch below hotels in price and facilities offered. They are a special class of accommodations—small, warm, family run, offering a personal touch at a (usually) budget price. They are the next best thing to staying with a local family, and even if hotels weren't more expensive, we'd choose this budget alternative.

Each country has these friendly accommodations in varying degrees of abundance and formality. They have different names and offer considerably different facilities from country to country, but they all have this in common: they satisfy the need for a place to stay that gives you the privacy of a hotel and the comforts of home at a price you can afford. While information on some of the more established places is available in many budget travel guidebooks, we have always found that the best information is found locally, through tourist information offices, room-finding services, or even from the local man waiting for his bus or selling mangoes. In fact, many times the information is brought to you. We will never forget struggling off a bus upon our arrival in Kuta Beach, Bali. A dozen teenaged boys and girls were begging us to spend the night at their families' places. Delighted, we made a snap decision and followed the most attractive offer to a very nice budget losmen accommodation.

Your private teak cabana, Sri Lanka

Losmen, the small guest houses of Indonesia, are basic but clean. Similar guest houses are found in Malaysia. Dramatically higher in price but still fairly basic and cheaper than hotels are minshuku, the family-run guest houses of Japan.

You'll find government rest houses in former British colonies— India, Pakistan, Sri Lanka, Myanmar (formerly Burma), and Malaysia. They usually range between $5 and $15 a night. (Foreigners are sometimes intentionally overcharged with the unspoken blessing of local tourist boards.) These accommodations are always basic, with barracks-style dorm beds or a bed, table, and chair in a spartan private room. There's not even a guarantee that you'll have electricity or running water. More modern government-sponsored tourist bungalows can be excellent values in these countries at $10 to $20 a double.

Sri Lanka has some friendly private guest houses for very reasonable prices. Nepal has many communal hotels and lodges for $10 or less a night. The last section of this book covers the guest houses in each country more fully.

Hostels

Because of the abundance of cheap alternatives, hostels are not as popular for budget travelers in Asia as they are in Europe. In Japan, South Korea, and Taiwan, however, hostels offer an important budget alternative to hotels.

Hostels are not hotels, not by a long shot. Many people hate hostels. Others love hostels and will be hostelers for the rest of their lives, regardless of their budget. Hosteling is a spirit. A hosteler trades service and privacy for a chance to live simply and communally with people from around the world.

A "youth" hostel is not limited to young people. In fact, the International Youth Hostel Federation offers a discount on membership cards to "youths" over the age of 55. People of any age can go hosteling if they have the international membership card, available at your local student travel office or youth hostel office. (It can also be ordered by writing to American Youth Hostels, P.O. Box 37613, Washington, D.C. 20013-7613, or from Europe Through the Back Door; see catalog.)

A hostel provides no frills accommodations in clean dormitories. Sexes are segregated, with 4 to 20 people per room. A few hostels have doubles and family rooms. The facilities vary, but most provide more than you would expect. Some serve hearty, cheap meals in family-style settings. Others have a self-service kitchen complete with utensils, pots, and pans. (Do your shopping at the grocery down the block.) The hostel's common room is our favorite. This is where people gather, play games, tell stories, share information, read, write, and team up for future travels. Solo travelers find a family wherever they go in hostels. They are ideal meeting places for those in search of a travel partner.

Now for the drawbacks.

Hostels have strict rules. They lock up during the day (usually from 10:00 a.m. to 5:00 p.m.), and they have a curfew at night (10:00 or 11:00 p.m., occasionally midnight). When the doors are locked, those outside stay there. These curfews are for the greater good—not to make you miserable. In the mountains, the curfew is early because most people are early-rising hikers. Big cities have later curfews. (In India, there are no curfews and no lockup hours.)

Pillows and blankets are provided but not sheets. You can bring a regular single bed sheet (sewn into a sack if you like), rent one each night ($1 each), or buy a regulation hostel sheet-sack at the first hostel you hit (light, ideal design at a bargain price).

Hostel rooms can be large and packed. The first half hour after "lights out" reminds us of Boy Scout camp—giggles, burps, jokes, and strange noises in many languages. Snoring is permitted and practiced openly.

Theft can be a problem in hostels, but the answer is simple: don't leave valuables lying around (in some countries, even dirty tennis shoes are valuable), and use the storage lockers that are available in many hostels.

Getting a hostel bed during school vacation periods can be tricky. The most popular hostels fill up every day. Written reservations are possible, but we've never bothered. Telephone bookings are wonderful when the warden will take them—about 50 percent of the time. We always call ahead to try to reserve and at least check on the availability of beds. Without a reservation, you can count on landing a bed if you arrive in the morning before the hostel closes. If you miss that, line up with the scruffy gang for the 5:00 p.m. opening of the office, when any remaining beds are doled out. Hostel bed availability is very unpredictable.

The latest international youth hostel directory (volume 2 covers Asia), available where you get your card, lists everything you could ever want to know about each of Asia's 550 hostels—some 380 of them in Japan. In the book, you'll find which day or season the hostel is closed, what train or bus goes there, the distance from the station, number of beds, cooking facilities, phone number, and a great map locating all the hostels.

A number of Asian countries have dormitory-style youth hostel alternatives. In Taiwan, the China Youth Corps has 15 hostels and 8 activity centers (with accommodations) around the island. If these aren't booked by school groups (as they often are in the January-February and July-September vacation periods), you can get a dorm bed for $5 a night and three square meals for another $8 a day. Private rooms are sometimes available at higher rates. Contact CYC Head-quarters (219 Sung-Kiang Road, Taipei, tel. 543-5858) for details and directions. In other countries, there are hostel-type accommodations that will be discussed in more detail in the last part of this book.

Temples and Monasteries

One of the most fascinating and culturally stimulating alternatives for accommodation in many parts of Asia is to make a temporary home in a temple. From Zen Buddhists to Sikhs to Roman Catholics, the brethren of many religious orders are happy to share their humble dwelling with respectful travelers from around the world.

Never be afraid to ask at a temple if lodging is available. Offer to make a small donation in exchange for floor space, and you'll often be accepted. This is especially true in Korea, Taiwan, Thailand, and other predominantly Buddhist countries. Traditionally, a temple was a haven where wayfarers could always be sure of finding shelter for a night.

More to come on temples in the last part of this book.

Camping

In Asia, camping is a practical consideration only in combination with hiking or trekking, or at the beach. And even when hiking, there are other, often preferable, options. In Japan and Taiwan, where mountain hiking is extremely popular with younger people, a network of mountain huts and youth hostels makes camping usually unnecessary. In the Himalayas, we prefer to stay in the homes of villagers along the trail for the cultural experience. Certain routes in the Himalayas, however, particularly in India, do require camping out.

Car camping, while unknown in many parts of Asia, is on the increase in others, particularly Japan. You'll find a number of campgrounds along the coast and in the mountains of Japan. The Japan tourist office can provide you with a current listing.

For information on what to bring, read "Choosing a Himalayan Trek" in the Back Door on Nepal.

Sleeping Free

There are still people traveling in Asia on $5 a day—and less. The one thing they have in common is that they sleep free. If cheap losmen and hostels are still too expensive for your budget, you too can sleep free. It's neither difficult nor dangerous if you pick your spots cautiously, but it's not always comfortable and convenient. This is not a vagabonding guide, but any traveler may have an occasional free night. Faking it until the sun returns can be, at least in the long run, a good memory.

Sleeping Out. Asia has plenty of places to throw your sleeping bag. This sort of vagabonding is a bad idea, however, in tightly governed countries like China or Myanmar; in countries with rampant thievery and property crime like Thailand; and in regions with undeclared civil wars like parts of Sri Lanka. Sleeping out in big-city parks is asking for trouble. Away from the cities, in the mountains or on beaches, you can sleep where you like (although thieves report to work at popular beaches). It's best to keep a low profile when camping unofficially. Some people crash on the tropical beach in Thailand wearing just a T-shirt and covered with a towel. We don't encumber ourselves with sleeping bags in Asia, but if you'll be vagabonding a lot, bring a light bag.

Host Families. A few organizations will set you up with a host family in any country. You normally need to join the organization and pay a small fee. One of the most popular and best run organizations is Servas. This organization promotes international goodwill though personal contact. It allows you to be a host of foreigners coming to the United States, or you can be a guest of someone abroad, or both. After applying, you will be interviewed by a representative in your city. Then you will receive a book with the addresses of hosts in the countries you plan to visit. You write in advance to let your host know you're coming. You can eat and stay overnight at the host's house at no cost. Servas asks that you spend no more than three days with a host, unless you're invited. For an application, write: United States Servas Committee, 11 John Street, Suite 706, New York, NY 10038. Allow at least a month for the whole process.

Friends and Relatives. The nicest way to sleep free is as a guest of friends or relatives. We've had nothing but good experiences (and good sleep) at our "addresses" in Asia. There are two kinds of addresses: Asian addresses from home and those you pick up on the road.

Before you leave, do some research. Find out if you have any friends or relatives living in Asia. No matter how distant they are, unless you are a real jerk, they'll be tickled to have an American visitor. We always send a card announcing our visit to their town and telling them when we will arrive. They answer either "Please come visit us" or "Have a good trip." It is obvious from their letter (or lack of letter) if we are invited to stop by. Follow the same procedure with indirect contacts. There is no better way to really enjoy a country or to establish lifelong friendships than as the guest of someone living there.

The other kind of address is the kind you pick up during your travels. Exchanging addresses is almost as common as a handshake in Asia.

When people meet, they invite each other to visit sometime. We warn our friends that we may very well show up someday at their house, whether it's in Bangkok, Frankfurt, New Zealand, or Ottawa. When we do (and we do), it's always a good experience.

We're not freeloaders when we stay with friends or relatives in Asia. We are freely invited. We honestly would welcome them into our homes in the Seattle area (although a Seattle-ite is pretty safe, living in such an untouristed corner of the world). Both parties benefit from such a visit. Never forget that a Japanese family is just as curious and interested in you as you are in them. Equipped with hometown postcards and pictures of our families, we make a point to give as much from our culture as we are taking from the culture of our hosts. In this sort of cultural exchange, there are only winners. We insist on no special treatment, telling our hosts that we are most comfortable when no fuss is made over us. We don't wear out our welcome, and we follow up each visit with postcards to share the rest of our trip with our friends.

It is appropriate, whenever you are invited to the home of an Asian family for any reason, to offer a small gift on your arrival. This is especially true in Japan. It needn't be expensive—we like to carry Space Needle keychains and hometown postcards—but it should express that you were thinking about them. Sometimes it's embarrassing when they shower you with expensive gifts in return.

Trains and Stations. Trains and stations can be great for sleeping free. On the trains, success hinges on getting enough room to stretch out. (See How to Sleep on the Train, chap. 2.)

When you have no place to go for the night in a city, you can retreat to the station for a safe place to spend the night for free (assuming the station stays open all night). Entering the main Delhi station at 3:00 a.m., you wonder if you're in a mission for the homeless in New York. You, too, are eligible to join the sea of bundled bodies on the expansive concrete floors. Your ticket or rail pass entitles you to a free night in the waiting room of any Indian train station. You're simply waiting for the early train.

We don't relish the mission scene in many stations, but we do just fine in the first-class waiting rooms. These are definitely not up to Western standards, but we feel more secure dozing off here. Most stations won't check for the required first-class ticket if you're a Westerner.

Be on guard for theft. Wear your money belt, and check your bags at the left baggage counter.

An airport lounge can be your bedroom after a late night landing or before a very early flight. We sometimes curl up in a chair or two here rather than hassle with a few hours sleep at a hotel.

Bathing beauty—Bangkok

It would be stretching things a bit to suggest that Asia is one big free hotel. But with a little imagination, you can sleep for free on beaches, in temples, you-name-it. Just carry your passport with you, attach your belongings to you so they don't get stolen, and use good judgment in your choice of a free bed.

Accommodation Traumas—Bathing, Mosquitoes, Laundry, Toilets, and Other Concerns

Bathing and mosquitoes may not be on your mind before a trip, but they will be once you're in Asia. Though we'll take a look at these in other parts of the book, let's take a peek at them in relation to your room.

Showers are a Yankee fetish. A night without a shower is traumatic to many of us; it can ruin a day. Here are some tips on survival in a world that doesn't start or end with squeaky hair.

First of all, get used to the idea that you won't have a shower every night. Depending on where you're traveling, you may not have a hot water shower for eight weeks. The real winners are those who persuade themselves how much they love to pour buckets of cold water over their heads. That's commonly what you'll find in tropical Asia—a plastic bucket full of water next to the water tap in the "shower" stall. In the bucket, you'll find a scooper you can use to pour cold water over yourself. Given the constant humidity of much of this part of the world, it will soon be something you'll look forward to.

In China, Taiwan, Hong Kong, Nepal, and other more temperate climates, guest houses will often have showers, but the water will be hot only at certain times. Hot water 24 hours a day is a luxury many of us take for granted. When you check in, ask if there's a best time to take a hot shower. If a shower is important to you, take it while you can. If there is no electricity, take a shower in the late afternoon after the basin has had a chance to warm up. A clever way to avoid a cold shower is to fill two buckets and set them out in the sun in the morning. By afternoon your shower's ready.

The mosquitoes in Asia are no worse than those in much of the U.S.A. Still, try to get a room with a good mosquito net. The best are made of synthetic. The worst are made of a densely woven cotton that stifles air circulation, even with a fan. Lighting a mosquito coil also helps.

Don't worry about those other little critters, like cockroaches. They're a fact of life in this part of the world. Try to see them in a positive light, as Asian roommates.

Travel Laundry

We have a photographer friend who travels extensively in Asia and Europe. He packs only black clothing—from shoes and socks right up to pants and shirt—on the theory that if the dirt doesn't show, he doesn't have to worry about laundry or too many friends.

Anybody traveling anywhere has to wash clothes. Our washer and dryer won't fit under the airplane seat, so we've learned to do without. Here are some tips.

Choose your travel wardrobe with washing and drying in mind: quick-dry and few wrinkles. Your self-service laundry kit should include a "travel clothesline." Stretch it over your bathtub or across your bedroom so your garments will dry while you slumber. Many hotel room sinks come without stopper to discourage in-room washing. Bring a universal sink stopper. It outperforms a stuffed-up sock in the drain. You can also line the sink with a large plastic bag and wash in that. A large zip-lock bag makes a good laundry bag. Small packets of laundry soap are available throughout Asia.

Hotel rooms around the world have multilingual "no washing clothes in the room" signs. This may be the most ignored rule on earth—after "eat your peas." Interpret this as "I have lots of good furniture and a fine carpet in this room and I don't want your drippy laundry ruining things" order. In other words, you can wash clothes very carefully, wring them nearly dry, and hang them in a nondestructive way.

Your laundry should keep a low profile. Even though a glance outside a Singapore housing estate might suggest otherwise (wet clothes dangle from four-foot rods like damp flags), check with the management before you hang your laundry out the window. You can always hang it quietly in the bathroom.

Some hotels will let your laundry join theirs on the lines out back or on the rooftop. Many guest houses will even do your laundry for a very nominal charge, labor costs being ridiculously cheap in most of Asia.

Wring your wet laundry as dry as possible. Rolling it in a towel can be helpful. Always separate the back and front of clothes to speed drying. Smooth out your wet clothing, button shirts, and set collars to encourage wrinkle-free drying. If your shirt or dress dries wrinkled, hang it in a steamy bathroom. (This precaution is unnecessary in the already steamy tropics.) In hot climates, we often rinse out a sweaty shirt several times a day and put it on immediately. It's wet, cool, refreshing . . . for a few minutes.

Japan and major Asian cities have self-service laundromats. They can be expensive and slow, but you can use the time to catch up on postcards and your journal or chat with the local crowd that's causing the delay. Full-service places are quicker—"just drop it off and come back this afternoon"—and even more common. The expense isn't outrageous for the occasional clean-clothes splurge, and every time we slip into a freshly cleaned pair of pants, we figure it was worth it.

Travelers' Toilet Trauma

Be prepared in Asia for toilets that are dirtier than and different from those at home. Americans who need disposable bibs to sit on and a paper sanitation-guaranteed strap draped over their toilet are in for toilet trauma. Those of us who need a throne to sit on are in the minority. Most humans, Asians in particular, sit on their haunches and nothing more.

John Gottberg, the previous co-author of this book, is an unrecognized expert in the field of toiletology. He says that the awkwardness with which Westerners approach Asian toilets is paralleled by the way Asians are traumatized by Western toilets. Most humans sit on their haunches. On a boat trip a few years ago from Java to Sumatra, few if any of the Asians traveling deck class with John had ever seen Western toilets, and that's what this new ship was equipped with. When John visited the toilet a few hours into the 60-hour journey, he discovered that (1) there were footprints on the rims, and (2) the concept of flushing was unknown to his Indonesian shipmates. By the second morning, the rest room was a cesspool. John quickly befriended some Canadians traveling cabin class and made arrangements to use their toilet. (You'll notice Asian airplanes have stick-figure decals over their toilets explaining to nonfrequent flyers how to use them.)

Traditional Asian toilets are of the squat-and-drop variety. They range in style from two slats over a hole to porcelain pots with built-in footprints. Some of them even flush. Other times, there may be a small can of lime to sprinkle over the droppings. More often, there's nothing more than flies in a holding pattern. Whatever you think of a pit toilet, it's a lot cleaner than a Western-style one would be in the same place.

Toilet paper, like silverware, is an "essential" that most people on our planet don't use. Throughout rural South and Southeast Asia, many pit toilets have a can of water sitting next to them, on the floor, on the left-hand side. We don't want to get too graphic in our description, but consider that a billion people in that corner of the world never eat with their left hands.

Some argue that water is a more sanitary cleaner than toilet paper. This is one case where we prefer not to go local. We prefer paper, and it's available everywhere in Asia . . . except in the rest rooms. You'll need to buy it in the shop and carry it with you. Or visit a first-class hotel or restaurant and borrow 10 or 12 yards of good soft stuff. Local grade T.P. is often closer to wax or crepe paper. But only Americans take the time to critique the stuff.

The importance of carrying toilet paper can't be overemphasized. Remember what we said about those sudden onsets of Delhi belly?

When you're on a long bus trip, a queasy tummy doesn't wait for the long intervals between rest stops. John recalls a bus trip from Kathmandu to New Delhi when half of the passengers (not including him, thankfully) had the runs. Every 20 minutes, someone would scream, "Stop the bus!" The bus would lurch off to the side of the road and the ailing party would scamper out of the bus, drop his drawers, and let go. It wasn't pretty, but without toilet paper, it would have been much worse.

Finding a public toilet that wouldn't gag a maggot can be tough. We count on subway or train stations, Western-style fast-food restaurants, government buildings, museums, classy hotels, and department stores in major cities.

No matter where you are, remember that any place serving food or drinks has a rest room. No restaurateur would label his toilet so those on the street could see, but you can walk into most cafés politely and confidently and find a toilet somewhere in the back. Some call this rude. We call it survival. Just smile and ask, "Toilet?" We're rarely turned down. Timid people buy a drink they don't want, but that's unnecessary. Just be polite and say thank you and good-bye.

In India and Nepal, particularly, many locals simply create a toilet. In some countries, especially Japan, it is a major faux pas to wear your shoes into a "water closet." You'll find a pair of W.C. slippers outside the door. Change into the slippers, wear them only inside the W.C., then leave them back outside the door when you change into your shoes.

On a bus ride in India and Nepal, you might stop in a small village where there is no public toilet. Men follow the men, and women follow the women. They're usually heading for an appropriate relief point outside the village. Long skirts allow women the same flexibility men enjoy.

Eating Cheap

Many vacations revolve around great meals. And for good reason: Asian restaurants serve some of the world's top cuisine at some of the best prices.

We're not gourmets, so most of our experience lies in eating well cheaply. In South and Southeast Asia, galloping gluttons thrive on $5 a day by frequenting outdoor food stands. In East Asia, you can get by for only slightly more at noodle shops and corner coffeehouses. Those with a more refined palate and a little more money can mix hawker stalls with satisfying, atmospheric, and enjoyable restaurant meals and manage just fine on $10 a day. This $10-a-day budget includes $2 for a light breakfast, $3 for lunch, and a $5 dinner.

Equate restaurant prices anywhere in the world with those in your hometown. The cost of eating is determined not by the local standard but by your personal standard. Many Americans can't find an edible meal for less than $20 in their hometown. Their neighbors enjoy eating out for half that. If you can enjoy a $10 meal in New York, Chicago, or San Francisco, you'll eat well in Tokyo, Calcutta, or Singapore for the same price.

Forget the scare stories. Anyone who spends $100 for a steak in Tokyo has no right to beef. In a land of few cows, smart travelers eat chicken, fish, rice, and vegetables.

Let us fill you in on filling up in Asia.

Restaurants

Restaurants are of various breeds. As in the United States, the range goes from the hot dog-type stand on the street to the expensive restaurant complete with a hovering waiter and endless fine food and drink. The street food in Asia is many notches above what you'd get here. And the price you pay in top-quality restaurants is much less.

Eating out consistently in the upper-end restaurants will ravage a tight budget. But it would be criminal to pass through Asia without sampling the local specialties served in good restaurants. You should relish a country's high cuisine; culturally, it's just as important as its museums.

To help with our budget, we look for an inexpensive restaurant with value in mind. Average tourists are attracted, like flies to cowpies, to the biggest neon sign that boasts, "We speak English and accept Visa cards." Wrong! The key to finding a good meal is to find a restaurant packed with loyal, local customers enjoying themselves. After a few days in an Asian country, you'll have no trouble telling a local hangout from a tourist trap. Take advantage of local favorites.

Restaurants listed in your guidebook are usually fine. Pay special attention to Lonely Planet recommendations. But know that the best bargains are often not found in any book.

You can find your own restaurant. Leave the tourist center, stroll around until you find a crowd of locals eating happily. Or ask your hotel clerk, or even someone on the street, for a good place. Many locals will assume you want an American-style meal. Make it clear you're interested in immersing your taste buds in local culture.

Some Asian restaurants post their menus outside. In Japan, eater-friendly wax models are often mounted and prices posted in the windows of reasonably priced cafés. In other countries, you may see cooked food displayed openly. Feel free to go inside, point, and ask prices before deciding to order.

Finding the right restaurant is half the battle. Then you need to order the right meal. Ordering in a foreign language can be fun, or it can be an ordeal. Restaurants in major tourist centers often have English menus lying around. Ask for one. If nothing else, you may get the waiter who speaks the goodest English. A pocket phrase book or menu reader can be helpful.

Japanese window displays make "reading the menu" easy

We prefer just pointing at food, whether it is displayed by the management or by another diner. You can't go wrong. People are usually helpful and understanding toward the poor monoglot tourist. If they aren't, you probably picked a place that sees too many of them. Asians who have the most patience with tourists are the ones who rarely deal with them.

Our rule of thumb is merely to get a basic idea of what's cooking, have some fun with the waiter, be loose and adventurous, and just order something. We never order the same meal as our partners. We share, sampling twice as many dishes. If you're really in the dark, it's best to order one high-risk and one low-risk meal. At worst, we learn what we don't like and split the chicken and rice.

In many countries, such as China and Thailand, sharing is made easy by "family-style" serving. In other words, the more, the merrier. Get a half-dozen people together, go out to a restaurant, have everybody pick something different from the menu (go for a variety: soup, vegetables, meat, and seafood), order a big bowl of rice for everyone to share, and you're on your way to a memorable meal. If anything, the waiters will be impressed by your willingness to dig into the native food. Very often they'll run over with a special treat for everyone to sample—like pigeon feet.

The best values in Asian entrées are fish, pork, and mutton. Beef, imported soda (like colas), and desserts are the worst values. Skipping those, we can enjoy some classy meals for $5 or less.

Before the bill comes, make a mental tally of roughly how much your meal should cost. When the bill comes (get it by catching the waiter's eye and, with raised hands, scribble with an imaginary pencil on your palm), it should vaguely resemble the figure you expected. It should have the same number of digits. If the total is a surprise, ask to have it itemized and explained. Sometimes waiters make the same "innocent" mistakes repeatedly, knowing most tourists are so befuddled by the money and menu that they'll pay whatever number lies at the bottom of the bill.

Food Stands, Noodle Shops, and the Like

By far, the cheapest and most colorful places to eat are at the small food stands that surround the market areas and bus stations of Southeast Asia and come out at night in places like Hong Kong and even Japan. Particularly in Thailand and Malaysia, you'll find some tasty and wonderful bargains on the street. In most cases, the food is safe and good to eat, if you heed the precautions covered later in this chapter.

MacFast

Fast-food places are everywhere in big cities. These may not be exciting, and their prices are often double what you'd pay in the States, but at least at McDonald's (and Kentucky Fried Chicken, and Burger King, and Wendy's—the list goes on) you know exactly what you're getting and how quickly. A hamburger, fries, and shake are fun halfway through your trip (we apologize if we've disillusioned anyone). Each country has its equivalent of the hamburger or hot dog stand. Whatever their origin, they're a hit with the young locals and a handy place for a quick bite.

Other Low Cuisine Value Spots

A sure value for your dollar, yen, or rupee is a department store cafeteria. Especially prevalent in Japan, these places are designed for the housewife who has a sharp eye for a good value.

In Bangkok, Singapore, and the larger cities of Malaysia, malls are springing up all too quickly. But one good side effect is the cheap restaurants you'll find inside. Though more expensive than what you'll find on the street, they offer predictable low-stress Western food for the homesick or culture shocked.

In most countries there are numerous cheap places (and potential English-speaking new friends) around the university districts. They can save you a lot of yen in Japan.

Tipping

We're not known for flashy tipping. In fact, we think it's a pretty archaic way of paying people. We're happy to report that most Asians feel the same way. People are paid for doing a job, and they don't expect more on top of it. In Japan, the most Westernized of all Asian lands, a 15 percent service charge is added onto the bill in more expensive restaurants, but no more is required. Most budget restaurants in Japan don't have a service charge. Nowhere are you expected to tip taxi drivers (although it's good form to tell him to keep the small change). If you're reading this book, you won't be staying in Intercontinental hotels, so don't worry about tipping bellboys. If a local person goes out of his way to show you some sight, a small gift (like one of those Statue of Liberty pens you're toting around) is more appropriate than a monetary reward.

Do not confuse tipping with baksheesh (payoffs), begging, or temple donations. They all have their places and their proper handling—which will be discussed in chapter 4, Finances and Money.

What Not to Eat and Drink and Why

Throughout Asia, you'll see some of the cheapest, most appetizing and nose-pleasing foods—as well as some of the most repulsive—offered by street vendors and at hawker stalls. The food may be perfectly fine, but think twice before ordering. Don't ask yourself if it has been hygienically prepared; on that basis, you'd never try any street food. Consider these questions: Has this food been thoroughly cooked? Has it been recently cooked, or has it been sitting all day in the sun exposed to flies? Has it been taken off the grill with a utensil rather than dirty hands? If it contains water, has it been boiled for several minutes?

Except in very Westernized societies with modern standards (Japan, Singapore, and better hotels in Hong Kong), don't drink water that hasn't been boiled. This includes lemonade and other water-based drinks, though tea and bottled drinks are normally fine. Peel all fruit before eating. Don't eat raw vegetables, including lettuce and tomatoes, even (especially) if they've been washed in local water. Try as you may, if you're wandering in the Third World, you won't be 100 percent successful at avoiding minor stomach ailments (a.k.a. Delhi belly, Tehran tummy, "The Big D"). But don't be so fanatically cautious that you brush your teeth in Coca-Cola. Study chapter 7, Health. Then go ahead, eating carefully and well. Food is a wonderful part of travel in Asia

Going Vegetarian

You don't have to philosophically agree that animals also have a right to live to receive the benefits of vegetarian eating. Since meat has a greater potential to carry the bugs that will make you sick, we recommend minimizing your meat intake in Asia. In more Westernized cities like Hong Kong and Singapore, there's not much risk. But on the road in India, we put restaurant meat one step above road kill and rarely in our stomachs.

You can get all the protein and nutrients you need by eating the right combination of foods. Grains and legumes together provide the protein needed. In most Asian countries, this combination is the normal diet, such as rice and lentils in India and rice and tofu in China and Japan.

You'll be surprised at how much better you feel in a hot climate eating a lighter vegetarian meal. And it may change your life-style. After going mostly vegetarian in Asia, we're no longer wowed by red meat. In fact, despite pressure from mid-Western relatives, we feel closer to the earth and healthier eating lower on the food chain.

Exotic Fruits

Perhaps tropical Asia's greatest taste treat is the incredible variety of colorful exotic fruits that travelers encounter here for the first time. Everyone knows the pineapple, the mango, and the banana, but how many have ever tasted the luscious purple mangosteen, whose colonial reputation was such that Queen Victoria offered a small fortune to have one delivered unspoiled to England? (No one succeeded.) Or the oddly shaped starfruit, its juicy pulp contained within a delicate yellow-orange flesh?

Look for the salak, its applelike pulp encased within a brown snake-like skin; the juicy sirsak, a large green fruit also known as a soursop; the jackfruit or nangka, the world's largest fruit, which makes excellent fruit drinks or (surprise!) curries; the rambutan, a furry red fruit related to the litchi; the mowiwowi, a leafy wonder that's eaten like an artichoke and tastes like a pomegranate; the pink-white mountain apple with its sugary pulp; and the notorious durian, which turns many

Westerners away with its offensive smell before they get close enough to savor its custardy interior. All but one of these delights await the Asian wanderer. Buy at a local market, peel, and enjoy.

How to Use Chopsticks

No one is really sure how chopsticks came to be the principal eating utensils of East Asia—one-third of all humankind. Were chopsticks developed to pick up the delicate medallions of chopped meat and vegetables typical of Chinese and Japanese cooking? Or was the cuisine fashioned to fit the means of eating it?

Whatever. If you can't use chopsticks, there's no point in puzzling over their origin. Here are a few tricks to minimize your feeble fumbling:

(1) Take one chopstick in your hand and place it firmly in the crotch between your thumb and forefinger. Now move the chopstick between your middle and ring finger and lock it in place.

(2) Take the second chopstick and hold it between the tips of your thumb and forefinger like a pencil.

(3) While the lower chopstick remains stationary and rigid, the upper one does all the work, opening and closing against the lower chopstick like a pincer. Remember: you eat with the thinner tips, not the thick ends of the utensils.

(4) Practice! Once you can pick up a peanut or a grain of rice and deliver it to your mouth, you've got it made. After a few days it becomes effortless and seems like the only appropriate way to enjoy East Asian food.

Aristocratic chopstickers rub the rough disposable kind together to smooth off the corners. It's rude to store your sticks stuck like a sword in your rice. Many believe lovers can see whose love is greater by breaking their sticks like Americans break a wishbone. He or she with the fattest chopstick loves the most.

Eating and Sleeping on a Budget—The Five Commandments

You could get eight good hours of sleep and three square meals in Asia for $10 a day if your budget required it. If you have any budget limitations at all, keep these rules in mind.

1. Budget for price variances. Prices more than triple from south to north and west to east. Budget more for Japan and large cities, and get by on less than your daily allowance in rural South and Southeast Asia. Exercise those budget alternatives where they will save you the most money (a hostel saves $30 in Japan but may save you nothing in India). If your trip will last only as long as your money does, travel fast in the northeast and hang out in the south.

2. Adapt to Asian tastes. Most unhappy people we meet in Asia could find the source of their problems if they examined their own stubborn desire to find the U.S.A. in Asia. If you accept and at least try doing things the Asian way, besides saving money, you'll be happier and learn a lot more on your trip. You cannot expect the local people to be warm and accepting of you if you don't accept them. Things are different in Asia. That's why you go. Asian travel is a package deal, and you have no choice but to accept the good with the "bad." If you require the comforts of home, you'll have a better vacation if you stay there.

3. Avoid the tourist centers. The best values are not in the places that boast with neon signs, "We speak English." Find local restaurants and hotels. You'll get more for your money.

4. Swallow pride and save money. This is a personal matter, dependent largely on your pride and your budget. Many people cringe every time we use the word "cheap"; others appreciate the directness. We're not talking about begging and groveling around Asia. We're talking about being able to ask a hotel clerk for the least expensive room; ordering water even if the waiter wants you to order wine; asking how much something costs before ordering it and saying, "No thanks" if the price isn't right. Demand equal and fair treatment as a tourist (unless it's not available), fight the price when appropriate, and search on. Remember, even if the same thing would cost much more at home, the local rate, as a matter of principle, should prevail.

5. Minimize the use of hotels and expensive restaurants. Enjoying the sights and culture of Asia has nothing to do with how much you're spending to eat and sleep. Take advantage of the many alternatives to hotels and restaurants.

You can spend your entire trip in Asia without going to a single hotel or expensive restaurant, and you'll likely learn, experience, and enjoy more than the tourist who spends in a day what you spend in a week.

4
Finances and Money

Traveler's Checks

Smart travelers use traveler's checks. They are replaceable if lost or stolen. Before you buy your checks, choose the best company, currency, and mix of denominations.

What Company?

Choose a big, well-known company. American Express (AmExCo), Visa, Bank of America, and First National City are all widely known in Asia, as are Cook's and Barclay's (both British). Traveler's checks cost only about 1.5 percent of purchase value, and it's not worth getting obscure checks to save. Any legitimate check is good at banks, but it's nice to have a check that private parties and small shops will recognize and honor. (In some countries, traveler's checks get a 2 to 3% better exchange rate than cash, so they can even save you money.)

If you go to India, it's wise to carry a traveler's check other than American Express, or at least another type along with AmExCo. Some banks there apparently have had trouble with check fraud.

Check into refund policies and services provided. We like AmExCo for its centrally located "landmark" offices, travel service, clients' mail service, refund policy, and universal recognition. The American Automobile Association sells AmExCo traveler's checks to members for free, a savings of 1.5 percent. Many savings and loans associations, credit unions, and so on, also sell major brand traveler's checks commission-free. Ask around.

You'll hear many stories about slow or fast refunds. None of them matters. Extenuating circumstances dictate the refund speed. Just keep your checks in your money belt and your money belt around your waist, and you'll probably never lose your checks.

What Kind of Currency?

You can buy traveler's checks in U.S. dollars, several European currencies, and the Japanese yen. We buy our traveler's checks in U.S. dollars. Not only are they stable but merchants around the world generally know what their currency is worth in dollars. Besides, it's simpler; we think in dollars. However, if your trip is going to be mostly in Japan, it's worth thinking about buying your checks in yen.

What Denomination Should You Choose?

Large bills and small bills each have advantages and disadvantages. Large checks save on signing and bulk. Small checks enable you to change money more accurately, saving money. Let's say you're only passing through a country and just need $10. If you have only $100 checks, you'll have to change back $90. Since there's a 4 to 5 percent difference between a bank's buying and selling rates, this sloppy money management (changing $100 to spend $10) costs you about $10. So spending $10 actually costs you $20. Also, with smaller checks, if you're out of cash and the banks are closed, it's easy to find a merchant or even another traveler who will change a $20 traveler's check. Changing a large check in that circumstance would be tough.

For $1,000 in checks, we would choose three $100, ten $50, and ten $20 checks. For longer trips (or bigger spenders), American Express issues $500 and $1,000 checks that can be broken into smaller denominations for free in most of its major offices throughout the world (except in Kathmandu).

Remember, traveler's checks are replaceable if lost or stolen, but you must keep track of the serial numbers. Leave a photocopy of all your check numbers (along with copies of your passport, plane ticket, and any other vital documents or statistics) with someone at home, and carry copies in your luggage and in your wallet. Update your traveler's check log frequently, so if you lose your checks, you'll know exactly which ones to claim a refund on.

Changing Money in Asia

Remember, it's expensive to change money. You lose money and time every time you change, so estimate carefully how much you'll need. In touristy places outside of major cities, bank charges can be high, and it's not uncommon to spend an hour in a bank line.

You need your passport to change a check at a bank. There are many "lost" checks floating around Asia, and no bank will change a check without a passport to match.

Many Asian countries also have licensed money changers. Their small shops or stalls are often concentrated near the financial centers of larger towns and cities. These merchants may handle fifty currencies from Asia and around the world. They give better rates than banks on cash, and if you have large denomination bills ($50 or $100), you may be able to bargain to get a better deal than their posted exchange rates.

Whenever possible, don't change money in hotels, shops, or nightclubs. Many of these places do change money but only at a substantial profit. An exception is Japan, where we always try to change our money at major hotels. Not only is the wait much shorter—in hotels you can just walk up to the exchange counter, while Japanese banks leave you sitting in a waiting lounge for a good half hour as your transaction is processed—but hotels usually give better rates! Technically, only hotel patrons are supposed to have this privilege. But if you intend to have lunch in their coffee shop, they'll be happy to help you . . . even if something comes up and you end up eating elsewhere.

Many Americans exclaim with glee, "Gee, they accept bank cards and dollars! There's no need to ever change money." Without knowing it, they're changing money every time they buy something—at a loss. Use the local cash.

Paper money of most Asian countries is accepted at banks anywhere else in Asia. The U.S. dollar is just one of many currencies floating in the international exchange market. If you leave Indonesia with paper money, that 10,000 rupiah note is just as good as dollars in Nepal. Many people change excess local money back to dollars, then change those dollars into the next country's currency. That needless double changing makes no sense and is expensive.

Coins, however, are generally worthless outside their country. Spend your coins or change them into paper before you cross the border. Otherwise, you've just bought a bunch of little souvenirs.

Credit cards are widely accepted in large hotels, tourist restaurants, and ritzy shops. This is exciting news to all the people who have gleefully put an extra middleman into our financial lives. Credit cards work in Asia—but not in the night market or at Akiko's Ryokan. They slam the "back door" shut on your travels. Be careful when you use your plastic money. Many people have been terribly ripped off. Take one for cash advances and major purchases (car rentals, plane tickets, and so on). But it's best to leave home with traveler's checks and change into local cash as you go.

The currencies of China, Myanmar, and a few of the other Communist and Socialist countries of Asia can't be exchanged outside their country. To discourage you from dealing dollars on their black market, and to encourage you to spend lots of money at the official value, these countries have installed a bureaucratic process known as the Currency Declaration Form. You'll be handed a form as you pass through immigration. On it, you are expected to declare all foreign currency (including traveler's checks) that you are bringing into the country, as well as luxury goods such as cameras and watches. This will be endorsed by customs, who can inspect your baggage if they want. In China, you can convert your traveler's checks into FECs (foreign exchange certificates) or renminbi at banks, hotels, airports, and railway stations in major cities. When you leave, your money and belongings will be checked against the Currency Declaration Form. If you don't have official government exchange receipts for all unaccounted-for currency and goods, you'll have to do some fast talking or be slapped with a big fine. You can convert unused currency back to dollars as you exit.

China and Myanmar have gone a step further by requiring that travelers pay for hotels, transportation, government store goods, and even postage with foreign exchange certificates (China) or with the local currency accompanied by proof of official exchange (Myanmar).

Cash

Carry some cash for the times when there isn't a bank around or it's closed. People always know roughly what an American dollar is worth, and you can easily exchange it. Several hundred dollars in cash stowed safely in your money belt comes in handy for emergencies.

Consider buying one day's budget in the currency of each country you'll be visiting before leaving home. Your bank (or AFEX, 1-800-366-2339) can sell you large bills from most countries for the same price you'll pay in Asia. Major airports have foreign exchange counters. Before flying out of Bangkok for Malaysia, for example, you can change leftover Thai baht into Malay dollars. Either way, you'll have enough money to get settled in each new country without worrying about banking as soon as you arrive. This is a wonderful convenience, especially if you arrive at night or on a weekend when banks are closed. Or you can wait in a line for a poor exchange rate at airport and railroad station currency counters.

When you arrive in a new country, get a good sampling of the local coins and bills and orient yourself monetarily. Many Americans refuse to understand the "strange" money of Asia. You won't find George Washington or Abe Lincoln, but it's all logical. Each system is decimalized just like ours. There are a hundred "little ones" (cents) in every "big one" (dollar). Only the names have changed—to confuse the tourist. In fact, most of the world's currency makes a lot more sense than American currency. Foreign visitors are confused to find all of our bills the same size and color. In most Asian countries and elsewhere (including Canada), bills change color and increase in size from smaller to larger denominations, so there's little chance of mistaking a $1 bill for a $20.

On arrival in a country, warm up your human exchange rate calculator. Equate the unit of currency (yen, baht, rupee, or whatever) into American cents. For example, if there are 25 Indian rupees in a U.S. dollar, each rupee is worth 4 cents. Keep it simple: think of a rupee as a nickel. If yogurt costs 2 rupees, then it costs a U.S. dime. There are 100 paise in a rupee. If a chapati costs 50 paise, it costs the equivalent of half a nickel. Two hundred rupees is $10. Quiz yourself. Some currencies are more difficult, but all are manageable. Survival on a budget requires getting comfortable with the local currency. Although we prefer to mentally adjust to the currency, some travelers simply use a small calculator.

Cash Advances and Other Options

More and more travelers are funding their travels with cash advances on their credit cards. Visa and MasterCard are best. If trends continue, traveler's checks may soon be a thing of the past. Banks that accept credit card advances usually give the best possible exchange rates with minimal paperwork. The disadvantage is that more places change traveler's checks than do credit card cash advances, and credit card advances cost you the 18 percent or whatever credit card interest rate from day one. Another concern is that those relying on credit card advances will need to change large amounts in big cities to cover them through the countryside. Many budget travelers on extended trips restock their traveler's check supply with cash advances, even though there is an extra loss from the double exchange necessary to do this. A "debit card" allows you to draw money without any interest expense directly from your existing home bank account. It's as simple as writing checks. Ask your bank for the latest on this quickly developing new convenience for travelers. You can use your American Express card at any American Express office to buy U.S. dollar traveler's checks.

You can either charge the checks or write a personal check on your bank account in America. This minimizes the loss in currency exchange and avoids interest expenses.

Major airports have cash machines for local currency. Before your trip, check with your bank or credit card company to see where you can use these.

Keys to Successful Bargaining

In much of the world, the price tag—if there is one—is only an excuse to argue. Bargaining is the accepted and expected method of finding a compromise between the wishful thinking of the merchant and buyer.

Prices are "soft" throughout much of Asia. The only exceptions are Japan and major stores in Hong Kong, Singapore, and other large cities. You should try to beat the price in street markets wherever you go.

While bargaining is important from a budgetary standpoint, it's also fun. Many travelers are addicted hagglers who would gladly skip a tour of a Buddhist ruin to fight it out with the crazy local merchants. Here are our ten commandments for the successful bargainer.

1. Determine whether bargaining is appropriate. It's bad shopping etiquette to make an offer for a wool sweater in a Tokyo department store. It's foolish not to do so at a Tibetan refugee weaving stall in Kathmandu. If there is no price tag, first ask, "How much?" When you hear the price, say, "It's just too much money." If there is a price tag, deliver the same response. In either case, you've put the merchant in a position to make the first offer. If he comes down even 2 percent, there's nothing sacred about the price. Haggle away.

2. Determine the merchant's cost. Many merchants will settle for a nickel profit rather than lose the sale entirely. Promise yourself that no matter how exciting the price becomes, you won't buy. Then work the cost down to rock bottom. When it seems to have fallen to a record low, rip yourself away. That last price he hollers out as you turn the corner and disappear out of sight is usually about a nickel above cost. Armed with this knowledge, you can confidently demand a fair price at the next souvenir stand—and probably get it.

3. Find out what the locals pay. If the price is not posted, you can assume that there is a double price standard—one for locals and one for tourists. If only tourists buy the item you're pricing, see what a Thai, Chinese, or Indian tourist would be charged. Rick thought he did very well in Singapore's Chinatown market until he learned his Indian friend bought an identical shirt for 40 percent less. Many merchants just assume that Americans and Europeans—expatriate residents as well as tourists—have more money to spend than Asians.

In a taxi, demand the meter. If there is no meter, or if it is conveniently "broken," negotiate a price with the driver before you close the door. Don't wait until you arrive at your destination and then allow the cabbie to "estimate" the price of the ride. Know what the locals pay.

4. Preprice each item. Remember that the price tags are totally meaningless and can serve only to distort your idea of an item's true worth. The merchant is playing a psychological game. People often feel that if they can cut the price 50 percent, they are doing great. Well, the merchant responds by quadrupling his prices. Then the tourist haggles the price in half and happily pays twice what that souvenir is worth. The best way to deal with crazy price tags is to ignore them. Before you even see the price tag, preprice the item you are interested in. Determine what it's worth to you, considering the hassles involved in packing it or shipping it home. This value, not the price tag, should be your guide in determining a souvenir's worth. Some merchants will even show you their "wholesale" cost to set a lower limit for bargaining. This is usually another ploy.

When you're in a market, stop by a number of vendors' stalls to compare prices. Quality and prices can vary widely.

It's a good idea to visit a government store, a handicraft center, or a large department store to price items before doing any serious shopping. Asian national capitals and many other large cities have such showcases. These offer a great opportunity to study the variety of souvenirs available in the country, get some idea of comparative quality, and learn the government-regulated ceiling price.

5. Don't hurry. Get to know the shopkeeper. Accept his offer for tea; talk with him. It is the Asian way of doing business. If you rush your purchase, you'll be seen as a typical tourist who has more money than time. If you take the time, you can get a better price, and more important, you can make a friend.

6. Be indifferent; never look impressed. To guarantee a fixed price, fall in love with that item right in front of the merchant. Look longingly into the eyes of that bronze Vishnu. As soon as the merchant perceives the "I gotta have that!" in you, you will never get the best price. He knows you have plenty of money to buy something you really want. He knows about American prices. Never be openly crazy about an item.

7. Impress him with your knowledge—real or otherwise. You'll gain the merchant's respect, and you'll be more likely to get good quality merchandise. Before Bob even started to talk price, he visited carpet shops in Kathmandu just to find out how the carpets were made and what to look for in a good one. He was then equipped to bargain confidently.

8. Employ a third person. Use a friend who is worried about the ever-dwindling budget, or who doesn't like the price, or who is bored and wants to return to the hotel. This trick may work to bring the price down faster.

9. Show the merchant your money. Physically offer him "all you have" to pay for whatever you are bickering over. He'll be tempted to just grab your money and say, "Oh, all right."

10. If the price is still too much, leave. Never worry about having taken too much of the merchant's time and tea. They are experts at making the tourist feel guilty for not buying. It's all part of the game. Most merchants, by local standards, are financially well off.

Souvenir Strategy

If your trip includes several countries, it's a good idea to save your souvenir shopping for the cheaper ones. You can buy an entire set of handcrafted leather shadow puppets in Java for the price of a single machine-molded Noh mask in Japan. On Asian trips, we do nearly all of our souvenir and gift shopping in South and Southeast Asia and rarely in large cities, with the notable exception of Hong Kong. By gift shopping in the cheaper countries, our dollar stretches farther.

In the interest of packing light, try to put off shopping until the end of the trip. Ideally, you'll end your trip in a cheap country, do all of your shopping, then fly home. If you insist on picking up something everywhere you visit, consider postage stamps. They're cheap (if you buy low denominations), colorful, unique to the country, and virtually without bulk or weight.

If you make major purchases before the end of your trip, it's easy and inexpensive to lighten your burden by sending a package home by surface mail. Do so, however, only in major cities in more Westernized countries to reduce the likelihood of mail theft. Be sure to wrap the package very carefully, and watch the postal workers cancel your stamps before leaving. (See Mail, chap. 10.)

Large department stores often have a souvenir section with prices much lower than those in the cute little tourist shops nearby. Never shop in a major hotel. Deal directly with artisans, or visit a street market—where most items have soft prices, and you can bargain like mad.

A Word of Caution to the Shopper

While shopping is an important part of the average person's trip, be careful not to lose control. All too often, slick marketing and cutesy romantic window displays can succeed in shifting the entire focus of your trip toward the tourist shops. It's a lucrative business for many merchants. This sort of tourist brainwashing can turn you into one of the hundreds of people who set out to see and experience Asia but find themselves wandering in a trancelike search for signs announcing, "We accept Visa cards." Don't let your tour degenerate into a glorified shopping trip.

We think it's wise to restrict your shopping to a stipulated time during the trip. Most people have an idea of what they want to buy in each country. Set aside a time to shop in each of these areas and stick to it. This way you avoid drifting through a day thinking only of souvenirs.

There are good and bad times to shop. If you are anxious to buy, that's a bad time. Shopkeepers will sense you really want something and won't budge on the price. If you're in a hurry, you may not look around enough before choosing and be disappointed later. Another bad time to shop is when tour buses are present or a cruise ship is in port. Prices will be artificially inflated.

When you are shopping, ask yourself if your enthusiasm is merited. Unless you're a real romantic, the thrill of where you bought something fades long before the item's usefulness. Our lives have more room for functional souvenirs than for useless symbols of places we visited. Bob, for example, collects musical instruments that he enjoys playing and sharing with others. But even thoughtful shoppers go overboard. We each have several large boxes in our garage or attic labeled "great souvenirs."

Begging and Bribery

Begging

"Sahib, rupee?" The pleading moans and outstretched hands are legion throughout most of South and Southeast Asia. But few beggars are in such a helpless condition that they really depend on donations from "rich" tourists such as yourself. In most cases, you're doing more harm than good by feeding their habit.

Bob remembers sipping a cup of tea across the street from several beggars in Bodhgaya, India. There were several blind and invalid children and an old crippled man. A tourist emerged from a nearby sweet shop with a big bag and began handing out sugary items to the children on the street. The old cripple exploded from his position on the road and outraced the blind boy to get to the sweets.

Certainly, not all beggars are scalawags like these. But many do make ends meet with this "business." Some beggars even give a percentage of their "earnings" to shopkeepers who agree to let them set up camp outside their stores.

Many beggars do need money. But where do you draw the line? In Calcutta, poverty-stricken street people have been known to lop off their children's hands to make them more pitiful as beggars. Tourists, through their donations, can actually encourage this cruel behavior.

Most Asian adults, like adults anywhere in the world, have too much pride to depend on the dole. Children don't yet have that emotional depth. It is sad to watch hordes of subteen kids mobbing a tour group of Americans to ask for money. It is even sadder to watch the tourists reach into their pockets to share their coins. The children learn that (1) tourists are suckers, and (2) you don't have to work to make money.

Our belief is that a person who really needs money will be willing to work for it. If a Nepalese teenager who obviously needs a few rupees offers to serve as a local guide, we'll often accept—and pay him for his trouble.

Incidentally, any monk or priest who puts his hands out to receive temple donations is bogus. Buddhist monks took vows not to touch money when they entered the Sangha, or brotherhood. We are happy to contribute a small amount to the upkeep of an ancient monument, but we'll put it in the appropriate offering box, not in the hands of a would-be monk.

While we generally ignore beggars, we find that travel gives us a broader appreciation of our human family and a more real understanding of material need. While we are not rich by American standards, we, like any Americans planning an Asian vacation, are wealthy on a global scale. There are plenty of effective and creative ways for an American who has been touched by the world through travel to touch it back in a helpful way. We are both giving all royalties earned from the sale of this book to nonprofit Third World relief and development organizations such as Oxfam and Bread for the World (see the back of the book). We are doing this nonanonymously in hopes that others can find creative ways through their work to get global.

The Other Kind of Handout

The difference between begging and baksheesh (bribery) is that people seeking bribes (1) don't need the money to survive, and (2) have you over a barrel. Throughout the Third World, not just in Asia, you'll encounter open palms (literally or metaphorically) from government officials and middlemen in any sort of business transaction. Some countries, such as Indonesia, are notorious for this behavior; others are less blatant but equally demanding. Unless you want to wait for hours or to be told to come back day after day, you may have to grease a palm to get things done.

This applies to some obvious situations—such as obtaining a seat on a train when there wasn't one a short time before or expediting the process of getting a visa renewal—and to some not-so-obvious ones— like sending a parcel back to the States and making sure it's not tampered with.

What is the proper way to pay a bribe? The person you're dealing with will probably make it clear. If you offer to pay an "additional service charge" of X rupees, you won't go far wrong. It isn't proper to allow your offer to be overheard by his fellow workers, though. Try to avoid baksheesh, but when it is necessary, be subtle.

Soft Currency and the Black Market

Sooner or later in your travels—sooner in lands with unstable currencies—you'll be approached by a local person wanting to buy money or goods from you. This is the "black market."

Most of the world's currencies have their true value determined by the international exchange market. Some countries, however, such as China, artificially overvalue their money. At a Chinese bank you'll be charged the "official" rate of exchange—more than that money is really worth on the street. The currency is "soft," difficult or impossible to change outside of the country. "Hard" currency, realistically valued, is in high demand in countries such as China for purchasing imported goods. A black market is created, and people everywhere seem to be in search of "real money" and the special items that only it can buy. Tourists are known to have plenty of hard money and will commonly be approached by people who are trying to gather enough hard cash to buy a stereo or camera that cannot be purchased with this country's soft currency.

Be extremely discreet in any dealings with the black market. Several Third World Asian countries have official exchange rates lower than the real value of currency, and here you'll find everyone from schoolteachers to customs officials quoting attractive exchange rates for your U.S. cash. (Myanmar is the most glaring example: the government exchange rate is 5 kyat to the U.S. dollar, but the black market offers about 40 to the dollar.) Many civil servants make well under 200 kyat a month and have a difficult time spending their money. What they want can only be purchased with hard foreign currency, so they will pay five or more times the official rate to acquire hard dollars. As governments continue to artificially control the value and flow of money and goods, they stimulate their own black markets.

Regardless of the supposed social status of the black market dealer—"Don't worry," said one, "my brother knows the president"—exchanging money this way is illegal. It can lead to heavy fines, prompt deportation for you, and prison for the native offender. Nevertheless, in many countries, the underground economy is the one that keeps things going. You will be tempted by the black market. Don't mess with it thoughtlessly. You should, however, know about it.

Many people subsidize their travels by playing the black market. They know what to buy, what to sell—and where. We're not talking about hard drugs and submachine guns. We're talking pettiness: a bottle of booze, the latest video, a carton of cigarettes, a Mickey Mouse watch, $50 bills. In Myanmar, the government requires tourists to show proof of foreign exchange for major expenses such as hotel and transportation costs. Many travelers finance all their meals and incidentals by buying a bottle of Johnny Walker and a carton of Dunhills at the Bangkok airport duty-free shop and selling it soon after arrival in Rangoon for six times what they paid for it. Other travelers buy bottles of Johnny Walker in the duty-free shop in Kathmandu before they board a flight to India; on arrival in India, they sell the liquor and use the profit to help defray the cost of their flight.

If you choose to use the black market, at least reduce your chances of getting ripped off. Deal with a friendly shop owner rather than a person on the street. He has an established business and reputation to maintain. Get the money first and count it before you exchange yours. Often you will be shortchanged. If you have to return for additional money, count it again. They will try to pull the same trick twice. Change money off the street where you aren't rushed. Often you'll be given a roll of bills, and you'll need time to count them. In several countries, old worthless paper money is routinely sold "at great rates" to naive tourists.

Black market dealings are illegal, and a traveler is expected to understand and obey the laws of the countries he is visiting. We just thought you might be interested.

5
Asia 101:
A Cultural Primer

Religion permeates Asian society. An appreciation of the people and
culture of Asia requires an understanding of their religious heritage.
The information in the following pages explains the basics of the major
Asian religious philosophies and makes your sightseeing less frustrating and more meaningful. For a more detailed look at Asian history,
art, and religion, see Kevin Chambers's *A Traveler's Guide to Asian Culture* (Santa Fe, N.M.: John Muir Publications). This chapter was written
mostly by John Gottberg.

Hinduism

Most Westerners think of Hinduism as reincarnation: "If you're good,
you'll come back as a cow; if you're bad, you'll come back as a slug."
Hinduism isn't that simple. But reincarnation and karma, the personi-
fied law of cause and effect, are certainly central to the belief system.
By working off your karma through devotion, knowledge, and duty,
you will harmonize with natural law (dharma) and assure a better
rebirth. Eventually, you will achieve moksha, spiritual liberation from
the cycle of rebirth. Of course, a life of bad deeds will push you farther
from your goal. These are the Hindu equivalents of Christian heaven
and hell.

Hinduism is a label given by the West to a diverse group of beliefs
with roots in a common set of ancient scriptures, the Vedas and Upanishads. These date back as far as 1000 B.C., when the traditional Dra-
vidian civilization was infiltrated by an Aryan migration from the west.
The great Rig Veda addresses subjects like creation in the ambiguous
manner that is typical of modern Indian religion: "Who knows, and
who can say, when creation came about? The world was created before
the gods. Who knows, then, when it first came into being? He, the first
origin of creation, whether he formed it all or did not form it, who
controls this world in highest heaven, he must know—or perhaps he
doesn't know!"

Equally metaphysical were the verses of the Upanishads:
"Bring me a banyan fruit."
"Here it is."
"Split it."
"It is split."
"What do you see inside it?"
"A number of rather fine seeds."
"Split one of them."
"It is split."
"What do you see inside it?"
"Nothing."
"This very fineness that you no longer can make out, it is by virtue of this fineness that this banyan tree stands so big. It is this very fineness which ensouls all this world. It is the true one—it is the soul. You are that."

In all forms of Hinduism, fire—literal or symbolic—is regarded as an element of transformation and purification. Fire represents oneness, uniting earth with air and heaven. The fire of passion burning between a man and a woman brings them together in one love. The inner fire of a yogi brings him to a oneness with the universe.

It is this search for identity with the universe that is the common thread in the diverse Hindu faith. Some meditate on the ancient scriptures; some focus on the postures and breathing exercises of yoga; most devote themselves to a particular god, particularly Shiva, Vishnu, or Krishna, with ritual offerings, chants, and the observation of festivals. Regardless of the spiritual discipline chosen, the Hindu should be guided by a guru, or spiritual teacher.

The Hindu social order, too, is based on an expression of oneness. The different castes of society represent the different parts of the body: from the Brahmin priests and scholars (the head) through the *kshatriya* soldiers and rulers (the arms) and *vaishya* merchants and craftsmen (the thighs) to the lowly *sudra* peasants (the feet). Each of these broad categories is further divided into many *jati*, or subcastes, each with its prescribed vocations, rituals, and rigid social laws. This social order is sacred, reflecting the oneness of the universe; the devout Hindu is expected to accept his place in this order in his quest for cosmic oneness.

The best example of accepting one's role is written in the Bhagavad Gita, a 2,000-year-old literary classic. The great warrior Arjuna is disturbed because it is his duty as a kshatriya to kill the opposing forces—even though many of his kinfolk are among them. He is advised by his charioteer, Krishna, a human incarnation of the god Vishnu, that one must take the actions of his station without attachment to their results, strictly for the sake of good; and that because souls cannot die, he will be killing only his relatives' outward physical form.

The polytheistic Hindu faith recognizes a trinity at the head of its pantheon—the creator, Brahma; the preserver, Vishnu; and the destroyer, Shiva. Brahma is almost deistic in concept: having created the universe, he now stands apart from it. Vishnu, assisted by such well-known human incarnations as Rama and Krishna, perpetuates the universe. It falls on Shiva to destroy—and in so doing, to make new creation possible. Thus, Shiva is the most dynamic of the gods and the most widely worshiped. His aspects are sometimes fierce, but he is basically a good god, destroying the evil and replacing it with good. Many temples symbolize his presence with a phallic lingam, and he is often found in iconography united sexually with his consort, Parvati.

The Hindu god, Hanuman

The Hindu pantheon is enormous. Here are a few of the gods and goddesses you might encounter in art and legend during your travels:

Agni—The ancient god of fire and sacrifice.

Aiyanar—The god of agriculture.

Annapurna—The goddess of abundance, a manifestation of Parvati. A famous Himalayan peak shares her name.

Bhairav—Shiva in his terrifying Tantric aspect, with a mouthful of sharp teeth and a necklace of skulls, intent on destroying everything he sees, especially ignorance.

Durga—Parvati's dark side; the female equivalent of Bhairav.

Ganesh—The elephant-headed boy, one of the most popular and unmistakable of all gods. Ganesh is the god of prosperity and wisdom. He decides between success and failure. He removes obstacles or creates them if he feels they are needed. According to legend, Ganesh was born in human form to Shiva and Parvati, but Shiva lopped off his son's head when he mistook him for a lover in bed with Parvati. Shiva was able to bring his son back to life but only by giving him the head of the first living thing he saw, which happened to be an elephant.

Garuda—The great eagle on whom Vishnu rides, a symbol of bravery and good (and the name of an Indonesian airline).

Hanuman—The white monkey, general of the ape armies and a symbol of loyalty.

Indra—Epic hero warrior god of ancient India. Equivalent to the Norse god, Thor.

Kali—Parvati in her fiercest aspect, wearing a garland of skulls as she demands sacrifices. Those seeking success on dangerous ventures make offerings to her.

Krishna—An extremely popular incarnation of the god Vishnu, he is famed for his dallying with the _gopis_, or milk maidens. Legend says he seduced them like Pan with his flute and, taking the form of as many men as there were maidens, made love to each of them in the way she personally liked best. Powerful yet sensitive, he is often painted blue and accompanied by consorts.

Lakshmi—The goddess of wealth and prosperity; Vishnu's consort.

Mahadev—Shiva as the lord of procreation and knowledge, symbolized by the phallic lingam.

Murugan—The god of war, eldest son of Shiva and Parvati, also known as Skanda and Kartikeya. In one South Indian form, he has 6 faces and 12 arms.

Nandi—A bull, Shiva's vehicle.

Narayana—An incarnation of Vishnu, the embodiment of universal love and knowledge.

Nataraja—Shiva as the cosmic dancer. In legend, his dance so stirred the cosmos that the earth was created.

Pashupati—A favorable aspect of Shiva, the developmental tutor of all species, particularly revered in Nepal.

Parvati—Shiva's consort, she is worshiped for fertility and abundance.

Pattini—The goddess of health, patience, steadfastness, and forgiveness.

Radha—Head of the gopi maidens; chief consort of Krishna.

Rama—Another incarnation of Vishnu. A prince, and the hero of the great Ramayana epic.

Saraswati—Goddess of learning; consort of Brahma.

A Hindu temple may be called a *mandir*, a *devala*, or a *kovil*. A portal of entry, a *gopuram*, tiered like a wedding cake and cloaked with a bridal party of colorfully carved gods and goddesses, makes it easy to spot. Worshipers wear a *tikka* (divine eye) on their foreheads, above and between their eyes. This pasty mixture of sandalwood ash symbolizes a sacred presence within the individual. The ritual offerings—*puja*—must be made of the five "elements": earth (incense or fruit), water (which can also be milk or coconut water), fire (usually the lighting of oil lamps), wind (fanning or incense smoke), and ether (sacred music and chanting).

Hinduism is the predominant religion in India, Nepal, and Bali and a significant force in Sri Lanka, Malaysia, and Singapore. A yogic offshoot of Hinduism called Tantrism has survived in Nepal and the Himalayas. An attempt to assimilate materialism with spirituality, Tantrism rejects contemplative meditation in favor of action and experience. Adherents try to go beyond their mental and physical limitations through mastery of the forces of nature. The sexually oriented Shakti cult is a hedonistic example; followers claim they are exploring the mystery inherent in human union (not to mention the bliss).

Buddhism

The founder of the Buddhist faith was a Hindu prince named Gautama Siddhartha, who lived 500 years before Christ in the eastern Ganges Valley of southern Nepal and northern India. In a life that appeared to be quite normal—he married and had a son—he grew increasingly dissatisfied with the decadence of palace society. His introduction to an old man, a cripple, and a corpse—and his charioteer's confirmation that "it happens to us all"—convinced him to seek an answer to man's suffering. At the age of 29, Gautama disappeared into the wilderness, where he wandered alone for over five years in his search for the truth. After nearly fasting to death, he abandoned himself to meditation. While seated beneath a large fig tree near Benares, he became enlightened and discovered the "Middle Way," rejecting all extremes of pain and pleasure.

Let local friends explain their religion

According to Buddha, literally, "the Enlightened One," all life contains the element of suffering. This suffering is caused by our attachment to people and things, even though we know that nothing in our world is permanent. To rid ourselves of suffering, we must relinquish this attachment or desire. We can do this by following the Noble Eightfold Path: living with wisdom (right views and right intent), morality (right speech, conduct, and livelihood), and mental discipline (right effort, mindfulness, and meditation).

The Buddha, who wandered and taught until his 80th year, explained that man's karma has trapped him in the endless, illusory cycle of rebirth. There is no permanent soul or "self," he said, because one's essence is forever changing. Thus, it is not the person who is reborn but the sum of his karma—much as a candle lit by a match bears a flame different from but dependent on the flame of the match. Man can escape the effects of karma and the cycle of rebirth by strictly following the dharma, the Buddhist doctrine. Nirvana, the end of desire and extinction of "self," is neither heaven nor annihilation; it might be defined as nonexistence, blissful nothingness.

Buddhism is nontheistic—but not atheistic. The Buddha avoided discussion of the question of God. He said it wasn't important to know whether a supreme being did or didn't exist: we must work out our own salvation in the here and now.

In the centuries following the Buddha's life, a number of doctrinal disputes emerged. Most significant was the schism that split the religion into the Mahayana ("great path") and Theravada or Hinayana ("lesser path") schools, much as Christianity divided into Catholicism and Protestantism.

Theravada is the more orthodox of the two and today predominates in Thailand, Myanmar, and Sri Lanka. The accumulation of merit for future rebirths is important in modern Theravada Buddhist communities. Some individuals even keep debit and credit account books! The giving of alms to monks is the number one merit-making activity, though meditation, preaching the dharma, and following moral behavior are all important. All Theravada Buddhists are expected to follow the Five Precepts—no killing, stealing, lying, sexual misconduct, or drinking of intoxicating liquors.

One of the central aspects of Mahayana Buddhism is a belief in *bodhisattvas*, "Buddhas-to-be." These are human beings who have achieved spiritual enlightenment but who have vowed not to enter Nirvana until all of us mortals attain the same level of consciousness. They are considered perfect teachers.

Zen (Ch'an in China) and Pure Land Buddhism are branches of Mahayana belief, just as Methodists and Lutherans are branches of Protestantism. Zen is found throughout East Asia, especially Japan. It's a school of meditation that often depends on the shock value of words and riddles to shake a disciple from his fixed view of life. The Pure Land school, dominant in Japan, requires only that followers repeat "Namu Amida Butsu" (Hail the Buddha) to earn salvation.

Tibetan Buddhism, sometimes called Lamaism (for its lamas, or priests), persists in Chinese Tibet despite the exile of its high priest, the Dalai Lama. It's also important in neighboring Nepal, even though Hinduism is the Himalayan kingdom's national religion.

Lamaism stresses the interrelatedness of individual human energies and the universal cosmic forces. Faithful meditation can carry a person to a state of altered consciousness wherein feats considered occult in the West—like levitation and incredibly rapid overland travel—are routinely possible. Meditation requires the chanting of a sacred mantra, syllables that intensify spiritual power, and visualization of a mandala, a sacred diagram that helps orient the meditator to the oneness of the universe.

Chinese Religion

The religious beliefs of the Chinese people don't fall into any single category. Yes, they are Buddhist. Yes, they are Confucianist. They are also Taoist. And they adhere strictly to ancestor worship and folk religion. Somehow, all philosophies coexist in harmony within the same minds.

Confucianism is a system of social philosophy attributed to a sixth-century B.C. civil servant named Kung Fu-tzu (Confucius). Confucius believed that the ultimate potential for goodness lay in the moral relationships between human beings.

According to Confucius, filial piety—the absolute respect of son for father—is the cornerstone of an ordered society and the basis for the family system, the veneration of ancestors, and recognition of the emperor as the earthly father and mediator with heaven.

While acknowledging heaven's power to affect man and his world, Confucius urged his followers to concentrate their attention on worldly things. They could do nothing about the supernatural. But their actions must harmonize with the natural moral order established by heaven. Confucius' optimistic vision of an ideal society was one in which all people individually achieved perfect virtue and benevolence, without which there was no escape from cruelty and violence.

A strong supporter of the ruling class, Confucius said that the true gentleman ruler was set apart from "inferior" beings by his power of vision and his keen moral sense. The gentleman-scholar's primary concern should be politics and "the proper ordering of the state." But Confucius also believed character to be more important than birthright, and he believed that man could improve his position through education.

Confucius' disciple Mencius expanded his tutor's teachings with his doctrine of human nature: all human beings have a basic tendency to do good. This may be no more than an instinct for right and wrong and an empathy for others' problems, but it can be cultivated and strengthened.

Everyone has heard a handful of Charlie Chan-isms beginning with "Confucius say . . . ," most of them tasteless. The true words of Master

Kung, as the Chinese know him, are found in *The Analects*. Here are a few examples:

"Do not do to others what you would not want others to do to you."

"Those who are born wise are the highest type of people; those who become wise through learning come next; those who learn by overcoming dullness come after that. Those who are dull but still won't learn are the lowest type of people."

"A young man's duty is to be filial to his parents at home and respectful to his elders abroad, to be circumspect and truthful, and, while overflowing with love for all men, to associate himself with benevolence. If, when all that is done, he has any energy to spare, then let him study the polite arts."

"In serving his parents, a son may gently remonstrate with them. If he sees that they are not inclined to follow his suggestion, he should resume his reverential attitude but not abandon his purpose. If he is belabored, he will not complain."

"Devote yourself to the proper demands of the people, respect the ghosts and spirits, but keep them at a distance—this may be called wisdom."

"It is only when art and nature are harmoniously blended that you have the gentleman. The gentleman understands what is right; the inferior man understands what is profitable."

"Lead the people by laws and regulate them by penalties, and the people will try to keep out of jail but will have no sense of shame. Lead the people by virtue and restrain them by the rules of decorum, and the people will have a sense of shame and moreover will become good."

The great importance placed on family in Chinese society is linked in part to traditional ancestor worship. Chinese believe that their own fortunes are affected by the well-being of their deceased relations. Each home has an ancestral shrine, usually in a special niche, with an altar containing wooden tablets with the names and dates of the deceased. Fruit and incense are offered daily, with special affection accorded during festival times and on birthdays and death anniversaries of the deceased. This often involves burning elaborate paper effigies of material goods—cars, televisions, and paper money, for example—for the deceased to use in the other life.

Another major religious influence on the Chinese people is Taoism (pronounced "Dowism"), a philosophy first articulated in the *Tao Te Ching* (The Book of the Way). The writings are attributed to the sixth-century B.C. sage Lao Tzu, about whom almost nothing is known. It is hard to imagine a philosophy more passive than the one he advocated—that one cannot do better than to do nothing at all.

Lao Tzu's writing portrayed a universal natural principle, the Tao (or "way"), beyond all definition. It extends far beyond the social and political emphasis of Confucianism. Only through intuition can the Tao be felt and heeded. When man has tuned into the Tao, he can flow with the processes of nature, responding to experience rather than reflecting on it, living and dying quietly according to *wu-wei* (nonaction).

The *Tao Te Ching* sets out the reasoning:

"Something and Nothing are two sides of a coin. Difficult and easy complement each other. Long and short offset each other. High and low incline toward each other. Note and sound harmonize with each other. Before and after follow each other.

"Therefore the wise man keeps to the deed that consists in taking no action and practices the teaching that uses no words."

While the *Tao Te Ching* doesn't specifically discuss the ancient Chinese concept of yin-yang, it embraces it literally and symbolically. The original meaning of the word *yang* was "sunny side of a hill," while *yin* meant "shadow." The pair of terms came to represent the eternal coexistence of opposites throughout nature—day and night, summer and winter, male and female, and so forth. The symbol of the Tao depicts how opposites are always represented within any single entity and are always a part of each other.

Later philosophers and mystics began to speak of the Tao as a place of total spiritual freedom, of union between man and heaven. As the common man tried to imagine an unimaginable Tao, romantic and occult elements became part of the religious fabric. By medieval times (and still today), Taoism boasted a colorful pantheon of gods, a priesthood whose lavish rites include exorcism and a series of alchemical, yogic, and magical practices designed to produce immortality and control spirits. Most alchemical experiments are based on the "five agents" theory—that wood, metal, fire, water, and earth (and various combinations thereof) are the sole elements determining all natural events.

Chinese temples housing the many Taoist deities are often elaborately ornate and gaudy. The images of deities and other fantastic creatures are intended to attract good fortune and repel evil from the temple and surrounding community.

Japanese Religion

It's hard to understand at first how 76 percent of the Japanese people can claim to be Shinto and 77 percent Buddhist. At the same time, a national study concludes that 69 percent of the people do not consider themselves religious. It has been our own observation that Japan is (on the surface) the most irreligious country in Asia. Yet there are 180,000 buildings of worship, not to mention millions of statuary and home altars, revealing the obvious importance of religion in society. What's the deal?

Except in the few Christian and Nichiren Shoshu communities, the Japanese don't observe a day of worship, their prayers are recitations whose content is of little importance, they pay little attention to questions of good-versus-bad or life-after-death, and their "holy day" festivals are social gatherings with little religious content.

Yet religion pervades their lives. Japanese parents will take their newborn child to be blessed by a Shinto priest, and when he enters school, they'll accompany him to a shrine to pray for good grades in the memory of a renowned scholar. Marriages are almost always performed by Shinto priests, but sickness and death are usually the realm of the Buddhists. A sick person may visit a temple known for its divine healing powers. A Buddhist priest will normally officiate at a funeral or cremation, after which the ashes will be placed in an urn and buried in a Buddhist cemetery or entombed in a Buddhist mausoleum. In addition, many homes have two worship niches—a *butsudan* (Buddhist altar) and a *kamidana* (Shinto god shelf)—where offerings of food, flowers, incense, and rice wine are made on days of special religious significance.

Shinto is the traditional religion of Japan, with roots in a system of rites and myths centered around Amaterasu, the sun goddess. Legend says she was the offspring of Izanagi and Izanami, the male and female deities who created the world, and a direct ancestor of the Japanese emperor. In other words, the emperor is himself of divine lineage—or, at least, he was until 1946, when Hirohito, under U.S. occupational pressure, renounced the myth.

Shinto is somewhat animistic in nature. *Kami* (spirits or gods) are believed to inhabit rivers and mountains, wind and rain, trees and rocks. Deceased heroes, famous scholars, and other admired persons likewise have become kami. Japanese traditionally recognize a common spiritual thread running through all objects, animate and inanimate, as well as in natural forces and phenomena. The more awe-inspiring a force or object, the more spiritual power it was credited with and the more reverence it was shown. People made offerings to the most powerful kami, along with requests for bountiful harvests, fertility, success in war, and recovery from disease.

The Shinto shrine, whether a great building in Tokyo or a tiny wooden structure in a remote grove of pines overlooking the ocean, is approached through a *torii*—a gateway of wood that reminds some visitors of a football goalpost. Two upright posts are joined overhead by crossbeams, the higher one curving slightly upward and projecting on each side. In ancient times, dead birds were hung from the crosspieces as offerings to the kami. The shrine lies beyond.

Shinto, with its animistic bent, has attracted a shamanistic leadership, and that influence has been felt in Japanese Buddhism as well. The charisma of a few great monks has shaped the different sects that dominate in Japan today. Shingon and Tendai, for example, both of which emerged in the Middle Ages, are almost Tibetan in approach: by techniques of chanting and visualization, said the monks, one could become a Buddha in this body and in this lifetime. Shingon even assimilated the Chinese theories of yin-yang and the five elements. But Zen and the Pure Land school have become the most popular schools of thought.

Islam

The Islamic faith has far more in common with Judaism and Christianity than with any of the so-called Eastern religions. Islam recognizes the Old and New Testaments and holds that there is but one God.

Islam began in the early seventh century, when a Mecca caravan manager named Muhammad became a medium for the revelation of the Qur'an, said to be the last and most perfect message communicated by Allah (God). Since then, the religion of the Muslim people has spread across much of the world, from Arabia west through North Africa and east to Indonesia and the southern Philippines.

Muslim reading the Koran

The Arabia of Muhammad's time (A.D. 570–632) was a primitive and rugged desert land, mainly inhabited by nomadic tribesmen who made their livings preying on the caravans that traversed the region. But those same caravans spread information about other religions to those who would listen, and Muhammad was certainly influenced by them.

Sometime around the age of 40, Muhammad began to have visions. Over the next ten years, he frequently retired to his garden, where Allah spoke through him on a regular basis. The most important points of his message were:

—There is only one God, and his power is absolute. Furthermore, His will is arbitrary and can be changed at His whim.

—Man's sole duty is to submit to God's will. "Allah leads astray whom he pleases and guides whom he pleases and no one knows the hosts of the Lord save himself. And every man's destiny have we fastened on his neck." (The word *Islam* means, literally, "submission." A follower of the faith is called a Muslim.)

—There are no priests, no sacraments, no intermediaries between man and Allah. Man can approach his God directly.

—On the judgment day, the dead will have their bodies restored, and they will be forced to walk the razor-thin bridge between heaven and hell. He who believes in one God will regain his youth and live a life of bacchanalian pleasure with wine and beautiful women.

Heavily persecuted, Muhammad and a small band of followers fled Mecca in 622 and took refuge in Medina, 320 miles north. There his movement grew in strength, and in 630, he returned to conquer Mecca by trickery and force. The concept of *jihad* (holy war) justifies any means to bring non-Islamic lands into the Islamic fold.

After Muhammad's death, a series of caliphs took the reins of the new faith and with swords flashing, spread it rapidly throughout the Middle East. A schism in leadership in the late seventh century led to the fractious Shi'a sect, dominant in Iran today, a messianic group that awaits the return of the Mahdi (guided one) to bring justice to the world. You'll find a significant number of Shi'ites in Pakistan. Most Muslims in Pakistan, however, as well as in Bangladesh, Indonesia, Malaysia, and the Philippines, are of the dominant Sunni sect.

The Five Pillars of Islam, as defined by Muhammad, still prescribe the duties that all Muslim faithful must follow.

First is daily recitation of a creed: "There is no God but Allah and Muhammad is his prophet."

Second is prayer, recited five times a day facing Mecca. Prayers consist of words of praise with requests for guidance and forgiveness and are never petitions for help. Wherever there's a mosque, you'll hear the voice of the muezzin (singer) summoning the faithful to prayer five times a day. In the mosque, prayers are led by an imam, a lay reader.

Third is the fast of Ramadan, a month-long period during which Muslims cannot consume food or drink, smoke cigarettes, or engage in sexual relations from sunrise to sunset. (Alcoholic drinks and pork, along with gambling, are always taboo.)

Fourth is almsgiving. The Muslim is obligated to provide assistance to fellow Muslims in need. Whatever he gives ties him closer to the Islamic "family" and allows him an opportunity to repent or atone.

Fifth is the _hajj_. Every Muslim man is duty-bound to make a pilgrimage to Mecca at least once in his lifetime, as long as his health and finances permit. Once he has made the trip, he can carry the honorific title _Haji_ before his name.

Before entering a mosque (major services are Friday afternoons), it is proper to remove your shoes. Be quiet, and don't cross in front of anyone who is praying. Women must not enter with their knees or arms exposed, during their periods, or within six weeks after childbirth.

You'll be interested to know, by the way, that a Muslim may have as many as four legal wives so long as he can provide financially and emotionally for all of them. He can obtain a divorce simply by saying, "I divorce you" on three separate occasions. The woman has no such recourse.

Sikhism

The Sikh religion has become quite prominent in world news. Its adherents, who number about 13 million, are advocating that their own independent country be created out of India's Punjab state. The conflict has escalated, and at times, the turbaned Sikhs, whose faith is founded on martyrdom, have had to defend their Golden Temple at Amritsar from attacks by Indian government troops. Resolution may be a long way off.

Sikhism was founded by Guru Nanak in the early 1500s as an attempt to mesh Hinduism and Islam. Most of the teachings found in its holy book, the Granth Sahib, are similar to Hinduism, but Sikhs recognize a monotheistic deity and are strongly opposed to any caste distinctions.

Sikh men are never supposed to cut their hair or beards, hiding it under a turban. This is one of the five symbols of their faith, along with a steel bracelet, a comb, a sword (often a symbolic miniature), and shorts (preferable to a loincloth when you're carrying a sword). In addition, all Sikhs bear the surname (or middle name) Singh, meaning "Lion."

Because of their military bearing, Sikhs are ideally suited for positions as soldiers, police, and guards. You'll see them throughout Asia—not just in the Punjab—in positions of responsibility. Their turbans make them hard to miss.

———

6
Hurdling the Language Barrier

Communicating in a Language You Don't Speak

That notorious language barrier is about two feet tall. It can keep you out of Asia, or with a few tricks, you can step right over it.

Bob has limited ability in several foreign languages, including Japanese and Indonesian. Rick speaks only optalk and English. But our linguistic limitations have never hindered our travels. Of course, if we spoke more languages, we could enjoy a much deeper understanding of the people and cultures we see. But logistically speaking—getting transportation, eating, sleeping, and seeing the sights—English-only people manage just fine. In fact, you can get by better in Asia speaking English than you can in most of Europe.

English is Asia's linguistic common denominator. In most of Asia, English is every schoolchild's second (or third) language. For centuries, England was the colonial mother to the Indian subcontinent, Burma, the Malay peninsula, and Hong Kong. France, Holland, Portugal, and the United States also left linguistic reminders of their presence in various parts of Asia. Students in multiethnic Singapore often speak four languages—English, Malay, Mandarin Chinese, and perhaps Tamil (a South Indian tongue)—in addition to their own family dialect. Japanese, Chinese, Indonesian, and other youngsters begin learning English in elementary school.

Imagine if each of our states spoke its own language. That's the Asian situation. Diverse countries like China, Indonesia, and India are actually catch-alls of hundreds of different languages! In India, when an Indian from the north meets one from the south, they communicate in English, because neither speaks the other's native language.

We English-speakers are a linguistic group that can be lazy and still travel easily. But those who try to pick up some of the Asian languages get closer to the people they're visiting. Asians love to see us trying their languages. You'll be showered with praise even if you only say Ohayo and Sayonara. Get a language phrase book and study it on the flight over. If you have time before you go, take a short language course or listen to tapes from the library in your car as you commute.

While English may be Asia's common language, communicating does require some skill. How well you communicate with the Asians you meet depends on how well you can get a basic idea across, not on how many words you know in a language.

Here are some tips on how to communicate with people who don't speak your language. Speak slowly and clearly with well-chosen words. The Voice of America, which is in the business to communicate, uses what they call "simple English." You're dealing with someone who learned English out of a book. Choose easy words, and pronounce each letter. ("Cris-py po-ta-to chips." Borrow a singer's enunciation exercises.) Most Americans speak louder when they aren't understood, and if they still can't communicate, they toss in a few extra words. Listen to other tourists, and you'll hear your own shortcomings.

Use no contractions. Cut out all slang. Our American dialect has become a super-deluxe slang chop suey not found on any Asian menu. The sentence "Cut out all slang," for example, would baffle the average Asian. "Speak no idioms" would be better understood. If you learned English in school, how would you respond to the American who exclaims, "What a day!"? Listen to yourself. If you want to be understood, talk like a Dick and Jane book.

Keep your messages and sentences caveman simple. When asking for something, a one-word question ("Photo?") is much more effective than an attempt at something more polite and grammatically correct ("May I take your picture, sir?").

Your first priority when communicating in Asia is to strip your message naked and transmit only the basic ideas. Even with no common language, rudimentary communication is easy. Don't be afraid to look like a fool. Butcher the language if you must, but communicate. Rick can't forget the lady in the local post office who flapped her arms and asked, "Tweet, tweet, tweet?" He understood immediately, answered with a nod, and she gave him the airmail stamps he needed. If you're hungry, clutch your stomach and growl. If you want a drink, put an imaginary bottle to your mouth and guzzle. If the liquor was too strong, simulate an atomic explosion starting in your stomach and mushrooming to your head.

Pick up some gestures, and avoid others. Every culture has peculiar—and fun—hand and face gestures. In Sri Lanka and southern India, a smile accompanied by a wobbling back-and-forth head motion (like someone just slapped one of those spring-necked Oriental dolls) indicates "probably yes." Shaking a limp hand as if strumming a ukelele often means "expensive." But pointing at someone or motioning with a crooked finger is very offensive. If you must point, point with your hand open, palm downward. Watch, listen, and learn.

A small note pad works wonders in a tough spot. The written word or number cannot be mispronounced. Our back-pocket note pads are among our handiest travel buddies. If you need to repeatedly communicate something difficult and important (medical instructions, "boiled water," "well-done meat," "your finest sake," and so on), have it written in the local language in your note pad. A hotel clerk or local student can help.

Some Asians are self-conscious about their English and would prefer not speaking at all to speaking broken English. If you are determined to communicate, and if you butcher their language doggedly enough, sooner or later they'll break down and surprise you with some English. After what you've done to their language, they'll be more comfortable messing up yours.

Your communicating job is made much easier if you choose a multilingual person to start with. Business people, urbanites, young well-dressed people, and those in the tourist trade are most likely to speak English. Older Asians are more likely to speak the language of the colonial power dominant in their country until the 1940s or 1950s. Thus, you could get by with Dutch in Indonesia, French in Laos, Japanese in Taiwan.

If you draw a complete blank with someone but you want to communicate, just start hurling bits and pieces at each other. Even if you don't speak Japanese, you can say "Toyota," "Sukiyaki," "Sayonara." Or pull out your note pad and start drawing pictures. If you can't entertain with words, at least you can do so with sketches.

You are surrounded by expert, native-speaking tutors in every country. Let them teach you. Spend bus and train rides learning. Start studying the language when you arrive. Psychologically, it's hard to start later because you'll be leaving so soon. We like to learn at least five new words a day. You'd be surprised how handy a working vocabulary of 20 to 50 words is. (The practical phrases listed near the end of this chapter are a good place to start. But the pronunciations should be tested with a native speaker on arrival. Asian languages just can't be accurately pronounced with our letters. Fine tune these lists with your own personal code, including melodic notes.)

Phrase books can give you the basics and are particularly helpful in countries with tonal languages. For instance, in China, a tourist may find it far easier to point to a phrase than pronounce it. Some phrase books, such as the Berlitz series, are overly complicated and stilted. We can't imagine anyone ever hauling out a phrase book to say, "I've broken my leg. Can you please show me to the nearest hospital?" In that case, a point and a scream works in any language.

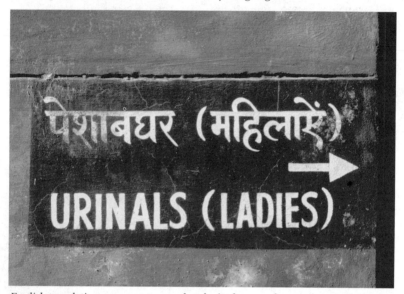

English translations are common . . . but don't always make sense

Assume you understand. Our master key to communication is that we make an educated guess at the meaning of a message, verbal or written, and act with confidence as if we understood it correctly. This applies to rudimentary things like instructions on customs forms, museum hours, menus, questions the hotel maid asks us, and so forth. We're correct 80 percent of the time. Half the time we're wrong we never know it, so it really doesn't matter. So 10 percent of the time we really blow it. Faking it this way makes our trip easier—or more interesting.

Let's take a border crossing as an example. We speak no Mongolian. At the border, a uniformed guard struts through our train car, stops, and asks a question. Not understanding a word he said but guessing what the average border guard would ask the average tourist, we look at him and answer with a solid "Nyet." He nods and continues past us to the next passenger. We're on our way, quick and easy. We could have reached into our rucksacks, struggled with the phrase book, and made a big deal out of it. But we'd rather fake it, assuming he was asking if we were smuggling anything in, and keep things simple. It works.

International Words

As our world shrinks, more and more words leap their linguistic boundaries and become international. Sensitive travelers develop a knack for choosing words most likely to be universally understood ("auto" instead of "car," "kaput" rather than "broken," "photo" and not "picture"). They also internationalize their pronunciation. "Restaurant," if you play around with its sound (rayss-tohr-awn), will be understood anywhere. Be creative. Here are a few internationally understood words. Remember, cut out the Yankee accent and give each word a pan-Asian sound.

restaurant	music
auto	police
kaput	telephone
tourist	communist
chai, cha (tea)	America's favorite 4-letter words
rock-n-roll	post (Pos)
English	Yankee, Americano
taxi	bye-bye
Disneyland (wonderful)	coffee
"Rambo" Stallone (he-man)	bank
hotel	OK
bus	photo
taboo	passport
beer	capitalist
Coke, cola	

Practical Foreign Phrases

Chinese

Chinese is spoken by more people than any other language. There are many dialects, such as Cantonese, but Mandarin is China's dominant language and the one we'll look at here.

Chinese is a tonal language. Words have up to four meanings depending on the melody you give them. In this phrase list, you'll see a number after each word. This indicates the pitch of that word: (1) normal, short, flat; (2) like a question; (3) a slow drawn-out sliding up question (e.g., whaaat?); (4) like a command. Obviously this can lead to some funny or embarrassing situations. Good luck!

Yes Shih (4)
No Poo (2) shih (4)
Good How (3)
Please Chin (3)
Thank you Shee' yeh (4) shee' yeh (4) nee (3)
Excuse me Too' ee (4) poo (4) chee (3)
Hello! Wy! (4)
Good morning Ts'ow (3)
Good-bye Ts'eye (4) chee'yen (4)
My name is Woh (3) teh (4) ming (2) tsuh (4) shih (4) . . .
Your name? Kweh (4) shing? (4)
How are you? Nee (2) how (3) poo (4) how? (3)
Do you understand? Nee (3) ming (2) pie (4) mah? (4)
Where? Nah (2) lee? (3)
Where is a good hotel? How (2) loo (2) kwahn (3) ts'eye (4) na (2) lee? (3)
Where is a good restaurant? Hoo (3) fahn (4) t'yen (4) ts'eye (4) na (2) lee? (3)
Water Shwee (3)
Delicious! Hen (3) how! (3)
When? Shem (2) mah (4) shee (2) hoo? (4)
When does it leave? Shem (2) ma (4) shih (2) hoo (4) lee (2) kah'ee? (4)
Now Shee'yen (4) ts'eye (4)
Later Yee (3) hoo (4)
How much? Too-who (1) shah-oh (3) chee'yen? (2)
One Yee (1)
Two Er (4)
Three Sahn (1)
Four Soo (4)
Five Woo (3)
Six Lee-yoo (4)
Seven Chee (1)
Eight Pah (1)
Nine Chee'yoo (3)
Ten Shee (2)
Entrance Roo (4) koo (3)
Exit Choo (1) koo (3)
How beautiful! Cheng (1) how (3) kan! (4)
You're very kind Nee (2) hen (3) keh (4) chee (4)
Stop! Ting (2) choo! (4)
Help! Ch'yoo (4) ming! (4)

Japanese

The language of Japan is very polite. Chopsticks (_hashi_) are called O Hashi (honorable chopsticks). It is fun and important to learn and use the polite words. Speak Japanese with no accented syllables. Anything ending in "des-kah" is a question. The written language uses several scripts with separate phonetic "alphabets" for borrowed and indigenous words. Howard Tomb's _Wicked Japanese for the Business Traveler_ will give you a lighter approach to this language with phrases like "Ugoki dasanai kachiku no niku, arimasenka?" (Do you serve any completely dead domestic animals?) If you're planning to spend several weeks in Japan, it's worthwhile to study the _katakana_ script (you'll quickly discover, for example, how to translate the three characters for "ho-te-ru" to "hotel" to find a room). The most common Japanese characters (_kanji_) are also worth learning. Many English words have been absorbed into Japanese. Some of our favorites are: _rashawa_ (rush hour), _sarariman_ (worker), _Sheendarera_ (Cinderella), _Makudonarudo_ (McDonald's), _Biggu Makku_ (Big Mac), _kissu_ (kiss), _beisuboru_ (baseball), _aissukurimu_ (ice cream), _poruno_ (pornography), and _shigaretto_.

Yes High
_No_ Ee-yeh
Good Ee
Please Doh-zoh
Thank you Ah-ree-gah-toh
You're welcome Doh-ee-ta-shee-mah-shi-teh
Excuse me Soo-mee-mah-sen
Good morning Oh-hah-yoh go-zai-mas
Good day Kohn-nee-chee-wah
Good evening Kohn-bahn-wah
Welcome! Ee-rah-shy-mah-seh!
Hello (on telephone only) Moshi moshi
My name is . . Wah-tahk-shee wah . . . des
Your name? Ah-nah-tah noh oh-nah-mah-ay wa?
How are you? Ee-kan-gah des-kah?
Do you speak English? En-goh oh hah-nah-shee-mas-kah?
A little Soo-kosh-ee
What? Nan des-kah? (literally "What is this?")
Where? Doh-koh?
Where is a good hotel? Yoh'ee hoh-tee-roo wah doh-koh des-kah? _Where is a good restaurant?_ Eee shoh-koo-doh wah doh-koh des-kah?
Delicious Oh-ee-shee
Cheers Kahm-pie

Expensive Tah-kie
Cheap Yah-soo-ee
Water Mee-zoo
Where is the market? Mah-keh-toh wah doh-koh des-kah?
To the railroad station Eh-kee eh
A ticket to . . . Yoo-kee noh ken . . .
Where is the train to Nikko? Neek-koh yoo-kee wah doh-koh des-kah?
When? Eet-soo?
When does it leave? Eet-soo shoo-pahts des-kah?
How much? Ee-koo-rah dehss-kah?
One Ee-chee (say "itchy")
Two Nee (say "knee")
Three Sahn
Four Shee (or) yohn
Five Goh
Six Roku
Seven Shee-chee (or) nah-nah
Eight Hah-chee
Nine Koo (or) kyu
Ten Ju
Entrance Ee-ree-yoo-chee
Exit Deh-goo-chee
I Wah-tas-shee
You Ah-nah-tah
Huh? Neh?
Really? Honto?
Healthy/happy Gen-kee
Stupid Bakka
How beautiful! Kee-ray des-neh!
Very interesting O-moh-shee-roy
Good luck Go-koon o
Have a good trip O-ghen-kee deh (literally, "Be healthy")
Look out! Ah-boo-nigh!
Stop! Toh-maht-teh!
Help! Tahss-keh-teh!

Hindi-Urdu

Hindi-Urdu or Urdu-Hindi, depending on where you're from, is the language of much of India (Hindi) and of Pakistan (Urdu). Each language is basically the same, but since the split in 1947, Urdu is drifting more toward Persian and Arabic, while Hindi is absorbing more Sanskrit, India's ancient language. Hindi and Urdu each have their own very squiggly script, and most travelers understandably focus their energy on conversational rather than writing skills. While English is widely spoken in Hindi-Urdu country, a few local phrases come in very handy.

Yes Hanh
No Hah-HEENH
Good Ah-TCHAH
Please MEH-hehr-bah-nee seh
Thank you SHOO-kree-yah
You're welcome Meh-ehr-bah-nee
Excuse me Moo-AHF-kee-JEE-eh
Greetings Sah-LAHM
Good-bye P'heer MEE-len-geh
My name is . . . MEH-rah nahm hay . . .
Your name? Ahp-kah-NAHM?
How are you? Ahp k'EYE-seh henh?
Do you speak English? K'yah ahp ahn-GREH-zee BOHL-teh henh?
A little Toh-REE-see
I like your country Mood-JEH ahp kah moolk pah-SAHND hay
What? K'yah?
Where? KAH-hanh?
Where is a good hotel? Koy-ee aht-CHAH HOH-tel kah-HAHN hay?
Where is the toilet? Pah-eh-KHAH-nah kah-HAHN hay?
Where is a good restaurant? Koh-EE aht-CHAH RESS-toh-rahn KAH-hahn hay?
Water PAH-nee
It was very good Bah-HOOT aht-CHAH thah
I would like MOODJ chah-hee-YEH
This Yeh
A ticket to . . . Kah-ehk TEE-kat . . .
I want to go to Bombay Mainh Bombay JAH-nah CHAH-tah hoonh
To the railroad station RAIL-vay is-TAH-shon koh
When? Kahb?
How much? KIT-NEH PIE-seh?
One Ehk
Two Doh
Three Teen
Four Chahr
Five Pahnch
Six Ch'heh
Seven Saht
Eight Ahth

Nine Now
Ten Dahss
I Mainh
You Ahp
How beautiful! Kit-HAH k'hoob-soo-raht!
Help! Mah-DAHD!

Malay-Indonesian

The people of Indonesia and Malaysia speak two different but mutually comprehensible languages. They're even closer linguistic cousins than Swedish and Norwegian. Bahasa Indonesia was developed by nationalists in the early twentieth century from the trade Malay spoken by merchants. The phrases that follow work for both countries. The language is now written in Roman letters and is easy to pronounce. There are a few fun quirks. When a noun is followed by a "2" it is plural.

Yes Yah
No Tee-DAHK
Good BAH-eek
Please See-LAH-kahn
Thank you TEH-ree-mah kah-SEE
You're welcome Kem-BAH-lee
I'm sorry Mah-ahf
Excuse me MAH-ahf
Good morning S'LAH-maht PAH-ghee
Good-bye S'LAH-maht teeng-gal (to person staying)
S'LAH-maht jah-LAHN (to person leaving)
My name is . . . NAH-mah SAH-yah . . .
What is your name? SYAH-pah NAH-mah, AH-pah?
How are you? Ah-pah kah-BAR? (literally, "What's news?")
Do you understand? Ah-PAH-kah men-GHER-tee?
What? AH-pah?
Where? Dee-MAH-nah?
Where is a good hotel? Dee-MAH-nah AH-dah hotel yahng bah-eek?
Where is a good restaurant? Dee-MAH-nah AH-dah ROO-mah-MAH-kahn yahng bah-eek?
Food Mah-KAHN
Water Ire-n'yah
Lunch? MAH-kahn-see-ahng?
Dinner? MAH-kahn-MAH-lahm?
Good eating! Seh-LAH-maht mah-kahn!
It was very delicious Mah-kah-nahn ee-too eh-nahk seh-kahl-lee

I would like SAH-yah mau
This EE-nee
That EE-too
A ticket to . . . SAH-too kart-yees oon-took keh . . .
To the railroad station Keh stah-s'yoon keh-REH-tah AH-pee
Where is the bus to Semarang? Dee-mah-NAH-kah bees oon-took per-
  ghee keh seh-MAH-rahng?
When does it leave? Bee-lah ah-KAHN beh-Rahng-kaht?
When? Bee-lah? (or) KAH-pahn?
Later Nahn-tee
How much? Beh-RAH-pah?
One Sah-too
Two Doo-ah
Three Tee-gah
Four Ehm-paht
Five Lee-mah
Six Eh-nahm
Seven Tood-joo
Eight Deh-LAH-pahn (in Malaysia, "LAH-pahn")
Nine SEM-bee-lahn
Ten Seh-POO-loo
I Sah-yah
I like it SAH-yah EE-too SOO-kah
Very good! Bah-GOOSE!
Good luck! Seh-LAH-maht!
Stop! Behr-HEHN-tee!
Help! Toh-long!

7
Health

Just a few words before you begin this chapter. After reading all the do's and don'ts, you may have some concerns about the risk of illness in Asia. And before you go, you'll likely hear the occasional horror story about a friend of a friend who contracted Japanese encephalitis in China and died. While you're in Asia, travelers will eagerly tell you their tales of woe about bouts of diarrhea. You may start to become paranoid. You may get a bit fanatic about what and where you eat and drink and where you go.

Well, stop yourself before you get to that point. If you know how to safeguard your health, you can travel almost anywhere. And if you are the unlucky one who picks up something more serious, you'll know what to do. More than likely, the only illness you'll encounter will be a short bout of diarrhea.

The medical advice that follows is a rough introduction to health for Asian travel from two rank amateurs (with help from two M.D.'s). Travelers should rely on medical advice from a medical professional.

Before Your Trip

Medical Checkup and Immunizations

Who to See

Just as you'd give your car a good checkup before a long journey, it's smart to get a general checkup before your trip. You'll also need immunizations, depending on your destination. You can start with your personal physician. However, only doctors who specialize in travel medicine keep up to date on travelers' needs. If your physician doesn't direct you, some good resources for information and immunizations are your county or state public health departments and the travel clinics sometimes associated with university medical clinics. Travel clinics are the experts and charge accordingly. Public health departments usually offer a sliding fee scale. Check first to see if your health insurance will cover the cost.

When to Go

If you need shots, get them well in advance so that you don't step onto the airplane feeling like a walking pincushion. Some immunizations require a series of two or three shots, several weeks apart. Others have short periods of effectiveness (gamma globulin lasts three to six months), so you'll want to get those shortly before you go. Antimalarial tablets are taken weekly or daily, beginning a few weeks before you enter the tropics and continuing for several weeks after you leave. Start your shots one to two months in advance.

What to Get

Countries "require" you to have shots to protect their population from you. "Recommended" shots are those that help protect you from them. You may not be required to have vaccinations prior to entering a country, but many areas still have diseases, and it's smart to get the shots to protect yourself.

Tell the doctor everywhere you plan to go and may go. Then you can have the flexibility to take that impulsive swing through Bangladesh and Myanmar knowing that you are prepared medically. The health situation changes in Asia, and you should get up-to-date advice before your trip. But we'll discuss some shots that are typically needed.

The "International Certificate of Vaccination" is a useful form on which to record your shots. Immigration could stop you from entering their country if there is a cholera outbreak and you don't have a shot officially recorded and stamped. Even though chances of this are rare, the form is a handy way to keep track of what you've had and when. State and local public health departments and travel clinics usually have forms in stock.

Cholera immunizations are no longer required for Asia. However, there are still scattered outbreaks, so check before you go. The vaccine is not very effective, unfortunately. For that reason, most travel clinics don't routinely administer it, but they may put a stamp in your Certificate of Vaccination form to satisfy possible immigration requirements.

A tetanus/diptheria shot is by needed by travelers and nontravelers alike every 5 to 10 years. All adult travelers should have a onetime polio booster after having completed their childhood immunizations. If you were born after 1956, you will need a measles booster, which will also protect you at home.

A gamma globulin shot to reduce the chance of hepatitis is important (more later on hepatitis).

You might want to get a series of rabies shots before your trip (more later on rabies).

Meningitis has been a problem at times in Nepal. Check with your public health department about the current situation before you go. There is a vaccine.

The plague and Japanese encephalitis sometimes occur. Consider shots for these if you plan to spend a lot of time in high-risk areas. Consult your doctor or a travel clinic.

What Else to Do

If you have an existing health problem, discuss it with your doctor, and find out what you need to know to monitor and maintain your health while traveling. It is wise to take with you to Asia a letter from your doctor describing your medical problem. Note your blood type, and pray that you never require a transfusion in Asia. (If you do, hope there is a friend with you who checks that the blood has been screened for AIDS). Bob carries a needle and syringe in his first aid kit in case he needs a shot in Asia. Some hospitals reuse needles, a dangerous practice that can transmit hepatitis and AIDS. You can buy needles and syringes at pharmacies throughout Asia.

Dental Checkup

Emergency dental care during your trip consumes time and money, and it can be hazardous and painful. Anesthetic, if it is used, is primitive in many developing countries, and dentists seem to anticipate a higher pain threshold than most Americans have. If it were absolutely necessary for us to get dental care in Asia, we'd head for Japan, Hong Kong, Singapore, or Bangkok.

Medical Insurance

Many policies cover travel outside the country; check to see if yours does. Most policies require that you pay the bills yourself and send in the statements for reimbursement.

If you need coverage, look into some of the insurance policies offered by travel agencies, insurance brokers, or some credit agencies, such as American Express. Some policies cover the high costs of emergency evacuation. For scuba divers, the Divers Alert Network (DAN) offers insurance for emergency evacuation for decompression illness and other diving emergencies.

Since medical costs in Asia (except Japan) are very reasonable, we go with a policy that takes care of the big costs. On Bob's long trips of over six months, he's protected by a $1,000 deductible policy that covers only major hospital costs. He pays out of pocket for the occasional $5 fee for a diarrhea diagnosis in India. The cost of antibiotics and other medicines is minimal in most Asian countries.

Doctors Abroad

Except in Japan, Hong Kong, Bangkok, and Singapore, the only places in Asia where you are assured of getting high-quality medical treatment are private or mission hospitals, European or American administered. The American embassy in every national capital maintains a list of recommended doctors, dentists, and other medical practitioners. Or check with the British or Canadian embassy, a large hotel, or a foreign aid organization such as the Peace Corps. It is important to visit a Western-trained doctor. Primitive medicine men are fun, unless your bed is the one they're dancing over.

If you want information on doctors before you go, contact IAMAT—International Association for Medical Assistance to Travelers, 417 Center Street, Lewiston, NY, 14092 (716/754-4883). They have a referral list of English-speaking doctors worldwide, a standardized fee schedule, and valuable information on subjects of interest to travelers.

Traveler's First-Aid Kit

We recommend the following first-aid kit, based on our personal experiences and the book *Health Hints for the Tropics*, published by the American Society of Tropical Medicine and Hygiene. But what you need depends on where and how long you go. If you're only visiting the cities, you'll be able to find almost everything you need. You may want to wait to get your medicines in Asia since they will be cheaper (except in Japan).

Highly Recommended Items
Bandaids, waterproof tape, gauze pads, moleskin, sterile cotton, small
  scissors, eyedropper, tweezers, needle.
Ace bandage.
Thermometer: one with a low temperature reading if risk of
  hypothermia, such as when mountain climbing.
Water purifying system (Potable-Aqua, Water Tech Water Purifier
  Cup, etc.).
Oral rehydration packets.
Aspirin or ibuprofen.
Antiseptic: Betadine.
Antibiotics for skin infection, diarrhea, bronchitis, and bladder
  infection (women).
Antidiarrheals: loperamide (Imodium).
Antifungal cream.
Antimalarials.
Insect repellent.

Insect spray for room or clothing.

Sunscreen, high SPF.

Skin medications for itch or sunburn.

Extra glasses or contact lenses (with cleaning solution), sunglasses, eyeglass or contact lens prescription.

Multivitamins (with flouride for children if extended travel).

Birth control drugs/devices, condoms.

Recommended Items

Pepto-Bismol.

Laxative.

Antacids.

Antimotion sickness: Scopolamine patch, Dramamine, Bonine.

Antibiotic skin cream: Bactroban.

Tincture of benzoin.

Mosquito net.

Insect sting emergency or allergy kit (if allergic).

Suture kit with scissors, skin suture material on a needle, small bottle of surgical soap, and local anesthetic such as Lidocaine (if hiking far from a town for extended periods).

Altitude sickness prevention/treatment: Diamox (if in high altitudes).

Disposable syringes and needles (with a note from physician explaining need for these).

Sleeping pills.

Codeine (Tylenol 3, Empirin 3), for emergencies such as a broken arm.

Medications for specific illnesses (diabetes, cardiac, allergies, etc.).

Later in this chapter we'll discuss how and when to use the medications above. But consult with your doctor before you use any of these drugs.

A thermometer is important. If you have a high fever, you should seek medical help. Asia uses a Celsius scale. To convert from Celsius to Fahrenheit, multiply by 9, divide by 5, and add 32. To convert from Fahrenheit to Celsius, subtract 32, multiply by 5, and divide by 9. If your temperature is 98.6 degrees Fahrenheit, it's 37 degrees Celsius.

Aspirin is a great general pain reliever for math-induced headaches, sore feet, sprains, bruises, hangovers, and many other minor problems. Supplemental vitamins (with iron, for women) are most effective when taken with the day's largest meal.

If you wear glasses, bring an extra pair in a solid protective case and a copy of your lens prescription in case your glasses are broken or lost. Glasses are cheap to replace in Asia. Contact lenses are used in many parts of Asia, and the required solutions for their care are easy to find in major cities. Hard contacts can be uncomfortable in the dusty cities; soft contacts are the better choice for travel. Consider bringing the disposable kind for easy maintenance. If you plan to wear your contacts regularly, it's wise to bring along a pair of glasses in case of loss or damage.

Health in Asia

We can't overemphasize prevention. Although on almost every trip to Asia, we get diarrhea, it's never been serious enough to ruin our plans. We credit our otherwise good health to careful eating, drinking, and living habits.

You Are What You Eat

Use good judgment when eating. You may want to start your trip by eating in Western-style restaurants and then expand into the local cuisine slowly to let your stomach adjust. But wherever you eat, there are some important rules to follow.

Eat only food that you know is properly cooked and still hot (ideally, food should be heated above 160 degrees F, but you'll get strange looks if you stick your thermometer in the chow mein). If cooked food has been sitting out all day with the flies, obviously, it's not safe. In India, some train station restaurants have fast turnover, so germs don't have time to congregate. But even there, be careful of what you eat. The locals feel that hot spices help control the germs. We don't know if that's true, but it does help control our appetite.

If the cook and restaurant staff look unhealthy, go elsewhere. You may want to carry your own eating utensils just to make sure they are clean.

Eat only thick-skinned peelable fruit. Who knows what was on the hand that picked that apple? Bananas are safe.

Stay away from fresh salads unless you know the vegetables were cleaned in water treated with iodine. (Animal dung, often used as fertilizer, can leave parasites on produce.) If you want a fresh salad or an apple, get your produce at the market, and then soak it for twenty minutes in water you've treated with iodine.

Except perhaps in Japan (where it's expensive), avoid red meat unless it's well cooked. A microwaved Big Mac in any country is probably safe.

An adequate diet is very important for a traveler. Traveling is hard work. You expend a lot of energy. The longer your trip, the more you will be affected by an inadequate diet. Too often, budget travelers try to stretch their dollars by eating more carbohydrates and less protein. This is the root of many nutritional problems encountered by travelers. Protein helps you resist infection and rebuild muscles. We bring supplemental vitamins, but these do not substitute for a well-balanced meal.

Bob goes vegetarian (except in Japan) on his trips to Asia. In most less-developed countries, meat is a luxury and the locals get their protein through a combination of grains and beans. In India, this is rice and dhal (lentils); in China and most countries in Southeast Asia, it's rice and tofu (soybean curd). Protein can also be found in dahi (yogurt) in India and Nepal. We eat yogurt whenever possible. It supplies good bacteria (acidophilus) that helps keep down the bad bacteria in your system. Bob brings along acidophilus pills from his local health food store for the times when there's no yogurt around.

If you're hooked on meat, visit a local outdoor market in Asia and take a look at the carcasses hanging in the sun. Tonight's beef steak is this morning's feast for the flies.

Don't Drink the Water

Some travelers claim they drink untreated water everywhere in Asia and never get sick. However, we advise that except in Japan, thoroughly Westernized Singapore and Hong Kong, and major (read "expensive") hotels with their own filtration systems, do not drink the water.

It's important to get sufficient fluids, especially in a hot climate where you sweat a lot. Water boiled for 10 minutes can be safely consumed. Beer and carbonated soft drinks are available and safe almost everywhere. Coconut milk from a freshly split coconut is very refreshing. Beware of the ice cubes in drinks; the ice likely wasn't made from safe filtered water.

Bottled water is available most places travelers go in Asia. Make sure the cap is properly sealed, or to be completely safe, drink carbonated water. Since bottled water is expensive by local standards, some entrepreneurs sell forgeries using discarded bottles (especially in India).

The most reliable way to purify water is to do it yourself. You can find small portable water filters at sporting goods stores such as REI and Eddie Bauer; the cost runs from $35 to $200. Consider the Water Tech Water Purifier Cup. Whatever model you use, check to see that it filters out giardia. None will remove viruses such as hepatitis. Adequately boiling water or treating it with iodine does remove viruses.

You can treat water with iodine-based tablets (very convenient) or iodine crystals. We throw in some real lemon or a dash of a powdered drink to kill the iodine taste.

The Rick-and-Bob preferred method is to ask our guest house to boil water for us in the morning. We carry this with us during the day in a quart water bottle in our day pack. Get a hard plastic bottle such as Nalgene which will accept boiling water.

It's a good idea to brush your teeth with safe water.

Other Preventions

Some people swear by Pepto Bismol to prevent diarrhea. You might try using this at the beginning until your stomach adjusts to the new foods. The tablets are easier to carry. Taking two tablets, chewed well, four times a day may help. Pepto Bismol contains aspirin, so avoid it if you are aspirin-sensitive.

If you plan on any long sea journeys or bus rides on winding mountain roads, consider taking a preventative for motion sickness. A Scopolamine patch placed behind the ear allows the medication to be slowly absorbed through the skin. Available by prescription, it is longer lasting and does not cause as much drowsiness as over-the-counter Dramamine.

Another useful item for long journeys is earplugs. The industrial type made of foam is the best and is readily available at most drugstores. You'll sleep better on buses and trains.

Remember, honor your body. One of the best ways to preserve your health is to take Asia slowly. Take rest days after a long tiring bus or train ride. Don't push yourself. Adapting to the new culture, food, and time change is stressful enough.

Malaria

Malaria is still found throughout Asia, excluding Japan and Korea. No medications offer a complete guarantee of prevention, but they can reduce the possibility and also lessen the symptoms if you do get it.

Malaria is a parasite transmitted by the bite of a mosquito. The symptoms are headaches, fever, sweating, and shivering. It can be fatal. Check with a travel clinic or the public health department to see which medicine is recommended for your area of travel.

At one time chloroquine was commonly prescribed to prevent malaria. Since malaria is now chloroquine-resistant throughout most of Asia, mefloquine is presently the drug of choice. However, there are already mefloquine-resistant strains of malaria along the Thai-Myanmar border.

One tablet of mefloquine should be taken once a week; we pick Sunday as the day to remember our pill. Start two weeks before going into an infected area, and continue four weeks after leaving. This drug is not recommended for scuba divers (per the Divers Alert Network), since it can cause spatial disorientation. One of the biggest drawbacks of this drug is its cost.

There are several alternatives to mefloquine, some less expensive, but with their own drawbacks. Doxycyline, which is taken orally once a day, can make your skin sensitive to the sun (leading to severe sunburn). Halofentrine is a very effective antimalarial drug; its drawback is that it isn't on the market yet—but may be by the time you read this.

Since drugs don't guarantee prevention, protect yourself from being bitten. The mosquitoes that transmit malaria bite from dusk to dawn. However, mosquitoes that transmit other diseases (e.g., dengue fever) bite during the daytime. Dengue fever is found mostly in the city, whereas malaria is a disease of the countryside.

How to reduce bites:

1. Wear long-sleeve shirts and long pants (as the heat permits). However, mosquitoes can bite through clothes.

2. Apply insect repellent to all exposed areas of the body. We recommend Ultrathon insect repellent by 3M Corporation (35% DEET) for adults. It gives up to 12 hours of protection. For children, use Skeedaddle repellent (10% DEET), made by Little Point Corporation.

3. Use a spray containing permethrin on your clothes and a mosquito net to keep the hungry at bay. Some of the sprays will last 2 to 3 weeks on clothes.

4. Make sure there is a mosquito net in your room. Not all rooms will have them. You may want to buy one in a sporting goods store in the United States. They are also available in Asian cities, usually cheaper than here. (Note that all mosquito netting is not created equal. The kind made of heavy cotton can be almost suffocating on a hot night. When getting a room or buying netting, look for the lighter nylon material.)

5. A very good deterrent to mosquitoes, available throughout Asia, is the mosquito coil. These flammable green spirals are installed on a small metal stand (it comes with the package) and then lit. As they burn like incense, they give off a distinctive odor that mosquitoes (and some humans) hate. Get the ones that last for eight hours. We burn these when caught short without netting. Also burn them under your table at night to keep bugs away from your ankles while you eat.

6. Find a room with window screens.

Taiwan has come out with a pen-sized electronic device that supposedly imitates the sound of a male mosquito. The female mosquito bites during egg-laying time, a time when she is repulsed by the sound of a male mosquito. Thus, the electronic sound is supposed to keep the females away. Bob tried one of these miracle cures on his last trip.

From the results, he figured he must have turned it on during the mating season.

A little preventative medicine can keep you out of the local clinics

Common Ailments

Diarrhea

Get used to the fact that travel is a package deal. You will probably get sick in Asia. You'll have diarrhea for a day, maybe three days. (Practice that thought in the mirror a few times.) If you're switching between several different cultures, it may happen again. When you get the runs, take it in stride. If you stay healthy, you'll feel lucky. Even if you faithfully follow all the rules—don't drink untreated water, peel all fruits, and so on—you may still get sick. The bacteria in Asian food and water is different from that in American food and water. Our systems are the most pampered on earth. We grew up on bread that rips in a straight line. We are capable of handling American bacteria with no problem at all, but some people can go to Hong Kong and get sick. Some Japanese people visit San Francisco and get sick. Some Americans travel around the world, eating and drinking everything in sight, and don't get sick. Others spend weeks on the toilet. It all depends on the person.

If you do get diarrhea, it will run its course. Don't panic. The current medical advice is to eat normally since your body needs the nutrients. Some find it best to initially eat only plain rice, avoiding fruit and milk. Caffeinated drinks are not helpful, but drink plenty of fluids. Personally, we choose to have only fluids for a day. It may be a myth, but we feel our system needs a rest. One benefit of a short fast is not having to spend the day on the toilet. Keep telling yourself that tomorrow you will feel much better. You will. Most conditions are self-limiting.

If you have diarrhea, it's very important to replenish lost liquids and minerals. Drinking a rehydration solution will help get you back on your feet sooner. A powder in a packet is available in most countries, or bring it with you as part of your first aid kit. In any case, water is most essential. Drink up!

During a bout of diarrhea, you'll lose potassium. Eat bananas. They will add potassium to your system and also help solidify your stool since they contain pectin, a binding agent.

Most travel clinics arm travelers with an antibiotic (usually a quinolone) and an antidiarrheal medication (Imodium, available at any drugstore) to take at the onset of moderate or severe diarrhea. However, Imodium is not recommended if you have a high fever or blood or pus in your stool. If this occurs, you should seek medical care. Remember, antibiotics are powerful drugs and will wipe out all the bacteria in your system. So you may want to wait it out if you have a light case of diarrhea. In Asia, certain medications sold over the counter (like Chloramphenicol and Enterovioform) are dangerous and should be avoided.

To just stop the flow, Imodium works great. It slows the bowels for a time. This is useful for a disastrous combination of diarrhea and a long bus ride with few pit stops.

Basic good hygiene is important. Keep your nails clean and wash your hands, especially before you use your hands to eat Indian-style. You can be your own worst enemy by reinfecting yourself after a bout of diarrhea.

Giardia

If, along with diarrhea, you have a puffed stomach, gas, and burps that taste like rotten eggs, you probably have the parasite giardia. Giardia is found in mountain streams as well as on plates and glasses washed in untreated water. Check with a local doctor if you think you have it.

We can testify that it's not fun, but it doesn't ruin your trip. Although we usually feel it's best to let your system handle things, we'd use antibiotics for giardia. If not treated, it may come and go for months. In the United States, flagyl is prescribed. However, a more effective treatment is tinidazole, available in Asia but not in the United States as it is not yet approved by the FDA. Four 500 mg tablets taken at the same time will most likely cure you.

Prevention is the key. Always treat or boil water, regardless of how clear and good it looks. Follow this advice even on hikes. A clear cold stream can seem irresistible but may be contaminated with giardia from animal or human feces. Avoid restaurants that look unsanitary. We disregard our own advice at times, and we're still alive.

Constipation

Constipation seems to be nearly as prevalent as diarrhea. Know what roughage is—fruits, vegetables, whole grains—and everything will come out all right in the end. Vigorous exercise helps to get things going.

Sickness from the Heat and Sun

Beware of the sun, especially in hot, humid climates. Wear a hat. Heat stroke and heat exhaustion can be disabling problems if not taken seriously. If you're feeling faint or nauseous, cool and clammy, or overly hot, do yourself a favor: take a break. Sit down for lunch or a cold drink, or end your sightseeing and take a taxi back to your hotel. The tropical sun is eager to burn your skin, so go easy at first and always use sunscreen (available in Asia).

Cuts and Scrapes

Any time you break your skin in Asia, take it seriously. Immediately clean the wound with soap and water. If your surroundings aren't too dirty, leave the wound open to dry. If it starts to become infected, see a doctor. An antibiotic treatment may be needed. If you get a blister, leave it alone. It is actually your best Band-aid. However, if it gets infected, you must treat it. Sterilize a needle with a flame from a match, and pop the blister. Clean it and cover it with a bandage, changing it daily. If the infection continues, antibiotics may be needed. For prevention, apply moleskin or a bandage over tender areas before they turn into blisters.

Strains and Sprains

A physical injury is often accompanied by swelling, which is painful and retards healing. For 48 hours after a sprain or strain occurs, you should elevate and apply ice to the injured area. Aspirin or ibuprofen often help relieve pain and inflammation. You can use an Ace bandage to immobilize the affected part, to stop swelling, and later to provide support. Do not "work out" a sprain.

More Serious Problems

Venereal Disease and AIDS

VD has reached pandemic proportions. And with AIDS on the rampage in Asia as well as everywhere, we think you're crazy if you mess around with an unknown partner, especially a prostitute. An effective way to lower one's sex drive is to learn what percent of Southeast Asia's prostitutes are HIV-positive. In certain Asian cities famed for sex for sale, some blocks are dotted with signs advertising "VD Clinic." Some mutated forms of VD have proven penicillin-resistant. Obviously, the best way to prevent VD and AIDS is to avoid exposure. A condom is fairly effective in preventing transmission for those too tempted to resist. Remember, many sexually transmitted diseases can come from oral sex. Wear a condom. Cleaning with soap and water before and after exposure to VD is also helpful. If you think you have something, head to a doctor.

Hepatitis

Hepatitis A is transmitted through food and water and can be contracted in unsanitary conditions anywhere. Although there is no vaccine to prevent it, a gamma globulin shot will fortify your system to resist it. Depending on the dose, the shots are effective up to six months. For maximum lasting power, get the shot just before you go. If you're on a long trip and need another shot, take care that the vaccine has been tested for AIDS since it is derived from blood. Try to get vaccine that has recently been screened in a Western country. Some Asian screening techniques may not be as effective. If you have doubts about the vaccine, don't risk it.

Hepatitis B is contracted through sex and intravenous injections and blood transfusions. There is a preventative vaccine. You should get this series of shots if you're considering having sexual contact in Southeast Asia.

Rabies

Many Westerners, Americans in particular, want to pat the head of every cute little doggie they see. In Asia, don't do it. Only Singapore is rabies-free. In Sri Lanka, for example, someone dies of rabies every day of the year. Give unknown animals of any kind—no matter how cuddly—a wide berth.

Although neither of us has ever been bitten in Asia, we've been with people who have. It's cause for concern, especially if you're not close to a major city. Scrub and clean the wound immediately. If possible, the dog should be observed and examined for rabies. If it remains healthy over the next ten days, you're safe.

Often it's not possible to either catch or observe the dog for long. Due to the high incidence of rabies in Asia, we recommend that if the bite breaks the skin, go for treatment. As soon as possible, head to a major city for the required series of shots. Some of the less-developed countries may not carry the newer human diploid cell vaccine that causes fewer reactions, so you may choose to fly to a more Western city such as Singapore or Hong Kong.

Some people get the fairly expensive rabies vaccine before they travel. Although this reduces the risk, you still need to follow up with a shorter series of shots if bitten.

Dengue Fever

This is a virus infection with symptoms of fever, rash, headache, muscle ache, and lymph node swelling. Like malaria, it's spread by mosquitoes. Use the same precautions to prevent being bitten. There is currently no medication for prevention, and there is no treatment other than bed rest and aspirin/Tylenol.

Snake Bite

We are often asked if you need to worry about snakes in Asia. Well, yes and no. There are poisonous snakes there. In our total of many years of travel there, the only ones we've encountered have been cobras in baskets in front of Indians playing flutes. However, throughout the Indian subcontinent, including Myanmar and Sri Lanka, snakebite is a common cause of death. Some of the pit vipers are far more deadly than even the cobra. Their venom can travel through the bloodstream so quickly that unless you're sitting on the hospital steps when you're bitten, and that hospital is fortunate enough to have the antivenin on ice, you're a goner. Don't go walking in thick jungle or bush unaccompanied by a local resident, unless you can see the path clearly and know exactly where you're going.

If someone is bitten, the old cut and suck method is out. Current advice is to immobilize the bitten limb (to decrease the spread of venom) and seek medical help pronto.

Altitude Illness

If you're going to be high in the Himalayas, you should take precautions to prevent altitude illness. The more likely and milder version of altitude illness is acute mountain sickness (AMS). Its most common symptom is a headache, but trekkers also may complain of nausea, light-headedness, and difficulty in sleeping. This will usually pass after a few days at a given altitude. The severer syndromes include high altitude pulmonary edema and cerebral edema—the accumulation of fluids in the lungs and brain. Symptoms may be confusion, staggering, worsening cough, and difficulty in breathing. If this happens to you, descend immediately. It can be fatal. Oxygen, acetazolamide (Diamox), steroids, or nifedipine may be used for treatment, but they are no substitute for prompt descent.

You can greatly reduce the chances of getting ill if you ascend slowly. Generally at 10,000 feet (but lower for some) you should start acclimatizing to the altitude before you move on. It's best to go at a pace of no more than 1,000 feet a day. If you have mild symptoms, either stay where you are until they stop or move on slowly, being alert for further problems. If the symptoms get more severe, descend 2,000 to 3,000 feet immediately. This normally does the trick. Scheduling rest days every few days when ascending will help.

Some people find acetazolamide useful when they fly into a high altitude to begin trekking. Consult a knowledgeable physician if you're thinking of using this medicine. It can cause side effects such as numbness and tingling of the skin.

Study this topic in more detail in some of the Asian mountain trekking books and in Dr. Stephen Bezruchka's *The Pocket Doctor*.

Small Things to Consider

Sooner or later—probably sooner—you're going to encounter the creepy crawlies that inhabit the tropical world. You'll definitely get to know mosquitoes and cockroaches on an intimate basis. Many travelers also encounter the unpleasant bedbug.

Cockroaches are said to be the most ancient of all surviving life forms—and the ones most likely to inherit the earth in the event of a nuclear holocaust. But they are more annoying than harmful. We don't like them in our food, because they can spread bacteria, but we try to tolerate them elsewhere.

Bedbugs are no fun. They leave welts that can take weeks to heal. They are frequent residents at especially dirty, seedy hotels. Check your mattress carefully before crawling into bed. When checking out a hotel room, step into it ahead of the clerk and flip the light on to catch the bugs by surprise. Count them as they scurry before you accept the room. If you do start itching during the night, turn the light on and the bugs may disappear. We carry a thin plastic sheet to throw over the mattress to contain them. The breeze of your fan discourages flying critters from landing on your body as you sleep.

Some get upset about the lizards that frequently inhabit Asian rooms. We consider these gekkos our friendly roommates. Not only do they serenade us but they lick up a lot of those pests ready to suck our blood.

Books and Other Information

A small handy book to take on your trip is Dr. Stephen Bezruchka's *The Pocket Doctor* (The Mountaineers, 1988). It's filled with good practical advice for the international traveler. *Health Information for International Travel* is available from: Center for Disease Control, Attn: Health Information, Center for Prevention Services, Division of Quarantine, Atlanta, GA 30333. Updated yearly, it has information on health problems specific to individual countries.

(Our thanks to Dr. Stacy Globerman and Dr. Eric Weiss for their substantial contributions to this chapter.)

Going local (minimize by reading this chapter twice)

8
The Woman Traveling Alone

Each year, more and more women are traveling in Asia. Melinda Williams, who recently returned from a ten-month trip, wrote this chapter to share her thoughts and experiences. While the information is primarily directed toward women traveling alone, much of it is applicable to two or more women traveling together and to male travelers as well.

A Woman Traveler

When I told friends that I was going to travel in Asia by myself for nearly a year, their first reaction was invariably either "Wow, you're really brave!" or "You must be crazy!"

Granted, a healthy dose of confidence and a dash of eccentricity will add immeasurably to your trip. But you don't have to be inordinately brave or insane to tackle Asia on your own. Women of all types and temperaments can and do travel alone and return home to brag about it. Really. I met women traveling alone in Asia who were nurses, students, retirees, businesswomen, homemakers, anthropologists, teachers, and volunteers. A few were just out of high school, and others were old enough to lie about their age.

Heidi, a 67-year-old German widow, had spent years resisting her daughter's attempts to get her out of the house and on the road. When I caught up to her on a beach in Thailand, she was talking about buying a little plot of land and never going back.

Going Solo

The solo traveler, male or female, has far more access to the lives and culture of local residents than those who travel in pairs or groups. As a general rule, women travelers receive more overall hospitality than men in similar situations. A woman traveling alone has even a further advantage. Locals are likely to find a lone woman more approachable than a male traveler or group of travelers, and will offer assistance, invite you to share their meals, teach you the language, and help you find your way around. Women, in particular, may treat you as a wayward daughter, drawing you into their homes to (over-)feed and mother you.

In addition to increasing your access to local culture, traveling alone can boost your confidence and independence. Many female travelers arrive in Asia, as I did, having never taken a trip of significant length alone. Most return home more confident and self-assured than when they left and with a renewed awareness of their own abilities and strengths.

Solo travelers have the freedom to indulge their whims. Some women report that solo travel is the one time in their lives when they truly follow their hearts on a day-to-day basis. With no one else to answer to, your only constraints as you travel are your own energy and interests. You can rise at dawn or sleep until noon, change your plans ten times, a hundred times, or even refuse to plan at all. Best of all, solo travel affords you the opportunity to learn to enjoy your own company. That alone is an irreplaceable gift to yourself.

Meeting the Locals

You don't have to go much out of your way to meet and befriend the local people. The key is a willingness to look beyond the usual buyer-seller relationship to the person you are dealing with. You may be surprised at how many tourists have never held a conversation with a local resident that did not begin with the words "How much . . . ?" or "Where is . . . ?" Those who do find their travels significantly enriched.

Knowledge of the local language is not a prerequisite for travel in most Asian countries. However, every word or phrase that you learn will bring you one step closer to the local people you encounter.

While traveling in Indonesia, my halting conversations with local residents enabled me to meet two families who "adopted" me for several weeks each. Living in the families' homes, I had a unique perspective of village life and became a participant rather than an observer. My rudimentary Bahasa Indonesia blossomed during my stay, I took part in spectacular local festivals as a "family member," and I gained friends and "family" to last a lifetime. And I hadn't known a word of the language before I left home.

Going My Way?

One of the best things about traveling alone is the freedom to choose when not to do so. While many women choose to travel with a partner from home, others leave home alone hoping to meet up with travelers along the way.

Whether you are just looking for someone to swap stories with or other travelers to partner up with for a few days or several months, one "hello" (or *namaste* or *salamat pagi*, or other local equivalent) is all it takes to get the ball rolling.

With all due respect to your mother, "don't talk to strangers" will not get you far if you're traveling solo. Shed your caution and strike up conversations with anyone who looks interesting. To meet other travelers, frequent dormitories, cafés, train stations, and tourist attractions. During a recent trip through Asia, I traveled with men and women from Canada, New Zealand, Germany, Great Britain, the United States, France, Sweden, and Australia. In addition to great companionship and conversation, I came away from my trip with friends to visit all around the globe.

If you meet someone you want to travel with, establish a clear understanding up front about how long you expect to travel together. While you can always alter your plans, common assumptions will help avoid misunderstandings later. If the partnership is less enjoyable than you had expected, or if you simply feel like traveling on your own again, sit down with your traveling partner and let her or him know that you are ready to move on. An honest, straightforward approach will help ensure that your friendship lasts well beyond the time you spend traveling together.

Travelers' romances are common and can sometimes lead to terrific long-term relationships. Most romances formed on the road, however, are both short-lived and relatively superficial. Be realistic about what you want and need from a relationship before you get into one.

If you do find yourself becoming romantically involved with a fellow traveler (or a local), be clear with him or her about your expectations. I have seen some wonderful trips go sour because of misunderstandings about the permanence of a travel romance. A broken heart makes a lousy travel partner, so think twice before you jump into anything.

Whatever you do, do it safely. The AIDS epidemic has invaded much of Asia at an alarming rate, a fact that affects a number of tourists. Don't assume that your travel companion—or local friend—automatically comes with a clean bill of health. (For information about contraception, see Women's Health, below.)

Who Is That Glamour Girl?

Regardless of how you travel through Asia, expect to attract a fair amount of attention along the way. No matter how "ordinary" you may find yourself, in most parts of Asia you are exotic. Different. Even glamorous.

The farther off the tourist trail you get, the more commotion you will cause. In smaller villages, you may be surrounded by crowds of gaping children pointing at your "enormous" nose or pushing close enough to tug the hair on your arms. If you're bothered by persistent stares or crowds gathering to marvel at you, try to remember it's just good-natured curiosity. Bring some humor to the situation. This is a great time to pull out the Groucho Marx glasses or the juggling balls you brought along for just these occasions, turning a slightly awkward situation into a standing-room-only performance.

Don't take yourself too seriously. It's all right to make a fool of yourself every so often. While I was in Asia, I found myself singing endless renditions of classic Western rock favorites (Eric Clapton, Beatles, and so on). The more I pleaded tone deafness, the more my Asian friends laughed and insisted that I sing. Despite my lousy voice, their response was always the same. "Sing another one!" Their delight at my willingness to play along far outweighed my embarrassment. I even grew to relish the sing-alongs. And I have perfected a pretty fair rendition of "Wonderful Tonight."

You may find, especially early on, that the stares and attention feel unwelcome or even threatening. Most of us are not used to being celebrities, and the adjustment can be difficult. In this context, it's imperative that female travelers learn to distinguish between local curiosity and sexual harassment (male travelers rarely face the latter). The situations I have described above stem from the natural interest locals have in someone different from themselves. Harassment is a very different situation, which I will cover later.

While it's easy to attract attention and strike up conversations with both locals and other travelers, at times you'll prefer to be left alone. It is perfectly acceptable to smile politely, shrug your shoulders, and walk away from a gathering crowd. There are several tactics you can use to carve out your own uninterrupted space. Pull out your journal or bury yourself in a book. Sit in the back of an empty café. Avoid dormitories. When you're ready for companionship again, head for the nearest travelers' center, check into a popular dormitory, or walk down to bargain at the local market.

Virgins, Wives, and Whores: Asian Views on Women

As you travel, you may have to contend with certain widely held beliefs about women, in general, and Western women, in particular. Don't expect to find a high degree of consciousness about equality or women's rights in Asia. There are a number of local women's groups working to raise awareness about the harsh economic and social conditions faced by a majority of women in Asia. However, most of the fruits of their labor have not yet trickled down to the general populace. In many Asian countries, a woman is somebody's wife, mother, sister, aunt, daughter, or cousin. Seldom is she considered a legitimate person in her own right.

As a result, a woman alone is an anomaly in most of Asia. Except in large cities, women are generally seen in groups and seldom travel farther than the outskirts of the village or *kampung* without a companion. Asians may wonder what kind of father you have who's let his daughter travel so far from home alone . . . or what kind of daughter is worth so little concern.

Rajiv, a university student I met in Bombay, told me with disdainful authority that there are three kinds of women in the world: virgins, wives, and whores. A virgin lives with her parents, a wife with her husband, and anyone else, by implication, falls into the third category. He left no doubts as to where he thought I belonged.

The Rules

Being "foreign," you will be exempt from many of the written and unwritten rules that govern local women. There exists an odd equation to which many Asian men subscribe: as a woman, you are of lesser status than they; as a Westerner, you are of higher status; and the combination of the two makes you roughly their equal. (I experienced this as a Caucasian woman and do not know whether or how it may differ for women of color.) Your status as an "honorary man" will enable you to travel with relative ease and allow you to participate in activities traditionally reserved for men, such as sporting or gambling events, conversing with strangers, smoking, and other "unladylike" ventures.

During a temple festival in Ubud, Bali, I was invited to a cockfight by the proprietor of my guest house. I was surprised to find myself not only the sole Westerner but also the only woman. When questioned, several nearby men explained that local women never attend the cockfights. They quickly assured me, however, that I was welcome. Indeed, following the cockfight, I was invited to several other male-only events and gathering places. On each occasion, I entered into conversations about social issues (division of labor, equal pay, politics) that most of the men would never consider discussing with their wives or daughters.

Despite our unequal treatment, I didn't find a barrier between myself and the local women. In fact, most of the women I met seemed

to accept me almost immediately as a sister or daughter. You will benefit immeasurably if you make an effort to meet and converse with the
local women. Relationships forged with them may be some of the most
meaningful and memorable aspects of your trip.

No Women Allowed

Despite your relatively high status as you travel, there are some
women-only prohibitions that will still apply.

Temples and other holy places may have "special" requirements for
women, which you will find posted near the entrance. A sign on the
gate outside a mosque in Old Delhi informs visitors that women cannot
enter "without the responsible male relatives." You may have irrespon-
sible male relatives or none at all, but never fear; any man will do. A
Jain temple I visited carries this ominous warning: "Entry of ladies in
monthly courses is strictly prohibited. Any lady in monthly course if
she enters any of the temples she may suffer." Compliance appears to
be voluntary, but I didn't take my chances. Before you get too frustrated, remember that you are in Asia to experience another culture, not
your own. There will be things you don't like, but it's not your responsibility or your right to try to change them. In fact, acting on your frustration is more likely to hinder than advance women's causes locally.
You may find that your sincere efforts on behalf of global sisterhood
are viewed with suspicion, even hostility, by the local women as well as
men. I'm not counseling you to leave your beliefs at home. But often
the most persuasive argument for improving local perceptions of
women is your own dignity, courtesy, and self-respect.

To support organizations promoting Asian women's rights and
opportunities, send a donation to or volunteer with the groups you
encounter while traveling. Educate yourself, before and while you
travel, about the work and experiences of women in those areas you
expect to visit.

Equally important, answer honestly and persuasively when you are
asked to share your views on equality, appropriate female roles, and
other sociopolitical issues pertaining to women. Local men may listen
to you more than they would to local women, because they perceive
you as somehow "more equal." You won't change the views of an
entire culture, but you may plant a seed.

Sex, Lies, and Videotape

Most Asian men only know about Western women from movies, newspapers, or other tourists. Some may act as though you are the glamorous
woman they saw in the latest soft-porn film. You may be seen as an exotic

and desirable sex object and a symbol of the "sexually free" West. Some negative stereotypes may be left over from the "free love" sixties, when many self-proclaimed hippies headed to Asia, searching for enlightenment and unwittingly lugging much of their own culture with them.

You are likely to encounter many confused notions. One young Asian man asked me with apparent sincerity, "Melinda, why is it that American women need to have more than six lovers in one day?" After viewing a recent movie, he assumed that this was normal behavior for American females.

Movies and other bearers of Western "culture" have depicted Western females as loose, immodest, and ready to have sex at the slightest provocation. While these stereotypes are patently unfair, there are a small number of women who, like some Western men, come to Asia on "sex vacations." Their exploitation of the local population certainly isn't the sole cause of negative stereotypes, but their behavior does make it more difficult for the women who follow.

Countering the Stereotypes: Basic Precautions

While some unwanted attention is inevitable, you can take precautions to minimize it. I'm not saying that you "ask for it" by wearing certain clothes or acting in a certain way. No woman deserves to be harassed. But remember that traveling in another culture is like visiting someone's home. Just as a smoker would refrain in a nonsmoker's residence, you must make accommodations to avoid offending your "hosts." Covering your thighs in a very conservative culture will not ruin your trip. It may, however, make the difference between being accepted and befriended by the locals or being shunned as just another Ugly American (or Canadian, or Swede, or . . .). You need not— and should not—be accommodating to the point of seriously compromising your own values or integrity. But don't sweat the small stuff.

You Are What You Wear

Don't reinforce stereotypes by dressing immodestly. Look around at what the local women are wearing, and take your cues from them. That isn't to say that you have to wear a sari in India or a sarong in Indonesia. But if the local women are covered from head to toe, you can safely assume that shorts and a bikini top are not appropriate. Don't expect to get a gorgeous, all-over tan in a small village on the east coast of Malaysia.

Loose, lightweight cotton clothing is your best bet in hot, humid climates. Leave your form-fitting clothing at home, where it is less likely

Western women should dress modestly and be sensitive to the local cultures

to be taken as an open invitation. Cotton is cool, easy to wash, and dries quickly. Tank tops, shorts, and bikinis are fine for the beach but will not do in the village surrounding it. Long pants or skirts and a cotton T-shirt or loose-fitting blouse will keep you cool and cool off potential "admirers," too. In some places, you should cover your shoulders. Save tight lycra and skimpy summer clothes for the beaches or resort areas. If you want to get to know the locals and gain their respect, avoid wearing clothing they consider indecent.

Try not to look as though you have been wearing and sleeping in the same outfit for two months, even if you have. A sign at the Thailand-Malaysia border illustrates the frustration some Asians feel about frequent invasions of raggedy-looking Westerners. Posted by the Thai Ministry of the Interior, the notice gives an eight-point description of the kind of "hippie appearance" that may bar you from the kingdom. These include: "A person who has long hair that appears untidy or dirty," and "A person who is dressed in an impolite and dirty-looking manner."

Don't worry excessively about what you wear as you travel. Just use some common sense, wash your clothes occasionally, be aware of the local standard, and try, within reason, to fit in.

A side note: leave the make-up at home. If you absolutely cannot do without it, take a bare minimum. The heat and humidity will send most of it running down your face. Keep it simple. You may be surprised at how easy it is to do without.

Cultural Body Language

Read up on the culture before you arrive. An awareness of cultural norms will keep you from unknowingly committing any serious social faux pas and enable you to better appreciate the people and cultures you encounter.

As a general rule, you should avoid anything that might be construed as a come-on. Establishing direct eye contact and flashing a big Colgate smile at men on the street may be considered an invitation. In questionable circumstances, learn to do the "New York strut": carry yourself with confidence, keep your eyes forward and your face impassive, hold your bags close to your body and stride like you know exactly where you are going, and don't intend to be put off by any two-bit mugger or street punk. A heavy dose of Attitude is usually all you need to carry you safely throughout Asia and anywhere else you choose to travel.

Harassment

Probably the single biggest factor that keeps women from taking off on their own is the fear of sexual harassment or assault. While it's true that an unaccompanied woman will attract a fair amount of attention in Asia, it's less dangerous than in most large Western cities. The random, everyday violence we take for granted in our own culture is unheard of in most of Asia. If you are aware of yourself and your surroundings and take reasonable care, everything should go smoothly.

You will encounter some men whose attention is irritating but essentially benign. Nonthreatening harassment can include the harmless but incessant, "Hello, miss, I love you!" shouted from a passing bus or motorcycle, camera-toting men ogling sunbathers at the beach, and construction site variety wolf whistles. Dressing conservatively and walking with confidence will go a long way toward keeping this kind of attention to a minimum. When it does happen, it's best to tune it out and keep walking. A cold stare will usually send beachgoing voyeurs scurrying, embarrassed at having been caught.

In travelers' hangouts like Yogyakarta or Kathmandu, you are likely to come across tourist "groupies": young men in their teens to mid-twenties sporting the latest Western clothes, packing guitars, and hanging around tourist areas in search of Western "girlfriends." You'll know them by their long hair, English slang, and perhaps the one or two Western women already in tow. Groupies are utterly harmless but may hound you with "Hey, baby's" and other macho mutterings. Once they know you're not interested, they will move on to more likely prospects.

To avoid persistent knocking at your door late at night, never tell strange men where you are staying in town.

There are, however, those rare instances that are frustrating and potentially threatening enough to merit a response. These can range from the "accidental" brush of an arm or shoulder across your breast to taunting jeers or a full grope in the middle of a crowded marketplace or busy street.

Don't be afraid to react to situations that are uncomfortable. Genuinely threatening or offensive actions merit more than a turned head. You may be reluctant to be confrontational for fear that you'll be culturally insensitive. But an Asian man who does something offensive to you—leering, touching, grabbing—is committing a serious breach of his own social customs. Go ahead and call him on it. Men may not like a woman who stands up for herself, but they will get out of her way.

Here are six steps for handling harassment:

1. Stay cool. Keep your head. Most situations can be defused simply by ignoring them and moving on.

2. An emphatic "NO!" is universally understood and will usually do the trick. In all likelihood, the offender was seeing how far he could go. If you let him know immediately that you won't tolerate harassment, he'll probably slink back to his corner and await a more timid victim.

3. If "No" doesn't do it, yell something else. Anything will do. Even if your words are unintelligible, your intent will be very clear. One well-practiced phrase in the local language can be highly effective and a lot of fun. An Indonesian friend taught me to say "You are a rude, dirty pig." In four months I only used the phrase twice, but it served me well both times. Both times, the aggressors blushed and hurried away, to the laughter of bystanders and my immense satisfaction.

4. Ad-lib. Defuse potentially threatening situations by whatever method occurs to you at the time. Wheel around and shout at your aggressor, pry straying fingers off and twist, stomp your feet, yell for your brother (wherever he may be), scream. I have never been able to cry on cue, especially when I'm angry, but if you can, have at it. A few well-placed tears can work wonders. Anything that draws attention to you will have the desired effect. Improvise.

One woman I know was being verbally harassed by a group of young men in Malaysia. She turned around with a crazed look on her face and marched swiftly toward the group. Their interest in deriding her vanished as they realized she was coming for them!

I once shook hands with a young man who grinned at me and tried to pull my hand down to his crotch. I obliged and hit him hard enough to send him sprawling on the floor, moaning and holding his crotch. I smiled sweetly, told him "Good night," and walked away confident that he would think twice the next time he considered pulling a similar stunt.

5. Trust your instincts. Always, always listen to what your instincts tell you. They will give you more practical, reliable advice than any guide-

Traveling alone, but friends are everywhere

book ever could. If a deal sounds fishy, say "no" and walk away. Do what you must to get out of situations you think are taking an ugly turn. Don't wait to see if you were right. For all practical purposes, you were.

6. Finally, don't judge an entire culture by the actions of a few Neanderthals. The more time you spend in a country, the more you'll be impressed by the hospitality and genuine warmth you are shown by both men and women. Every country, including yours, has its share of jerks. Don't let the few you encounter spoil your experience in this fascinating part of the world.

A Note on Theft

As a symbol of the affluent West, you will encounter those who are more than happy to relieve you of the burden of your wealth. Hustlers, thieves, and wily shopkeepers will all vie for your money at one time or another. Although female travelers may be targeted more often men, guidelines for dealing with theft and related problems are the same for both sexes. (See Theft and the Tourist, chap. 9.)

Women's Health

The previous chapter dealt with general health issues for travelers in Asia. This section will address physical and health-related issues that relate particularly to women.

Menstruation

Western-brand tampons and sanitary pads are available in large cities such as Bangkok and Jakarta. However, it's good to carry a small supply of anything you consider a necessity.

Some women find that their menstrual periods become irregular and even stop for some time as they travel. In many cases, this is due simply to the stresses of travel. However, the most common reason for missed menstrual periods is pregnancy. Consider carrying a small, over-the-counter pregnancy test with you if you plan to travel for an extended period of time.

If an unplanned pregnancy occurs while you're traveling, and if termination is a consideration, return home immediately to ensure that you receive proper medical attention. Pregnant women should consult with their doctors prior to embarking on a trip overseas.

Contraception

Don't leave home on a long trip without considering what your contraception needs may be. An acquaintance tells of trying to communicate her need for contraception to an overseas pharmacist who did not understand English. In an elaborate game of charades, she pantomimed holding and caring for a baby and then snapped her heels together, stood at attention, and thrust her right hand straight out to signal "Stop!" Her reenactment is hilarious, but she admits that she didn't find the situation particularly funny at the time. Probably the best way to avoid uncertainty and frustration is to bring your own "baby stoppers" from home.

I recommend condoms over birth control pills or any other form of contraception for one important reason: condoms protect against sexually transmitted diseases. Asian condoms are available in larger cities in most countries. However, you may want to bring a small supply from home to be on the safe side. (Especially in Japan, where local condoms may be a bit small for some. No joke.)

If you choose to use birth control pills, you should know that certain antibiotics can limit their effectiveness. Consult with your doctor to be certain of the risks.

Urinary Infection

Urinary infections are not uncommon in women, especially in conjunction with a new sexual partner or renewed sexual activity. Bloody urine or frequent burning urination can indicate infection. Drinking large amounts of liquid may clear up minor problems in a day or so. More serious infections require a course of antibiotics.

Prior to leaving on your trip, ask your doctor to prescribe a multi-purpose antibiotic to carry with you. Make sure that she or he writes out for you the proper dosage necessary to treat urinary and other common infections.

Yeast Infection

Unfortunately, while antibiotics will clear up most minor infections, they can sometimes cause yeast infection. Unusual discharge and genital itching, especially following a course of antibiotics, may signal the presence of a yeast infection. Yeast infection is easily cured with over-the-counter treatments such as Gyne-Lotrimin and Monostat 7. However, these treatments may not be available in most parts of Asia. Add one or both of them (or ask your doctor for his or her recommendation) to your medical kit.

* * * *

Book your flight! In trying to alert you to potential problems, I have probably painted a bleaker picture than what you are likely to encounter as you travel in Asia.

What you will find are warm, hospitable people, fascinating cultures, and some of the most varied and beautiful scenery in the world.

If you're lucky, you may even discover a bit of yourself along the way.

9
Coping Abroad

Step by Step on the Plane and from the Airport

You've arrived at your first stop in Asia. Now what? The next few hours and days are an adapting period to new sights, tastes, smells, and ways. We always find that if we've mentally organized the steps we plan to follow during this time, our adjustment is a lot easier.

On the Plane

1. Prepare and plan before you land. Often we don't have much time to do this before we leave, so those eight or more hours on the flight come in handy.

2. Look through the guidebook to decide where you want to stay. If we're exhausted from a hectic time packing and leaving home, then we sometimes decide to stay in a nice hotel the first night or so. Leaving our bags there, we roam to find the perfect little guest house and move later.

3. Study your language phrase book to learn some of the basics. We practice "hello," "good-bye," and "how much" and start learning the numbers. We know we can get by in English, but we also know the locals will appreciate our efforts at their language. Develop a language study sheet with key phrases to keep handy in your pocket.

4. Read about the local currency and practice converting dollars amounts, first on paper, and then mentally. We decide how much we need from the airport bank to last until we can go to a bank in the city (airport banks usually give lower exchange rates).

At the Airport

1. Go to the tourist information booth. You can get help there finding a hotel, maps of the city and country, bus and train schedules, and all sorts of useful information.

2. Find a hotel. You can start with help from the tourist information booth. Tell them you're a budget traveler and how much you can spend a night. They don't always keep up with the smaller and cheaper hotels and guest houses, so you may need to find a telephone and call the guest house in your guidebook. If they are in the guidebook, they'll speak English. Ask someone at the information booth how to use the phone; it's a bit different in each country. Or just ask the information person to call for you.

If you make the call, ask for directions. If it's late at night, we often just splurge on a taxi. If we arrive during the day, we'll likely get into town by bus. There is usually a public bus route connecting the airport and the city.

3. On arrival, reconfirm your flight back or onward. Especially in India and Nepal, your seat may be dropped if you don't reconfirm.

4. Change money. We usually find $20 is enough to get us into town and have a bite to eat. Then we change more in town at a better rate. You may need to change more than $20 at the airport if you arrive on a Saturday night with the banks closed the next day. Count your change before you leave the bank window. We've been short-changed a few times.

5. Before you take a taxi, ask at the tourist information booth how much it costs to take a taxi into town. Then let the taxi driver know what you'll pay before you get in. There's often a standardized fare from the airport into town. If the driver refuses to be fair, you can try another cab or walk out of the airport to the main street, flag down a less aggressive cabbie, and save a lot of money.

First Days in the City

1. Relax and recover the first day or so. Lounge around the hotel, read, go for walks. Plan what you want to do over the next few weeks.

2. Go light on food and alcohol. Don't dive into the hot spices yet. Give your stomach a chance to acclimatize.

3. Force yourself to fit into the new time zone. Even if it is midnight in America and your body says to go to sleep, stay up (reread Jet Lag, chap. 1).

4. Book train or domestic plane flights soon after you arrive. During certain seasons, you may need to schedule these at least three or more days in advance.

Urban Survival

Many Americans are overwhelmed by Asian big city shock. Struggling with the L.A.'s, Chicagos, and New Yorks of Asia is easier if you follow three rules: (1) get and use information; (2) orient yourself; (3) take advantage of taxis and the public transportation system.

Information

Without information and planning, you'll be a lost toad in a large city. Read and ask questions to find out where you want to stay and what you want to see. Your sightseeing strategy should cover the city systematically, grouping sights by area. Find out when museums are closed before you get there. Plan free days.

Get a good map. The best and cheapest map is often the public transit map obtainable from the tourist information office. Or try a bookstore. Get a map that shows bus lines, subway stops, boat taxi routes (Bangkok), and major sights. If you get a map in English, also get one in the local language. People on the street can point to where you are on the latter, and you can reference it against the English version.

Big Asian cities vibrate with entertainment and nightlife. But it won't come to you. Without the right information, it's easy to be completely oblivious to a once-a-year event erupting just across the bridge. All major cities publish an activity guide in English, usually with a name like "This Week in . . ." You'll find it in major hotels, train stations, airports, and newsstands.

Ask at your hotel and at the tourist office about entertainment. Read the newspapers, and ask local tourist guides. Many countries have a year-round roster of special events, holidays, and temple festivals.

All big cities have English-language bookstores, and large bookstores and university bookstores have English sections. Often you'll find guidebooks, local fiction, and books on the language and culture. Some cities, such as Bangkok and Kathmandu, have used bookstores where you can swap your novels and find used travel guidebooks for many Asian countries (Lonely Planet books, Moon, this one, and others). Knowing this can save you up to ten pounds of guidebooks on a long trip. At bookstores you can also find Asian editions of American newsmagazines. There are weekly Asian editions of _Time_ and _Newsweek_. The _International Herald Tribune_, published by the _New York Times_ and _Washington Post_, comes out daily except Sunday. Tokyo has four English-language dailies; the _South China Morning Post_ (Hong Kong), the _Straits Times_ (Singapore), and the _Times of India_ (New Delhi) are the leading journalistic English voices of their respective countries. Many hotels often have the best selection of English-language guidebooks and newspapers in town.

Orientation

Get the feel of the city. Once you get oriented, you'll feel more at home. Study the map to understand the city's layout. Relate the location of landmarks—your hotel, major sights, the harbor, main streets, the station—to each other. Use any view point—a tower, hilltop, or penthouse restaurant—to look over the city. Tokyo has Tokyo Tower; Hong Kong has Victoria Peak. Retrace where you've been, and see where you're going. Back on the ground you won't need your map quite so often.

Public Transportation

When you master a city's bus or subway system, you've got it by the tail. Asia's public transit systems are so good that most Asians never own a car. (Then again, most can't afford a car.) Trains, buses, subways, and other ad-lib forms (see chap. 2) are their wheels.

The buses and subways all work logically and are run by people who are happy to help the lost tourist locate himself. Anyone can decipher the code to cheap and easy urban transportation, even in Japan. Too many timid tourists never venture into the subways or onto buses and end up spending needless money on taxis.

Tokyo has by far the most extensive, and the most needed, subway system. The city bends over backward to provide the monolingual American visitor with English-language subway signs and maps. As long as you pay attention, it's hard to get lost. That's even truer of Hong Kong and Singapore, where English is the lingua franca and everything is printed for Americans (or British) to read.

Subways are speedy and comfortable, never slowed by traffic jams. Trains and buses are more scenic. In most cities, the systems are interconnected: you can step off the subway and continue to your destination by bus. They are often under the jurisdiction of a common transport authority. It's sometimes possible for tourists to buy a one-day pass for unlimited travel on all routes, a handy way to get an overview of all the major sights.

Make a point to get adequate transit information. Have a local person explain your ticket to you. A dollar may seem expensive for the bus ride until you learn that your ticket is good for two hours, a round-trip, or several transfers. Bus drivers and local people sitting around you will generally mother you through your ride. Just make sure they know where you want to go.

Taxis are often a reasonable option. Outside of Japan, they are cheap; even in Japan, a group of three or four people can often travel cheaper by cab (for short distances) than by buying three or four bus tickets. (That's not true if you're going all the way from downtown Tokyo to Narita airport.) Your driver may not speak English; have a local person write your destination in the native language on a piece of paper. Don't be bullied by cabbie con men. Taxis intimidate too many tourists. If we're charged a ridiculous price for a ride, we put a reasonable sum on the seat and say good-bye.

When we really want to experience an Asian city, we walk. We see all the little things we miss while aboard a bus, stop and chat with storekeepers, and explore small shrines down hidden alleyways. The three rules we faithfully observe when walking, however, are these: (1) be extremely careful in crossing streets, mindful that most Asian drivers don't stop for pedestrians; (2) don't walk at night in dimly lit areas, for the same reasons you wouldn't do so in large American cities; and (3) pace yourself in hot, humid climates. If you're feeling faint, or overly hot and sweaty, take a break from your stroll. Sit down for lunch or a cold drink, or end your walk and take a taxi back to your hotel. Heatstroke and sunstroke can be temporarily disabling problems if not taken seriously.

Rural Survival

Many Asian travelers spend as much time in rural locations as they do in major cities. We'd much rather be on the beach at Ko Samui, Thailand, or in the mountains outside Pokhara, Nepal, than pent up in a hotel room in Calcutta or Manila. But just as big cities require orientation and adjustment, so do small villages.

The best part of Asia is found by just heading down a dirt road or side street near your guest house. Chances are that not many travelers have done this because there's no special sight at the end. However, this is how to have a special experience with the locals. Since few have passed this way before, people will be curious about you. You'll probably be invited in for tea or to talk with the local schoolteacher who knows some English. You'll see the daily life, not the daily deal ("Hello. You want buy carpet?"). Relax, observe life around you. This is one of our favorite pastimes. Try it at home sometime, too.

Often maps and tourist information in small rural areas are hard to find. But check with your guest house; it may have put together its own map of the area. And guidebooks such as this and the Lonely Planet and Moon publications can help you. It's usually best to take a personal tour by foot from your lodging, establishing the various landmarks in your mind as you go. You may only need to know how far and which direction it is from your inn to the bus station, beach, and local café. But you've still got to know.

Language is far more likely to be a problem in an isolated village, especially a nontouristy one, than in a large town or city. Body language will get you a long way. But even in remote islands of Indonesia, English is taught in schools, and though it might sound strange to you the way it's spoken, you'll have a common ground to begin conversation. So look for the local schoolteacher or a student.

Rural towns won't have the selection of food or rooms that you find in cities, and you'll have to settle for what you find, but it will almost inevitably be extremely cheap. Be prepared to be a curiosity among the local people.

Local fascination with white skin and blond hair can be ego nourishing at first, but it quickly gets old as you find it nearly impossible to do anything without attracting a crowd when you're away from big cities and resort areas. All you have to do in many parts of India is to sit down in a local café for a cup of tea, and before it's delivered, you'll be surrounded by a three-deep circle of onlookers craning their necks to see you sip your chai. This is no exaggeration. All you have to do in rural Indonesian villages off the tourist track is stroll down the village path, and you'll have two dozen children either yelling "Take picture!"

or—in rare instances—throwing rocks. A German friend of ours had a tried-and-true way of dealing with curious Indians. With typical Teutonic discipline, he'd draw a line (or indicate an imaginary one) and order the onlookers: "No one is to step over this line!" He never got any argument. Then, to hush the babble of questions coming from a dozen different mouths, he'd designate one person as the Indians' "spokesman" and request that all questions be uttered by him only. It worked.

Theft and the Tourist

Thieves plague tourists throughout the world. As the economy gets tighter, pickpockets and purse snatchers get hungrier, and tourists become very tempting targets.

Many countries depend on the United States economically. When we experience a recession, they suffer. In much of the world, your camera is worth one year of hard labor to the man on the street. Gross inequities like this enable many thieves to rationalize their crimes.

If you are not constantly on guard, your possessions will disappear. One summer, four out of five friends Rick traveled with lost their cameras in one way or another. ("Don't look at me!" he says.) We have heard countless stories of tourists getting ripped off: camera slipped right off the neck of a man napping in Bangkok; bag pulled off the shoulder of a woman by a passing motorcyclist in Yogyakarta; pickpocketed in the middle of a busy bazaar in Kathmandu; pack taken by a friendly man who volunteered to "watch it for just a minute" while the tourist ran to relieve himself in Hong Kong. And so on.

You can't be too careful. Tourists are easy targets. Loaded down with all their valuables in a strange new environment, they are favorite victims of robbers, many of whom specialize solely in the tourist trade. We read of people whose trips are ruined by thieves who snatch their purse or wallet. There is no excuse for this kind of vulnerability. Nearly all crimes suffered by tourists are nonviolent and are avoidable. If you exercise the proper caution and are not overly trusting, you should have no problem. Here are some helpful hints to reduce the rip-offs.

Limit your loss. First of all, don't bring things that will ruin your trip if they are lost, broken, or stolen. If you're going to worry the whole trip about that camcorder, expensive camera, or top-of-the-line Walkman, leave it at home. Bring a used camera and a cheap Walkman instead.

Keep your valuables under your clothes. Rick puts everything crucial in his money belt. A money belt is a small nylon zipper bag that ties

around your waist under your clothes and tucks under your pants like a shirttail. Bob thinks a money pouch is much cooler to wear in Asia. A pouch hangs on a thong around your neck and under your shirt. Either costs only a few dollars. In it, keep your passport, plastic money, cash, traveler's checks, train pass, plane ticket, and any very important documents, vouchers, or identity cards. But first place these inside a zip-lock baggie to prevent damage from sweat stain and rain.

Pouches worn outside your clothes are at risk. Fanny packs and pouches that attach to your belt are not thief-proof. We've talked to more than one traveler who has had a razor blade artist cut through the bottom of these in a crowded bus.

We keep bulky or replaceable documents in a small zipper bag (a three-ring notebook pencil bag or a second money belt) that we tie or sew to the inside of our rucksack or suitcase. It's important to keep the money belt or pouch slim so it's worn comfortably and hidden. We wear our respective "safes" all trip long, even sleeping with them when necessary, and they are never uncomfortable (see Back Door Catalog).

With our money belt or pouch safely on us, our trip can't be ruined even if our baggage is stolen. We can reoutfit ourselves for $200 and carry on. The photographic equipment and film would be the only real loss, and we consider that risk when we decide to pack it in the first place.

Expect to get your wallet picked or your purse snatched. Use a wallet—but only for one day's spending money and a funny note to the thief, not for irreplaceables. Use inside pockets for small money or the left front pocket on pants. Since the right side is universally preferred, that's the one thieves target. Fasten your wallet pocket shut with a button, zipper, or Velcro.

If traveling in couples, keep your own passports and money. If you get separated unexpectedly, you'll need your own money and identity. And if one of you is robbed, the other will still have money.

Get a photocopy of your valuable documents and tickets. It is a lot easier to replace a lost or stolen plane ticket, rail pass, or passport if you have a picture proving that you really owned what you are claiming is lost.

Carry bulky valuables with you at high-risk times. When we're on a train or bus, we keep our bulky valuables—camera, binoculars, exposed film, trip journal—with us at all times. Or if we're staying at a dorm and we have to leave our rucksacks unattended during the day, we take our valuables with us in our day packs.

Use a padlock. Carry a small padlock or a combination lock to use with your pack, on doors, or to quiet a jabbering friend. Padlocks are available throughout Asia; combination locks are not. Bob uses a padlock because he has a bad memory and even forgets where he writes down the combination numbers. Rick loses keys, so he goes with the combination.

Don't appear obvious. Luxurious luggage lures thieves like a well-polished flasher attracts fish. Why brag to the thief that your luggage is the most expensive? The robber assumes the most impressive suitcase in the pile is full of the most impress-thy-neighbors valuables.

Our cameras are, to a potential thief, the most tempting item in our luggage. We never leave them laying around where hotel workers and others can see them and be tempted. They are either worn around our necks or tucked safely out of sight in our day packs.

In your room. Check out your room to see if a thief could enter. Are there adjacent balconies? Is the window easy to climb up and into? Can the window be locked securely? Are there outside screws on the windows and door that a thief could easily remove? If you're staying in a thatched beach bungalow, are the walls or floor easy to get through?

If everything seems to be secure, you may want to leave your camera and other bulky valuables inside, but only if you put your own padlock on the door. Except in the more expensive hotels, there is usually a latch on the door where you can put your own lock.

If you can't trust the security, carry your camera with you in your day pack. If you're sharing a room or dorm with other travelers you don't know well, it's best to keep all valuables with you. There are some travelers who pay for their trip by preying on others. Fortunately they are few. And regardless of how safe our hotel seems, we always wear our money belts.

On the beach. What do you do when you go swimming? We leave our valuables, including our money belt, with the owner of the guest house or hotel. Inventory your checks and other items. Present a copy to the manager, and keep a copy. Count your checks when you return.

One exception to the above is credit cards. If you're close to the city, it's best not to leave your cards in anyone's care. In Chiang Mai, Thailand, trekking agencies will keep all your things, including credit cards, while you're on one of their two- to three-day hikes in the hills. Some travelers returned to the United States to find their credit cards had been used in both Chiang Mai and Bangkok during that time. If you're on a remote island, chances of this are slim. Use your judgment.

If your room looks impenetrable, you can lock it with your own lock and leave your valuables inside.

Another idea is to take along a waterproof fanny pack. You can snorkel and swim with your passport and traveler's checks (fun companions if alone). These are available at some larger sporting goods stores. One brand is Seal Line by Cascade Designs of Seattle.

In left baggage rooms. Often it's convenient to leave items at the left baggage rooms at train stations, airports, and hotels. Even small guest houses will store things. Evaluate the situation. Often in small guest houses, left luggage is put in a locked room. However, many have access to the key, and other travelers can go through your bag while they are getting theirs. In such a case, it's best to remove valuable items and check them personally with the guest house owner. Or take them with you. At left luggage rooms at airports and train stations, we leave our bags but keep our cameras and other valuables with us.

On the train. Be especially careful in train stations. These are the thieves' hangouts. Never leave your bag unattended. If you have a big bag, you may have an awkward time even using the toilet. If you need to leave your bag temporarily, you can ask another traveler to watch it, seek out a family, or leave it in the left baggage room at the station. Don't leave it with someone who comes up to you and asks to watch it.

In stations in India, occasionally someone may ask to help you carry your bags onto the train. This is a risk. Bob watched two well-dressed young Indian men help two Western women with their bags. They were within eyesight all the way through the crowded aisle to the compartment. The women turned around to talk to Bob. Thirty seconds later, they turned to find helpers and bags gone. If you want help at a station, ask a porter. For a few rupees, your bags will be safe and you'll help a hardworking man feed his family.

On the train, place your bag where you can keep a watchful eye on it. Get to know others sitting next to you. Ask them to watch your bags when you go to the toilet. We keep our bulky valuables in a day pack by our feet. Turn your rucksack's straps into an anchor. Wind and tie them around a luggage rack so a thief can't just grab and run. The slightest hindrance will put off most thieves. Some people carry a thin bicycle cable to lock their bags to the rack. We've slept attached to our bags a few times—not comfortably.

On the bus. On long trips, you'll probably have to store your rucksack on the roof. Is it safe? Well, we've never had anything stolen and only heard of one person who did. There are many local people who ride the roof and will be sitting near your luggage. Take precautions. If possible, strap your bag to the rack, or lock it on using a bike cable. Remove bulky valuables and keep them with you in your day pack. We like to ride on top of the bus for the views and fresh air and to keep an eye on our bag.

Crowded city buses are the playground of pickpockets. Keep your valuables in your money belt or neck pouch, safely hidden under your clothes.

On the street. Be on guard for the imaginative artful dodgers of our time. Thief teams often create a street scene or commotion to distract their curious victims. A favorite in South Asia is the snake charmer. While the wizard with the cobra sways back and forth, playing the snake to the rhythm of his flute, your purse or rucksack is being delicately rifled. Keep things zipped, buttoned, and secure. Be alert and aware! Somewhere, sometime, when you least expect it, you'll meet the snake charmer.

Relax

After all this, you're probably thinking, "No way. I'm staying home where it's safe." Keep in mind that we tried to cover all the possibilities, not the probabilities. A section like this on travel in the United States would be just as long. But it would also include suggestions on how to avoid being murdered.

Take the precautions we mention, and relax. There's no sense in letting fear limit your vacation. Most people in every country are on your side. If you exercise adequate discretion and don't put yourself into risky situations, your travels will be about as dangerous as hometown grocery shopping. In forty-six months of Asian travel between us, we have only lost one insignificant bag, binoculars, a $20 watch, and a few bundles of innocence. And these could have been prevented. Please don't travel afraid. Just travel carefully.

Drugs

Drugs of many kinds are available very cheaply throughout Asia. They are also illegal throughout Asia. We highly recommend that travelers steer clear of drugs of any kind during their journeys. There's not a thing that any U.S. embassy can do for you if you're arrested and jailed on drug charges. While possession of marijuana might mean only a fine and deportation from some countries, possession of marketable quantities of narcotics can in some cases lead to a death sentence.

Since some of you may indulge anyway, we feel obligated to keep you informed so you know what you're getting into. Even if you think you know about drugs, the danger is the dosage and purity. In Asia, types and mixtures are different, and you risk overdose and death on certain drugs.

A highly potent type of marijuana known as "elephant grass" or "Thai stick" is sold very cheaply throughout Southeast Asia. Hallucinogenic mushrooms are used by several chefs on Kuta Beach, Bali, and on some islands in Thailand. If you see a "special" mushroom omelet or soup on the menu, that doesn't mean "low cal." Opium dens (found in cities with large Chinese populations) cater mainly to elderly Chinese but willingly share the Alice in Wonderland experience with visitors. A puff on the opium pipe is often offered by the elderly locals to trekkers through the villages of northern Thailand. Hashish is the preferred poison in India and Nepal. Take care before you order a "special" brownie on the menu in Kathmandu. Have nothing to do with any drugs near borders. And be sure nothing has been put inside your bag before a border crossing.

A legal drug (like alcohol or tobacco) that tourists often find repulsive is betel nut. It is found throughout rural South and Southeast Asia, and its telltale sign is a pool of red spittle. You can spot a user—usually a middle-aged or elderly peasant—by his or her red-stained teeth and gums. Betel is a tropical nut that is ground, then chewed, not unlike chewing tobacco. It has a very mild narcotic effect.

Locally brewed alcohol is generally safe. The alcohol content is often enough to kill what's in the water, although that's not necessarily true with local beers. Be cautious of high percentages of alcohol in whiskey. There is the rare report of death due to the ignorant or willful addition of poisonous methanol to give whiskey an extra kick. Use common sense. If they've been drinking the stuff in the village for years, and they still look sane, it's probably O.K.

Mail

Where to Pick It Up

Minimize mail stops. If you know where you're going, select a few places along the way and let friends know when you'll be there. Tell them they'll have to write a few weeks in advance of the date you arrive.

All post offices have a general delivery section, and all towns large enough to be on a map have a post office. In a city, the main post office is called General Post Office. Since you probably don't know the location of the smaller city post offices, have your friends send mail to you in care of the general delivery section of the main one. Address the letter like this: Rick <u>STEVES</u>, Poste Restante, General Post Office, Kathmandu, Nepal.

Poste Restante is international lingo—French, actually—for general delivery. Tell your friends to print your last name in capital letters and underline it. This will help postal clerks figure out which name is your last name so they can file the letter properly (because of this problem, also have them check for mail under your first name). Often the general post offices in big cities are crowded, so pick a smaller city if possible. Avoid small towns, though, as your mail may take longer or may not reach you.

American Express offices in major Asian capitals offer a free clients' mail service for holders of an AmEx card or traveler's checks. They will hold your mail for a month and will forward it on for a charge. If you change your destination plans, you can try having your mail sent from the American Express office you missed. This has worked for a few people we know—no guarantee. We always carry at least a few AmEx traveler's checks just so we can use their postal service.

Other possibilities are having your mail sent to a particular hotel or to friends and relatives overseas. We wouldn't suggest picking a guest house or small hotel out of a guidebook and giving out the address to friends. Businesses can go out of business. Check with other travelers to see if the place still exists. Larger hotels are safer.

Mail pickup commitments can be a pain. Don't design your trip around stale mail. Every year, our mail stops get farther apart. Once a month is comfortable. If you get homesick, mail just teases you, stirring those emotions and aggravating the problem. The best remedy for homesickness is to think of Asia as your home.

How Long It Takes

In general, tell your friends to allow at least two weeks for mail to reach you. But if you're in Japan, Hong Kong, or Singapore, you'll get your mail from the United States in about five days. Mail sent from most Asian countries takes about two weeks to get to the United States. Packages coming and going take about one to three weeks for airmail and three to six months by sea. Sea mail is the cheapest way to send packages.

How Safe It Is

Mail is one of the worst milieus for corruption. When sending a letter from many Third World countries, don't leave the counter until you see the postal worker cancel your stamps. Direct him to do so, if necessary. Many letters and packages never reach their destinations simply because the uncanceled stamps are removed and cashed in by poorly paid postal workers. If sending a particularly important letter or package, register it.

Incoming letters are usually received. However, packages sent to you have a greater chance of being "lost" in poorer countries. Bob received a Christmas package intact in Bangkok. Another year, one sent to Nepal disappeared. Nepalese postal workers were probably buzzing for days on the Starbucks coffee and chocolate chip cookies.

There are always stories about lost packages from Third World countries. Bob has his own:

"I'd heard tales about the post office in this small town in India. Travelers told me they'd found their letters (with stamps removed) littering the fields. So when I entered the two-man post office, I was cautious. Gifts and my film were at stake. I distracted the clerk from his cup of tea, and he started me on my package-sending odyssey. First I went to the rice stand across the road to have my package weighed. Back at the post office, the clerk rummaged through a stack of papers until he found a torn scribbled-up sheet listing the cost of sea mail packages. He handed me four large sheets of stamps. Then he sent me up the street for glue. Back at the post office, I presented my totally stamped and wrapped package to the manager. He gave me a blank sheet of paper and asked me to make a customs form. All set, I had the clerk cancel my stamps so my package wouldn't end up in the field out back. I waited and pointed out the stamps he'd missed. He canceled them all and then set my package on top of a filing cabinet. I inquired about insurance. I could imagine the manager chuckling to himself as he said, 'Don't worry. Your package will arrive.'"

To Bob's surprise, the package appeared in Seattle four months later. We may have been lucky, but we've always gotten what we've sent.

Tips on Mailing

Know the local requirements. Each country has its own rules. Wrapping requirements are different everywhere. For example, in India, you must stitch up the package in cloth and seal the seams with wax (tailor shops will do this for you). The postal clerk may ask for a bill of sale for items purchased in the country to verify the cost. In Nepal, you must have a certificate from the Department of Archaeology if the item looks old. To save yourself a hassle, check with the post office or the local tourist office about the requirements ahead of time.

Get help. In major cities, you can usually find someone to do the packaging and mailing for you for a small charge. Often this is done in shops or stands just outside the main post office. In Bangkok, there is a packaging service inside the general post office. Local shipping companies will also pack and ship items.

Allow enough time. Figure about two hours or more at the post office if you do it yourself. At the General Post Office in Bangkok on a busy Saturday morning, we've spent three hours mailing a package. This included standing in line to get a box, packing the box, and standing in line again to have it weighed and to get stamps. And standing in yet another line to send it.

There are other alternatives. Check your return airline for the cost of sending your package home as unaccompanied baggage. This could be cheaper than airmail. You can send some items ahead to your next destination, and they will be stored at the airport at a daily rate, which may be expensive.

Send parcels as gifts. Gifts can be shipped from Asia to friends and family in the United States free of tax and duty. The recipient can receive one gift shipment per day with a value up to $50.

The outer package of the gift must be marked with the following: "unsolicited gift," the nature of the gift, and the fair retail value of the gift.

Gifts can be consolidated in one parcel if individually wrapped and labeled. The box should be marked as "Consolidated Gift Parcel" on the outside. List the names of the recipients and the value of each gift. You can't send a gift to yourself.

Learn about duty-free items. Some less-developed countries are given preferred nation trading status, and certain items purchased in the country are duty-free. For details, check with the nearest U.S. Customs office. Helpful brochures are: "Know Before You Go—Custom Hints For Returning Residents" and "Generalized System of Preferences—GSP and the Traveler."

If you're sending home clothes and other personal belongings, mark the package: "American Goods Returned." They will be duty-free.

Telephoning in Asia

The more we travel, the more we use the telephone. We call hotels and ryokans to make or confirm reservations, tourist information offices to check our sightseeing plans, restaurants, train stations, and local friends. In every country, the phone can save you lots of time and money. Each country's phone system is different, but each one works logically.

The key to figuring out a foreign phone is to approach it without comparing it to yours back home. Instead of putting in a coin as soon as you get a dial tone, for example, you often must wait for the other party to answer before quickly depositing your coins. In most countries, you can find phone booths with multilingual instructions. Study these before dialing. Operators generally speak English and are helpful. International codes, instructions, and international assistance numbers can usually be located in the front of the phone book. If the phone book is in a non-Roman script, or if we otherwise can't manage in a strange phone booth, we let a nearby local person help us out. They are happy not only to dial for us but, if necessary, to do our talking as well.

Area codes are a common source of phone booth frustration. They are usually listed by city in the phone book. When calling long distance in Asia, you must dial the area code first. Area codes start with a zero, which is replaced with the country code if you're calling between countries. Local numbers vary in length from three to seven digits.

Once you've made the connection, the real challenge—communication—begins. With no visual aids, getting your message across in a language you don't speak requires some artistry.

Some key rules are as follows. Speak slowly and clearly, pronouncing every consonant. Keep it very simple; don't clutter your message with anything less than essential. Don't overcommunicate; many things are already understood and don't need to be said. Use international or carefully chosen English words. When all else fails, let a local person on your end do the talking after you explain to him or her, with visual help, the message.

Let us illustrate with a hypothetical conversation with a hotel receptionist in Nagoya. We're at the station, just came into town, read our guidebook's list of budget hotels, and like Akiko's Ryokan. We call from a phone booth, and here's what happens:

Someone picks up the phone and says, "*Moshi moshi. Akiko Ryokan.*" (In Japan, this is a phone greeting.)

We reply, "*Moshi moshi.*"

Remember not to overcommunicate. You don't need to tell her

you're a tourist looking for a bed. Who else calls a hotel in a foreign accent? Now you must communicate just a few things, like how many beds you need. We've already checked our Japanese phrase book and decided before we called the easiest thing to say.

"*Ni America-jin.*" We let her know "two Americans" are coming. And then ask, "*O.K.?*" (O.K. is a good international word, widely used in Japan and other Asian countries.)

"*Hai* (yes), *O.K.*," she says, understanding you want beds for two Americans. And we say, "*O.K.*" If there was no room, she'd say, "*Heya wa nai* (No room)" and hang up. If she's still talking to you, she's interested in your business.

Now she'll rattle off a bunch of questions, asking you if you know the directions, if you want supper, and so on. You don't understand and can't answer, so you just say, "*Sanju-pun* (thirty minutes), *O.K.?*"

She figures you mean you'll be there in thirty minutes, and says, "*Hai.*" Since you didn't answer her questions, she knows you don't speak much Japanese. You have the address in your guidebook, so you can ask for directions at the tourist booth at the station. You can point to things in your phrase book once you're at Akiko's to answer other questions.

We say, "*Arigato, sayonara* (Thank you, good-bye)."

Thirty minutes later, we walk in the door and remove our shoes, and Akiko greets us with, "*Konnichi wa.*"

We could have taken the easy way out by just asking someone at the tourist information booth at the station to call. But we enjoy the challenge.

Phoning Home

Most Asian countries have direct connections to the U.S.A. It's not cheap—about $3 a minute—but when you're on the road, it's worth it to hear a familiar voice from time to time.

You can call home in several ways. Calling collect is usually expensive. Your telephone credit card could be less expensive, but you'll need to check the rates before you go. Telephoning through your hotel's phone system may be easy or difficult, but it's invariably very expensive.

Most national capitals and other good-sized cities and towns have an international telephone and telegraph office with booths that are metered. You apply at a desk, give the clerk the number you want to call, and have a seat in the lounge. Within five minutes or so, you'll be called to a booth where the international operator will already be dialing your number. Keep it short and sweet, and you'll pay immediately after you hang up at the desk.

Public phone booths are reliable for long-distance dialing in Japan, Korea, Hong Kong, Taiwan, Singapore, and parts of Malaysia and the Philippines. Some countries such as Japan have phone booths that are specifically for international calls and others for domestic. Check with tourist information. If you feel confident about calling this way, get a pile of coins together, put one in the slot, and dial: first, international code, wait for tone; second, country code; third, area code; and fourth, seven-digit number. Every country has its quirks. Try pausing between codes if you're having trouble, or dial the international operator. Remember you crossed the date line, so it's yesterday in the States.

We start with a coin worth 50 cents to be sure we get the person we need or can say, "We're calling back in five minutes. Wake him up." Then we plug in more coins. We keep one last sign-off coin ready. When our time is done, we pop it in and say good-bye. The booth tells you when you're about to be cut off.

It's cheaper and easier (coin-free) if you have your friend call you back, dialing direct from the States. Give your local area code (without the first zero) and number. They can get the international and country codes from their American operator.

USA Direct services offered by AT&T, MCI, and SPRINT are a new convenience allowing travelers to call the U.S.A. direct toll-free from any place covered in Asia. The call costs about $2.50 for the service charge plus the (much cheaper than Asia) American rate of about a dollar a minute. You'll break even by talking for three minutes. After that you'll save about $2 a minute over the pay-in-Asia rate. Before leaving home, check with your phone company to get your access number and the number for their Asian operators.

Finding Street Addresses

Labeling houses and buildings in numerical order from one end of a street to the other may seem to Americans to be the only logical way to identify street addresses. Some Asians would agree. Many others do not.

Unsuspecting Yankees find Japan a nightmare to get around. Although our Japanese friends insist their system makes sense, we still insist on getting a street map whenever we're trying to find an address. The basic problem lies in the fact that buildings are numbered according to the order in which they were built—not in the order in which they are physically organized—and that those numbers apply to a four-sided block rather than to an individual street.

Let's take a typical Japanese address: a foreign language institute at 2-Bancho 4-27, Takamatsu-shi, Kagawa-ken. "Ken" refers to the prefecture (state), this particular one being on the island of Shikoku. "Shi" is the city—Takamatsu—within that prefecture. "2-Bancho" means this address is in section 2 of the Bancho district. Each square block within this section is numbered in logical numerical order. The address we seek is in block 4. Once we've come this far (if indeed we have), we simply walk around the block until we find number 27.

If it's important to find a particular address anywhere in Asia, we rely on local taxi drivers. Whenever possible, we have an address written in the local language or script to hand to the cabbie. In Hong Kong and Singapore, you won't have too much trouble.

Measuring up to Asia

Asians use the metric system. Even in Americanized Japan, kilometers are used instead of miles, kilograms instead of pounds, and Celsius temperatures rather than Fahrenheit. The standard unit of measurement is the meter, which is equal to 39.37 inches, or just a little over a yard. The meter is divided into 100 units—centimeters—of which there are 30 to a foot, or 2 to an inch. One thousand meters equals a kilometer, which is 0.62 mile. So if Jarkarta is 100 kilometers away, that's about 60 miles (0.6 x 100 kilometers).

Grams, the unit of dry measurement, are a little harder. There are about 28 grams to an ounce, 455 to a pound. One kilogram (1,000 grams) is equal to 2.2 pounds. One hundred grams is about a quarter of a pound. For liquid measurement, use liters instead of quarts or gallons: a liter is slightly more than a quart, and there are 3.8 liters in a gallon.

For temperatures, it's easy to remember that 0 degrees Celsius (Centigrade) is freezing (32°F) and 100 degrees C is boiling (212°F). The exact formula to convert is $1.8 \times C + 32 = $ Fahrenheit. We just use 2 instead of 1.8. So if it's 35 degrees Celsius, then $2 \times 35 + 32$ equals 102 degrees F (actually 95, but you know you're hot in any case.) An easy memory aid: 28°C = 82°F, hot enough to swim.

Throughout Asia, as in Europe, the 24-hour clock is used in any official timetable, whether train or plane. Learn to use it quickly and easily. Everything is the same until 12 noon. Then, instead of starting over again at 1:00 p.m., keep on going—13:00 (1:00 p.m.), 14:00 (2:00 p.m.), 15:00 (3:00 p.m.), to 24:00 (12 midnight). Thus, 8:35 p.m. would be 20:35 on the 24-hour clock.

Most countries number the floors of buildings differently from the United States. The first floor is called the ground floor. What we would call the second floor is an Asian's first floor. If your room is on the second floor (Asian), you will be on the third floor (American).

In numbered dates, the day and month are reversed, logically moving from smallest unit (day) to larger units (month and year). Therefore, Christmas is 25-12-94 instead of 12-25-94 as we would write it. An exception is Japan, where the year is written first: 94-12-25.

Self-Defense on Guided Tours

Throughout your trip, you'll encounter sightseeing tours. There are several kinds of tours. Orientation tours are fast, inexpensive, and superficial. Rarely do you even get out of the bus. Their only redeeming virtue is that they serve to orient the traveler. If you had only five hours in Hong Kong, for example, the Round Hong Kong Bus Tour would be the best you could do to "see" the colony.

Fancy coach tours, the kind organized by major travel brokerages, can be of value to the budget-minded do-it-yourselfer. Pick up the brochure, and you have a well-thought-out tour itinerary. Now do it on your own, taking local buses at your leisure, touring every sight with fewer time restrictions for a fraction of the cost.

Walking Tours

These are our favorite. They are thorough, covering only a small part of a city. They are usually conducted by a well-trained local person who is sharing his town for the purpose of giving you an appreciation of the city's history, people, and culture—not to make a lot of money. The walking tour is personal, inexpensive, and a valuable education. We can't recall a bad walking tour. Ask about them at local tourist offices and expatriate associations.

Local Tours for Asians

We've been more impressed with local tours operated by Asians for Asians. These often take in sights that the standard tours ignore, and the cost is inevitably less because it's geared to the Asian, not the American, pocketbook. Surprisingly, many are in English—the language of travel.

All-Inclusive Tours

Many do-it-yourselfers take escorted air-and-bus tours year after year only for the hotels, meals, and transportation provided. Every day they do their own sightseeing, applying the skills of independent travel to their tour. This can be very economical and an easy way to go "on your own."

Most inclusive tours do not include the daily sightseeing programs. These are optional. Budget tours are highly competitive, and profit margins on the base cost are thin. For this reason, it's very important for the guide to sell the "options."

Discriminate among options. Some are great, but others are not worth the time or money. We have found that, in general, the half-day sightseeing tours of cities are a good value. A local guide will usually show you his or her city in a much more thorough fashion than you would be able to do on your own, given your time limitations. After-dinner entertainment options are less worthwhile. Usually, several tour groups combine for an "evening of local color." Two hundred tourists having a sip of sake while actresses dressed as geishas perform on stage and buses line up outside isn't really local. We would prefer to save $20 by taking a subway or bus downtown to just poke around.

The guide may pressure you into taking the options. Stand firm. In spite of what you may be told, you are capable of doing plenty on your own. Maintain your independence. Get maps and tourist information from your hotel desk (or another hotel desk) or a tourist information office. Ask the man or woman behind the hotel desk how to get downtown by public transportation. Taxis are always a possibility, and with a small group, they're not expensive.

Team up with others on your tour to explore on your own. No Asian city is dead after the shops are closed. Go downtown and stroll.

Do your own research. Know what you want to see. The guide will be happy to feed you Asia, but it will be from his menu. This often distorts the importance of sights to fit the tour. When you travel with your own guidebook, you become what tour guides call "an informed passenger"—bad for their income.

Many people make their Asian holiday one long shopping spree. The guide is happy to promote this. A tour guide commonly receives a 15 percent commission from stores to which he brings a busload of tourists. Don't necessarily reject your guide's shopping tips; just keep in mind that the prices you see often include that 15 percent kickback. Shop around, and never swallow the line, "This is a special price available only to your tour, but you must buy now." The salesmen who prey on tour buses zero right in on the timid and gullible group member who has no idea what a good buy is. Use this time to price items and do your shopping in your free time.

Remember that the best-selling tours are the ones that promise you the most in the time you have available. No tour can give you more than 24 hours in a day or seven days in a week. What the "blitz" tour can do is give you more hours on the plane and bus. Choose carefully among the itineraries available, and don't assume that more is better. In Asia, pace yourself. Be satisfied with what you can see comfortably.

10
Attitude Adjustment for a Better Trip

The Ugly American

Asia sees two kinds of travelers: those who view Asia through airport corridors and air-conditioned tour bus windows, socializing with their American friends and collecting painted fans, and those who are taking a vacation from America, immersing themselves in different cultures, experiencing different people and life-styles, broadening their perspective.

Asians will judge you as an individual, not based on your government. We have never been treated like Ugly Americans. Our Americanness in Asia has been, if anything, an asset. Ugly Americans do exist and not in small numbers. Asians recognize them and treat them accordingly, often souring their vacation. Ugly Americanism is a disease easily cured by a change in attitude.

How do you identify an Ugly American? Easy. He lacks respect and understanding for strange customs and cultural differences. Only a Hindu can truly understand the value of India's sacred cows. Only a devout Muslim really sees the virtue in a woman covering her face. No American has the right, as a visitor, to show disrespect for these customs.

An Ugly American demands the niceties of American life in Asia—orange juice and eggs (sunny-side up) for breakfast, long wide beds, English menus, punctuality in India or Napa Valley wine in Korea. He should remember that he is visiting a land that enjoys rice for breakfast (lunch and dinner), that doesn't grow six-foot, four-inch men, that speaks a different language (with every right to do so), that lacks the "fast-food efficiency" of the U.S.A., and drinks beer at room temperature. Live as an Asian for a few weeks; it's cheaper, and you'll make more friends and have a better trip.

An Ugly American is ethnocentric, traveling in packs, more or less invading each country while making no effort to communicate with "the natives." He talks at Asians in a condescending manner. He finds satisfaction in flaunting his relative affluence and rates well-being by material consumption. (Americans, of course, are not the only "ugly" tourists. Packs of Japanese tourists often set a similarly bad example when traveling in the U.S.A and Europe.)

The Culturally Sensitive Traveler

You can be a "Beautiful American." Your fate as a tourist lies in your own hands. A graduate of the Back Door School of Touristic Beauty:

—maintains a modest sense of humility, not flashing signs of affluence, such as overtipping, overdonating to beggars, or joking about the local money.

—not only accepts but seeks out Asian styles of living and learns to deal with a little discomfort.

—is genuinely interested in the people and cultures she visits and learns enough about the culture not to make any major cultural faux pas (see Cultural No No's, chap. 11).

—makes an effort to bridge that flimsy language barrier. Rudimentary communication in any language is fun and simple with a few basic words. While a debate over the economics of Marx on the train to Mandalay (with a common vocabulary of 20 words) can be frustrating, you'll be surprised at how well you can communicate—if you only break the ice and try. Don't worry about the language. Communicate! (See chap. 6, Hurdling the Language Barrier.)

—is positive and optimistic in the extreme. Discipline yourself to focus on the good points of each country. Don't dwell on problems. You can't go wrong with a militantly positive attitude.

—above all else, keeps a sense of humor. Look for the absurdity in a situation and laugh at yourself.

We've been accepted as American friends everywhere we've traveled in Asia and the Pacific, not to mention Europe, Russia, the Middle East, and North Africa. Coming as American visitors, we've been embraced by Nepalese Sherpas in the remote Langtang Province; motorcycled around Bali with a Sumatran engineer, learning Indonesian and teaching English; expressed joy that our Japanese hosts baked a special American-style "Christmas cake" for our visit; been invited to a Sikh wedding party in Amritsar; and explained to a frustrated young Thai man that American women really would prefer talking with a man rather than being treated as a sex object.

The Ugly American sees Asia through ugly eyes. There is no excuse for being an Ugly American. Go as a guest, act like one, and you'll be treated with hospitality and respect.

Be Open-minded

Travel is reality. It's rocky for romantics. Between the palaces, temples, and museums you'll find a living civilization—grasping for the future while we tourists grope for its past.

Today's Asia is a complex mixed bag of tricks. It can rudely slap you in the face if you aren't prepared to accept it with open eyes and an open mind. Many will find that parts of Asia are crowded, tense, and seedy, hardly a homogeneous fairy-tale land. If they come expecting everyone to be a yogi or Zen Buddhist, they'll be sadly disappointed.

If you're not mentally braced for some shocks, local trends can tinge your travels. The centuries-old wooden temples of Kathmandu are soiled with excrement—human as well as canine—by sunrise every morning. A McDonald's sits just around the corner from Bangkok's massage parlors and VD clinics. Every village in Bali has a troupe of children who will assault you with carved wooden images and "antiqued" ivory for sale. You may meet an Indian hotel keeper who would consider himself a disgrace to his sex if he didn't follow a woman to her room (he's turned away as easily as a Girl Scout selling cookies). You're part of a wave of muffled grimaces as four-foot, six-inch Hong Kong grandmothers elbow their way through a crowded bus. Ten-year-old Javanese boys spit a steady stream of betel from their mouths, their lips stained crimson red.

Contemporary Asia is alive and groping. Today's problems will fill tomorrow's museums. Feel privileged to walk the crazy streets of Asia as a sponge, not a judge. Absorb, accept, learn, and at all costs, be open-minded.

Don't Be a Creative Worrier

Travelers tend to be creative worriers. Many sit at home before their trip, all alone, just thinking of things to be stressed about. Travel problems are always there, but you don't notice them until they're yours. Every year there are air traffic controller strikes, train crashes, terrorist attacks, and so forth—new problems and old problems turning over new leaves.

The competent traveler learns to ad-lib and to conquer each surprise problem he encounters. Make an art out of taking the unexpected in stride. Those with the tightest itineraries, like those who ski with locked knees, are least able to handle travel's mogels. Relax: you're on the other side of the world. Be a good sport. Enjoy the uncertainty, and have fun.

Tackling problems with relish opens some exciting doors. Even the worst times will become cherished memories after your journal is shelved and your trip is stored neatly in the slide carousel of your mind.

The KISS Rule: "Keep It Simple, Stupid!"

Don't complicate your trip. Simplify! Travelers get upset over the silliest things. Here are some common complexities that can suffocate a happy holiday: registering your camera with customs before leaving home, spending several hours trying to phone home on a sunny day in Bali, worrying about the correct answers to meaningless bureaucratic forms, making a long-distance hotel reservation in a strange language and then trying to settle on what's served for breakfast, sending away for Japanese hotel vouchers.

People can complicate their trips with movie cameras, lead-lined film bags, special tickets for free entry to all the sights they won't see in India, instant coffee, 65 Handi-wipes, and a special calculator that figures the value of the yen out to the fifth decimal.

Travel more like Gandhi—with simple clothes, open eyes, and an uncluttered mind.

Be Militantly Humble

As one of the world's elite who is rich and free enough to enjoy international travel, you are leaving home to experience a different culture. If things aren't to your liking, don't try to change those things; instead, change your liking.

Legions of tourists tramp through Asia as though they're at the zoo—throwing peanuts to the monkeys, asking the India in the white dhoti to charm a cobra, and bellowing "Banzai!" out Yokohama hotel windows. If a culture misperforms or doesn't perform, they feel gypped. Treat Asia like a royal but spoiled child who is always right (even if undeservedly so). By demanding nothing—approaching it like

Oliver Twist, humbly but firmly asking for "more soup"—we leave the Genghis Khan-type tourists mired in a swamp of complaints.

Throughout our travels, we're pushing for bargains. Tourists and locals often clash, especially where money is involved, and many tourists' trips are soured. When we catch a Malay merchant short-changing us, we correct the bill, smile, and say, "Selamat tinggal" (Good-bye). An Indian taxi driver may demand more money than agreed. Rather than get angry, we firmly state the agreed price, place the money on the seat, and leave. Being calmly assertive but never demanding "justice," we usually see the person come to his senses and work things out or simply go away.

"Turn the other cheek" applies perfectly to those riding Asia's magic carousel. If you fight the slaps, the ride is over. The militantly humble can spin forever.

Swallow Pride, Ask Questions, Be Crazy

If you are too proud to ask questions and be crazy, your trip may well be dignified—and dull. Make yourself an extrovert, even if you aren't. Be a catalyst for adventure and excitement. Make things happen, or often they won't.

Neither of us is naturally a "wild and crazy guy." But when we're shy and quiet, things don't happen. We try to keep ourselves out of that rut when we're traveling. It's not easy, but this special awareness can really pay off. Let us describe the same evening twice—first, with the mild and lazy us, and then, with the wild and crazy us:

The traffic held us up, so by the time we got to that great temple that we've always wanted to see, it was six minutes before closing. No one was allowed to enter. Disappointed, we walked over to a restaurant and couldn't make heads or tails out of the menu. We shrugged and asked for "chow mein." On the way back to the hotel, we looked into a very colorful local bar, but there were obviously no tourists in there, so we walked on. As we walked down a residential street, we were talking rather loudly, and a couple came out on their balcony and told us to be quiet. We went back to our room and did some washing.

That is not a night to be proud of. A better traveler's journal entry would read like this:

We were late and got to the temple only six minutes before closing. The security guard said no one could go in now, but we begged, joked, and pleaded with him. We had traveled all the way to see this place and we would be leaving early in the morning. We assured him that we would be out by 6 o'clock, and he gave us a glorious six minutes in the temple. You can do a lot in six minutes when you are excited. Across the street at a restaurant that the same guard recommended, we couldn't make heads or tails out of the menu. Inviting ourselves into the kitchen, we met the cooks and got a firsthand look at "what's cookin'." Now we could order an exciting local dish and know just what we were getting. It was delicious. On the way home, we passed a classic local bar, and while it was dark and sort of uninviting to a foreigner, we stepped in and were met by the only guy in the place who spoke any English. He proudly befriended us and told us, in very broken English, of the old days when the British navy often visited town, while treating us to his favorite local drink. We'll never forget that guy or that evening. Later, as we chatted loudly while walking down a residential street, a middle-aged couple shouted something that clearly meant "shut up." We quietly continued the conversation, and they eventually invited us up to their apartment. We joked around—not understanding a lot of what we were saying to each other—and they invited us to join them on a trip to the market the next day. What a lucky break! There is no better way to learn about this country than to spend an afternoon with a local family. And to think that we could have been back in our room doing the laundry!

Many tourists are actually afraid or too timid to ask a local person a question. The meek may inherit the earth, but they make lousy tourists. Local sources offer a wealth of information. People are happy to help a traveler. Hurdle the language barrier. Use a paper and pencil, charades, or whatever it takes to be understood. Don't be afraid to butcher the language.

Ask questions or be lost. Create adventure, or bring home a boring journal. Perceive friendliness, and you'll find it.

If the kids are staring, entertain

11
Terrorism, Culture Shock, and Getting Back to "Normal"

Terrorism and Tourism

Over the last decade, terrorism has become a hot topic. And as tourists, we feel threatened by it. But believe it or not, terrorism is nothing new. There have always been terrorists, and there always will be. What's new is that Americans are among those targeted, and our media brings it into our houses in living color.

Certainly we need to respect, understand, and minimize the risk of terrorism, but it shouldn't keep us from traveling. We have the option of accepting the risks or settling for a lifetime of armchair and TV show travel. We're still traveling.

Consider the odds. Every year, about 25 million Americans travel—and a handful are killed by terrorists overseas. Every year, about a half dozen hijackings make headlines. People dwell on this.

Every day, in the United States alone, more than 160,000 airplanes take off and land safely. Several hundred people die in plane crashes each year in the United States. We say a quick prayer before each take-off, and we travel. Thousands hike (and a few die) in the Himalayas. Hundreds of pedestrians are run down on the streets of Bangkok annually. But we go anyway—and look both ways before crossing.

The point is that nothing dangerous is likely to happen to you. And if it does, it's more likely to be something other than a terrorist attack. It seems that most tourists take these other serious but less glamorous risks in stride.

People who don't travel because of a fear of terrorism should be reminded that in our country more than 8,000 people a year are killed by handguns—compared to fewer than 10 a year in Canada, Japan, and Great Britain. Our government chooses to ignore this kind of ter-rorism. What our government defines and our media publicize as ter-rorism is very subjective. We hate to see political hang-ups and adver-tisement-boosting sensationalism put hurdles between you and the travel experience of a lifetime.

Many Asian countries, large and small, are dealing with serious or potentially serious internal threats. Some of them make our own 6 o'clock news. Most do not. The Punjabi Sikhs are challenging the government of India for an independent state. Tamil Hindus and Sinhalese Buddhists are waging an undeclared civil war in Sri Lanka. The Burmese (now Myanmar) government has continually struggled to squash domestic opponents since its independence four decades ago. Indonesia is still grappling with guerrillas in the former Portuguese territory of East Timor. The Philippines has the triple threat of Communist insurgents in the north, Muslim separatists in the south, and pro-Marcos holdouts everywhere. South Korea has a large, vocal, and oppressed political opposition. And all Americans are well aware of the continuing troubles in the Indochinese countries such as Kampuchea (Cambodia). While none of these movements specifically targets Americans, trends are directing more terrorist violence in our direction.

You don't have to dig too deep to start discovering why. Regardless of who's right or wrong, we in the U.S.A.—with about 5 percent of the world's population—control about 30 percent of the world's wealth and are trying to gather more. (This is why we sport "Buy American" bumper stickers and outlaw DDT while continuing to produce it for export sales.)

Recently, fundamentalist Muslims are lashing out at us because our high-tech, capitalistic, Christian life-style is threatening theirs. They target the high-profile fingers of our world: airports and airplanes, luxury cruise ships, famous and elegant hotels and restaurants, embassies and consulates. Terrorists also target places where American soldiers hang out. Avoid those spots. Sensitive travelers stay in local-style accommodations and, without even trying, minimize the potential for being targets. We're staying in the corner guest house, a local B&B, or a thatched hut. Terrorists don't bomb these kinds of places; that's where they sleep. Killing Colonel Khaddafi won't stop terrorism, and staying home won't make it go away. While "good guys" and "bad guys" is a matter of perspective, the only way to end terrorism is to recognize and deal with terrorism's root cause.

America is a leader in God-given truths. We proudly fight and die for self-evident truths like "all men are created equal." When Thomas Jefferson and our Founding Fathers (many of whom owned slaves) penned those words, every American knew "all men" meant all white, landowning males were created equal. Slowly we've made room for nonlandowners, nonwhites, and women. So now we find it self-evident that all Americans are created equal. As the world grows smaller and we grow bigger, the distinction between equal Americans and the rest of the global community will become more and more painfully obvious. An attempt to at least understand and recognize the needs of people who reside outside the First World would help reduce terrorism.

Terrorism is caused by a lack of understanding. Travel teaches global understanding. It has taught many Yankees (including ourselves):

1. There are values other than American ones (democratic, materialistic, Christian) for which patriots will fight and die. Without denying that "God blessed America," we must understand that every country has its Nathan Hales who regret that they have but one life to give for their national cause.

2. Like whales, nationalities can be endangered species. Five languages die out each year. As foreign Nathan Hale types resort to desperate means to preserve their nationalities, the demands of postrevolutionary fat and happy America to play by the rules are hard to take seriously.

3. America is a giant but young and rambunctious nation with a 220-year heritage from which to draw. After following the news from a foreign perspective, many American travelers are surprised to find that other nations—with less bulk and more history—view the world with a broader perspective, more depth, and at least as much understanding.

Travel can broaden your perspective, enabling you to rise above the 6 o'clock news and see things as a citizen of the world. While monuments from the past are worthy of your sightseeing energy, travel plugs you directly into the present. There are many peoples fighting the same thrilling battles we won 200 years ago, and while your globe may paint Pakistan green and India pink, no political boundaries—no matter how carefully drawn—can divide racial, linguistic, or religious groups so simply.

Look beyond the beaches and hotels in your tourist brochures for background on how your vacation destination's cultural, racial, and religious makeup is causing problems today or may bring grief tomorrow. With this foundation and awareness, you can enjoy the nearly unavoidable opportunities to talk with involved locals about complex current situations.

If you're looking to "talk politics," you must be approachable—free from the American mob on the air-conditioned coach. Like it or not, people around the world look at "capitalist Americans" as the kingpins of a global game of Monopoly. On their board, "Baltic Avenue" and "Boardwalk" are separated by much more than two squares. Young, well-dressed people are more likely to speak (and want to speak) English. Universities are the perfect place to solve the world's problems in English with a liberal, open-minded foreigner.

Search out a conversation at a Tokyo bookstore coffee shop, and you'll come away with a better understanding of what Americans tend to call Japanese "protectionism" but the Japanese see as economic survival. Befriend a student in Beijing and learn how many Chinese now view their government. In a Bangkok temple, a saffron-robed Buddhist monk will explain to you what "guided democracy" means in Southeast Asia while you school him in some American slang. Your Singapore taxi driver may give you a half-dozen reasons why Prime Minister Lee Kuan Yew's "Speak Mandarin" campaign benefits not just the Chinese population but all Singaporeans.

Understand a country's linguistic divisions. It's next to impossible to keep everyone in a multilingual country happy. India and Indonesia, for example, have literally hundreds of different languages.

It's refreshing to be so out of touch while traveling that you forget what day it is. But it's always wise to be up on the news. American and English-language newspapers are available in most of Asia, as are English radio broadcasts. Other tourists can be valuable links with the outside world as well. Most important, the nearest American or British consulate can advise you on problems that merit concern.

Terrorism is caused by a lack of understanding. Travel teaches understanding. And since we're all trapped here on this little globe in a high-tech drama that will sooner or later force us to choose between living together or dying together, what could be better than to continue to travel and thereby help the world take a much-needed step toward global harmony?

Travelers who want to stay aware of global danger zones can get an informative map, updated bimonthly, which demarcates areas of war, civil unrest, and epidemic disease. The World Status Map can be obtained for $6 by writing to Box 466, Merrifield, VA 22116.

Culture Shock

Many Americans have their vacations marred by "culture shock," a psychological disorientation caused by sudden immersion in a different culture. It can make a traveler bitter, resentful, and depressed and can bring on all sorts of psychosomatic illnesses. The best way to fight this upset is not to close yourself off from the strange new culture but to open to it. Learn to understand the real differences so as not to fear the unknown.

Each group of people on this planet has its own behavioral patterns, transmitted from one generation to the next. This life-style provides logical answers to their basic needs. Sensitive intercultural travelers must realize that there's more than one way to crack an egg. Most solutions to life's problems are neither right nor wrong; they're just different, and that's what distinguishes cultures. About the only thing that all cultures have in common is that, to some degree, they're all ethnocentric. They think their own way is the best way.

We Americans, like all groups, have our own peculiar traits. It's fun to look at our culture from a grander perspective and see how shocking our culture may look to others. For instance, we consider ourselves very clean and commonly criticize other cultures as dirty. In the bathtub, we soak, clean, and rinse, all in the same water, though we'd never wash our dishes that way. A Japanese visitor, who washes before entering the bath and rinses off after soaking, might find our way of bathing strange, even disgusting.

India's Hindus, who vastly outnumber Americans, normally eat with their own freshly cleaned fingers. They are convinced this is cleaner and more civil than putting metal objects in their mouths.

Many cultures spit in public and blow their noses right onto the street. They couldn't imagine doing that into a small cloth, then storing it in their pockets to be used again and again.

Too often, we think of the world in terms of a pyramid with "civilized" (us) on top and "primitive" (them) at the bottom. This judgment may be based on comparing their ability or interest in keeping up with us in material consumption, science, and technology. If we were to measure the components of civilization differently—perhaps according to stress, loneliness, heart attacks, hours spent in traffic jams, or family togetherness—the ratings might stack up much differently.

It's best not to "rate" at all. All societies are complex and highly developed in their own ways. Lay them side by side with varying degrees of overlap, but reserve judgment. Try to understand your own cultural baggage. People will recognize you as an American no matter what you do. There's something about us that is very hard to mask. But why should we mask it?

Just as we have a stereotypical view of most other peoples, they have a typical Uncle Sam image imprinted in their minds. Consider the average Abdullah on the street, who's seen plenty of American movies and TV shows, read the craziest Yankee news stories, and watched tourists in his city. To him we are outgoing, aggressive, ambitious, informal, extravagant, overconfident, in a hurry, and likely to disregard class distinctions and authority.

Some of these traits are positive, and others aren't. Remember, there is no absolute good or bad when it comes to life-styles. While we may proudly ignore class ranks and think of our extroversion as a virtue, a Hindu might be shocked at our ignorance of caste lines, and a Japanese might see our "good old boy," slap-on-the-back warmth as downright rude.

As you struggle to adapt, you may find it hard to get simple views across. How can you explain to the Hindu next to you on the train that you aren't rich? He makes $500 a year, and you make that much in a week. Why are you traveling alone? Why do Americans put their parents in nursing homes when they get old? Psychologically, you may find yourself reeling as many personal values that you once regarded as absolutes are challenged.

A prescription to minimize culture shock would include these instructions:

1. Learn as much as you can about your host culture.

2. Assume that "strange" habits in a "strange" land are logical. Think of them as clever solutions to life's problems.

3. Be militantly positive. Avoid the temptation to commiserate with negative Americans. Don't joke negatively about the culture you're trying to understand.

4. Be patient. Banks may guarantee you five-minute service at home, but don't expect that speediness in lands where time is not money.

5. Make a local friend whom you can confide in and learn from.

6. Have faith in yourself, in the culture you're adapting to, and in a happy ending.

Cultural No No's

Before you land, you should at least know a few things that would shock the locals. Then you can decide whether you want to do just that or to fit in. The following are some cultural faux pas that apply to most places in Asia.

Saving Face

Throughout Asia, and especially in Japan and China, saving face is more important than being right. Though there are words for "No" in the various Asian languages, you won't often hear them spoken. The Japanese have a hundred ways of saying no without actually saying "No." The Indians are likely to say "Yes"—even if they really don't know—instead of saying "No" or displaying any degree of ignorance. Learn to read between the phrases.

Likewise, you'll be taking giant steps backward if you get angry, if you raise your voice and shout when you're not getting the service you expect or are otherwise frustrated. Not only will you be causing the person on whom you vent your anger a loss of face but you yourself will lose respect in their eyes, which you can't expect to regain.

Body Language

Be modest. Don't assume you can begin a first-name relationship at first introduction. Unless you are intimate with someone of the opposite sex, you should not touch him (or her). It's perfectly acceptable for men to walk in purely macho friendship with their arms around each other or for women to hold hands walking down the street; but it is not proper to give a bear hug to an old (or new) friend of the opposite sex. Also, it's improper to be too personal in your conversations. Don't boast about your family or possessions: Asians will hold you in more esteem if you are self-deprecating.

Be sensitive to the local cultures

The following gestures are regarded as universally offensive or obscene throughout Asia: pointing with your forefinger (use your open hand); beckoning someone (including a taxi) with a crooked forefinger (use your whole hand, palm down, waving toward you); making a fist and hitting it against your open palm (it's like the American middle-finger gesture).

Many Asians feel the head is the home of the soul. Resist patting even small children on the beanie; it's disrespectful.

Don't use your left hand to shake hands, eat, touch someone, or point. Since the left hand is often used to clean oneself after a trip to the toilet, you'll get a reaction if you use it for anything else around others.

Never point your feet in anyone's direction, such as when sitting or resting on the floor. This will insult someone as the feet are considered to be the lowest and dirtiest part of your body.

If someone laughs or smiles at a seemingly inappropriate moment, don't be surprised. Smiles and laughter are used to cover up embarrassment and shock as well as to show happiness. In many Asian cultures (as well as in America), strong feelings are not shown in public. While working in Osaka, Bob told a Japanese co-worker that his father was gravely ill in America. The man smiled while he expressed concern. Having heard of this sort of reaction before, Bob understood that this was just a mask for what were sincere feelings of regret.

In general, dress conservatively. In temples and mosques, anticipate modesty dress codes: keep your upper arms and back covered, and don't wear shorts. You may need to take your shoes off before entering a religious place. If in doubt, watch what the locals are doing.

When visiting a private home, be observant. In many countries, you'll remove your shoes before you enter. Often a small gift (especially in Japan) is appreciated. We carry some lightweight souvenirs for this, such as pens with "Seattle" on the side, balloons, and so on. Or we pick up some sweets to take over.

Cultural Knowledge

We highly recommend reading *Culture Shock* by JoAnn Craig (Singapore: Times Books International). It covers the ins and outs of custom, courtesy, and behavior in the Chinese, Malay, and Indian communities. Also *The Traveler's Guide to Asian Customs and Manners* by Kevin Chambers (New York: Meadowbrook) is very useful for all of Asia. To better understand the Japanese, look at *The Japanese* by Jack Seward (Tuttle: Rutland, Vt., and Tokyo).

Readjusting to Life in the U.S.A.

Each time we travel to Asia, even for a short period, we come back changed. The way we look at ourself, others, and our way of life is altered. Some things that we never thought about before now disturb us, such as seeing two and more cars in front of people's houses (even our own) or witnessing the amount and type of food being carted out of grocery stores. Materialism emerges as the flip side of spirituality.

Something also seems to be missing when we return. In Asia, life was spread before us. Walking the streets there, we watched men playing cards in front of their homes, women washing clothes, children coasting on their crude wooden carts. We passed through open markets where locals bargained for their daily produce and said hello to their neighbor. We winked at babies peering out from bundles of cloth, strapped around the back of an older sister. We heard music pour from wedding parades snaking through the street. We witnessed processions of mourners slowly moving toward the riverside cremation.

Life is so neatly tucked away in the United States. Driving the street at night, we pass endless rows of ranch-style houses, couples silhouetted against the glare from the tube. Bikes left parked in the garage, forsaken for the latest Nintendo game. Cars intent on getting someplace. Funeral homes hiding bodies so they don't disturb our thoughts. Here are the cars, here are the steeples, but where do you look to find all the people?

Back home, we can feel isolated and removed from life. Unlike Asia, it's hard to feel a sense of community. So many people go their individual ways. Individualism, which has helped America accomplish so many wonderful things, also limits us.

If you've been trekking in Asia, spending time on an island, or tuning into the sunset, the return to the city for many of us is also a shock. We soon realize how calming nature has been for us, and what we're missing.

All of these things may add up to a greater reentry shock than our culture shock in Asia. We may be left confused, disturbed, lonely, disgusted, and even angry.

Both of us constantly look at our reactions on returning from travel and talk with others about theirs (Bob, being a psychologist by profession, and Rick out of interest). We've tried to isolate the most important things from the travel experience that we're now missing. And then figure out how to incorporate that into our lives here.

We find what we enjoy most from travel is slowing down, living in the moment, trying new things, learning from different cultures and people, and feeling a part of life. When we return home, we miss and seek these things. Here are some ideas that help us and may also give you that "travel quality of life" in your work-a-day world at home between trips.

1. Try something new. Take a class on Japanese brush calligraphy, improvisational acting, or massage.

2. Drive to work a different way, even if it's longer.

3. Join activities to meet fun and interesting people. Check into dance classes, biking or hiking clubs, and reading or storytelling circles.

4. Slow down and appreciate life. You did on your trip, and that's probably why you liked it so much. Have a cup of tea while you people-watch. Pause to feel the warm sun on your skin, the breeze through your hair, the chirping of birds in your trees.

5. Pause to really look at yourself and others. Who is that person you've seen in the mirror all these years? And who is that person, really, across from you at work or the dinner table?

6. Join in ethnic activities in your community. Is there a Chinese New Year? Do any Indian music or dance groups come to town? Can you help with them?

7. Be a host to a foreign student. Many colleges and universities have programs for foreign students. They usually look for host friends, not necessarily a live-in situation. Also many refugee programs need people to help in various ways.

8. Look for ways to help you get in contact with the moment. Try meditation, yoga, herbal flying, or a Tai Chi class.

9. Seek out other travelers or an understanding friend to share your new insights and changes. Don't worry too much about "explaining India" to people who have never been there.

10. Plan your next trip.

Part Two
Thirty Asian Back Doors

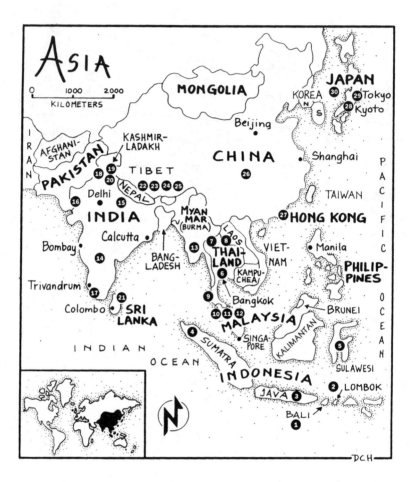

Now that you've learned the hows and whys, it's time to take a look at the wheres. In the following pages, we'll introduce you to our thirty favorite Asian destinations—some of them well known, others off the beaten track.

To make for less tedious reading, we've stowed the navigation-type details in the fine print Nitty-Gritty, Country by Country section in the back of the book. Read the Back Doors to stack up and sort out your travel dreams. We trust you'll use our nitty gritty details and a country-specific guidebook for your actual travels.

Thirty Asian Back Doors

INDONESIA

1. Bali—
Worth Jumping Ship For

Bali, a Hindi-animist planet in the diverse Indonesian galaxy, is seductively alien, hauntingly beautiful, and genuinely welcoming. When Captain Cook first landed here, his men jumped ship and there was nothing he could do about it.

Similar in size to Hawaii's Big Island, Bali is a tropical land of gleaming white beaches, live volcanoes, and lush green terraced fields of rice. Most of all, the island is home to three million gentle, smiling people whose hypnotic music, remarkable artistry, and kaleidoscope of festivals only hint at the complexity of their culture.

Despite its increasing fame among tourists, much of Bali (pronounce it "Bah-lee," not "Bally") is unspoiled. But tourism, and all it represents, has brought more motorbikes, more Walkmans, more opportunistic locals organizing festival tours. Thankfully, the package tourists hang out at Sanur Beach, budget travelers gravitate to less-developed northern beaches or the hedonistic Kuta Beach, and most of the interior is left to the rare explorer.

Bali is cheap, accommodations abound, eating is a delight, transportation is a snap, and most Balinese who deal with tourists speak English.

The Balinese bed and breakfast is called a *losmen*. Lists and particular recommendations aren't worth the trouble. Lovable losmen are everywhere—$10 a day for a double room with a big fruit and black rice salad for breakfast. Expect a bamboo hut with a thatched roof, concrete floor, covered front porch, lantern (when there's no electricity), sturdy bed and clean sheet (no need for a blanket), and *mandi*, the local-style bathroom. For a few extra dollars you'll get a hot shower, overhead fan, and more comfort.

Your mandi, a tub of water with a big plastic scoop, serves as your sink, your shower, and your flusher (for that porcelain hole in the ground). For your shower, you may have the option of raising a pail of water from the backyard well and dumping it over your head. Most bathrooms come with a lizard who eats your bugs. His friends live in your roof—heard but unseen.

Bali

Bali's roads, most of them asphalted, are a parade of minibuses and *bemos* (pickup trucks outfitted with two benches and a canopy). Schedules don't apply. Buses take off every few minutes, whenever they're reasonably full. Soon more people jump in, and they become unreasonably full. Most rides cost just pennies. Watch what the locals pay, and follow suit.

During your visit to Bali, explore towns and villages—like those below—that represent Bali's distinctly different elements. If you're flying in and out for a short visit, consider checking all but a tiny day bag of essentials at the airport so you can do Bali like Dorothy did Oz.

Kuta, on a broad stretch of white sand only five minutes bemo ride from the airport, is a Balinese version of L.A.'s Venice Beach, without the roller skates and musclemen. It's a perfect hangout for the frugal hedonist wanting Western decadence with an Eastern flair. It seems that at any point in time, half the tourists in Bali are at Kuta, savoring mellow-dramatic sunsets or passing time in international-style tropical bars and loud, dull discos. Hawkers on the beach sell drinks and sunglasses. In town, their goods tend more toward the illicit. Kuta cuisine is Balinese-American, featuring mango pancakes, coconut milk shakes, and hallucinogenic mushroom omelets.

Ubud is raw Bali. Surrounded by *padi* (rice) fields, it's the island's cultural center and most atmospheric large village. It's artsy, with museums, galleries, shops, temples, handicrafts, live gamelan music, folk dancing, and even a sacred monkey forest. Ubud is famous for its festivals. Plenty of losmen hide in the back alleys, and good little restaurants line the main streets. Pedal a rental bike through some of Bali's most beautiful countryside, to nearby villages where the locals will take your hand on an impromptu personalized tour or invite you into their home for a cup of tea. Ubud can ruin a tight itinerary.

Lovina Beach, on the north coast, is Bali's undiscovered "Kuta." With great snorkeling, a black volcanic sand beach, and plenty of lazy losmen, it's hard not to linger. Pay a local fisherman to wake you at dawn and take you in his boat to watch schools of dolphin jumping in the orange-pink sunrise. Break out of a nap by feasting on big chunks of fresh pineapple, expertly skinned and sliced for you by a beaming five-year-old salesman. Wander the beach at sunset, and don't be surprised if you're joined by a herd of goats and a few stray chickens. A simple three-room cottage (bed, bath, and sitting room) goes for $5, with tea and bananas for breakfast.

The proud and dignified village of **Tenganan** lies at the end of a road on Bali's east coast. It's an isolationist stronghold of Balinese traditions predating the arrival, 400 years ago, of Bali's modern Hindu culture. Its 300 people welcome visitors but shun change. It's a sort of utopian walled commune. Its residents follow strict laws or are exiled to the "East Road" (to live with those who have divorced, married outside the village, or chosen to lead unacceptable Western-style lives). Spend a day in this peaceful haven, watching traditional artisans weave exquisite double-ikat cloth (unique to Tenganan) and huge intricate baskets or listening to the village gamelan maker demonstrate his handmade bamboo xylophone.

A proud citizen of Tenganan, Bali

Candidasa, a growing east coast beach town, is a good base for exploring eastern Bali. Despite its increasing popularity, Candidasa is still a lazy sun-soaked refuge. When the beach nearly disappears at high tide, hop on a rented bicycle or flag down a passing bemo and explore the lush surrounding countryside. Candidasa has dozens of first-class restaurants at third-class prices, and you can still find several small _warungs_ (simple, local-style cafés) where excellent Indonesian staples like _nasi goreng_ (fried rice) and _gado gado_ (vegetables in peanut sauce) are served up at local prices.

Tirtigangga (eight miles from Candidasa by bemo or bus) is spectacularly set amid terraced rice fields, palm forests, and rolling green hillsides. It's famous for its water palace complex, a wet wonderland of carved stone fountains and swimming pools. You'll find a warm welcome at one of its many idyllic losmen.

Padangbai, a small, friendly port town on Bali's southeastern coast, is the jumping-off point for Lombok (four hours) and islands beyond. Most tourists step off the boat and directly onto a bus bound for Kuta or Sanur. Buck the trend. Hang out. Hitch a ride on one of the local fishing boats sporting colorfully painted "faces," or stroll along the back road, past children playing "king of the Balinese mountain" on huge piles of sand-filled burlap bags. Cheap eats and sleeps and a laid-back atmosphere prevail. The Topi Inn, at the far end of the beach, has fine food, a large open sitting area with beach view, private rooms, and a good dormitory.

Bali rewards its visitors with experiences and surprises that'll make any journal read like a Dali painting. We treasure our favorite Bali memories. Here's one that Rick penned while sitting under a thatched roof, writing by flickering light while the smoke from his mosquito coil quietly danced:

"Lanterns painted a rutted dirt road through the new darkness. Thin unloved street dogs played with my shadow as it walked before me to the candlelit temple. Batik smiles ushered me to a bamboo chair where I joined a couple dozen villagers seething like barnacle tongues to the churning beat of a twenty-piece gamelan orchestra.

"Gamelan is Bali's traditional orchestra of bamboo xylophones, gongs, flutes, and stringed instruments. To the casual tourist, it's a jumble of jungle noise worth little more than a snapshot and an ear glance. But if you look into the musicians' eyes, you see that they're dancing as one, making music in tongues, pure as Mozart. Children hide attentively on performers' laps, and all are lost in the same beat.

"The temple was a peacock of happy candles. Its warm outline against a starry black backdrop stood protectively above the music. Through the temple's door danced a goddess-gowned girl. Her icon eyes dug deep into mine as she quivered like a butterfly on a lotus flower. Then there were four dancers waving like seaweed in the tide. Their eyes and fingers, like the gamelan mallets, were puppets from paradise tied to the same god's strings. They throbbed with the gong and flute like fish Eskimo-kissing, intensifying as the speeding gamelan churns like a train in heaven. As Orion reached for the temple, I found myself breathing heavy in this seductive tidepool."

Back Door traveler Melinda Williams (who wrote our chapter on women traveling in Asia and some of our Indonesia Back Doors) reported this "Pineapples in Paradise" experience in her journal:

"A boy of four or five wanders the beach with a small pineapple and a large knife, calling 'Hello, pineapple!' through a toothy grin. Though I pretend to be engrossed in my book, he plants himself in the sand at eye level and launches into a well-practiced sales routine. '500 rupiahs,' he announces, holding up his tiny prize. I laugh at his ridiculously high offer, and counter with an equally ridiculous low one. '100,' I say, glancing up from my book. The boy rolls his eyes, shakes his head sadly, raises his hands to the heavens and cries, 'Oh my dog! My dog!' apparently hoping that some Western god would overlook his mispronunciation and help me see the light. '450!' he says, waving the pineapple authoritatively in front of me. I shake my head and offer 200, nearly bringing tears to his eyes. 'Bankrut! Bankrut!' (bankrupt) he moans, falling backward on the sand. He opens one eye and, seeing me return to my book, sits up on his knees. He pleads. He pouts. He points frantically at the pineapple. Finally he walks away, dragging his feet in the sand to allow me to catch up. After a minute he runs back, plops down in front of me with a huge grin, declares '300, O.K.!' and begins peeling. I trade him 3 worn bills for one overpriced pineapple and bite into the juicy treat as he skips away down the beach, turning every four or five steps to wave happily back at his gullible newfound friend."

2. Lombok— Bali's Quiet Cousin

Mellow Mangsit Beach—With its stunning sunsets, deserted white sand beaches, and fascinating traditional village culture, Lombok may well be Indonesia's next Bali. But for now, Lombok is less discovered, and, at least in the interior and the east, you can travel for days without seeing another traveler. Beautiful crafts—ikat cloth, tightly woven rattan baskets, pottery, and wooden carvings—are made on the island by the Muslim Sasaks, who make up three-fourths of the population. Many travelers mistake the Sasak's shy, reserved nature—especially compared to the gregarious Hindu Balinese—as unfriendly. Don't let these misleading rumors keep you away.

After the four-hour ferry trip from Bali, we hopped a bemo straight to Sengiggi, a palm-studded beach 18 miles from the ferry terminal on the island's more touristy west side. With clear, turquoise water, sparkling white sand, snorkeling right off the beach, and good food and lodging, we shouldn't have been surprised to find all the rooms taken.

Fortunately, about 2 miles up the road is a quiet little haven called Mangsit. This untouristy mini-Sengiggi must have Indonesia's best losmen (guest house). We were driven there by Iwan, who promised that Pearl, the losmen's British proprietress, would find room for us.

Pearl and her Indonesian husband call their guest house Santai. That's "relax" in Indonesian, and "relax" is this place's forte. The guest house's half-dozen roomy bamboo bungalows each have private bathrooms and large covered porches. They stand in a jungle of exotic trees and flowers, linked to one another by a winding footpath leading down to the deserted beach.

We awoke in the morning to coffee and tea on our porch, then sat back against comfy throw pillows to await a delicious breakfast of sweet black bean porridge and bananas. After a day of exploring nearby villages and an impromptu game of soccer with a group of rowdy teenagers, we strolled to the beach for the day's main event: the stunning, multicolored sunset melting across the sea behind Bali's Mount Agung.

Lombok

Gili Trawangan: Snorkelers' Shangri-La—North of Sengiggi off Lombok's northwestern coast are the three tiny Gili Islands. Head directly to the most distant, Gili Trawangan, about an hour from the mainland. Like Senggigi and Mangsit, Trawangan has fascinating coral, exotic fish, and snorkeling a minute's stroll from your bungalow. (The beachside stands rent snorkels.) The island's half-dozen losmen are primitive thatched bungalows with wood floors, rickety porches, shared toilets, and communal eating areas.

The best part of Trawangan is its sleepy pace. Lack of electricity sends many travelers to bed with the sun (though the noisy generators may wake them up soon after). There are no vehicles, no shops to speak of, and no need for your wristwatch. A burst of energy will take you all the way around the island in an easy three hours. Recover from your jaunt with a tall, cool Bintang beer at the Excellent Pub. When it's time to leave, wander over to the beach and flag down an outgoing boat.

Mystical Mount Rinjani—A Lombok highlight is a hike up the island's magnificent Mount Rinjani. It's a tough but otherworldly journey.

Rinjani's highest peak overlooks the brilliant blue-green waters of its crater lake, Segara Anak. The typical traveler's goal is over the rim to the crater floor, for a peaceful night at the lakeside camp. It's a strenuous three or four day round-trip hike from the village of Batu Kok. In Batu Kok, you can arrange for a guide (who doubles as a cook) and rent sleeping bags and tents. Bring warm clothes.

Getting an early morning start, we hiked through thick, misty forests sliced by shafts of sunlight. A recent rain made the trail slippery. It's an 8-hour hike to the base camp, where most spend the first night. While we set up camp, our guide prepared a feast of rice, vegetables, and ramen-style noodles.

The next morning we reached the breathtaking crater rim view point. At the far side of the crater, the "new" volcano, Gunung Baru-jari, reminded visitors of the awesome forces that slumbered (and occasionally snorted) below.

A steep and beautiful 6-hour descent from the rim brought us to the lake. Rinjani is sacred to Lombok's Muslims and Hindus. After the long hike, we were eager to join the pilgrims for a soak in the mystical hot springs at Kokok Putih. Full moon is prime time for a pilgrimage and the most interesting time to visit Rinjani.

—Melinda Williams

Soaking in the sacred hot springs at Lombok's Mt. Rinjani

3. Java—
Beyond the Coffee Beans

Yogyakarta: Center of Javanese Culture—Throughout Asia, the eyes of Back Door travelers twinkle when the Javanese city of Yogyakarta is mentioned. It even has a pet name, "Jogja," after its earlier Dutch spelling.

The traditional center of Javanese culture and history, Yogyakarta has been the home of Java's most powerful sultan since the mid-eighteenth century (his palace is still the focus of the city). Jogja is also the center of a thriving batik industry and other traditional arts. The great Buddhist monument of Borobudur and the Hindu temple complex of Prambanan are each a short trip out of town. Add to this a great variety of low-cost accommodations and delicious food, and you've tickled this budget traveler's fancy.

The biggest concentration of low-cost, comfortable losmen and good travelers' restaurants are south of the train station, on two long alleyways (Gang I and Gang II). Eat at Superman I and II and Anna's (try the pizza). Shoppers find great bargains at nearby Malioboro Street. Wall-to-wall hawkers line the sidewalk, selling everything from batik cards and fabrics to leather goods and wooden puppets. You'll pay two bucks for batik clothes that sell for fifty in your hometown import shop. Stop by at night, when traveling "restaurants" cook up spicy *sate ayam* (chicken satay) and corn on the cob.

To really feel the city, head south down Jalan Jenderal A. Yani, a gauntlet of jackfruit milk shakes, durian ice cream, and lines of waiting bicycle "taxis," which leads to the Kraton, or sultan's palace. Tall thick walls enclose a market, schools, mosques, shops, offices, home industries, and even a medical school. This is a private city within the city. Ask one of the turbaned men squatting outside about Taman Sari, the "water palace," once a maze of canals and pools, now a ruin. Follow the squawking and screeching to the bird market a few blocks to the north.

Jogja is the center of batik, an intricate process of patterning a piece of cloth by waxing, dyeing, and boiling. Look for beautifully colored shirts, skirts, and batik "paintings."

Don't miss a *wayang* (puppet theater) performance. *Wayang golek* (three-dimensional wooden puppetry) is charming, but *wayang kulit* (leather shadow puppetry) is more entertaining. Both draw their story lines from the folkloric Ramayana or Mahabharata sagas. Modern playwrights use these ancient soap operas when they want to satirize modern Indonesian politics.

From May to October, once a month for four nights, classical Javanese dancers perform the Ramayana Ballet under the full moon at Prambana. This ancient Hindu temple is an enjoyable 11-mile bike ride east of Jogja.

Twenty-five miles west of Jogja is Borobudur, a massive, thousand-year-old Buddhist monument representing the mystical "center of the universe." Built with over two million cubic feet of stone, this is one of Southeast Asia's most impressive sights, with 472 Buddha images tucked in niches and beneath bell-shaped stupas and nearly 300 relief pictures carved into its walls.

Borobudur is quiet and most enjoyable in the morning. By afternoon, you may want to charge admission yourself. You will have become the main attraction for hundreds of Indonesian tourists who will line up to have their photos taken by your side!

Placid **Pangandaran**, a small fishing village on the Indian Ocean and gateway to the magnificent Cagar Alam Panajung wildlife reserve, is a welcome respite from the rigors of sightseeing. The west side of town is your typical travelers' beach hangout. The "back door" is on Pangandaran's less-visited eastern side.

From Melinda Williams's journal: "I arrived at the beach before dawn, to find dozens of fishermen hauling their heavy wooden boats from the water. Before heading home, they took time to share cigarettes and a little camaraderie. Swallowing my caution, I called out 'Selamat pagi!' (good morning) and joined them. We talked, passing my dictionary back and forth, and filled in the blanks with pantomime and laughter.

"In the afternoon, the boats left to retrieve their floating nets. As they returned, dozens of men and women gathered on the beach. As if in a methodical net-gathering contra dance, they walked to the water's edge in twos, taking hold of the net and dragging it slowly up the sand. As they moved backward, others joined at the front of the net. Women in conical hats stooped over the net, filling their baskets with fish. When the 'dance' was over, they walked to the market—heavy baskets on their heads, surrounded by darting children and brightly colored butterfly kites.

"South of the beach past several tea stalls is the wildlife reserve. The map (available at the entrance) directs you into a world of fascinating wildlife. Swaggering monkeys and graceful flying squirrels seem to enjoy the lush and exotic vegetation. You can relax on the beautiful white sand beaches or explore the limestone caves.

"Traveling to Pangandaran is half the fun. From Yogyakarta, minibuses make the 4-hour trip to the Cilicap (pronounced "chill-a-chop") ferry landing. From there, ride the Kalipucang boat past tiny river villages built on stilts, women washing laundry in the river, and fishermen in small wooden dugouts. Shout 'Apa kabar?!' (How are you) to the children splashing and playing in the water. Mini-buses go regularly from Kalipucang to Pangandaran, where you'll hop a becak (three-wheeled bicycle with a passenger seat, pronounced bay-cha) to your guest house."

4. Sumatra—Laid-Back Lake Toba and Beyond

Laid-back Lake Toba, a 635-square-mile blue-green crater lake, on the island of Sumatra is rarely visited. It's as remarkable for its native inhabitants—the Batak—as for its setting. The Batak, who migrated from the Himalayan foothills 1,500 years ago, have preserved their unique culture in part by eating their neighbors. Only in the 1850s did German and Dutch missionaries convert the Batak to a sort of animistic Christianity. With the cannibals gone, today the island is most famous for its huge traditional houses with roofs that sweep up like the horns of a buffalo.

Catch a boat from the resort town of Prapat, halfway up the lake's eastern shore, directly to Samosir Island. The best selection of losmen is on Samosir's Tuk Tuk Peninsula. The flexible ferries drop you off at the front door of any losmen.

We shared our seat from Prapat with Murni, a delightful Batak woman who invited us to stay at her losmen, cleverly named Murni's. Blood pressure runs low on laid-back Lake Toba. After swimming from your front yard, order a towering fruit salad and a tall lemonade. Digest, then stroll the village, admiring Batak houses and craft shops. Socially, locals and travelers mix well on Lake Toba.

Samosir offers plenty more. You can hike to tombs and stone sculptures of dead ancestors, remnants of the Batak's pre-Christian culture. Tomok, a 45-minute walk from Tuk Tuk, offers woven textiles, wood carvings, musical instruments, and other works of art. Ambarita, an hour stroll from Tuk Tuk, boasts ancient tombs and a cannibal's kitchen, where prisoners were butchered and cooked with buffalo meat.

Brastagi, a cool, sunny market town in the north Sumatran highlands, is another stay-put-for-a-while kind of place. It's also a fine base for day trips to nearby villages and a climb up the Sibayak volcano north of town.

Stay in Brastagi's Wisma Sibayak, a well-lit, sunny, and friendly hostel with double and single rooms and a very sleepable dorm. Travelers sun themselves like lazy reptiles in the huge yard, reading, playing cards, and trading travel tips. The proprietors arrange river, moun-

Batak homes, Sumatra

tain, and jungle trips, provide maps for walks to nearby sites, give you a riveting thumbnail history of area, and serve incredible fruit salads— topped with a squeeze of the tangy marquisa fruit—and melt-in-your-mouth avocado salads.

The nearby Sipisopiso Waterfall is spectacular. A series of bemos will jostle you from Brastagi to a poorly marked junction between Merek and Tongging, where a tiny, hand-lettered sign points the way to the falls. An hour climb, past rice fields dotted with workers, rewards you with a stunning view of Lake Toba, the mountains, the thundering falls, and the lush valley below.

From the lookout, a steep, little-used trail leads to the base of the falls a hundred yards below. On the valley floor we entered a cool jungle swimming in mist. The violent crash of the falls filled the world. A rainbow of light split the mist as we stood mesmerized, watching the water bounce high off the rocks, until our shivering forced us reluctantly back up the trail and into the sunlight.

Bukittinggi—Only the most energetic travelers in Sumatra make it as far as Bukittinggi, a relaxing highland town set in some of the most stunning scenery on the island. Those who make the head-bumping, seat-bruising 20-hour bus ride south from Prapat or Medan are rewarded with a cultural, scenic, and gastronomic feast.

Bukittinggi is the heart of the Minangkabau culture, a matrilineal society where all property, titles, and family names are handed down through the women (who control even the TV remote stick). It stands apart with its remarkably high literacy rate and high degree of political, social, and sexual equality. The Minang, who balance a strong belief in Islam with their female-oriented culture, are one of the most fascinating societies in Southeast Asia.

Several of the guest houses in Bukittinggi can arrange Back Door-style tours to nearby villages. These tours are your best chance to understand this culture. Choose a guide who understands the Minang culture and your desire to learn, not one who will take you to his cousin's curio shop.

Bukittinggi's market entertains with a fun blend of Asian crafts, Western clothing, freak show oddities, and the usual produce. Wednesdays and Saturdays, the biggest market days, feature contortionists and fire eaters. Crowds of believers are transfixed by hawkers touting the magical powers of their just-bottled potions. From baldness to impotence—you'll find a cure at Bukittinggi's amazing market.

There are abundant food stalls and restaurants serving the fiery Padang food, tasty buffalo yogurt (to put out that Padang fire), and quasi-American fare.

Use Bukittinggi as a base from which to explore. Get up early and walk to Panorama Park to enjoy a mystical view of Ngarai Canyon with the impressive Gunung Singgalang mountain rising beyond. East of town, visit the maze of tunnels and pillboxes built into the hills by the Japanese in World War II. Ride a bemo or rented motorbike through gorgeous countryside to Lakes Maninjau and Singaraja. At Singaraja, frolic in inner tubes (borrowed from the Jayakarta Hotel) in the cool, clean lake.

Within walking distance from Bukittinggi are several villages known for their skilled artisans. Kota Gadang is a silver-working center. Pandaisikat and Silungkang are known for their intricate wood carvings. Other villages produce beautiful embroidery work and loom-woven cloth. All come with children eager to be your impromptu guides.

Another memorable Bukittinggi diversion is the weekly buffalo fight at nearby Kotabaru. The list goes on and on, causing many to wish they gave Bukittinggi a bigger part of their itinerary.

5. Sulawesi— Grave Entertainment

Exotic tour operators have plastered their brochures with Sulawesi for years. But most independent travelers have yet to discover this island treasure. Between Bali and the Philippines, Sulawesi is off the "Lake Toba to Kuta Beach" beaten path—and worth the extra boat or plane ride.

Of the island's many wonders, intriguing Tana Toraga, "land of the Torajans," with its high fertile plateaus, superb views from the mountains, elaborate festivals, and fascinating traditions, deserves the most time.

Rantepao, Toraja's main town, is friendly and remarkably relaxed. Ringed by blue mountains and rich vegetation, it's an excellent base for hiking and exploring. The best time to visit is between September and November, during festival season but after the June–August rush. Visitors fly or ferry to Ujung Pandang, the Sulawesi capital. Toraja is 7 hours by bus from there.

Fine losmen and *wisma* (family homes with guest rooms) abound. Our favorite is Wisma Surya, perched above a bend in the river at the north end of town. The Bobi family will treat you as one of their own, even inviting you to share in their family festivals.

The Torajans place tremendous importance on their funerals. Tradition has it that the dead hang around town in a funk until they're sent off in style. The resulting **Pesta Mati** or **Festival of the Dead** is one of Asia's most exotic spectacles.

At death, bodies are wrapped in cloth, partially embalmed, and kept in or near the home until the family can raise enough money for the extravagant funeral. Depending on the person's station, this can take months or even years. Family members come in from all over Indonesia for the preparations. Elaborate two-story bamboo dwellings are built around the ritual field, where guests will be fed and entertained during the funeral. Then, despite all the work, the festival community is broken apart and burned at the ceremony's close.

The funeral itself can last up to two weeks, with thousands taking part. It's an intense but joyous medley of chanting in the moonlight, formal processions, offerings, dancing, pig feasts with palm wine, buffalo fights, buffalo sacrifice, kick boxing, and more.

At the end of the funeral, an effigy in wood and cloth (*tau tau*) is made by family members. All mourners then proceed to a field ringed with boulders, each a monument to a departed relative. The decorated coffin is hauled with ropes up the cliff and slid into a hole cut in the rock. The effigy is stood next to effigies from previous funerals on high balconies carved out of the cliff. Each protects the souls of those buried within.

Faces of the dead decorate the cliff graves of Sulawesi's Tana Toraja

From the journal, the first day of a Torajan funeral: "Several black-clad men carried the coffin from the house to where the mourners waited. A young girl threw herself at the coffin, wailing 'Bapak!' (Father!). The men loaded the coffin into a red and black miniature house, placed it on large bamboo poles, and hoisted it on their shoulders. A second curtained box on poles carried the widow and daughters. Heading to a field below, the men playfully dipped and jumped and shook the women. Tripping, they crashed to the ground, sending up a roar of laughter from the crowd.

"Hundreds of us trailed along behind the procession. At a field the coffin was placed alongside the widow and daughters. Eight young women in shimmering orange and yellow sarongs performed a series of elegant fan dances in their honor.

"The funeral festivities went on in waves. More chanting, singing, then the slaughter of the buffalo. This gory but fascinating aspect of the ceremony is performed with one quick slice of the neck. The animals are carved up where they fall, and the meat is distributed to the guests according to rank.

"The chanting and dancing rolled deep into the night. A sense of playfulness and celebration pervaded. I was encouraged to join in. My efforts to keep up with the chanting added to the light mood. Just when I thought I had mastered the rhythm, some secret signal seemed to go out and everyone stopped. Suddenly, I found myself chanting at full force . . . solo. The group roared with laughter at their trick. It was a full five minutes before they could muster the dignity necessary to continue the funeral."

—Melinda Williams

THAILAND

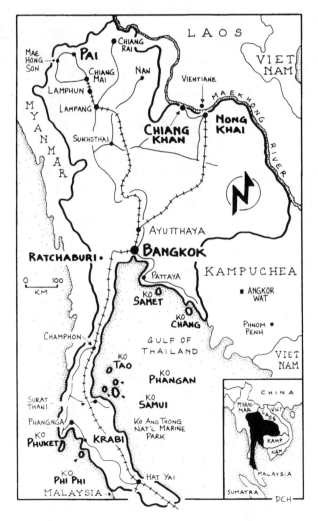

6. Bizarre Bangkok

Few cities on this planet are as frenzied or exciting as Thailand's capital, Bangkok. Pack yourself like a simmering sardine in a city bus, then climb off to explore an open-air silk market. Buy a cheap meal from a passing boat while floating down a canal. Yuk it up with saffron-robed monks. Share a three-wheeled taxi with fifty coconuts as you putt-putt wildly through Asia's noisiest city. Take your hat off to King Bhumipol as he walks down a carpeted path with flowers strewn all about him. Watch two "boxers" kick each other to a pulp before thousands of cheering onlookers.

If you find traffic too slow aboard a crowded bus, or the weather too humid to walk any distance, hail a motorized trishaw (negotiate your price first) to weave in and out of the traffic lanes in a modern-day white-knuckle chariot race.

Bangkok's Grand Palace, Southeast Asia's most spectacular building, is a colorful walled city that mysteriously mixes Italian Renaissance architecture with traditional Thai styles. Within, various spires shoot above the city like a frozen fireworks display. Next door is Wat Phra Keo, where the Emerald Buddha resides in Their Majesties' Private Chapel. King Bhumipol Adulyadej personally changes the icon's bejeweled robe with the advent of each season—hot, wet, and dry. It's a major event. As crowds of wide-eyed Thais scatter flower petals ahead of the king and he strolls regally down his fragrant red carpet, you may find yourself getting wrapped up in this typically Thai form of king worship. But true Thai political power rests with either the prime minister—rubber-stamped by the king—or the army, depending on who you ask and when. The king represents stability, which is appreciated in a country with a government that changes so often. The king also represents spiritual sovereignty, very important in Thailand.

At nearby Wat Pho, known for its huge reclining Buddha image, you'll get a good look at Thai monastic life. It's considered an honor—and in many families, an obligation—for a man to devote a couple of years to the Sangha, the brotherhood of monks. While some adult men wait until retirement age to do their "hitch," it's more common for children (ages 10 or 12) to be sent to study with the monks. Some of these youngsters make a career of the monkhood. Many wats (temples), therefore, are schools where the visitor can wander into a corridor and find a math or writing lesson in progress—twenty saffron-robed youngsters listening to a similarly garbed instructor. After the lesson, make a friend. You'll get a personal guide for a tour of the wat, and he can practice his English.

Another fine temple is Wat Arun, across the river from Wat Pho (take the small ferry from the river landing near Wat Pho). The "Temple of Dawn" towers 280 feet above the river. Go in the late afternoon to miss the crowds and walk up its steep steps for views over the city.

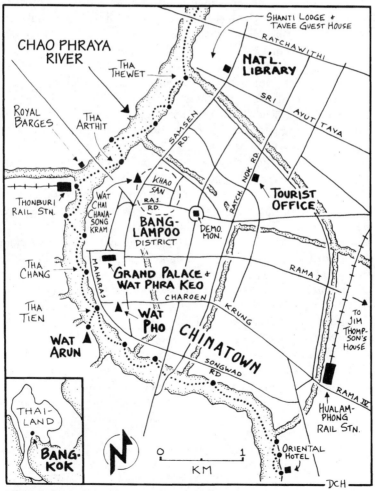

Bangkok

To see Thailand through the eyes of a mysterious *farang* (foreigner), visit Jim Thompson's house. Thompson, the prince of postwar expatriate society in Bangkok, founded a silk company that still bears his name. He filled his luxurious canalside wood house with an incredible art collection, much of it quite ancient, from throughout Thailand. Today, the home is a museum. And Thompson? His disappearance a couple of decades ago while on a hike in Malaysia is still one of the great mysteries of Asia, a topic bandied about at cocktail parties of old Asia hands whenever conversation lulls. Was he captured by guerrillas? Eaten by a tiger? Or did he simply "drop out" and go into hidden exile? We're not telling (although we hint at it in our Back Door on the Cameron Highlands).

To see the "real" Bangkok, explore this "Venice of the East" by boat. More than a million people live in houseboats or in canalside homes on stilts. For a city boat tour, bargain hard with the "long tail" boatmen at the Chao Phraya river landings for the Wat Phra Keo, Wat Pho, and the Oriental Hotel.

Most tourists head for the touristy Floating Market, where each morning countless long, narrow sampans sell vegetables, rice, flowers, and other merchandise to the canal communities. For a less touristed and much larger floating market, head out of town to the Damnoen Saduak Floating Market, in Ratchaburi, 50 miles southwest of Bangkok. The market is best before 9:30 a.m. Buses (leaving very early from the Southern Bus Terminal) go regularly. Floating Market Guest House, next to the market, is good for those staying overnight.

For a touch of classic Oriental violence, go to a kick-boxing match (nightly at either Lumpini Stadium or Rajdamnern Stadium). Anything goes. Knees, feet, fists, and elbows, the boxers go at it like minks making love for five three-minute rounds punctuated by two-minute intermissions. In bizarre Bangkok fashion, a small orchestra plays Thai music "to give the boxers rhythm and encouragement."

Fortunately or unfortunately, depending on your point of view, Bangkok is most famous among international travelers for its bar girls. Any taxi driver will gladly tell you, whether you ask or not, what's hot and where. Bangkok's sex scene has brought lots of negative press lately with the exposure of the booming organized sex tour business (mostly from Japan, other Asian countries, and Europe), child prostitution, and the explosion of AIDS in Thailand. For some reason, the Thai government has been slow to recognize the problem. Today, a shocking percent of the Thai prostitutes are HIV positive.

Bangkok has plenty of lodging at any price range. On the high end, the Oriental Hotel is one of the best in the world. We usually stay in one of the basic and clean guest houses for less than $10 a night for a single (dorms are cheaper). There are countless small guest houses in the Banglampoo area. Here, along Khao San Road, you'll find many guest houses, small restaurants, and budget travel agents (Bangkok is still a good place to get cheap international flights). There are also used bookstores, street vendors with fake but quality designer clothes, bootlegged tapes, and almost anything the budget traveler wants—and doesn't want, like the masses of other budget travelers. To find a decent guest house, central but a bit away from the Western crowds, walk toward the river past the Wat Chai Chanasongkram (temple).

We stay in a quieter area behind the National Library (a 10-minute bus ride north of Khao San Road, at the end of Sri Ayutthaya Road, west of Samsen Road near the river). Try the Shanti Lodge at 37 Sri Ayutthaya Road (tel. 281-2497). Quality changes yearly, so use an up-to-date guidebook's listings or tips you pick up from other travelers.

To get around town without the noisy, choking traffic, ride the Chao Phraya Express boats. These go all day long to nearly any place you'd want to visit. Bangkok maps show riverboat landings and routes.

7. Pai—
Trekking in North Thailand

"If you'll fall in love with Asia, you'll do it in Chiang Mai." That used to be true, but travel-hardened vagabonds return to the capital of North Thailand and find the mellow magic gone. Once the laid-back staging point to visit the ethnic minorities of North Thailand, now every restaurant, hotel, and guest house in town was giving the hard sell for their "unspoiled hill tribe trek" and travelers are left looking for the untouristed Chiang Mai. That'll cost you a ticket to Pai, 4 hours by bus from Chiang Mai.

Pai, small and quiet, still has easygoing, friendly locals. The food, from local specialties to vegetarian lasagna and yogurt milk shakes, is traveler-friendly. Cheap thatched roofed bungalows with river and mountain views abound.

While many come here to trek, Pai is also a place to just enjoy the people and the countryside. East across the river and twenty minutes up a dirt road, a hilltop Buddhist temple offers commanding views of the countryside. Several miles farther, a hot springs soothes trekkers' muscles. About 4 miles to the west along another dirt road is a pleasant waterfall. These attractions, while not spectacular, are good excuses to plug you into Thailand. You'll walk or bike through nearby villages of different ethnic minorities and feel welcome to glimpse their fairly traditional life-style. You'll see mostly Burmese Shan people as well as the Lahu, the Lisu, and refugees from China. Bicycles and motorbikes may be rented at guest houses. Pia's guest houses provide handy and free maps.

Pai is a fine springboard for trips to the more remote hill tribes. Some trek on their own, but most go with a guide. Pai's guides seem to be knowledgeable, friendly, and not hard-sell as in Chiang Mai. In choosing my trek, I looked through books of recent recommendations at their offices and talked with trek leaders and potential trekkers to answer some important questions.

A hill tribe maiden of northern Thailand

How many people are going? A group of five or six allows you to become more intimate and also to blend in and not overwhelm the small villages. More than ten becomes a Western civilization road trip.

How long and difficult are the daily walks? The average traveler can handle the normal five to six hours of daily walking. If you want more or less, arrange this with your guide before the trek. The terrain is hilly. Trails can be slippery.

Am I physically compatible with the other people? If three or four hours walking a day is enough, your guide can find others who would also prefer that pace. The guide and group should set an itinerary that fits the weakest person. Ann, an Aussie women, who joined a group that didn't, had this story: "I wasn't in very good shape, but I didn't think there would be so many hills. Utterly exhausted from two days of up and down, I plopped down and demanded a helicopter to fly me out. I knew it was crazy and impossible to arrange, but I'd had it. I did struggle to the finish, and was glad I went." The others on her trek may not have been so glad. Prevent this by discussing and planning.

Will I enjoy the other people? Talk with them to see if you're compatible. Even one jerk can spoil it. I met two Brits who wanted a third for their trek. After ten minutes of talking, I found that our personalities clashed. I found another group that worked out great.

Am I going to unspoiled villages? Look through the trekking companies' book of recommendations to see what others say. If they don't have recommendations, don't go. Talk to those who just returned. Find out from your potential guide if other trekking companies also frequent the villages.

Does the trek include elephants and rafting? Many treks include both, at an added cost. Normally, this means that for one day you walk to an elephant camp in the forest and take a one- to four-hour ride toward your next destination. Swaying to and fro on a bamboo platform strapped to your giant gray machine, you stride over streams and brush past branches. Although great fun, these rides are popular, and they ensure that you'll run into other trekking groups in the area at least for a day or so. Consider trekking without elephants and doing a short elephant camp trip when you are done. Rafting, which also means running into other groups, is thrilling and can be dangerous. Bamboo is tied together to make a raft and steered with poles. When rivers are swollen by the monsoon, chances of a wipeout are high. Life jackets are usually not used. If you do go, enclose your things in a plastic bag, especially your camera.

What should I bring? Ask the trekking company what they furnish. Many provide backpacks for you to carry your clothing and possibly a blanket or sleeping bag. Some have blankets stored at the villages they visit. Normally, the guide buys most of the food at the village and brings along extras such as cookies and bread. If you bring your own backpack (probably better quality), store the rest of your stuff with the trekking company or your guest house manager. If you leave your valuables behind, inventory them so each of you can keep a copy. There's been some problem with leaving credit cards behind for safekeeping in Chiang Mai (too big of a temptation). Bring along a flashlight, insect repellent, water bottle, lightweight rain jacket, and sweater. Even in the hot season, the hills get cool at night. Quick-dry nylon running or walking shoes are better than hiking boots as you'll be going through streams. Thongs or sport sandals are good for walking through streams or wearing around the village while your other shoes dry. Without an inflatable or foam sleeping mat, you'll be sleeping local-style, on a woven straw mat.

How long is the trek? Treks can be tailored to your time and conditioning. For some, a three-day trek is more than enough. Many find that it takes four days to even begin to appreciate the quiet, beauty, and culture.

What is the cost? Prices vary from $10 to $20 a day for food, lodging, and guide. The upper end usually includes elephants.

If you're having doubts whether a trek is worth it, the following from my journal may help you decide.

"Day Two: Rewarded after a long haul to the top by a great view of the surrounding hills. Then a sunset, beautiful light. We raced the darkness to the village below. It was slippery. We couldn't see our footing. Everyone stumbled and complained. It seemed dangerous. Aniko, Clay, and I pulled out our flashlights. The four Danes had none.

"It was dark as we pulled into the village of Lahu people. Sith, our guide, meeting with a silhouette under a large thatched-roof house on stilts, motioned us to throw our bags on the bamboo platform and climb the ladder.

"The head of the village and his family greet us. As we join them at the open fire, a girl in a frilly satin blouse and a bright sarong serves tea. Two pantless young boys watch us from behind their squatting father. I cut veggies and peppers while Sith chops bits of pork. Smoke swirls around us and up through the roof. Some local boys bring in six cans of sardines with tomatoes, which Sith curries into a soup. Hungry and tired, we eat rice, curried veggies, and a thick soup without talking.

"After supper, the grandfather lays in the corner on his straw mat. He lights a small kerosene lamp and places a glass globe over it. He then stuffs his pipe with a sticky glob of the regional specialty, opium. Heating it over the globe, he takes a long draw and then puffs a hand-rolled cigarette bursting with tobacco. Children sit around the fire poking it with sticks. We talk. Grandfather puffs.

"Pigs whine and squeal beneath our stilted floor. It's louder than last night and reminds me of a scene out of 'The Ghouls from Hell.' Grandfather motions us to have a puff. I decline. The setting is euphoric enough. The wife sits with a half-opened blouse nursing her baby. Sith gives me a blanket for the night. It's not big enough to double around me, but the fire's coals keep me warm.

"A few hours later, I wake up shivering. The fire's out. Remembering wilderness survival training, I stuff my hiking shorts in the raincoat I'm wearing and over my stomach for warmth. Everyone is asleep except grandfather. His face is dimly lit by the globe, as he sucks on his pipe and gazes into the night. It's quiet—even the pigs, having fought themselves to sleep. A second awakening to the sound of a cock and the smell of coffee and toast. Sith has been cooking. While we eat and talk, he pours two cans of condensed sweetened milk into the big pot of cooking rice and has the Danes taste test. Pouring coconut milk over the top, we dish in. Carbs for the day's walk."

Trekking is roughing it. But there's no better way to experience the quickly disappearing traditional life of Thailand's colorful hill tribes.

For travel specifics, see the Back Door Survival information under Thailand in the Nitty Gritty section.

8. A Swig of Mekong— River Towns of Thailand's Northeast

As I walked out on the balcony, kerosene lanterns were just being lit in the Laotian village across the brown Mekong. The stillness was only broken by the chugging of a small boat heading for Thai immigration.

A few days earlier, fellow travelers wondered why I was going to Chiangkhan. In fact, no one I had met in the previous two months had been or was going there. This in itself recommended and added a spark of adventure to the trip.

Chiangkhan is unpromoted. It doesn't really offer what most travel agents think people want. This small town has one sandy riverside beach, a few small bars, and a usually vacant disco— where the town's two prostitutes hang out.

Here, however, is a chance to experience the Northeast, where the people are among Thailand's friendliest and most traditional. In Chiangkhan, life is slow, and if you're not, you'll miss the subtleties.

Here's a slice of life from my journal:

"November 25, 6:30 a.m., the outdoor market is already winding down. Fruits and vegetables spread on the ground before the saronged women. A more fashionable class of townswomen wander up and down, bargaining for what will become today's meal. For breakfast I dunk donuts into warm sweetened soya milk and munch a grilled rice cake on a stick. The woman behind the grill encourages me with a big smile. A young man, chopping coconuts in the next aisle asks, 'Where you from?' 'Pom ja pai America,' I respond. He smiles, 'Thai . . . you,' and gives me a bold thumbs up.

"The farm women are folding up their blankets and packing their baskets. I buy the few remaining finger bananas from an old lady, leaving her with only a small pile of unsold tobacco.

"Walking back, I pass two round tents in the small park along the river. They are long-handled umbrellas stuck in the ground with an orange cotton screen enclosing each. A monk is hanging his saffron-colored robe out to dry. By one tent an older monk sits talking with a half-dozen elderly Thais who present him their offering of rice, fruit, and vegetables.

"Tired from the early start, I go home to be greeted by the owner of my large teak guest house. His wife is feeding their two young children. From my riverside balcony, I look across the river at the rolling forested hills, read, write a few letters, and see how low I can get my pulse."

Another important aspect of life in Chiangkhan also starts early in the morning when young orange-clad monks with shaven heads file down the streets holding their pots for alms. People stand at their doorways parceling out rice, a little to each monk. In Northeast Thailand, the farmers are quite poor, so many send their boys to the wat (Buddhist temple) for their education. The locals, though poor, freely support the monks. Since most only give rice, if you visit one of the seven local wats with cakes, cookies, or other treats, you'll be a big hit. Check first to see how many monks are there, and bring a little for all.

Chiangkhan has Thailand's hottest and coldest weather. It can freeze in winter. Combine those temperatures with the local cotton, and you'll find blankets. When walking the streets, look through open doors at dollar-a-day women making thick cotton blankets famous throughout Thailand.

November is harvest time. You may be invited to be part of _Ngarn_, which means both work and party. Teams of locals eat, drink, dance, sing . . . and cut rice. Stopping to watch, people in the field yelled and waved me over and handed me a sickle. All laughed at the way I cut the rice. Soon one woman took me on as her intern.

Head up the Mekong on a dugout teak boat equipped with driver and motor. This can be arranged through Rob at Chiangkhan's Nong Sam Guest House. We headed west on the Mekong and up the Mae Nam Hueang, a sleepy tributary that divides Thailand from Laos, enjoying views of thick forested hills of Laos and the riverside gardens of Thailand.

The surrounding area is great to explore. One-speed bikes or small motorbikes can be rented from the Nong Sam Guest House. Fairly flat roads wind though the jutting hills, making pedaling easy. For a short trip, head 3 miles east of town on the main paved road to Kaeng Khut Khu park for a fine Mekong view. In the dry winter season, sandbars emerge and swimming improves.

Food treats abound in Chiangkhan's evening market stalls. _Gai yang_, lightly spiced grilled chicken on a bamboo skewer, is a Northeast specialty. Ask for _khao neeow_, the sticky rice popular around here. Then find the _somtom_ vendor. A woman will shred unripened green papaya into a large wooden bowl. Then come roasted peanuts, small red

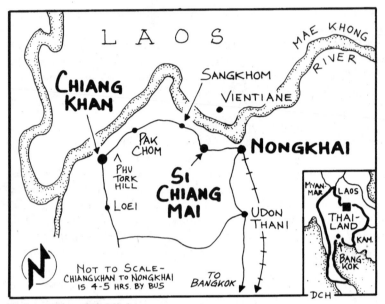

Mekong River Highlights

tomatoes, and two lime halves. Next she'll point to small crabs or potent-smelling fish. Shake your head no at this point, unless you enjoy a risk. Out come "mouse shit" peppers and a questioning look at you. Put up one or two fingers, or let her decide how much fire your mouth can handle. Memorize "Nit noi pric" (just a few chilies). With a large pestle, she blends everything, places it in a plastic bag, and says "Ha baht." Give her the 5 baht. She's impressed. You're giving the local food a try.

Onward Trip Down the Mekong, Chiangkhan to Nongkai—Take a trip east along the Mekong to Nongkai through a land of hilly country-side, small towns, and friendly people. Catch the *songthaew* (small truck) from Chiangkhan to Pak Chom, an hour ride. In Pak Chom, take the 90-minute bus trip to Sangkhom. This relaxing village, with several riverside guest houses (D.D. Guest House and the River Hut are both good) is near the soothing Thanthip waterfalls.

Si Chiangmai is larger but just as visitor-friendly. It's an hour past Sangkhom, across the Mekong from Vientiane, the low-key capital of Laos. From the dusty and drab bus stop neighborhood, follow the signs to the riverside and Tim's Guest House. During the ten-minute walk things cheer up, children shout hello, and people wave.

At the guest house, Daniel, a Swiss man, and his Thai wife, Tim, offer basic but clean rooms, prepare good Thai or Western food, and are helpful with information and arranging excursions.

As in Chiangkhan, this is a place to observe and join in the traditional life. The local Thais and the Vietnamese, who have recently settled here, make a visitor feel welcome. You'll be invited in to watch the process of making spring roll paste, the major source of income. The town is littered with pizza-shaped sheets drying on bamboo screens.

Rent a bike for a quiet riverside pedal. A pleasant Thai temple is a short trip to the west along this road. Stop and say "Sawatdee" (Thai for "hello") to people. The next small road to the right takes you to a sandy river beach with views of Vientiane in Laos.

Take an excursion to Ban Pheu National Park, interesting for its recently excavated temples and dwellings dug into the strange rock formations. These date back over a thousand years. Some may go back four thousand years.

An hour bus ride east from Si Chiangmai is **Nongkhai**, a small city with a French Indochina colonial feel, including baguettes and French pastries. Nongkhai, at the end of the Bangkok rail line, is where you catch the ferry into Laos. There are more than enough budget beds to accommodate its many tourists. Niyana's Guest House, on Meechai Road near Pochai Road, has a few more interesting annex cottages along the river. Sitting on the old veranda, I watched the neighboring Thai family eat, play, and till their garden. Boats moved along the river. In the nearby temple, young monks did their chores. The friendly Niyana staff arranged a monk-run herbal sauna, relaxing inside and out.

Tour the town by bicycle rickshaw or on a rental bike (your guest house has a map). The Chaiya Porn Market (not what it sounds like) on the corner of Meechai and Chaiporn roads is interesting. A small handicraft and jewelry market is at Thasadet ferry pier. The Village Weaver Handicraft Center (on Prajak Road just before Korakarn Road) has handwoven local-style clothes.

Wat Khaek is a Disneyland of Deities (bike, rickshaw, or songthaew 2 miles east of town, just off Highway 212). Since 1978, followers of Luang Pu, a priest who tried to integrate Hinduism and Buddhism, have been building some very large and incredibly strange Buddhist and Hindu figures.

From Nongkhai, trains and buses leave daily to return to Bangkok. Or head into Laos. In 1993, Laos was open to tourists, but an expensive visa (available in Bangkok, hard to get in Nongkai) was needed. Things are changing quickly in Laos, so check with the Laotian embassy (2222 S Street NW, Washington, D.C. 20008). If you can't get a visa there, try the Laotian embassy in Bangkok or one of the travel agencies on Bangkok's Khao San Road. With a visa, you can catch the ferry to Laos and go by taxi to Vientiane, the capital. Depending on who's running the country when you visit, you may be limited to only Vientiane.

Consider biking from Nongkhai to Chiangkhan, or vice versa. The paved road follows the river most of the way, and traffic is sparse. Rent a one-speed, or bring your own. Tim's Guest House in Si Chiangmai may be able to rent bikes for a one-way trip to Chiangkhan (to be returned by bus). American mountain bikers reported that the ride was great on their bikes. (Recommended itinerary: Day 1—Nongkhai to Si Chiangmai, 34 miles; Day 2—Si Chiangmai to Sangkhom, 24 miles; Day 3—Sangkhom to Pak Chom, 36 miles; Day 4—Pak Chom to Chiangkhan, 24 miles. All these places have guest houses.)

For travel specifics, see the Back Door Survival information under Thailand in the Nitty Gritty section.

9. A Beach for Every Dream

Another Monday morning. You wake to the roar of the surf and thin rays of light streaming through the thatched walls of your bungalow. After an early morning swim, breakfast—coffee, toast, and a big bowl of fresh mixed tropical fruit sprinkled with coconut with other travelers at the beachside restaurant. Decisions, decisions . . . to read, write a letter, take a walk on the beach, or lay in the hammock between the palms. It's a walk on the beach, and save the hammock for the afternoon. Hot and hungry, you go home for a blended fruit drink and chicken fried rice. Time for the hammock. The Aussie got it first, so it's letter-writing time. A warm breeze and rustling palms talk you into a nap. Aussie still in the hammock, a woven mat on the sand is good enough. Later the English chap two bungalows away reminds you it's time to join the others for the sunset. Inner silence, surging sea, infinite horizon of color, hunger. The group heads for supper. Fresh fish from the reef, rice, and cooked mixed vegetables. The Danish couple at the next table pass around the Mekong whiskey. The Frenchman says this island is his favorite, but the young New Zealand woman knows of a beach with better snorkeling. This day seems pretty much like the last, and tomorrow will probably be about the same. That's life off the road in Thailand.

If you have never been to a Thai beach, then any would seem like paradise—squeaky white sand, clear water, good food, Thai hospitality. But in Thailand you have your choice of paradises. One with nightlife or with quiet, day and night? Primitive, luxury, or somewhere in the middle? Here's a quick rundown.

East Coast Islands

Ko Samui (Ko means island in Thai) once laid back, is now Thailand's prime beach target. Each of its many beaches is unique. Chaweng Beach on the west end is the prettiest, with the most tourists, bars, discos, and prostitutes. There are a variety of lodgings, cheap to steep.

Mae-nam Beach in the north has less tourists, less nightlife, and less beach. We like Mae-nam for the quiet and ride the songthaews (truck taxis) to Chaweng for the white sand. The island is circled by a paved road, and most guest houses rent motorbikes. For something really peaceful, try a ten-day meditation retreat at the Buddhist wat (temple) Pang Bua at Rawaeng Beach. Retreats are at the beginning of April, July, and November. Contact Acharn Poh at the wat.

Ko Phangan is less touristed than Ko Samui. The rocky beaches in the north end are especially quiet. You can stay in the nearby fishing village. The west end of the island has the better beaches with more people and bungalows. In the south, near the port town, there are a few bungalows and a nothing special beach.

Ko Tao, a little-touristed island to the north of Ko Phangan, is a place to really experience the relaxed island life.

Ko Samet, the most accessible island from Bangkok, is busy on the weekends with city day-trippers but quieter during the weekdays than many of the islands. Ko Samet has fine beaches and bungalows.

Ko Chang, close to Cambodia and off the beaten path, is unspoiled. It's destined to become another Ko Samui, lined with bungalows. Head for Mae Bae Beach. As with the other islands, some beaches are quieter than others. We hope you'll get there before the masses discover it.

West Coast Islands and Beaches

Ko Phuket spells entertainment. Busy bars, discos, and movies keep Phuket town and some of the island's beaches throbbing late into the night. This, with its many pretty beaches, clear water, fine range of accommodations, and international airport attracts everyone—from vagabonds to package tour groups to jet-setters.

Ko Phi Phi, a very pretty island with plenty of bungalows, is also a national park. It's popular with day tours from Phuket and Krabi, but those who settle in are glad they did.

Krabi, a town on the mainland west of Phuket island, is surrounded by good beaches. The area is popular, but you can still find your own quiet beach, like Phra Nang (accessible only by boat from Krabi).

All of the above islands have been discovered, so deserted beaches are rare. But part of the area's beauty is an opportunity to meet other international travelers as well as Thais. Whether you crave a disco at the beach or only the sound of the surf, there's a place for you.

These days, most beach bungalows show videos in their restaurants at night, so you may have to walk down the beach to sit under the moon in silence. We pick an individual bungalow away from the restaurant or a place that doesn't show videos. There were some on the north beaches of Ko Phangan, on Ko Tao, and Ko Chang.

For travel specifics, see the Back Door Survival information under Thailand in the Nitty Gritty section.

MALAYSIA

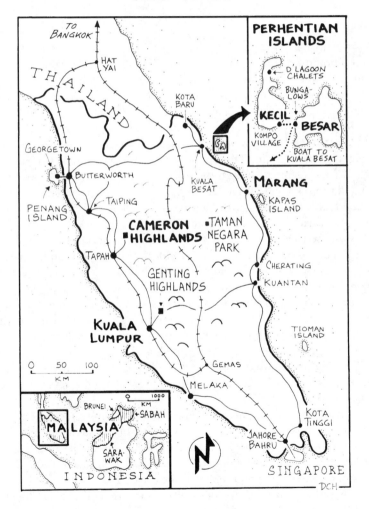

10. Cameron Highlands— Jungle Walks for the Faint of Heart

Jim Thompson, the legendary Thai silk tycoon, disappeared in the jungles of the Cameron Highlands years ago. Search parties and huge rewards couldn't bring him back. The Cameron Highlands became more than just a place to beat the heat of the coast, play golf, and walk in the forest. It was a place of mystery and adventure.

As I told the Jim Thompson story to Georgina, a British traveler, her eyes got big. "Jim Thompson!" she said, "I saw him. I mean . . . when I was coming through the jungle interior on the train, we came to a stop in a small village. A older English fellow came on the platform, handed his card through the window, and walked away. I don't have the card now, but I'm certain it said Jim Thompson."

Most travelers, however, visit these highlands not to search for poor old Jim but to commune with this wonderful chunk of Asian nature.

"A plateau with gentle slopes shut in by loftier mountains, which, from the plateau's elevation of 4,500 feet, appear comparatively low," reported William Cameron in his 1885 British government survey. Since this time, the highlands have become a popular resort for the locals as well as a national park. There are several small towns on the plateau, a golf course, a few resort hotels and tea plantations.

The highlands are not really off the beaten path. But they offer a beautiful setting, friendly locals, pleasant walks, a cool climate, and an enjoyable stay.

Tanah Rata, fairly quiet and sitting among the forested hills alongside a stream, is the most pleasant town. The main road, lined by small hotels, shops, and restaurants, quickly gives way to nature and a number of the jungle walks. On occasion, a small night market with food vendors, games, and goods enlivens the evening.

The restaurants offer inexpensive and tasty Indian, Malay, Chinese, and Western food. The adjoining Indian restaurants, the Kuman and the Thanam, are especially good. The *murtabak*, a pancake-thin pastry stuffed with vegetables and chicken, was good and cheap. The clay pot rice bowls are also tasty. The local breakfast roti is a light pancake stuffed as you like with egg, banana, jam, or any combination.

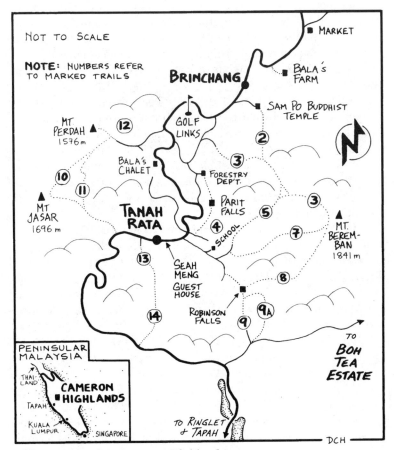

NOT TO SCALE

NOTE: NUMBERS REFER TO MARKED TRAILS

Walks in Malaysia's Cameron Highlands

Well-marked (in English) trails of all difficulties start near Tanah Rata. Rough hotel maps will lead you, not always accurately, through forest and thick jungles. Hike smart with raingear, flashlight, basic first aid kit, water, and food. Sneakers are good enough. Sandals will cause blisters. It's not wise to hike alone. Here are some sample hikes.

Tanah Rata to Boh Tea Plantation (Walking time: 2.5 hr., easy downhill 1.5 hr., then gentle uphill along a road for 1 hr., or catch the bus. Return by bus.)—Up the main road just past town take a right on the first road going toward the playground and school (Persiaran Dayang Endah Road). Past the school at the end of the road, turn left across a small bridge and walk 500 yards to Robinson Waterfalls (path

9). After the falls, stay to the left on path 9A. Don't go through the gate at the fence. A nice gradual trail descends through forest into the farmland below. From town, it takes 90 minutes to reach the farms and the road below. Go left up the paved road through farmland for one hour to the Boh Tea Estates. With luck or planning, you can catch a bus to the Estates coming from the town of Ringlet. There are four buses a day (check the schedule at your hotel or the Tanah Rata bus station).

The groomed hillsides of the Boh Tea Estates, the largest in Malaysia, are dotted by hardworking tea-pickers. Tours of the tea drying and sorting plant are available any time between 10:00 a.m. and 5:00 p.m. (closed Sunday or Monday, call 05/996032 to check).

You can ride the bus from Boh Tea Estates back into Tanah Rata. Take the bus from Boh down to the junction of the Ringlet–Tanah Rata road. At the junction, wait in the small restaurant for the hourly bus going to Tanah Rata.

Tanah Rata to Gunong (Mount) Jasar and Return (Walking time: 2 hr. if you skip the mountain summit. Fairly level walk. Going to summit adds a steep 30 minutes.)—Walk 10 minutes out of town toward Ringlet. Turn right at Highland Villas and go past the Oly apartments. The start of path 10 and 11 (combined at the beginning) is marked here. A stirring chorus of birds and insects serenade you along the clear and level path through the rain forest. After 1.5 miles (1 hr.), path 10 makes a side trip (to the left) up and over Gunong Jasar (5,365 ft.) and back to path 11. For the easy route back (1 hr.), skip this detour and continue on path 11. Later, both paths join path 12. At path 12, go right and onto a dirt road (not far from Hilltop Bungalow). Stay to the right at all forks on the dirt road to get back to town. Without a local map, these directions should get you wonderfully lost.

Tanah Rata to Gunong Beremban to Sam Poh Buddhist Temple (Walking time: 4 hr. of steep ups and downs. Return by bus or taxi.)— This more adventurous path is confusing, steep and slippery when wet. It's your chance in a lifetime to swing on vines like Tarzan (at least like Tarzan outtakes when the vines broke).

Path 8 is steeper and more confusing than number 7. At the edge of town, off the main road, take the first right going toward the playground and school (Persiaran Dayang Endah Road). Then turn left and cross a bridge 200 yards beyond the school to the Malaysia Agriculture Research and Development Institute (MARDI). Behind MARDI, follow the sign for path 7. The jungle is interesting along the 1.5-mile moderately steep trail. The view from the top of Gunong Beremban (6,041 ft.) is basically nearby jungle foliage. Return the way you came. You can return via the Sam Poh Buddhist temple (on path

3, then 2, then 5) just outside the town of Brinchang. From the temple, walk the half mile to Brinchang to catch a bus or taxi back to Tanah Rata.

For travel specifics, see Back Door Survival information under Malaysia in the Nitty Gritty section.

11. Marang—Hooked on a Malaysian Fishing Village

At the edge of town the sign read, "Warning—Achtung. No bikinis. No beer. No kissing and cuddling. Please. Try to live in a Malay Community. Don't force us to do something bad." Marang is a somewhat conservative Moslem town, sitting next to a beautiful beach where foreigners came for the reasons listed in the warning. A young Moslem man in shorts and a striped beach shirt was hammering the sign back into position. "What is the something bad?" I asked. "Maybe shouting, maybe fighting," he said. "We getting mad. People see sign, but still come to Marang and do these things. O.K. at beach, not town."

Marang is a worth a visit. If you abide by Moslem custom, the people in town are friendly enough. Outside of one door was even a sign, "Free room. Tourists welcome." Nice offer (assuming this wasn't a trap where you would be sacrificed for the sins of those who had cuddled in the streets).

Visit the nearby fishing village, a five-minute walk toward the sea on the beachside road. Between the palms, a cluster of wooden houses with corrugated rusting roofs rise above the sand on stilts. Saronged, barefoot fishermen play cards or sleep in the shade. A few painted wooden boats list in the inlet mud, waiting for the evening tide and the night's fishing. Children draw lines in the sand and play a game like four square. Women, ankle-deep in the inlet mud, scrub white shirts.

From my journal: "I watched several men raking about thirty yards offshore, surf breaking over their fully clothed bodies. One waved me out. I felt a bit underdressed wearing only my swim trunks but joined them. 'You try,' he said, handing me the rake. He pointed to the clams he had in his basket. I pulled the rake, and he stopped me to reposition the handle on my shoulder. I soon struck something in the sand, bent over, and was knocked down by the next wave. I came up with a rock. After fifteen futile minutes, I finally raked one in. 'I bring two rakes tomorrow,' he said, seeing my delight and handing me a couple of clams. 'I come here everyday after work in town. Food for my family.'"

Marang has a long stretch of gold sand, palm trees, and few people. The clean water and calm surf make for good swimming. Single women in bathing suits may be harassed by the local boys. Cover up in a sarong, or go to the beach with a male traveler from your guest house. Swimsuits are okay on the beach but not in town.

For a more remote, undeveloped (and hassle-free) beach, take the daily 30-minute boat ride to Kapas Island, which offers good beaches, interesting coral for snorkeling, and a selection of budget sleeps and eats. You can simply catch the midmorning ferry or book a trip through your guest house ($10 for the day with snorkeling).

For travel specifics, see Back Door Survival information under Malaysia in the Nitty Gritty section.

12. The Perhentian Islands—Rats in Paradise

From the journal (evening reflections on Perhentian Island): "Light beams across the water from the village. Fishing boats on the horizon. A quarter moon breaks through a patch in the billowing clouds. Palm trees silhouetted. A sun-warmed rock contrasts the evening cool. Monkeys chatter from the trees. Poetry swinging all around."

Hearing the young travelers across the bus aisle buzz about Malaysian beaches, I was direct. "I'm looking for the perfect island— beautiful white sand, clear waters, no roads, jungle, quiet, friendly locals, good snorkeling, and a few interesting travelers to talk with." One women paused to reflect. "We've been to most places along the East Coast, and there's one place— the Perhentian islands. That's paradise . . . at least until somebody puts it in a guidebook." Ha!

Two days later, as my boat neared the islands, I was elated. It looked like not one but two paradises. Near the island of Perhentian Besar (big) lay Perhentian Kecil (small).

Staying on Perhentian Besar confirmed my initial impression— wonderful. The mainland ferry stops on the west side at a white sand beach where most of the bungalows and restaurants are. From this beach, you can walk on paths (there are no roads) to more deserted ones or into the surrounding hillside jungle. The beach bungalows organize daily boat trips around the island for excellent clear water snorkeling. There's particularly good snorkeling on the west side near the island's one beach resort. The bungalows rent kayaks and snorkeling gear.

Check out Kompo, the fishing village a quarter mile away on the small island, Perhentian Kecil. I accompanied Yee, the owner of Coco-hut Bungalows, on his daily shopping trip there. Wandering alone through the cluster of houses and shacks, I enjoyed a warm welcome but found no English spoken. They lit up when I spoke the little Malay I knew. Yee and I met, bought some *pisang goreng* (fried bananas) and sat in a small *kedai kopi* (coffee shop) with a number of fishermen. Most were playing cards, others chatting on the small thatched deck next to the restaurant. The older men were topless, turbaned, and wrapped in sarongs. The younger men were in trousers and T-shirts. Fishing at night, relaxing during the day . . . hooked on a Malaysian fishing village.

Beach life on Malaysia's Perhentian Islands

A five-foot-long Besar sea turtle swam with us as we returned to the big island. The giant turtles come to shore to lay eggs at night around September. To see them, you either have to take turns at guard with a flashlight or pay someone else. Unlike humans, the turtles don't mind people watching as they dig a hole in the sand and deposit their eggs. They probably do mind someone picking up their eggs (which is illegal) or hopping on their backs as they trudge toward the sea (which is stupid). Beat up anybody you see doing this.

For an even quieter spot, take a small motorboat to one of the small beaches on the small island. On the northeast end of the island, miles from the fishing village, you'll find a small cove, surf, jungle, and the D'Lagoon Chalet and Restaurant. The tiny beach is cluttered with painful coral. You can swim comfortably and float through a colorful world of coral from a nearby anchored raft. There are dog-eating clams and psychedelic fish. If that's not exciting enough, you may spy a man-sized turtle or a stray barracuda or shark. (Locals claim there's no danger of being attacked. But watch out for the clam.)

D'Lagoon Chalet, a few basic thatched bungalows on stilts with kerosene lanterns and a thatched restaurant, is run by a "real" character named Razak. His menu is dictated by the skills of the current cook. You can borrow snorkeling gear or arrange a fishing expedition. Ask Razak to tell stories of his three years with aborigines in the central jungles of Malaysia.

The local animal life adds to the remote feel of this place. Five-foot lizards lay in the brush waiting for their next meal. There are even a few pleasant-looking rats that sneak around the bungalows. (One evening in the restaurant, Gerrit and Klasina, a Dutch couple pondered the question, "Are there rats in paradise?")

Turtle Beach is a ten-minute jungle walk across this narrow neck of the island. The rocky beach offers good snorkeling in the nearby coral. While no turtles visited, I did see some walking fish climb the rocks with their fins to feed on stranded algae.

For travel specifics, see Back Door Survival information under Malaysia in the Nitty Gritty section.

MYANMAR (formerly Burma)

13. Only Travelers Exit the Black Hole

Burma now calls itself Myanmar. The name may be new, but the country still spells mystique to travelers and oppression to its people. Its socialist-military government has restricted everything from trade and travel to democracy since the 1950s. The country stands still. Little comes, little goes. It's a black hole.

Tourist visas are limited to fourteen days with no renewals. The leaders don't need Westerners kicking around democratic ideals with the locals. "Just spend your money and get out." Current problems have forced many university students into the jungles with the rebellious tribes. Even monks are agitated.

Bob was in Myanmar during an uprising: "As I rode in the taxi, yesterday's strife was apparent. A few gawkers wandered the streets surveying the damage. The cautious stayed inside. Trees lay across the street—impromptu tank barriers. Power lines were down.

"I saw the demonstrations start just a few days before in the small town of Pagan. The small group of Burmese, charged and chattering, grew into a large force by the time it reached town. Farmers, students, shopkeepers, government workers, the young— their energy was contagious and kept peaceful. They wanted democracy, to be free of torture, to make a decent living.

"Rangoon's huge demonstrations were also peaceful. Tens of thousands gathered and grew until the government felt threatened. The foreign press was escorted out of the country. Foreigners were moved outside the city to make way for troops and tanks. The leaders ordered the troops to open fire on the crowd. Thousands of peaceful demonstrators died.

"The cabbie wanted me to see. At the hospital, flowers marked the spot where a doctor and nurse were gunned down as they worked. A young man lay in bed with his leg blown off. An old woman rested, shot through the shoulder. The driver said, 'Buddhist ideals prevented local retaliation. The people were defeated now, but change would come—leaders die, new ones are born.'"

Travelers wonder if it's "politically correct" (and safe) to visit a country such as Myanmar (or China) where the government is repressive. These governments don't appreciate the "international presence," but the locals do. Your visit is important. The people need contact with the West and welcome a chance to talk. As for safety, chances are slim you'd be near any violence. The government is careful to keep foreigners safe and, if there is unrest, out of harm's way. Tourists have never been allowed in the wartorn jungles of the northeast, and in particularly troubled times, Myanmar closes its doors to tourists altogether.

Currently, to get a visa, you must go on a "tour." This can be "a tour of one" where hotels and transportation are prepaid, but you're on your own. Many traveler's take advantage of a loophole. They pay for a three-day package, then spend the rest of their fourteen days entirely on their own. This means coordinating hotels and transportation on your own with the Myanmar Travel and Tours (formerly Tourist Burma) Office. At times, the $5-a-night guest houses are allowed to operate. At others, you're restricted to officially sanctioned $20-per-double hotels. Away from Rangoon, things relax, and you may be able to deal directly with the hotel or guest house.

While you can arrange a tour from the U.S.A., Myanmar tour prices are cheapest when arranged in Bangkok (from agencies along Khao San Road in the Banglampoo area). A four-day on-your-own tour including visa, hotels, ground transport, and round-trip airfare from Bangkok, costs about $550; an eight-day program, around $700. About $250 of that is for the round-trip Thai International flight (Bangkok to Rangoon three times a week). Allow five days to process your visa in Bangkok. Consider this basic tour program: 1st night— Rangoon (renamed Yangon); 2nd night—train to Mandalay; 3rd and 4th night—Mandalay; 5th night— Bus to Pagan; 6th and 7th night— Pagan; 8th night—bus to Rangoon.

You can't see it all in fourteen days. Land transport is slow and grueling. Flights are finicky. Get reservations early as trains and planes book quickly. Frightening as Myanmar Airways is, we fly as much as possible to save time.

A good guidebook is essential. Lonely Planet's *Burma: A Travel Survival Kit* and Apa Productions' *Insight Guide: Burma* are best. The situation constantly changes in Burma, I mean Myanmar. So consult a knowledgeable travel agent in the U.S., check with the Burmese Tourist Information Office (see Appendix), and talk with other travelers and travel agents in Bangkok. Thankfully, the Burmese people are more gracious and gentler than their government.

Since the only way into Myanmar is by air, you'll start your visit in Rangoon. As you leave the airport, you'll be greeted by a chorus singing, "Change money?" You'll hear this in your taxi, at the entrance to your hotel, and through the stall of the toilet.

The black market gives ten times the official rate. Remember, it's hard to blow black market windfalls. You must pay for hotels, planes, and trains with officially changed money (noted on your currency declaration form). For meals, taxis, and souvenirs, you're on the honor system. Some travelers bring cigarettes (the 555 brand is a local favorite), cosmetics, whiskey, Walkmans, and other Western goods to barter or to sell at 1,000% margins.

Rangoon's charm lies in the fact that it's much the same as when the British left it in the 1940s. Crumbling buildings, vintage taxis, street vendors, and as much pollution as industry—almost none.

Rangoon is slow. Tour it that way. Walk a block from the hotel and rest at a tea shop. Soon a university student will wander over and offer to buy tea. Students have plenty of idle time; the government routinely closes schools at any sign of unrest. Politics is the leading topic of conversation in the capital.

Ride a bicycle rickshaw to the Shwedagon Pagoda, the most sacred temple in this very Buddhist country. This gold-plated, gem-studded stupa towers over the city. Buy some gold leaf (paper-thin and dirt-cheap) as you ascend the covered steps to the pagoda platform, and contribute to the sacred wealth by pasting it on a stupa. Another

The Wonder Monk of Myanmar

impressive but often-missed sight is the 230-foot-long lounging Buddha at the Chauk Htat Gyi Pagoda (on Shwegondine Road, near the Shwedagon Pagoda).

Take your taste buds on a tour of the local cuisine. Try the Burmese staple, _ngapi_ (a heavily spiced and highly pungent fish or shrimp paste), _mohinga_ (a fish soup with rice noodles), and _kaukswe_ (chicken and noodles in coconut milk). And no visit is complete without a belly full of fried grasshoppers.

On arrival in Rangoon, book your plane or train onward. Tickets go fast. Those who decide to suffer with the masses in third class do.

The deserted city of **Pagan** is Myanmar's most remarkable sight. Pagan was the center of Burmese (and Buddhist) culture from the eleventh to the thirteenth century. During this period, its kings built thousands of temples and pagodas—only to see most of them destroyed when Kublai Khan invaded in 1287. Despite decay and a major 1975 earthquake, hundreds of shrines are in decent shape, and the top temples have been restored.

Tour the temples by horse-drawn cart (_tonga_) or rental bike. Find relief from the midday sun in the cool vaults of the towering white Ananda Temple. Climb to the top of Thatbinnyu Temple to watch the sun set the great plains on fire before it dips into the muddy Irrawaddy River.

If you're into body parts, the Shwezigon Pagoda near the village of Nyaung U houses a number of relics, including Buddha's collarbone. The young monks at the monastery next door, starved for entertainment, enjoyed my impromptu harmonica concert.

The colorful Burmese lacquer ware in Pagan offers great sport for hagglers. The small workshops offer the best prices. Even it you don't buy, hang around to watch and talk with the craftspeople.

Pagan's many shrines are well explained in the government-produced "Guide to Pagan" and in the Lonely Planet and Apa Guides to Burma. Respectfully wear long pants or dresses, remove your shoes before entering any religious place, and tour the shrines by walking in a clockwise direction.

For an escape from the heat of the lowlands and a chance to see colorful ethnic tribes—complete with a village on stilts and floating gardens—head for **Inle Lake**. The small town of Yaunghwe, on the north end of the lake, is the handiest place to stay and a good place to experience Burmese life. Start your day by giving rice or treats to boy monks making their daily ration rounds.

Arrange a boat tour to Ywama, a village on stilts. Try to hit the floating market (here every fifth day). On the way you'll pass floating gardens growing from a layer of mud on floating reed mats and fishermen whose legs do the rowing so they can fling bamboo fish traps.

At the floating market in Ywama, drift among a tangle of boats filled with hill tribe people and their produce. Old women puffing long pipes or chomping huge cigars sell tobacco and other more interesting smokeables. Colorful turbaned men and women shove bananas at you. Toss out a price, and let the haggling begin.

Inle is most easily reached by flying from Pagan, Mandalay, or Rangoon. From Rangoon, it's 18 hours of train and truck travel (connection in Thazi). From Pagan and Mandalay, it's a ten-hour Datsun ride.

Maymyo, a former British hill station, worth a visit if you have time after Pagan and Inle, is an enjoyable three-hour jeep ride from Mandalay into the hills of the Shan Plateau. Maymyo will take you back in the colonial days. The Candacraig, now the Maymyo Government Rest House, will provide a faded memory of the English country house. Picnic and meet Burmese travelers at Maymyo's botanical garden. Get around on small horse-drawn taxis.

Cruising for a picnic on Inle Lake's floating market

INDIA

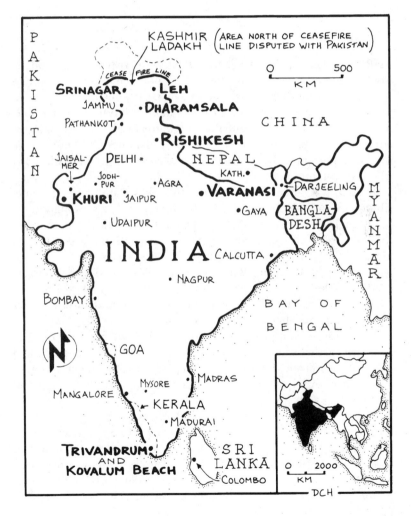

14. Intense India

As Rick picked up his ticket to Bombay, his travel agent said he wouldn't go to India if you paid him. But India is our favorite country. India enchants or disgusts—depending on what you're looking for.

No country is more diverse or offers more cultural thrills per mile, minute, and dollar. While India has a few great sights, its real fans are attracted by its basic day-to-day life—its "Indian-ness." Where you go isn't as important as how you go. The magic of India shines brightly wherever you find her people.

India is a strange mix of leaving this planet and coming home. Things are radically but nonchalantly different. It's disarmingly "normal": English is India's language of travel, India's rail system is one of the most extensive on earth (left by the British), and a boy named Shiva will serve tea, toast, and marmalade for breakfast.

And it's very different. Bankers and beggars eat with their fingers off disposable banana leaf plates. Many street scenes look like the zoo escaped. Classical musicians play rhythms that would thrill any jazz fan. And time has almost nothing to do with money.

If you approach it properly, travel in India is intense but easy. The language barrier is minimal. While India is as diverse linguistically and culturally as Europe, English is the language of government, business, and tourism. After a few weeks you may even develop an accent and start bobbing your head.

The British heritage is evident in India's passion for signs. In museums, displays are protected by signs saying, "Keep yourself away." Hotels entice the visitor with welcome signs reading, "Please Get Here" and provide service with a flair: "The flattening of underwear with pleasure is the job of the chambermaid." Many copycat businesses do their best, but some—like Bangalore's "Kentacky Fried Chicken"—fall short of perfection.

India is one of the cheapest countries on earth, but its intensity makes occasional splurging for first-class rooms, meals, and transporta-

Dipping into the Taj Mahal

tion a necessity for many. Even so, you'll find it easy on the pocket-book. Plan on spending $2 to $10 a night for sleepable hotels and $1 to $5 for restaurant meals. Bus and train rides are slow but cost under a dollar an hour. India's almost endless supply of workers has driven the cost of labor to ridiculous lows. While we Americans look at time as a commodity to save, spend, waste, or invest, Indians have a different perspective. Labor-intensive treats—massage, bicycle rickshaw joyriding, and having the chambermaid do your laundry—are a cheap and fun part of travel in India. We see these "treats" as employing (rather than taking advantage of) a hard and eager worker.

India's wonderful cuisine varies from state to state. Try regional specialties. We eat better by going vegetarian in the south. The curries aren't as fiery as many fear. Splurge royally at least once in each state. Ten dollars buys the best meal in town, and that memory is an easy-to-pack souvenir. Go local, be adventurous, let new friends help you out. If you eat with your hands—the norm in India—wash at the sink that every restaurant provides before you use the five-fingered fork God gave you.

While accommodations in India can be dirt cheap, most travelers feel more comfortable staying in midrange $8 to $15 per double hotels. We've never used or needed reservations. We simply catch a rickshaw from the station to a guidebook's or traveler's best recommendation. Don't miss the opportunity to sleep in one of the many maharajah's palaces that now make aristocratic ends meet by doubling as hotels. India also has some wonderful British-style hotels left over from the colonial days.

Transportation is the bugaboo of many Indian trips. We solve the frustrating problem of sold-out trains and planes by, when necessary, letting the available departures dictate our major transportation needs and shape our itinerary. For smaller connections, reserve bus or train seats as soon as you get into town. India's cheap but sometimes scary bus system has rides going just about everywhere all the time. And with a day's notice, tickets are easy to get. We use•buses for any ride shorter than five hours. The trains—cheap, more comfortable than buses, but slower—are best for medium to long rides (4 to 20 hours). They're often booked long in advance. Our Nitty Gritty section at the end of the book explains how to break into the "quota" system for last-minute tickets. Flying is a great value. Flights will cost you from $30 to about $150. Reservations can be difficult. Make several as far in advance as you can in one tedious sitting at a big-city Indian Airlines office.

The joy of India is in getting beyond its basically mediocre sights. Make friends, get caught up in the local news, joyride in bicycle rickshaws, go to political rallies and concerts, and talk to students at universities. Indian zoos are great for people- as well as animal-watching.

A Hindi movie is another Indian treat. The theaters are the domain of the young crowd. Your hotel receptionist can direct you to the hottest Hindi film. They are so melodramatic, you'll have no trouble enjoying the show—even in Hindi. The plots are generally variations on a Romeo and Juliet theme broken with musical interludes. India's cinema is its MTV, featuring the country's hottest heartthrobs singing India's top hits. Swooning is a big part of Indian moviegoing. Romance runs rampant but rarely gets beyond longing looks. Sex is normally only implied, but the hinting can get wonderfully heated. Not long ago, Indian filmgoers enjoyed their first screen kiss—quite a sensation. Don't miss an Indian movie, and be sure it's in Hindi. The hottest shows are usually sold out, but a tourist will nearly always attract a scalper, and even those prices are cheap.

15. Varanasi and the Ganges—Holy Water, Batman

Along the banks of the Ganges, sacred cows wander, eating garbage. Hindu holy men, *sadhus*, sit erect in the lotus position on the riverside steps (*ghat*). Facing the rising sun, they chant prayers. Some are half-naked with long matted hair. Others are wrapped in orange or bright white cotton. Young boys chase each other. Men stretch out fifty-foot-long strands of silk and individually separate them for weaving saris. A young man in Western-style trousers and shirt scoops out chai (tea) from a continuously boiling pot. His open-front tea shop, the size of three phone booths, is stocked with cookies, cigarettes, and candy. Sitting on the wooden bench in front, several men talk excitedly. A gaggle of women stand in the water, beating their dirty laundry against the steps and building a rainbow mosaic of drying clothes. Men, young and old, bathe nearly naked in the river.

Along the riverbank, several bodies, wrapped in cloth from the head down, wait their turn on the funeral pyre. A family sits on the ground next to one body in flames. Feet stick out of the smoke. A priest doubles them back onto the body to burn. Behind this ghat, a new electric crematory stands above the river, a government attempt to clean up the Ganges. Not all can afford to buy enough wood for a thorough cremation, so partially burned bodies are tossed into the river. The priests, making their living off the traditional method, warn people that salvation requires a wood-burning fire.

Varanasi shines a brutal light on Indian life. Everything is on display. In our world, things are properly contained and controlled: bathing in tubs, cows behind fences, people in houses, kids in car seats, music digitalized, and dead bodies in funeral homes. In Varanasi, reality wields a crowbar. Life is beyond our control. This is scary. Nagging waves of death lap at our feet on the banks of the Ganges. Some travel thousands of miles to peep at India and find themselves.

Over 2,000 years ago, people started coming to Varanasi, also called Benares, for their spiritual and practical learning. It's still one of the

Pilgrims cleansing their sins in the Ganges

most important Hindu pilgrimage spots and an educational and cultural center as well. For a Hindu, the holiest way to go is to be cremated here and have one's ashes tossed in the Ganges. And bathing in the river removes sins. Others come here to study at the schools and universities dedicated to classical language, music, and arts.

"Benares is to the Indian the rough equivalent of Rome to the Christian, with an intensity and transcendence which Rome may have had but has lost," writes Edward Rice in "The Ganges: A Personal Encounter." For the Hindu pilgrim, Benares is not just a city, and the Ganges not just a river. The city was called Kashi, "that which illumines," and is known as "the resplendent city of Shiva," with this god's most sacred temples. Looking at the universe symbolically—as a human body—Kashi is the head, where knowledge dwells, and thus the center of Hindu studies. And Benares is where the three arteries of this symbolic universal body meet. These arteries are the three forms of the Ganges: the visible river, the celestial Ganges (the Milky Way), and the Underworld Ganges.

"It is understood, throughout India, that Ganges water is pure. No matter how muddy, dirty, and refuse-strewn the river may seem to be, her waters bear no disease or germs and are considered clean. Locals safely bathe in the Ganges, wash in her, and drink her water without fear of getting sick."

The Ghats—The bank of the river is where to find it, whatever you're looking for. The areas where steps lead down to the water are

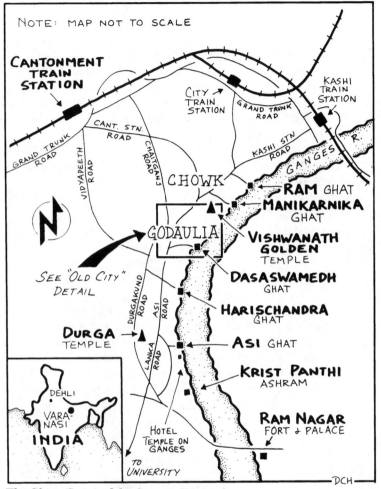

The Ghats (Steps) of the Ganges, Varanasi

called ghats. Each of the many ghats are a bit different. You'll witness weddings, bathing, meditation, clothes washing, death, martial arts, and play . . . simultaneously. There's no better place to observe India in all its intensity.

Acclimatize slowly by starting upstream at the **Asi Ghat**. Take a rickshaw here from anywhere in the city. The drivers know all the ghats. This ghat, near the Benares Hindu University in the south of the city, is relatively quiet and undeveloped. It's the first of five ghats in which pilgrims bathe. Since there's more open space, it's also popular for wedding parties. People pack into rowboats with a brass band and head across the river.

Walk upstream. "Boat, ten rupees," will ring out from men next to wooden boats lining the banks. Temples and old stone buildings tower over the river. A fifteen-minute walk (allow an hour) brings you to **Harischandra Ghat**, busy with fires and cremations. It's fine to sit and watch, but taking pictures wears out your welcome in a flash.

Another fifteen minutes brings you to the **Dasaswamedh Ghat**, the central, most visited, and first essential ghat. A quick tour of the ghats should start here. A busy street market leads to it. Each morning this ghat is packed with bathing pilgrims.

At the **Manikarnika Ghat**, ten more minutes upstream, climb the steps to a concrete deck with a grand river view. This ghat is the main area for cremations.

The Ganges—Everyone cruises the Ganges. Don't miss this experience. Hire a boat for a sunrise and sunset cruise.

Sunrise is the cleansing time. Pilgrims bath to cleanse their sins. Laundry wallahs come to beat clothes on the rocks with a force that demolishes shirts after a few cleanings. Meditators chant inward to their god while waiting for the morning light. The views are best from a boat.

Sunset is quieter. Watch the large red sun sink behind the old buildings and temples that line the river from a boat. Consider crossing the river to the Ramnagar Fort in the late afternoon and returning as the sun sets. This fortress, home of the maharajah of Benares, is in bad condition. Its museum is mediocre, but the sunset isn't.

Men with wooden rowboats compete for your business at all the ghats. Prices are inflated. Bargain hard. An hour boat ride should cost around $1 or $2 for the boat, not per person. The ride from Asi Ghat to Ramnagar Fort is about $2 or $3 for the boat, from ghats farther downstream a bit more.

The Temples—As you tour the ghats, squeeze in a few temples. From Asi Ghat, walk twenty minutes to the **Durga Temple**, also called the Monkey Temple. Although small, it's one of the most famous in Varanasi. Since the eighteenth century, it's been the home to the goddess Durga and to many monkeys. Varanasi reveres the god Shiva. Durga is the destructive side of his beautiful consort, Parvati. In Hindu philosophy, there are two sides to everything. That includes the seemingly playful monkeys. They have a passion for grabbing tourist's glasses.

While visiting the Manikarnika Ghat, head to Lord Shiva's famous **Golden Temple**, also called the Vishwanath temple. Shiva, the god of destruction, destroys ignorance, greed, and lawyers. He also does a lot of reproducing. You'll see his phallic representations (Shiva lingams) being worshiped under a ton of gold.

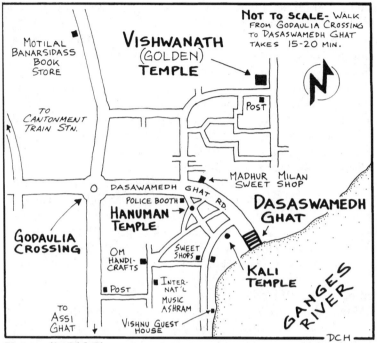

Varanasi's Old City

Follow a Cow—Cows are travel gurus. Be one. Meander slowly with them through the small streets and alleys. They frequently stop, stare, and browse. They aren't intimidated by crowds or rickshaws. They could care less how fast the rest of the world is moving. Since the cow is sacred to the Hindu, the crowds part as they come through. Even buses give cows (and tourists drafting behind them) the right of way.

The best place for being a cow is just above the Dasaswamedh Ghat. As you head toward the ghat on Dasaswamedh Road, you'll come to the street market just before the steps of the ghat. Wander right or left. It's all the same in this oldest part of the city. Wind through lanes too narrow even for rickshaws, with traffic jams of people and cows who wish their horns could honk. You'll get lost, but just ask for one of the ghats or say "Ganga." Someone will point you back toward the river.

If cows are too fast, sit yourself in a chai stall and watch the river of Indian life meander by. (Try the Madhur Milan Café on Dasaswamedh Road between the ghat and Godaulia Circle.) With your chai, try some of Varanasi's famous sweets. The fudgelike cashew burfi is made from boiled milk, sugar, and nuts.

Silk seekers enjoy Varanasi. Often woven with fine silver and gold strands, Varanasi silk is near and dear to the wealthy Indian's heart.

The friendly "Hello, where are you from" on the street invariably leads to "My brother has a shop with silk . . . the best price for you." Experience at least one shop. You'll be taken down a narrow back street, into a small shop, seated on a floor cushion, and served chai. The owner will ask you about you, your family, and your country. Yes, he'll have a brother or cousin living very near you . . . in New York City. Next comes the silk saris, the wraparound dress of Indian women. Eighteen-foot party favors of color are shot out one after the other. The shop owner watches for something that catches your eye before he stops. If nothing catches your eye, all of his shop will be at your feet.

Krist Panthi Ashram—A visit with Father Francis at this ashram is inspiring. A Dutch missionary for a Catholic relief organization, he's been working on local housing, education, and health problems here for eleven years by providing long-term loans. This alternative to charity allows the people to maintain their self-respect. He invites travelers to visit and even stay. Take a rickshaw past the Asi Ghat toward the university to Lanka Nagua. Then ask anyone for Krist Panthi Ashram. Most likely, some eager young boy will lead you straight to the mud house of Father Francis.

Music—Ravi Shankar doesn't live in Varanasi for the swimming. Varanasi is India's classical music capital and home to many of her greatest musicians. Many foreigners come here to study or to just listen. Toward evening, boys walk along Dasaswamedh Road near the ghat and hand out flyers for the nightly concerts. Two good places for music in the Dasaswamedh area are the International Music Center (at D 33/81, Khalishpura) and the Music Yogashram Academy (at D 33/32, Khalishpura). They are near the main road but back down some winding lanes, so ask the boys to lead you there. Both offer lessons in sitar, tabla, flute, and dance. It takes at least a month to learn the basic skills. You can also find a music teacher at the Benares Hindu University. Inquire at the fine arts college, or check with some of the foreign students you'll see on campus.

Festivals—If you're traveling in February, don't miss Varanasi's Shivaratri festival for Lord Shiva. Shiva is big in Varanasi, and so is ganja (hashish) during festival time. During the day, thousands come to the ghats to bathe. Before the evening parade many people have a yogurt drink with ganja, called a bong. So the street procession gets pretty wild. It's definitely worth experiencing. Hundreds of people carry large flashing neon lights on top of their heads and drag portable generators on wooden carts. There are charmed snakes, magicians igniting their heads in flames, bands in bright full dress uniforms and thongs, and so on.

Home, Home, on the Ghats—A big part of the experience in Varanasi is where you stay. The Hotel Temple on Ganges (tel. 312340) is by the quieter Asi Ghat but just a twenty-minute walk from the old city action. The small family-run hotel has a nice view looking over the garden onto the river. The pleasant, clean rooms range from $2 to $7. Mr. Pandey may invite you to play music with his family on the roof.

If you have a particular place in mind, like the above, rickshaw and taxi drivers will try to talk you out of it. They'll say it's closed, burned down, there's violence in the area—anything to get you to go where they want to take you. That is, to a place from which they get a commission.

16. Camel Khuri— Tasting the Desert

Khuri is where good eating and good camels come together. In the desert of Rajasthan near the Pakistan border, this tiny village offers the adventurous overnight camel excursions, an opportunity to live life as the locals do, and the peace of the desert. There is no shopping, no movies, and only one place to eat. Tourists hate this place. Travelers wanting to experience life in the desert stay.

To get off the beaten path in India, travelers are going to the town of Jasailmer in the state of Rajasthan. They've heard this is a wonderful old walled town at the edge of the desert. It is. They've also heard this is a good place to go on a camel trek in the desert. It is. But from Khuri, your trek is more remote, it's less businesslike, and it's cheaper.

Head to Jasailmer for a splash in Rajasthan culture, then leave it in the sand. Your experience will start when you tell the bus driver in Jasailmer to drop you off in Khuri. You'll be the only foreigner on the bus as it slowly moves from people and villages into sandy nothingness. In two hours the bus will drop you in the middle of the Thar desert with a 360-degree view of sand. Only sand. Don't panic. Just follow a few of the locals down the path toward the dots of houses a quarter mile away.

Khuri is beautiful in its simplicity, only twenty or so houses of mud and straw, each painted with a unique Persian carpetlike design of golds, reds, browns, and blues. Walk the wide sandy paths through the village past kids playing, camels chewing, and locals talking. There are no cars, motorcycles, TVs. People are clean and friendly and don't beg. A few speak English. And there is Mama.

Mama's Guest House is where you'll be directed when you walk into town. It's the only lodging, but luckily it's a good one and reason enough to come to Khuri. Mama will greet you with hospitality and great cooking. She'll put you up in a basic but clean room, with thick mattresses on a concrete floor. There's an outhouse, and she'll heat up buckets of water for your bath. Her porch is a good place to linger with a book, have an occasional chat with a local, or just observe life.

Mama's meals are not basic. She cooks up quite a spread: delicious potato and eggplant curries, spicy chickpeas, dhal (lentils), rice, and breads. You'll be graciously served tea by her daughter. Mama makes sure you're comfortable, while honoring your privacy.

And Mama arranges camel treks. You can go from one to three nights, or even do a half-day trip. Claire McIntyre, one of our Back Door travelers, had this to say about her recent ride:

"The two-day trek was wonderful but definitely long enough. Mama arranged two guides for myself and another female traveler, one on each camel. We rode on the front in a saddle of thick blankets. The turbaned guides steered from their rear seat with long leather reins and a constant clicking noise.

"From Khuri, we headed through absolutely barren land. There were no trees, shrubs, or grass . . . only sand. The desert alternated between flat lands and rolling sand dunes. The camels plodded slowly through the sand. Sometimes the guides would bring them to a trot. Even at a walk, we had to hold onto the saddle to keep from bouncing off the side. We moved our legs to one side and then another. No position seemed to feel good for very long. And bending forward to hold onto the saddle was a bear after a while. Humans weren't meant to ride camels.

Hoofing it in Rajastan; khuri up

"We were more than ready when we stopped for camp. The guides lowered the camels to their knees, and we crawled off. We brought

'Mama's To-Go' curries, bread, and crackers. Our guides warmed the food over a grill so black and sooty we didn't know if we wanted to eat. They joked in their limited English during dinner, then moved away to give us privacy.

"The intense yellow of the sun expanded into bands of brilliant colors as it slowly drifted into the sand. Vibrant oranges, yellows, and reds, such as only the desert could produce. The fading light gave way to the evening cool.

"With no fire, we soon crawled into our sleeping bags. We heard the guides chatting about thirty feet away. Since they worked for Mama, we trusted them. They were polite and punctual. We didn't worry that they'd make unwanted advances, and they didn't.

"An intense dark came. When our guides fell asleep, we lay in awe of the absolute quiet. In our bags looking up at the countless stars, we thought of being in the desert in India, far from the nearest town, farther yet from anyone we knew. It was all so romantic, but there was that camel ride back tomorrow."

For travel specifics, see Back Door Survival information under India in the Nitty Gritty section.

17. Kovalum—
India's Greek Beach

On the south tip of India, at just about the end of the tourist world, is one of India's finest beaches, Kovalum. Just 7 miles from Trivandrum, Kovalum offers the atmosphere and facilities of a Greek island. Many travelers complain that they dropped in for a few days and got lost for weeks. It's tough to plunge back into the intensity of India after a taste of this easy oasis.

Kovalum is two perfect white sand crescent beaches, an international-class hotel, and a hip community of vagabonds served by a fringe of cheap hotels and restaurants, backed up by a very traditional palm-centric village world. It's a mix of sand, sun, surf, Western decadence, simplicity, and traditional village life—for about the cheapest price on earth.

The beach is the focal point of the visitor's world here. By mid-morning, the mats are out, and the sand is littered with lazy bodies. Naked toddlers frolic dark-skinned and water-winged while mom is lost in a third-hand paperback. The waves are made for body surfing (beware of the strong rip tides), and small clouds soothe this world with brief but cool shadows. A lovely Australian savors a coconut oil massage by a bristly old local who charges $2 for half an hour. A woman, looking colorfully Jamaican, wearing a bulging basket of fruit as a hat, caresses the beach with the soft tempting chant, "Papaya, pineapple, banana, cheeeep price, very goooood." Her shadow covers my body, and she offers, "Two papaya, one pineapple, 10 rupees" (US$1 = 28 rupees). With great effort she dismounts the basket, sits cross-legged, and pulls out a lush pineapple. I say, "Pineapple—5 rupees." As I lay back, close my eyes, and return to the sun, she says, "O.K., pineapple—8 rupees." I counter, not firmly enough, "Five." With a note of finality, she says, "You take pineapple and papaya—6 rupees." She peels and quarters it before I can say a thing. With a lus-cious fresh-off-the-tree and nicely peeled pineapple in hand on a hot beach, a beautiful smiling tropical woman sitting by me, and all the palm trees in the world waving "take it," I give in and hand over two dimes worth of rupees. She leaves, promising, "Tomorrow I come again."

In a strange flip-flop, the tourists of Kovalum actually become tourist attractions as proudly plump big-city Indians in slacks and sleek shoes stroll awkwardly along the beach filling the corners of their eyes with each topless bronzed or burned European sun worshiper. It's strange how the Indian badge of success is to be fully covered in European clothes, while the cheeky Frenchman's ideal is the almost heathen sheaf and G-string.

The beach world of Kovalum will put the word "mellow" back into your vocabulary. Backpacker-type travelers and a few refugees from the 1970s eat, sleep, and casually smoke local marijuana at places with names like Woodstock Lodge and Velvet Dawn. Nobody checks anyone's urine. Mellow yellowed posters of Rod Stewart and Bob Marley decorate the hangout of Europeans who said, "Stop the world, I want to get off," and really meant it. The only activity seems to be snorkeling, sing-alongs, yoga, katakali dancing, watching video films in the waterfront cafés, going into town to buy cashews, and watching the sunset.

Behind this international community of experts in lethargy is a traditional village world of farmers, fishermen, mud huts, elevated mud walkways, gardens, rice paddies, woven palm-leaf fences, dugout canoes, and jungle-wise children. It's a great place to get lost.

You can live like a monkey-king here for $10 a day—$5 rooms and $2 meals. Canoe rides, endless fresh fruit, coconut oil rubdowns, and other diversions bump up a bum's budget. But life on this beach is basic. Water is limited and not heated, tea is served in chipped china or in far-from-clean plastic, and the local crowd would probably disgust your grandma. But with the appropriate attitude, Kovalum is seductive.

Kovalum is just one slice of **Kerala**, one of India's most interesting states. Stretching along India's southwest coast, Kerala is unique, boasting the first freely elected Communist government on earth and the highest literacy in India. It's also the most Christian part of the teeming Indian subcontinent. Kerala, literally the "land of palms," is a romantic's India. With a relatively equal distribution of wealth, the people enjoy a simple but, for India, comfortable life. The visitor sees none of the harsh poverty so prevalent in other states.

After Kovalum, be sure to cruise north on Kerala's picturesque backwaters for a day and explore the historic town of Cochin.

India is primarily rural. To see just its diesel-stained nerve-wrenching cities is disillusioning. Your best chance to fall in love with the magic of India is to take the eight-hour commuter boat ride from Quilon to Alleppey. This milk run goes daily, stopping at every palm-trunked dock. It normally hits its last landing two or three hours late. The ride costs just a few rupees. No reservations, just show up. Most tourists join the pilot on the rusty tin roof for the best view. The battered old boat, with its rolled-up burlap window shades and trapdoor latrine hanging over the stern, seats about a hundred. You'll enjoy an endless parade of greeting parties at each dock, idyllic tropical villages, adorable snot-nosed kids wearing happy face T-shirts and nothing more, and a lagoon world of lazy palm trees, fishing nets, smooth canoes, birds, and commuters coming and going throughout the ride.

Cochin, an easy hour-long bus ride from the Alleppey boat dock, is one of India's more interesting cities. With its sleepy port, it has a Mediterranean atmosphere. The city is laid out like San Francisco with a bay and ferries connecting downtown with local communities across the water. Ernakulam, the noisy local Oakland, is where most visitors sleep, eat, and tour from. Steeped in European history, Cochin offers India's oldest church, the tomb of Vasco da Gama (1524), and a 500-year-old synagogue.

Any city tour will show you these European sights and take you on a brief cruise through the harbor filled with phantomlike freighters. If you take a city tour, leave it after the fishnets to gain some free time in the old town and miss the last worthless stop on Bolgatty Island. Cochin's famous Hindu murals at Mattancherry Palace are arguably the finest paintings in India. The fascinating cantilevered Chinese fishing nets can be traced to the court of Kublai Khan. Visit the interesting Jewish quarters.

If you see just one dance-drama in India, see the Kathakali show in Ernakulam (Cochin Cultural Center, tel. 37866, in the rustic, traditional-style theater on Durbar Hall Road next to the Cochin Museum, shows nightly). While a real performance lasts most of the night, tourist shows last two hours, starting with a wonderfully helpful orientation lesson and finishing with the audience crying for more. Drop in late in the afternoon to observe the ritualistic and tedious application of the colorful makeup. Reserve a front seat (leaving a shirt or something on it several hours before show time) to get a close look at the facial expressions, fascinating right down to the eye movements (eggplant flowers are tucked under the eyelids to turn the whites of the eyes a dark red).

The more intense and very Hindu state of Tamil Nadu is a scenic all-day bus ride east of Cochin. A great game plan for south India is to fly into Trivandrum, enjoy a vacation from your vacation on Kovalum Beach, cruise the backwaters from Quilon to Alleppey, explore

Cochin-Ernakulam, bus into Tamil Nadu stopping to explore the Periyar Wildlife Sanctuary, enjoy the cool and relaxing hill station of Kodaikanal, and bus into the bustling and exotic city of Madurai with its fascinating Shree Meenakshi temple. Bangalore is an overnight train ride north, and from there you can enjoy Mysore, an exciting South India city.

18. Kashmir—Houseboats in the Himalayas

Writing about Kashmir is an exercise in superlatives. If we were Cupid, we'd send all honeymooners to Kashmir. You won't really understand the magic of this place until you pop out of that one-lane mountain tunnel and are greeted by the cheery sign, "Welcome to Kashmir. You're now in Paradise."

The valley of Kashmir, a romantic mix of gardens, lakes, smiles, Hindu fertility, British gentility, and Muslim mystery, is kept pure by a towering ring of Himalaya Mountains. Struggling to keep China, India, Pakistan, and the modern world at bay, Kashmiris have maintained their cultural independence. Although Hindu-ruled, the population of Kashmir (India's northernmost state) is mainly Muslim. Hindu-Muslim tensions have occasionally erupted into skirmishes along the India-Pakistan border, including Kashmir.

Although the occasional conflicts between India and Pakistan don't affect the visitor, you should know the latest before traveling into Kashmir. (The American embassy in New Delhi can give you the latest on the local situation before you head north.) Off and on the Indian government has cautioned tourists against going to Kashmir. Some of our Back Door travelers have gone during these warning periods and haven't felt personally threatened. They report hearing shots in the distance at night, and the next morning, stories from Kashmiris of what happened the night before. Houseboat owners can be overly protective and insist you go everywhere in Srinagar with a guide (they usually have a cousin who is eager to be employed). But as long as you are back on the houseboat by dark, travelers have felt safe browsing the streets alone. However, since there is some guerrilla activity in the countryside, you should check in town for places to avoid if you head out.

With this in mind, we feel any visit to India should include Kashmir. Srinagar, the capital, is just a one-hour flight from Delhi. The adventurous take the overland trip to Kashmir, enjoying two days of chaos and anarchy on Indian trains and buses, and fly back.

Srinagar is a good home base for wandering the Vale of Kashmir. Again, check with the locals about what to avoid. Like many Asian cities, its old town is intense, while its new town offers a more comfortable refuge to visitors. Old Srinagar, seething with activity, begs to be explored. Bridges tremble across the Jhelum River, and mosques rise peacefully above the busy tangle. Cows munch newspapers in the streets. Ornately carved buildings are painted ever darker by hot summers and violent winters. Crazy three-wheeled buses seating ten (or thirty in a pinch) take you anywhere for a rupee. Animals clog the streets. At times, it seems as if an entire zoo has escaped.

Go on a photo safari. Run the gauntlet of pleading merchants in one of India's largest bazaars. Study craftsmen in action. Kashmir is a shopper's mecca. Finely crafted leather, jewels, furs, silk, wool, and carvings can be had for great prices. Kashmiri carpets are closely related to Persian, with the same high quality at better prices.

Pedal a rental bike around the lake. Stop for tea at the Shalimar Gardens. Stop and talk to the kids that will come running after your bike.

English is India's language of government, travel, and business. India's wealthy have always vacationed in Kashmir, where tourists are handled in style—and in English. The climate, at 5,700 feet, is comfortable and very refreshing after the mucky heat and sheetless nights of most of India.

In the days of British India, the independent-minded Kashmiris ruled that no outsider could own land. Rich vacationers beat the law by building houseboats. Today more than a thousand of these boats remain, many quite palatial. They provide visitors with Old World royal accommodations, unique and ridiculously cheap.

Arriving at the dock in Srinagar, you feel very popular. Everyone wants to take you to their houseboat. Reservations? Unnecessary. Skirting the "boatlords," we hired a private shikara (gondola-type boat) and had a local boy in the traditional pajamas take us houseboat shopping. He couldn't speak English, but he loved to sing.

We cruised past everything from rotten rafts to floating palaces, getting a feel for the market. We chose a "Grade A" boat offering "boat and board" and a family of servants for $20 a day. We realized we were paying top rupee, and there were plenty of fine places for half the price. But this one felt like home. And at those prices, who wants to haggle?

Our boat had a royally furnished living room with a small dining table, two double bedrooms, two bathrooms, and a sun deck upstairs. The host family lived in a much smaller boat out back. We had a local

shikara at our disposal, and for a price, we could even have our home
relocated for a fresh view of the surrounding mountains.

Muzaffer, the owner, cooked roast duck, potatoes, spinach, rice,
sweet baked apples in syrup, a wonderful Persian tea, and chilled
boiled water that was safe to drink. He thoughtfully described the
Kashmiri food, explaining, for instance, that the spinach was really "a
local vegetable much spicier and more packed with iron." Muzaffer
beamed with pride when we attacked his meal. All this service made us
uncomfortable at first, but we got used to it. If you're going to be king
for a day, you've got to wear the crown.

For travel specifics, see Back Door Survival information under
India in the Nitty Gritty section.

Kashmir and Ladakh

19. Ladakh—India's Loft

To feel the Buddha within, rise above the earthly beauty and pleasures of Kashmir into the high of Ladakh. Roaming past steep monastic walls that project above the moonscape, I experienced a serenity and openness to man and nature that only comes in the lofty Himalayas. Within that openness, something deep was touched by the warm gentleness of the Ladakhis, their special character shaped by the harsh but starkly beautiful environment and their Buddhist views. In Ladakh, it seems, man and nature shared the same cradle.

The long, breathtaking bus ride from Srinagar (the capital of Kashmir) to Leh, Ladakh's capital, eases you in without the cultural bends. While no buses have shocks, the "super-deluxe" ones have padded seats. The road is generally clear of snow and open between June and October. For maximum Himalayan views, I'd fly one way and bus the other. Flights connect Leh regularly with Srinagar, Delhi, and Chandigarh. Make plane reservations before you get to Leh. India's violent summer monsoons cause many flights to be canceled. So, if you have to be out on a certain day, try to fly in and bus out.

Once in Ladakh, you can visit the many monasteries, trek, and just practice "being" in Leh, a miniature Kathmandu—without "freak street." The many monastery festivals immerse you in fascinating Buddhist rituals. In mid-July, be at the Phange Monastery, near Leh, for two swirling, twirling days of horns, drums, and demonically costumed monks.

To best experience Ladakh, trek the valleys and passes. For example, on the six-day trek from Lamayuru to Alchi, you'll wander through small isolated villages, encounter herders with their grazing flocks, and huff and puff over a 15,000-foot pass. Read Lonely Planet's *Trekking in the Indian Himalayas* for a variety of trekking ideas. Bring along your own supplies, as villages are often far apart and have no Eddie Bauers—or go Ladakhi style and subsist on tsampa, ground barley flour. Lighten your load by renting a donkey—$3 a day with

Gompa (monastery), Ladakh

unlimited mileage. Donkeys come complete with a "donkey man." Having a donkey man (as they call themselves) along takes a huge load off your back and gives you a great opportunity to get intimate with the Ladakh culture. His friends and family become yours, too.

May to October is warm and the best time to visit. The winter is brittle cold, but you can fly into a tourist-free Leh. In any case, go now. The modern tide is rolling in on lofty Ladakh.

20. Rishikesh and Dharamsala—Truth in a Rucksack

For many travelers, India's top sights are those they discover within themselves, and its most scenic roads are those that take them close to God. Many visit first as normal snapshot tourists and, inspired by the nakedness of Indian life, come again without their camera.

Indian life is spread-eagle real. You're swimming in birth, life, and death. And though the average Indian is no saint, some come close. While many gurus are con-artists primed to take you for a ride, some offer a real spiritual lift. For inspiration, guidance, and insight, visit Rishikesh and Dharamsala. These Hindu and Buddhist spiritual centers both entertain the traveler and reward the seeker.

Rishikesh—Sanctuary of Saints and Sages

Where the sacred Ganges leaves the Himalayas for the plains of India sits Rishikesh, one of the great Hindu pilgrimage centers. Saints and sages from all over India wander here on foot, bus, and train. Some live and practice their faith alone in caves or huts along the river. Others are the gurus of the many ashrams or Hindu religious communities. Many Hindus with the time and money come to the ashrams to strengthen their faith through meditation, yoga, discussions, and reading the scriptures. For others, it's merely a vacation in a spiritual Disneyland.

From our journal: "Feb. 16—Arrived at Hardwar on the overnight train. An old man in a pilgrim's orange robes tagged along with me to catch a taxi for the thirty-minute ride into Rishikesh. The first stop was his ashram—several plain concrete motellike buildings with a nice garden. The manager insisted I come in to clean up and have tea. Warming ourselves around a bowl of coals, we looked at pictures of their guru, Sawamaji, sitting in flames, unharmed. The manager, explaining that Sawamaji could even stop the river, invited me back to see him.

"I caught a three-wheeled scooter taxi to Ram Jhula, the footbridge north of town. Across the bridge was a different India. Far from the noise and dust of the busy little town, the pedestrian-only path wound peacefully past small clean shops, ornate temples, and ashrams. Well-dressed Indians strolled the lane lined with beggars and religious curio peddlers. A clean India—except for the occasional cow splat.

"At the end of the line of ashrams was the Ved Niketan. This ashram is popular with travelers since its daily regimen is a breeze—no requirement to do anything but follow the rules: no alcohol, no smoking, and pursue the spiritual path. They did offer morning yoga and evening meditation and discussion for those interested. Most travelers used it for a cheap hotel—$30 a month for a room with bath. More than twenty years ago, John, Paul, George, and Ringo sat cross-legged, just next door, with the Mahesh Yogi.

"Feb. 22—Walked to my favorite chai shop to eat breakfast and read the India Times newspaper. Along the path, an old woman sits against the wall. We've come to recognize each other and she nods. I toss a rupee coin into her bowl. Another woman nods and yells out, "Money, rupee." I walk by. With so many beggars, I've decided to give only when moved, not out of guilt.

"Monkeys play on the roof of the produce stall across the lane. A cow lays next to a man selling piles of coins, ready change for beggars. An alert shopkeeper flings a rock. The monkey dives. Another swings in. I throw my banana peel to the cow for his breakfast. Life goes on in Rishikesh.

"Feb. 28—Tonight is a special one. Several of us walk up the moon-lit mountain to Muni Baba's cave. Muni (meaning silent) has spoken only one night a year for thirteen years. Tonight, the evening before the religious holiday of Holi, is the night. Muni will sing. In the dimly lit cave, Muni sits, with his three-pronged spear of Lord Shiva, next to his mud fireplace. He wears only a loincloth, the rest of him covered in ashes. His braided hair coils up a foot above his head, and his beard hangs just as far below. Since he has vowed not to talk, he welcomes us with clicking sounds.

"One of the travelers brought his guitar, and another brought tablas (Indian drums). We sang simple Hindu Badras (religious songs). Muni Baba made a clicking sound and motioned that he wanted us to tape him on our Walkman as he broke his long silence. Then, all attention was focused on Muni. With gusto, he sang and sang, repeating the songs, working to get them just right. Soon we wished Muni would go back to his silence.

"An apprentice sadhu (holy man) was also staying with Muni. He was in his 20s and spoke English fluently (every day). His spent his days wandering and living in the jungle. He said India was bad now. Everyone wanted things. So he needed to help by wandering, nearly naked, seeking the spiritual. He said when he became a master, he wouldn't need to worry in the jungle. A master would be seen by a tiger as a master tiger, by a snake as a master snake. Nothing would harm him.

"That night we slept outside the cave in the forest. The tigerlike sounds of the peacocks woke me from time to time. I wasn't even an apprentice, but I felt safe with the master's dog curled up next to me."

New friends at a Rishikesh ashram

Dharamsala—The Dalai Lama's Mountain Exile

Dharamsala is soothing. That's rare in India. Nestled in the forests at the foot of the northwest Himalayas, Dharamsala offers the crowd-weary traveler a reprieve. This isn't your average hangout. For the last thirty years, it's been the home of the Dalai Lama, the exiled spiritual leader of Tibet. Since the domination of Tibet by China in 1959, the inspiration for millions of Tibetans to continue their struggle for freedom has come from Dharamsala. Culturally, visiting Dharamsala is side tripping out of India.

There are two distinct town sites; the predominantly Hindu Dharamsala at the head of the valley, and the Tibetan village of MacLeod Ganj on the hilltop, twenty minutes away by bus. Although Dharamsala offers a lively bazaar and a few comfortable hotels and restaurants, the magic increases with the altitude. Just before reaching MacLeod Ganj, you might notice the picturesque St. John's Church tucked quietly among the trees, a relic of the British Raj.

However, it isn't the remnants of the British Empire that attract the multitude of visitors. MacLeod Ganj is a remarkable community of Tibetans, Tibet scholars, and spiritual seekers (Western and Eastern) who have gathered around the Dalai Lama. A rich cultural spectrum flavors the simple Tibetan village life. Austere Buddhist monastic practices flourish in a community of bustling hotels and restaurants catering to perhaps the last of the hippies. It's hard not to be charmed by MacLeod Ganj.

The local Tibetan Library is the world's foremost resource for information on Tibet and Tibetan Buddhism. Meditation classes or Buddhist talks offered by eminent lamas are open to visitors most mornings. The nearby Medical School offers a truly holistic approach to healing. Body, mind, and spirit are diagnosed. Students spend about seven years studying this ancient tradition, which includes the art and science of herbal medicines. The students are involved in collecting herbs in the mountains for the school's modernized facility that may combine up to seventy ingredients into one very potent pill.

Near MacLeod Ganj is the Dalai Lama's monastery, which actively educates Tibetan monks, and for Westerners there is a retreat center called Tuschita. The Tibetan Children's Village, just outside MacLeod Ganj, is also worth a visit. It was established to give home and education to the many "orphaned" children who are still arriving from Tibet. Many parents in Tibet have their children smuggled out to MacLeod Ganj to avoid the fate of a secular Chinese "education" and the consequential loss of their traditions and values.

Good trails take hikers from MacLeod Ganj into the magnificent Dhauladhar mountains. Choose from four-hour walks or four-day treks in rugged terrain. Go on your own, or join an organized hike. Come prepared with your own hiking gear.

Dharamsala, in the state of Himachal Pradesh, is reached by bus in four hours from Pathankot (which is on the Delhi-Jammu train line). A unique place, these days it's more Tibetan than Tibet.

SRI LANKA

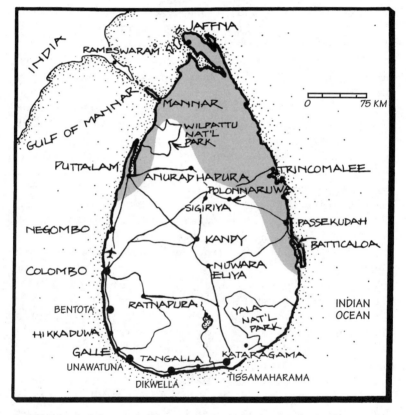

In 1993 the shaded areas on this map were basically closed to tourism because of Sri Lanka's simmering civil war.

21. Serendipitous Sri Lanka

When ancient Arab mariners first visited this teardrop-shaped island centuries before Christ, they named it Serendib. Serendipity—a happy surprise! Today, while a bit frayed at the edges after centuries of internal strife and colonial occupation, West Virginia-sized Sri Lanka is still a traveler's delight. It offers dreamy sandy beaches, mountains cloaked in teak plantations, rich and teeming wildlife refuges, ancient cities, fabulous Buddhist and Hindu temples, piles of sapphires and rubies, cheap comfortable guest houses, exquisite curry dishes, incredible festivals, and a hunger to make its visitors happy.

The current hostilities between the Tamil Hindu minority and Sinhalese Buddhist majority, the latest chapter in a 2,000-year-old conflict, have devastated Sri Lankan tourism. While tourists are advised to avoid Sri Lanka's Tamil region in the north and east, including the wonderful east coast beach resorts, the area from Colombo and Kandy south, where tourism is unrestricted, is packed with interesting sights and fine beaches.

If your time is limited, the best way to get around the island (known as Ceylon during the Dutch, Portuguese, and British colonial periods, which ended in 1948) is by hired car and hired driver. The cost to be driven usually works out less than self-drive when you add on insurance.

Throughout the country, you can stay in the rest houses. The Ceylon Hotel Corporation can book a place anywhere you're going. You can pay ahead of time in Colombo, and you'll get a receipt to show when you arrive. A pamphlet describes each place. Most are basic but clean with their own baths. Rooms are about $10 for a double. Check on these with the Ceylon Tourist Board, Steuart Place, in Colombo, opposite the Oberoi Hotel (tel. 437059).

Your taste buds will also enjoy Sri Lanka. Sri Lankan curries, white, brown, red, and black, are each prepared with coconut milk. A typical home-cooked meal is rice with a half-dozen meat, fish, and vegetable curries, all with different spices. Seek out and swallow the cashew curry.

Guard against the local tendency to protect you from the authentic cuisine. The Western food served is so-so to bad. Ask locals to point you toward a good *lamprais* (rice cooked in stock, placed in a bed of mixed curries, wrapped in a banana leaf and baked). A fine breakfast food is *indi appa*, or "string hoppers" (rice-flour spaghetti steamed like bird's nests and served with light curries). Plain hoppers or egg hoppers are the local pancakes. Sip *thambili* (coconut water) out of the shell, or see if you can enjoy a "toddy," the potent fermented coconut sap. You'll pay about $2 for a decent dinner. Laurie Rich, a veteran Back Door traveler of Sri Lanka, reports that Colombo still has no McDonald's. Imagine.

Sri Lanka in Twelve Days

If we had a dozen days and the services of a driver-guide to explore this exotic culture as well as pamper ourselves on Sri Lanka's lovely beaches, here's how we'd do it:

Day 1—Fly into Colombo. Change money at the airport and taxi downtown. A good cheap, central, and decent place to stay is the YMCA in the fort (old town). Don't miss their breakfast. It'll squash any doubt that this isn't Kansas anymore. Arrange for your rental car and driver. (Try Walkers Tour Ltd at 130 Glennie Street in Colombo. L. D. Sarath Jayantha is a good driver.)

Day 2—See Colombo, drive to Hikkaduwa or Bentota Beach. See the highlights of Colombo—the president's house, post office, Galle Face Hotel, and other reminders of British colonial extravagances. Enjoy a drink and the best view in town with your driver in the Harbour Room of the Taprobane Hotel and drive south. Hikkaduwa, the country's most famous beach, is great but touristy. It's a thin three-mile strand of beachfront hotels and guest houses (Sunils Beach Hotel is good), simple shops, and thatched family restaurants that separate thick jungle from a lazy world of white sand and surf. Haggle with local craftspeople or try a surfside massage. Rent bikes and ride fifteen minutes south to a fishing village for sunset when the boats are launched. Boredom is not an option.

For a less touristed alternative, stop at Bentota Beach. A good place to stay is at the Warahena Walauwa (a five-minute taxi ride south of Bentota, tel. 5374, or call in Colombo, tel. 29161). A double including three meals is $25. They serve good Western and Sri Lankan food. There are other cheaper guest houses in the area.

Day 3—Free Day on Bentota Beach. Bentota offers golden sand, beautiful sunsets, sandy-bottomed water shallow enough for good swimming, and body surfing. There is a resort here, but Bentota is most popular with Sri Lankans. It's great for quiet walks along the palm beach. For nightlife, drive thirty minutes farther south to Hikkaduwa.

Day 4—Galle, Unawatuna Beach, evening in Tangalla. Your driver will take you south to historic Galle, three hours from Colombo. The old section of town in enclosed in the remaining walls of an old Por-

A happy Tangalla family

tuguese fort. A white-washed lighthouse rises above. Visit the little library, have a drink, and relax in chairs with foldout leg props at the elegant New Oriental Hotel. Despite the name, it's one of the oldest hotels in Sri Lanka. Down the street from the hotel is the Groote Kerk (Great Church), originally built in the 1600s. Tombstones here date back to the early ships that arrived from Portugal and Holland. Walk on the old fort walls most of the way around town. See Galle in a day, and head to Tangalla for the evening. On the way, stop to snorkel at the postcard-perfect Unawatuna Beach, three miles south of Galle.

Check into one of the many inexpensive guest houses in Tangalla. (Ask for the Paradise Palm Cabanas on the north edge of town.) Walk along the beach. Chat with friendly villagers along the way. Get invited in, eat exotic fruit, and browse through family scrapbooks. Fireflies, moon shadows, and a soothing surf serenade tonight.

Day 5—Tangalla Beach, Dikwella. After a free morning on the beach (caution: dangerous body surfing), take a day trip to Dikwella. Backtrack about a half hour toward Matara to see the biggest Buddha in the country. This spiritual giant is eight stories high.

Day 6—Kataragama temple pilgrimage. Drive east to Tissamaharama. Stop at a curd stand for a tasty local snack. Set up in safari-type hotel or bungalow near Tissamaharama. Spend the day at the teeming pilgrimage temples of Kataragama. Sri Lanka's holiest site, Kataragama, is basically a Hindu pilgrimage site, but Buddhists, Muslims, and local Christians also pay their respects to Skanda, the god who lives here. Your senses will be bombarded as crowds of pilgrims line up to present flowers, fruit, and incense to the icons. Eat a hopper, follow the pilgrims through the entire complex, learn about the rituals that turn this cultural tidepool into a whirlpool.

Day 7—Yala Wildlife Preserve Safari. From Tissamaharama, drive north into the hill country. Arrange a jeep with your hotel. Join with other travelers to split the costs. Your jeep and special guide will be waiting at 5:00 a.m. Your hotel's sack breakfast probably isn't worth the trouble. Spend the morning searching out elephants, monkeys, crocodiles, buffalo, and lots of colorful birds. Your guide will undoubtedly demonstrate the local specialty, "monkey-disco." By late morning, you'll be back at the hotel. After a rest, drive north out of the coconut plantations and into the hills and rubber forests. Have a very scenic lunch at the Ella Rest House. Sleep 6,200 feet above sea level in the old British hill station of Nuwara Eliya at the Grosvenor Hotel ($15, funky, colonial, tel. 0522-307, 4 Haddon Hill Road). For more than enough colonial decadence, dine at the Hill Club. Ties are required; the bartender will rent you one to go with your T-shirt.

Days 8 and 9—Explore the Sri Lankan hill and tea country, evening at Kandy. Break the very scenic drive to Kandy with a tour of a tea plantation. Plenty of photo fun today. Spend midday at the incredible Peradeniya Botanical Gardens (three miles out of Kandy). The Royal Gardens Cafeteria there serves fine lunches. Kandy was Sri Lanka's political capital for centuries. Today, it's still the island's cultural and spiritual center. Check into the Queens Hotel, tops in Kandy's Old World elegance (tel. 08-22121) and right in the center of our favorite Sri Lankan city. Plan your evening carefully; there's a nightly religious ceremony (6 o'clock) at the Dalada Maligawa, the Temple of the Tooth, where a tooth of the Buddha—symbol of Sri Lankan sovereignty—is locked away. See the famous Kandyan dance shows, complete with fire eating and fire walking (nightly at several locations, tickets easy through your hotel). The dances at the Kandy Lake Club are very good. If you're lucky enough to be in Kandy in

August, you may see the Kandy Perahera, possibly the most spectacular festival in Asia. For two weeks, from the new moon to the full moon, a burgeoning procession of tusked and cloaked elephants, jeweled dancers, jugglers, whip-crackers, and fire-eaters march around the city, beginning and ending at the Temple of the Tooth. The last day is the most spectacular. (Rooms are booked long in advance.) To see some elephants (even if you're not considering adoption), go to the Pinnewala Elephant Orphanage. This is about an hour from Kandy on the way to Colombo near Kegalle. Be warned: the babies are awfully cute.

Have your driver (or taxi) take you on a temple loop drive outside of Kandy (described in detail in Lonely Planet's _Sri Lanka: A Travel Survival Kit_). The temples aren't incredible, but the views over the hills are.

Day 10—Drive north to Dambulla, stay in Sigiriya. Rising above Dambulla on a rock face are several 2,000-year-old Buddhist cave temples featuring hundreds of statues of the Buddha. Ten miles north, the fascinating ancient rock fortress of Sigiriya rises like a giant Phoenix from the scrub jungle. This huge rock is capped by the 1,500-year-old palace of a paranoid patricidal king. The precarious climb to the top of Sri Lanka's best ancient site takes you past 1,000-year-old graffiti and frescoes of topless "celestial maidens." Sleep at the nearby Sigiriya Rest House (tel. 066-8234).

Days 11 and 12—Polonnaruwa and Anuradhapura, ancient Sri Lanka. Spend the morning driving to Polonnaruwa, capital of Sri Lanka a thousand years ago. The best of the many impressive temples is the Gal Vihara, a giant rock face carved with three Buddha images, one of them reclining. Spend the day exploring. The Polonnaruwa Rest House, off the main road to the ruins, has good rooms and a terrace overlooking ancient reservoirs (created thousands of years ago by farsighted Sri Lankan rulers to provide their monsoon-dependent kingdom with water for drinking and irrigation). If you're up for more temples, go to Anuradhapura. If it's a choice between the two areas, Polonnaruwa has a better setting and is easier to get around.

Two-thousand-year-old Anuradhapura is the island's best-preserved and biggest ancient city. Your visit to the fascinating and sprawling sight is best on a rental bike and with the fine USESCO guidebook (available locally). The Tissawewa Rest House (tel. 025-2299) offers a quiet night among the ruins.

NEPAL

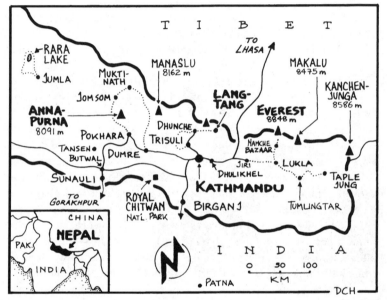

Nepal and Its Top Treks

22. Kathmandu— Repulsively Wonderful

Kathmandu is a living museum, a cultural circus, a story that needs no plot. Don't try to understand every shrine or mystery. Just put your guidebook away and immerse yourself in this city of pagodas, sleeping dogs, beggars, holy men, and trouserless small kids in raggy-baggy shirts.

Opened to the West only in the 1950s, this medieval capital refuses to join the twentieth century. Even though it's changed since we first visited fourteen years ago, it's still a mystical place. But don't read "mystical" to mean "wondrous"—illiteracy and infant mortality rates are very high, and the place is filthy. You'll see hungry homeless dogs eating the undigested rice out of human excrement in small lanes, butchers tossing water buffalo heads into the street gutters for the blood to drain off, and so on. Amazingly, you won't think much about these after a while; they'll just be part of the story.

While repulsion was a part of our experience, fascination with the Nepalese culture was a bigger part. Kathmandu offers enough in the way of temples, back streets, food, shopping, and interesting people to keep you from the surrounding mountains for a while.

Start with a visit to the tourist information center on Ganga Path near the Crystal Hotel (west end of New Road). Pick up a city map and information about the temples. Many bookstores also have maps and books on the history of the city (see the well-stocked Pilgrim's Book House near the Kathmandu Guest House in the Thamel area).

The palaces and temples always beckon. One of the largest and best-known clusters is at Durbar Square, a few minutes walk west on Ganga Path from the tourist information center. Ogle the Hanuman Dhoka, the former Royal Palace, surrounded by Hindu temples whose pillars are carved with all imaginable forms of people and animals having sex. These erotic and often kinky displays are offensive to the virgin temperament of the goddess of lightning and thus keep the palace safe from storms. The ploy apparently works, since these and many

similarly protected structures have survived the centuries unscathed.
Once you get your eyes off the erotic, notice the other intricately
carved buildings and towers. The 800-year-old Kasthamandap temple,
at the southwest end of the square, is one of the world's oldest wooden
buildings.

Kathmandu

You might see a living goddess, the Kumari Devi, as she looks out
her window from her three-storied "home" in Durbar Square. This
young girl is honored from about the age of five until she reaches

puberty. The tradition started centuries ago when a king had intercourse with a young girl and as a result she died. To atone for his sins, he was instructed during a dream to select and worship the Kumari. She goes through a long process of selection, with one final trial for the young girls. All are put in a dark room. Noises, frightening masks, and slaughtered buffalo heads are all around. Whoever emerges without fear is selected. The Kumari appears in public during the major festivals and is paraded through the streets in her chariot during the Indra Jatra festival in September.

The all-seeing eyes of Buddha will pull you toward a few other temples near Kathmandu. Within eyesight from the west side of the city, Swayambhunath (a.k.a. the "monkey temple") sits on a hilltop. The temple dates back about 700 years, although locals have worshiped on the site for 2,000 years. You leave your earthly existence as you climb the long steep flight of steps to the temple. Monkeys chase each other across the steps and screech. At the top, a stupa rises like a huge golden-nippled breast with eyes. Tibetan pilgrims circle the stupa clockwise, spinning the many brass prayer wheels at its base. With each turn of the wheel, the embossed words "om mani padme hom" (literally, there is a jewel in the lotus) is spun into the universe. Women worship in their wraparound woolen dresses, striped aprons, and black braided hair. You'll see old men with dark, furrowed faces and feet sporting running shoes or red-dyed yak wool boots. Some pilgrims spin small hand-held prayer wheels. Others push prayer beads one by one on their string. Mixed in are Western-dressed pilgrims and tourists with cameras. Purple-robed monks of all ages carry out their duties or rituals for pilgrims, answer the questions of visitors, and chase away an occasional disruptive monkey. The monks also chant, clash gongs, and blow trumpets during their daily late afternoon service. Soon after, the last soft rays of the sun bathe the stupa and offer a last lingering impression of the Kathmandu valley below.

You can either walk (40 minutes from Durbar Square), take a taxi, or bike to Swayambhunath. Bikers enjoy an easy coast back into town after a long uphill climb. Near the temple steps, young boys will want a few rupees to guard your bike. I see this as a way for these ragtag kids to earn money and enjoy employing them. If you don't agree, bring your air pump.

A few of the other temples near Kathmandu are at Patan, Bodhnath, and Bhaktapur. Avoid the crowds by arriving early or late. Take a bus, taxi, or bike to these. There are many bike rental shops in the Thamel area of Kathmandu. One-speeds are fine for around the city and cost less than a dollar a day. Rent a mountain bike (starting at $3 a day) for side trips from Kathmandu. Taxis are reasonable.

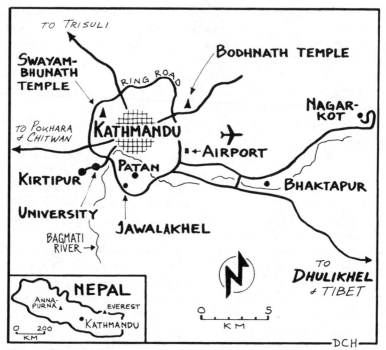

TO TRISULI

SWAYAM-
BHUNATH
TEMPLE

BODHNATH TEMPLE

RING ROAD

TO POKHARA
& CHITWAN

KATHMANDU

NAGAR-
KOT

✈ ←AIRPORT

KIRTIPUR

PATAN

BHAKTAPUR

UNIVERSITY

JAWALAKHEL

BAGMATI
RIVER →

N

TO
DHULIKHEL
& TIBET

0   5
KM

NEPAL

ANNA-
PURNA ▲

EVEREST
▲
•KATHMANDU

0   200
KM

DCH

Greater Kathmandu

With more temples and less tourists than in Kathmandu, the Durbar (Palace) Square in Patan is a place to see and feel history. Patan's palace and temples are beautiful examples of the local architecture—intricately carved wood and brick structures. There are also many Buddhist temples in the city. The Mahabouddha Temple (the temple of one thousand Buddhas) is worth a visit. Each brick of the temple has an image of Buddha; thus, its name. Although a tall structure, it's surrounded by buildings, and you must enter a courtyard to see it. Walk about 10 minutes southeast of the Durbar Square to the Sundhara area of town. People will point the way. Patan itself is just south of Kathmandu across the Bagmati River.

The largest stupa (Buddhist temple) in Nepal and community of Tibetan refugees is at Bodhnath, about 5 miles northeast of Kathmandu (north of the airport). Bargain for the many Tibetan handicrafts at the shops. If you bike, take any number of roads west to Ring Road, head to Chabhil, and go west again.

Farther away (10 miles) and less changed than either Kathmandu or Patan, is the third-biggest town of the valley, Bhaktapur, also known as Bhadgaun. The large Durbar Square here has the openness of a plaza. This plus the small amount of traffic creates a more relaxed atmosphere for visiting the palace and Hindu temples. Just down the street is Taumadhi Tole, a square known for the Nyatapola temple, the tallest and one of the finest in the valley. Watch the activity of the square over tea upstairs at the Nyatapola Café, a converted temple. To enjoy the town with no other Westerners, spend the night at one of the guest houses around the Durbar Square. Buses from Kathmandu leave from the east side of the city at Bagh Bazaar. The trolley leaves from Tripureswar in the south of Kathmandu. Taxis cost about $8.

When you're templed-out, simply roam the streets of downtown Kathmandu (ideally between the Thamel area in the north and New Road). In the busy street markets, city women in colorful saris bargain with their saronged country counterparts over vegetables. Small lanes open into courtyards and temples. Men with brimless Nepalese caps chat over tea in small open-front shops. Hire a bicycle rickshaw to take you on a tour, then walk back to the interesting areas. At night, singing to the beat of a drum and tune of a harmonium will often flow from a temple. Stop and listen. You'll be welcome.

For a long day trip, pedal out to the Ring Road, and bike the loop around Kathmandu and Patan. This paved road takes you through countryside and suburbs without much traffic to deal with. It's best on a mountain bike. Near the loop's east end, you can visit Bodhnath Stupa. From the west end, bike to nearby Swayambhunath Temple. Jawalakhel with the Tibetan Handicraft Center is near the south end. The nearby zoo is the only one in Nepal. Like many Third World zoos, it's interesting but small and poorly funded. Take an elephant out for a spin.

A highlight of the loop is a trip to the small ridgetop town of Kirtipur. In the southwest, just before Ring Road goes east across the Bagmati River, turn right on the road going to Tribhuvan University. On the hill beyond the university is Kirtipur. (You can also take a bus to the university and walk.) All of these side trips aren't possible in a day but could be done a section at a time.

From the travel journal: "Coasting out of town, I came first to the impressive Tribhuvan University. I stopped for a cafeteria lunch with the intelligentsia and future of a more modern Nepal. After strange food and good conversation, it was on to Kirtipur.

"Climbed the stone stairs into the town center. I came upon the perfect medieval square. Martin Luther could have just burned his papal bull. Buildings were decorated with food drying in the sun. People washed in the rectangular pond next to the well, the men gathered under eaves, ornately carved and aged windows framed grandparents and their dog, yarn was spun while ladies daydreamed. It could have been a Brueghel painting: so much was going on, but everything was small and nothing dominated.

"I 'namastayed' my way through the long village, following the road to a ridge marking the highest point in town. Here I joined the local people admiring the pastoral view of the Kathmandu Valley. Content, happy, and at peace, I sat there silently—me, new friends, and the Nepali sunset."

Spend a Kathmandu evening experiencing the Nepali culture through folk dance and music. The Hotel Yak and Yeti entertains travelers with free (if you order something) dance performances every evening in their main dining room (tel. 2-22635). The Hotel Annapurna presents folk dances by the Everest Cultural Society (every evening, $4, tel. 2-20676). Both hotels are near Durbar Marg (road). The Hotel Shankar also has shows (north end of town in the Lazimpat area, tel. 4-10151). Check with the tourist information office for other dances and music (tel. 2-20818). The Aangan Restaurant and Bar gives its customers good food and live Nepalese/Indian music each night (Thamel area on Tridevi Marg, tel. 2-25388, ext. 331).

Kathmandu Valley is the place for the latest in Tibetan yak wool hats and prayer wheels. For Tibetan items, especially carpets, go to the Jawalakhel area of Patan. The Tibetan Handicraft Center buzzes with women of all ages weaving carpets. The road between the handicraft center and the zoo is lined with small carpet shops. Shops that cater to travelers' Christmas shopping lists are in Kathmandu's Thamel and Durbar Square areas. The bookstores carry rice paper stationery, wood block print calendars featuring the Hindu god or goddess of the month, and wooden stamps carved with yetis (abominable snowmen), Buddha eyes, or om mani padme hom. Hanging from shop doors and windows are colorful handmade wool sweaters, hats, and carpets. Watch men on foot pump sewing machines embroider T-shirts. My favorite and a most practical one says, "No Hashish. No Carpet. No One Rupee. No Change Money. No Rickshaw. No Problem." After shopping or just walking the streets around the Thamel area, you'll want this. As merchants called out, I just pointed to the appropriate answer.

The T-shirt brings up a few topics. People will ask you to buy hashish. In fact, a few shops still sell "special" brownies and cookies. Drugs are illegal here, but, except at border crossings, little effort is made to clamp down on users or sellers.

"One rupee. One rupee," pleads the little kid with beautiful eyes. The scruffy lice-ridden kids are needy. But giving to young beggars encourages a life of begging. Your charity is generally most effective when channeled through the properly chosen stateside agency.

You will often be approached to change money. This is also illegal but not watched. Black market exchange rates vary but usually beat the bank rates by around 10 percent for traveler's checks and up to 20 percent for $50 and $100 bills. (Big bills get the best rates.) Hustlers earn their commission by getting you to a money-changing shop. You can do better by going directly to a shop alone and asking if they change money. Plan ahead, though. When you leave, you can change back only 10 percent of the Nepali money you officially changed or the last amount you changed, whichever is largest. You also need to show you changed $20 a day for each day you want to extend your visa.

"You, rickshaw?" After being asked this question twenty times in ten minutes, an enlightened response finally emerged, "No, I am not a rickshaw." Rickshaws are another dilemma Western travelers have faced since the East became a destination. Many Westerners—super rich by Nepali standards—feel awkward having someone straining on the bike pedals to move us down the street to an Italian dinner. Remembering that this work means food for the bike rickshaw man and his family, we are happy rickshaw riders. And he'll usually charge you more than the locals, so with this "tourist surcharge," you're a bonus. More rickshaws also mean fewer taxis, and the city is getting polluted and congested enough.

If you don't want to buy the T-shirt, just ignore the questions. Westerners often feel they have to be polite and say, "No, thank you" to every solicitor. In some tourist areas, there are just too many. Don't feel you're being rude by just looking straight ahead and saying nothing.

Hanging out in Kathmandu

Apple pie, lasagna, cinnamon rolls, burritos, pizza, yak burgers—Kathmandu's many small restaurants know how to keep travelers happy. Since the advent of the freak scene here in the 1960s and early 1970s, Kathmandu has catered to the whims of the Western taste bud. In the Thamel area around the Kathmandu Guest House, young Nepalese who once only cooked rice and lentils now specialize in Italian, Chinese, German, French, and New Age healthy vegetarian. What they do is usually tasty and often an interesting variation on the norm.

A big part of the experience in Kathmandu depends on where you stay. Kathmandu has from the cheap cheap to the luxury with casino. Budget places abound. We prefer the smaller places where we get to know the staff. Since there are so many similar and decent places, just pick the area of town you want and wander. The Thamel area is a popular travelers' base. It's filled with fun eateries filled with happy travelers. Unfortunately, the Nepalese you'll meet here are usually pestering you to buy something. The streets are jammed with rickshaws, taxis, and people. It's handy for its many good restaurants, bookstores, trekking shops, and the visa extension/trekking permit office. The Paknajol area, a 5-minute walk northwest of Thamel, has decent hotels and none of the Thamel congestion.

Around Durbar Square are several low-budget lodges, especially along Freak Street. Since there are fewer tourists staying here and many temples and the old palace, you'll get a better feel of the city. You won't find the variety of lodges and restaurants that Thamel offers, and you won't be hassled as much by the merchants.

Every land has its own special rhythm, and the only way to really get inside a foreign culture is to get in step with that rhythm. Kathmandu has a very special rhythm: gentle-natured people, cowpies in front of luxury hotels, broad grins from Tibetans smelling of yak butter, stone images of gods with six arms wearing wreaths of human skulls, fruit yogurt shakes, and chocolate "space cakes."

For travel specifics, see the Back Door Survival information under Nepal in the Nitty Gritty section.

23. Dhulikhel—A Mini-Trek with Maxi Views

An unobstructed view of 200 miles of the snowcapped Himalayas is worth a one-hour drive. Especially since it's from a small ridgetop town with cobbled streets, interesting old buildings and temples, and friendly locals.

Dhulikhel is known for these attributes and by the foreigners living in Kathmandu as a place just to get way from the city and relax. Fortunately, not many tourists know about it. It's a convenient place to experience life in a small Nepalese town and take a variety of walks in the countryside.

The town sits on a ridgetop at 5,100 feet. The one main street in town has a few old temples and worn brick buildings on the west end and wonderful Himalayan views on the east. Foreigners aren't a novelty, neither are they abundant, so the people are still gracious. You can wander and observe life without feeling you are intruding. The town is also the district headquarters and has a number of administrative offices. Walking through town in the evening, you'll probably meet a young man assigned to work here who is eager to practice his English or just find out about you.

For good views of the mountains without walking too far, head to the soccer field on the east end of town. This is especially nice at sunrise or sunset. A better view is from the Kali Temple, about a 30-minute walk up the hill from the soccer field. Follow either the winding dirt road or the direct footpath to the temple for views of the entire central Himalayan range, from Mt. Langtang in the west to Mt. Everest in the east.

There are several longer walks in the area that someone in average shape can handle. The most interesting is a circular walk through small villages and past great views to Namobuddha Stupa and a small Buddhist monastery. It takes three hours to the stupa and three hours back. The Dhulikhel Lodge in town has hand-drawn maps of the route. The lodge will also prepare a lunch for you to take, but there

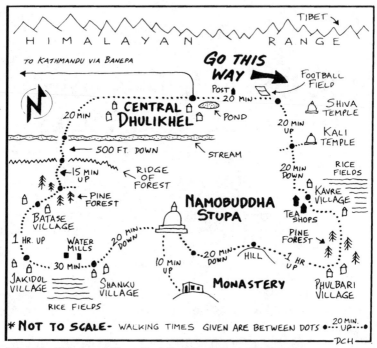

The Dhulikhel and Namobuddha Maxi-View Mini-Trek

are a few tea shops along the way. All the locals along the way know exactly where you must be heading and will point out the way the moment you look confused. If you want to practice your Nepalese, just say "Namobuddha jaane," which means "I go to Namobuddha."

Namobuddha means "hail to the Buddha." This has been a holy site for centuries. Pilgrims will be circling the stupa, chanting, and spinning prayer wheels. There are some tea shops here with basic food and drink. From the stupa, walk about 10 minutes to the top of the hill. Here is a small monastery, more stupas, and a stone slab depicting the legend of Namobuddha. Supposedly at this spot Buddha found a starving tigress and her cubs. He was so moved by compassion that he offered his body as food.

Walk back to the stupa, and follow the path 20 minutes downhill to Shanku village. Walk another 30 minutes past a few water mills on to Jakidol village, then up about an hour to Batase village. Next walk through the pine forest. Stay to your left where the trail splits. In about 15 minutes, climb up 10 feet of broken sand steps, and head 500 feet down through a bush area. Cross the tiny stream and walk the 20 minutes back to Dhulikhel.

A shorter hike goes to the village of Panuati, southwest of Dhulikhel, where you'll find the old and finely carved Indreshwar Mahadev Temple, among others. Off the beaten path, the village offers a peek into the slow traditional Nepalese life-style. From Panauti, either walk the 4 miles to the roadside town of Banepa or take a bus. In Banepa, there are regular buses for the short distance to Dulikhel or to Kathmandu.

Part of the pleasure in staying in town is the Dhulikhel Lodge. It still offers the same warm hospitality it did when we first came here nine years ago. It's an older twenty-room building in the local Newari style. The rooms are basic but clean. There's a quiet garden in the back where tea and meals are served during the day. At night, sit on covered mattresses around low tables in the sitting room and restaurant. Spun wool blankets carpet the floor. The intimate atmosphere here brings travelers together in discussion about travel, philosophy, and stool samples. Bob recalls, "In this room over tea in 1981, I learned from a traveler that China was unofficially open to independent travelers. This changed the course of my trip and the next two years of my life." If you don't get such profound tips from travelers, Prem Shrestha, the owner, will at least fill you with information about getting around the local area. The lodge will be moving to a different building. We hope it's as cozy as the present one.

If you don't have time or energy in Nepal to go on a longer trek in the mountains, at least get out of Kathmandu to Dhulikhel for a mini-trek with maxi views.

For travel specifics, see the Back Door Survival information under Nepal in the Nitty Gritty section.

24. Himalayan Treks or Treats

"I'm not sure which line to stand in," an American woman said at the entrance to the trekking permit office in Kathmandu. French, German, Italian, and Spanish whirled around us as fingers traced routes on stretched-out maps. Above the front counters, signs stirred and beckoned us: Everest/Khumbu, Langtang/Helambu, Annapurna. Noticing "The Slug Who Ate Seattle" emblazoned on Bob's T-shirt, the woman looked our way and added, "I really don't know which trek to go on. Where are you guys going?" It can be confusing. Here are our ideas on the whys, hows, and wheres of trekking in Nepal.

Why not hike instead of trek? Trekking is not just an exotic way of saying hiking. There is a fundamental difference. A hike is "a long, vigorous walk." A trek is a "journey," with a journey being "passage from one experience to another." Thus, in the Rocky Mountains, you might hike the trails and look at nature. When you trek in Nepal, you walk, have chiyaa at tea shops, huddle with Sherpas in smoky one-room houses, and get chased off the trail by stubborn yaks.

Trekking in Nepal isn't typically a wilderness experience. There are some isolated areas, but the mountains are dotted with small villages until you reach the very high altitudes. While the lofty peaks are awesome, a great part of the experience is the interaction with a different culture. You'll get insights into a slower, ancient, and in many ways more satisfying life-style. Settling into the different pace, observing different customs and attitudes, you start to examine and question your own patterns and values.

When deciding if a trek is for you, consider whether you want to interact with a new culture. This means learning about and observing the local customs. It also means making the effort to share something about yourself through words, pictures, or music (we always bring photos from home and a flute or harmonica). Trekking tries your patience and tolerance. Here is an example of that from the travel journal.

"The snow is now rain, and my REI jacket is soaked. So are my Gortex-lined boots. I'm tired of sliding in the mud. I hope it's not much farther to the next village; it'll be getting dark soon. We come to a fork in the trail. It's not on the map. Should we go up or down to the stream? We slide down through wet brush. The trail ends at a stream running through a high walled narrow gorge. The water is fast and about waist deep. I don't see the trail on the other side but can't really tell in the dim light. So we muck our way back up the steep hill. At the fork, the other trail narrows as it traverses the steep gorge wall. We decide to walk back twenty minutes to a small hut and ask directions. A family of three sits around a fire in a straw lean-to nestled against a cliff. I stand at the entrance and try my few words of Nepalese. They just look at me. I say the name of the next town, 'Dunche.' They still stare. I point up and ask, 'Dunche?' They nod their heads from side to side. Does this mean yes or no? I point down and ask, 'Dunche?' They nod. Rain drips off my saturated wool cap and down my neck. I point both up and down. They nod again. I'm frustrated, irritated, and angry. I feel like screaming and shaking these people. Somehow I manage a 'namaste.' They nod good-bye. We head back and take the high trail. Fortunately, it leads past the gorge and connects to a trail across the stream. At the lean-to I had a chance to observe my anger, as the Buddhists would say. To watch negativity arise and then go."

Trekking in Nepal usually includes food and lodging along the way. The lodging ranges from sleeping around the fire with a family in a small stone hut to staying in a separate room with bed, mattress, and pot-bellied stove. Some lodges have only dhal bhat (lentil soup and cooked rice); others may serve pizza, Tibetan momos, and chocolate pudding.

For a solo wilderness experience in the mountains, hike the Rockies or Sierras. For a cultural journey in a spectacular setting, trek Nepal.

Are you in good enough shape? Anyone who's in decent physical condition can find a suitable trek. If possible, get into some aerobics and go on a few hikes before leaving for Nepal. Or start your trek by walking only a few hours each day and then adding more hours as you strengthen. If we walk no more than four or five hours a day, we can meet people in the villages, take pictures, and enjoy the views. We plan rest days for just hanging around the village.

You can match your trek to your condition. Your route can be short or long, low or high. You can hire a porter or guide to carry all or part of your gear. To work into shape, consider hiring a porter to carry your pack for the beginning of your trek. You can also hire porters in the villages along the way. This way you can carry your pack at low

A trekkers' bed and breakfast . . . with the abominable Yeti

altitudes and then have someone carry it over the high passes, or when you want a break.

With or without a guide? There are pros and cons to trekking with a guide. With a guide there's a feeling of security that comes with having your own private expert. The guide is a ready resource in planning. He can also increase your interaction with the Nepalese, since he may have friends or family in the area you're going. Depending on his English, he can tell you about the area and the people and also interpret. You'll probably learn a lot about him—and maybe gain a friend. A guide can take you off on side trips if you plan in advance. Some guides will carry part of your load and cook, although these are usually the jobs of a porter. For women trekking alone, a woman guide or porter will make it safer (although incidents of crime are still rare). Nepalese women don't travel alone, and you won't seem so strange or of questionable morals if you don't either.

Taking a porter will reduce your load. You can be free to just walk and enjoy the people and scenery. Porters usually don't guide and rarely speak much English. They may know people along the way, so this could increase your interaction with the locals.

Without a guide or porter, you gain the rewards of self-reliance: freedom, self-confidence, and the satisfaction and knowledge of figuring out a new situation on your own. You'll enjoy the freedom of being able to set your own pace without worrying about the porter keeping up. This is more a problem when the porters are carrying a lot of equipment. Or if the porters have had too much _chang_ (beer) the night before. If it's just you and a guide, it's usually not an issue. You may need to stick to a schedule, though, if the guide has to return for another trek. Without a guide, you talk to the locals and other trekkers to find out directions, order your own food, and make your own decisions, such as if there is too much snow in the pass to continue.

If you do take a guide, keep your group small. Large organized treks feel separate from the culture. You spend your time talking to others in your group, not with the locals or even your guide. Organize your own trek, and keep it to two or three people.

Consider your style of trekking. Do you want the works, where a guide leads you and porters carry a tent, food, and your things? This allows you to visit areas where there are no villages. You don't need to stay in lodges with other travelers. And with your own tents, on the popular treks in the busier fall season, there's no need to worry about finding room in the lodges.

Other options are to hire one guide and porter, but don't plan to be completely independent. You can stay in the lodges and carry very little. Or bring along a tent and a few supplies, getting the rest in the villages. This would allow you to camp out sometimes and also stay in the village lodges. You will meet more locals and other travelers this way.

When making your arrangements, understand the system. Usually, guides won't carry, and porters won't guide. So you will probably have to hire both if you want total service. If you hire only a porter and you don't plan to stay close to the villages, you are responsible for his food and shelter. You must also make sure he has adequate clothing and shoes for the route. We've seen some parties turn around at high snow-covered passes because the porters were barefoot. Porters are usually not educated and speak little English. They may be less reliable than a guide and could decide to turn back or be difficult to get started in the morning. If you hire a guide, he will arrange for and manage the porter. Guides usually speak a little, if not good, English. You'll need to establish the wages per day before you leave. The guide and porter are expected to buy their food from this, so discuss this at the start. Also, if you provide clothing, they'll want to keep it. If you don't plan on that, then let them know.

The easy and expensive way to arrange a trek is to go through a trekking company in Kathmandu or through a travel agency in the United States who deals with them. You can save money if you do this in Kathmandu (allow several days for the arrangements). They'll arrange food, tent, trekking permits, guide, and porters. In Kathmandu, the cost will be at least $30 per day per person depending on the number of people going, the route, and so on. Some trekking agencies offer a cheaper barebones trek of basically a permit and a guide.

If you arrange a guide or porter yourself, you save the cost of the middleman agency. Best places to check for them are at trekking equipment rental shops or at the Association of Sherpa Guides. Interview the guides to see how well they know the area you plan to go and if this is the person you want to spend a lot of time with. Ask to see their book of recommendations from other treks. Guides charge $5 a day and up depending on their reputation and skills. The regulated wage for porters averages about $2 a day but depends on the altitude.

On your own? Like many things in life, the most difficult part of trekking on your own is just getting started. The unknown is frightening. To go to a strange land, head into the mountains, and stay in village houses without any help sounds adventurous . . . maybe too adventurous. We'll be evangelists for a minute. There are only two reasons you couldn't trek on your own: (1) You're completely out of shape and don't want to bother getting back into condition; and (2) you totally lack the patience, time, or interest to get to know another culture. Otherwise, just prepare and jump into it like the rest of us.

You need your gear, a map, and a Nepalese-language phrase book (and you could get by without that). Either bring hiking equipment or rent it at one of the trekking shops in Kathmandu. If you're only going to Nepal and have your own gear, bring it. If you're going to be traveling outside of Nepal, rent your gear in Kathmandu. Down sleeping bags and jackets and foam sleeping mats are easy to find. Hiking boots are available, but your feet will probably be happier with a broken-in pair of your own. Good backpacks are in short supply, though there are some decent used ones for sale. There are a limited number of lightweight stoves and tents. Most items rent for around a dollar a day.

If you bring your own equipment and will be traveling around before coming to Nepal, you can (for a charge) leave your things at the left baggage office at the airports. You can also take it with you into any city and leave it at your first hotel or guest house. Most places will store your things for little or no charge. For example, on our last trip, we stored our hiking gear at the guest house in Bangkok for free.

Then we traveled around Malaysia and Thailand for two months, picked up our stuff, and flew to Kathmandu. Make sure you don't leave any valuables in storage, though. You can also ship your things back from Kathmandu or sell them to the trekking shops there.

Trekking maps and phrase books are available at Kathmandu bookstores. The tourist information office also has maps. You'll need to arrange a trekking permit from the Immigration and Trekking Office in Kathmandu.

Picking a trek. Now down to the heart of the matter—which trek. In choosing, look first at your personal constraints and what you want from the trek. Your constraints will be your physical condition, the season, and your time. In considering what you want from the trek, think about: Do you want to take it easy, be on the move all day, or something in between? Do you want to have nice lodges and good food, or do you want to rough it? Are you interested in certain types of people such as Tibetans or Sherpas? Do you want to be around other travelers? Do you want to be on your own, or go someplace where you'll need a guide? How much do you want to carry?

Think about these questions when looking through the following short trek descriptions. You should find one that fits. Then get one of several detailed trekking books to use as you actually do the trek.

Ridgetop trekking in Nepal's Annapurna range

Annapurna Himalayas

The Annapurna range, north of Pokara in the central area of Nepal, offers short and long treks. The longer and most popular trek, the Annapurna Circuit, goes completely around the range and takes twenty days. The trail goes from lush vegetation and rice paddies into rhododendron forests, up through the impressive Kali Gandaki gorge, to arid countryside extending into the Tibetan plateau. Then it goes over Thorung La pass (17,700 ft. and often closed by snow from December through mid-April). The trail then passes along the north side of the range, providing spectacular views. This trek specializes in grand views. In addition to the varied landscape, the ethnic groups along the way are quite different. There are good lodges along the way.

The shorter and also very popular trek to Jomsom and return only takes ten days. Most prefer to go on to Muktinath, a Buddhist and Hindu pilgrimage site at 12,500 feet, which adds a few more days. This Jomsom trek is part of the Annapurna Circuit. It has the most comfortable lodges and best food of the treks in Nepal. It's open year-round, and there are no high passes.

The Annapurna Sanctuary is worth a side trip off the Jomosom or Annapurna Circuit trek, or make it a trip in itself. You'll need at least ten days. The trek takes you to around 13,000 feet, and there you are surrounded by the giants of the Annapurna range towering more than another 10,000 feet above. There are small lodges along the way. In the winter, the sanctuary may be closed due to snow or avalanches.

Around the Pokara area, there are a number of one- to five-day treks. Several of the trekking guide books mentioned later discuss these.

Advantages: Varied geography and ethnic groups. Spectacular mountain views. Options of short or long trips. Good lodging and food. From Pokara, easy access to the start of the treks. Pokara is a visit-worthy town.

Disadvantages: Most popular trekking area. During the peak months of October and November, you may have to stop early to get a bed in a lodge. The lodges are more comfortable than other treks, but they also alter the feeling of the villages. Some places even have videos. Some of the treks will be closed due to snow in the winter.

Langtang/Helambu, North of Kathmandu

The regions of Langtang and Helambu can be done as individual treks or connected by crossing a mountain pass. The areas do not quite match the variety of ethnic groups and geography of the Annapurna area. On the Langtang trek, however, you'll find terraced rice fields and forests at the lower elevations and yak pastureland and Tibetans among glaciated peaks at the higher. And as you near the Tibetan border at the upper reaches of the Langtang River, the mountains jut above the 12,000-foot valley floor. Some small peaks (such as Yala, at 16,000 ft.) are worth the extra hike for the views of the surrounding mountains. Several side trips, such as to the Gosainkund Lakes at 14,000 feet, are worth considering. The Langtang trek is through sparsely populated areas, and the upper elevations are uninhabited except during the summer when the yak herds graze. There is lodging all along the way. The Langtang trek is a 6-hour ride from Kathmandu, although most people take the 12-hour ride to Dunche to save a two-day walk. From Dunche, the Langtang trek takes about seven days. Langtang is trekked less than either Annapurna or Everest.

The Helambu area does not have great mountain views (unless you cross the 15,000-foot pass near Gosainkund into the Langtang area—which may be closed by snow in the winter). The Sherpa people live here. Helambu does have the easiest access from Kathmandu of any of the popular hikes. It's only about an hour ride. And Helambu gets relatively few trekkers. From Kathmandu, the Helambu trek takes seven days.

Advantages: Good for those wanting a shorter trek. Fewer trekkers here than Annapurna or Everest, especially in Helambu. Right among the high peaks in the upper Langtang valley. Not closed due to snow, except for the passes between Helambu and Langtang. Both have villages and easy-to-reach uninhabited areas. There are lodges the entire way which are less sophisticated than on the Annapurna Circuit.

Everest (Solo-Khumbu)

Mt. Everest is this area's main draw, but a trek here has more to offer than just the mountains. The Sherpa people in this area are known for their friendly and industrious nature. Their hard work has also put many foreign climbers on the top of Everest. You have spectacular mountain views once you're in the Khumbu area. Many people come to trek to the Everest Base Camp (17,500 ft.) just to say they made it to the big one. Another popular destination is Kala Patar (18,500 ft.), which has a good view of Everest. There are other trekking possibilities in the area if you don't want to struggle into the higher elevations.

The largest Sherpa settlement in the area is Namche Bazaar. It caters to trekkers with comfortable lodges and small hotels, shops, and restaurants. Definitely not the traditional small village atmosphere.

Along the trek there are other smaller villages with lodges, and there are also places to stay in the higher uninhabited areas.

Unless you fly in, you'll climb and descend (from the nearest road-side town, Jiri) for eight days to the Khumbu area. It's another eight days walk to the Everest Base Camp. There are flights to Lukla in the Khumbu, a six-day hike from the Base Camp (12 days round-trip). Weather often delays flights. It's common to have up to a hundred people waiting to get out of Lukla on the small planes.

From the travel journal: "This morning we started the eight-hour hike back to Lukla. When we got there, an American in a cowboy hat stopped us. He wanted to know if we had plane tickets. We said we were supposed to fly out the next day. Then he told us that no planes had flown out for the last four days and some people had been waiting for a flight to Kathmandu for nine days. He asked that we turn our plane tickets over to him, and he would put us on a waiting list. He said the airline officials weren't handling things like people wanted, so he had volunteered to take charge up here. We refused and went to the flight control office. The mountains were socked in and there must have been 200 people hanging out in the village. We were told that the day before passengers had marched around the one-room control tower with ice axes, shouting and threatening the officials. They all wanted to be flown out the day it cleared.

"The next day it did clear. An army helicopter flew in first, and armed soldiers were posted next to the control tower. When the first plane landed, the officials escorted us to the plane. We flew out, and fortunately everyone else got out also."

Considering this story, along with the fact that more people fly out, you might want to fly into Lukla (9,200 ft.) and walk out. This would take twenty days to do the Base Camp. The problem with this is the sudden change in altitude. You'll have to take more rest days to adjust. There are also some other airstrips at lower elevations that you could use. Flights aren't as frequent as to Lukla, but you wouldn't have to deal with the sudden high altitude.

As you climb you need to acclimatize to the changes in elevation by pausing for a day at certain elevations to allow your body to adjust. The most likely candidate for altitude sickness is the one who thinks he's in such great condition he won't get it. We saw one group of French Alpine guides who raced from Lukla to the Base Camp in three days (9,000 ft. to 17,500 ft.). One man went into a coma, and some of the others were very sick. Take acclimatization seriously. Just take it slowly and watch for symptoms. If they occur, go to a lower altitude for relief and rest. Some people use the drug Diamox to help with high altitude. Trekking guidebooks discuss altitude sickness in more detail.

Advantages: The thrill of trekking to Mt. Everest. Spectacular scenery. The Sherpa people. Interesting short as well as long treks. Open year-round, although more difficult and few views during the monsoons.

Disadvantages: Need to acclimatize to high elevations. Long walk in or possible delays on flights. More trekkers here than Langtang but fewer than Annapurna.

For travel specifics, see the Back Door Survival information under Nepal in the Nitty Gritty section.

Wannabe porter

25. Rhinos and Tigers and Gurus, Oh My!

This section is a catch-all for a variety of things to try in Nepal. If you have the time after Kathmandu and trekking, head south to Chitwan National Park to see the rhinos and tigers. A meditation retreat offered by one of several Buddhist centers in Kathmandu will guide you up some entirely different mountains. White-water rafting will test any tranquillity gained from your meditation. And if you can't bring yourself to leave this wonderful kingdom, you can look for volunteer or paid jobs.

Chitwan National Park

From the travel journal: "We lay on our bellies and crawled along the banks of the river, our camera cases dragging to the side. We wanted to get within range of the two rhinos in the water. We moved a few yards at a time, gaining more courage as the rhinos hadn't picked up our scent. Finally, close enough to get a decent shot with our 150 mm lenses, we stopped. We lay for about ten minutes just watching these strange-looking creatures. Then keeping low, we backed up into the brush. We continued on the path through the six-foot-high elephant grass. Suddenly there were snorts, stomps, and rustling on each side of us. As a wild boar broke through the grass at full speed, we both sprang up trees. We were relieved that it wasn't a rhino, or worse, a tiger. After we caught our breath, we ran the rest of the way to the platform and scampered up the ladder . . . closing the trapdoor to keep nature where it belonged."

All the ingredients for an adventure are in Chitwan National Park. There are hundreds of rhinos, some tigers, sloths, bears, monkeys, deer, crocodiles, and many species of birds. You'll have to look for them more carefully than you would in the parks in Africa. But that's part of the excitement.

Chitwan National Park sits along the border with India about equal distance between Kathmandu and Pokara. It's near the Terai, the hot plains of Nepal, and next to several rivers. The park has both grasslands and forest. In the earlier days, the royalty of Nepal and other countries hunted here for tiger skin rugs. Now it's lowlife poachers killing rhinos so some fellow in Hong Kong can cure his impotence with a magic potion of powdered horn.

You can explore by elephant, walking, or canoe. Many tourists let the expensive lodges in the park arrange it all. By doing it on your own, you'll save $280 a day—enough to pay for your film. In the village of Sauraha, adjacent to the park, are a number of small inexpensive lodges that will help you arrange everything.

Swaying on the back of an elephant above the tall grass, you won't be worried about charging rhinos. An elephant is the safest and most fun way to go through the park. And there is a good chance you'll see some rhinos. Rides can be arranged with the government-run elephant camp at Sauraha or through your lodge. Get your name on the list early. The two-hour $10 rides are popular.

Hire a guide in the village to take you on a walk through the forest. Although not an official guide, the young man leading us knew a lot about the animals and where to look for them. There were groups of monkeys chattering and swinging above, a variety of birds along the river, and an occasional deer and wild boar. The guide also spotted some bear droppings. He apologized that we didn't run into more animals that day. Guides cost about $2 per person. Your lodge can find you someone. You can go on your own, save $2 a day, and maybe even become a wild boar's snack.

A canoe trip down the nearby Rapti River and up the small streams provides views of birds, sometimes crocodiles along the banks. Inexpensive canoes can be arranged through the lodges in Sauraha.

Sauraha has a number of inexpensive lodges for the do-it-yourself traveler. Look around and compare. Basic thatched-roof huts with verandas, shared baths, and nice gardens cost about $3. A few places have classier $8 rooms with private baths. Most places will help you find guides and arrange for elephant rides and canoe trips.

The more expensive lodges can be arranged through travel agencies in Kathmandu. For these, two-night/three-day packages run from $150 to $600. Packages include transportation, meals, park fees, and other things such as elephant rides or raft trips. Many of the lodges (like the Elephant Camp Lodge in Sauraha) offer dances at night by the Tharu people of the area. It's usually a good show.

The entry fee for the park is about $10, which you'll pay each time you enter. There is a visitors' center at the edge of Sauraha with some exhibits and information about the park.

To get to Chitwan, you can take a plane, bus, taxi, or raft. The cheap way is an eight-hour bus trip from Kathmandu or Pokara to Tadi Bazaar. If you're coming up from India, the bus takes about four hours (and $2) from the border towns of Birganj or Sunauli. It's four miles from Tadi Bazaar to Sauraha. You can catch a ride on a jeep or truck, rent a bike, or walk. A taxi from Kathmandu can cut several hours off the trip but runs more than $100 for a return trip. The driver will wait for a few days there. If shared with several others, this may be affordable. The half-hour flights by Royal Nepal Airlines go to nearby Meghauli and Bharatpur. Many of the expensive lodges offer rafting on the way to the park. Some travel agencies in Kathmandu also arrange rafting trips into the park.

The best time to go is during the cooler and dry months of mid-October to February. It's warm during the days and cool at night. The monsoon season (June to September) is the worst time because of flooding and the heat. The locals cut the park's high elephant grass in February, so this is a good time to see the animals.

Bring light cotton clothes and a sweater and light jacket for the months of December and January. Also take a brimmed cotton hat for the sun, mosquito repellent, and compact binoculars.

A visit of two or three days at the park should be enough to see things, although you could spend a few more relaxing days here. Allow a day to get down and a day to get back.

A final piece of advice. If a rhino charges, go up a tree. If there is no tree, run in an arc. They have bad eyesight, so they usually charge straight ahead. Rhinos don't really want to hurt you. They just can't see well enough to know whether you want to take their picture or shoot them.

Rafting

Several Nepali rivers are great for rafting. Travel agencies in Kathmandu can arrange trips of various lengths for $30 a day and up. The fairly gentle Trisuli River heads to the south of Nepal toward Chitwan National Park. The Sun Kosi River, originating in the Everest region and flowing west toward Kathmandu, offers some good white-water rafting. The rivers are too swollen for rafting during the monsoon season (June to September). October, November, February, and March are good. December and January are fine but cool to cold. In April and May, the water is getting low and the weather hot.

Meditation and Buddhism

Travelers to Nepal are often struck by how people with so little love life so much. In the mountain villages, old women smile and joke while molding yak dung into paddies for fuel. Ragged, dirty children laugh and shoot small pebbles across the dirt as in a game of marbles. At the end of a long day, sooty-faced women with babies strapped to their backs hover for hours over a smoky fire cooking, yet never seem to lose patience and their zest for life.

Many feel part of the mountain people's wonderful nature is due to the influence of Buddhism and are drawn to look at the religion. In doing so, the idea of the word "religion" changes. It's interesting to see that people don't go to buildings to worship on Sunday and the rest of the week get involved in other work. Religion here is an everyday part of life. You see it in the way some walk down the trail muttering prayers and carrying strings of prayer beads. You see it in stones along the paths engraved with the prayer, "Om mani padme hom." You feel it in their kindness to travelers.

To understand what makes Buddhism such a vital force in the people's lives, attend a discussion on the religion, or better yet, join a meditation retreat. Both are offered in Kathmandu. For either talks or retreats, check with the Himalayan Yogic Institute (tel. 4-13094) in the north part of the city near the Russian embassy. The Nepal Vipassana Meditation Center offers courses each month (Jyoti Bhawan, Kanti Path, in Kathmandu, 4:00-5:30 p.m. except Saturdays, tel. 2-25490 or 2-26327). If you wish more information, write the Vipassana Center, c/o Mr. Maniharsha Jyoti, Box 133, Kathmandu, Nepal. Around the Thamel area, you'll also see notices for discussions and classes on Buddhism and Yoga. Check with the Pilgrim's Book House and on the bulletin board of the Kathmandu Guest House.

Volunteer and Paid Work

Some people just can't leave Nepal and find a way to stay. There are some volunteer and paid positions available. Getting a work permit, technically necessary for paid positions, can be tricky. For studying, or teaching at a university, you may be able to get a longer visa. You may wish to work as long as your tourist visa allows (about three months), side-trip to India, and return for another three months.

There are many volunteer agencies in Nepal, but most hire from outside the country. To work with the Tibetan refugees (e.g., teaching English), talk with Karma Tashi of the Snow Lion Foundation at the Tibetan Refugee Handicraft Center in the Jawalakel area of Patan (tel.

5-21241). Also check with Save the Children-USA near the Russian embassy in the north part of Kathmandu (tel. 4-12447 or 4-12598). The American Peace Corps (tel. 4-13875) in Kathmandu and CARE (tel. 5-22153) in Patan is worth a visit. Nurses can check with the hospitals and clinics. The foreign-operated clinic, CIWEC, may have some ideas.

The best way to land a rare paid position is through a local contact. On his last trip to Nepal, Bob was offered a job teaching at a university in Kathmandu. The pay wasn't great, basically subsistence and a small room. The most obvious positions are teaching English. Talk with the colleges and universities and private elementary and secondary schools.

CHINA

26. The Back Door China Closet

China provides the best and worst of traveling. It's frustrating, exciting, overwhelming, and enlightening all at once. After hassling with a rigid, unconcerned government tourist agent for a train ticket, a helpful middle-aged worker will lovingly guide you down the street to the station. It's a vast land filled with places that have never seen an American. You can also visit touristed places that serve hamburgers and Coke with gourmet ten-year-old eggs.

It's dreary. And it's spectacular. Mundane concrete cities cloaked in coal dust are springboards for visits to some of the world's greatest wonders—both man-made and natural. There's the Great Wall, the sculpted terra-cotta army of Qin Shi Huangdi in Xian, and the 230-foot Buddha carved from the cliffs in Leshan. There are also the tropical jungles in the south, Mt. Everest in Tibet, and the vast Gobi Desert.

The Chinese are a mixed bag of temperaments and ethnic backgrounds. The city folk of the industrialized and crowded east could appall a New Yorker in their pushiness and rudeness. But one on one, they're usually considerate and pleasant. The people in the countryside, especially in the ethnic areas along the borders, are easier going and easier to like. As anywhere, those less rushed and cramped have time and energy to say hello.

One of China's great walls is the language barrier. While more and more Chinese are learning English, expect communication problems outside the normal tourist areas. Venture off the beaten path only with a good Chinese-language phrase book, a small Chinese-English dictionary, and a ready pointer. Compile a list of useful Chinese character phrases.

While we're generally handy at managing with the Asian languages, we find Mandarin (the official dialect of China) difficult. When Bob practiced his skills, a Chinese friend would usually ask, "Are you speaking Mandarin or English?" But locals appreciate your struggles and work hard to understand you. Creativity and pantomiming helps.

Chinese, especially students, wanting to practice English, go to a regular spot, an "English Corner," usually in a city park. Ask at your hotel or guest house. You'll make Chinese friends who will often speak openly and frankly about themselves and China. If they invite you to their home, bring a small gift such as fruit, sweets, or something from home: postcards, music tape, and so on.

For many, Chinese food is most enjoyable outside of China. Quality varies. Variety is often limited. While some places offer outstanding local cuisine, others may serve only a dish that looks and tastes like brutally hacked pork parts rescued from an oil slick.

Food is best at local restaurants. Except for breakfast, avoid hotels and other tourist establishments. Normal Chinese breakfasts consist of sour or salty rolls and watery soup. The tourist hotels serve Western-style breakfasts. For other meals, follow the recommendations of your guidebook, the hotel staff, and other travelers. Get a group together so you can order a number of dishes. A full meal of rice and several dishes costs less than $2 per person. The small street food stalls can be good or at least memorable.

While common sense is important, travelers generally find China less of a health risk than other Asian destinations. Boiled water is readily available and food is usually well cooked.

While China is fascinating any way you travel, you'll smell the most cultural roses by bike or on foot. Head out slowly through any city and discover an old man in a sidewalk kiosk shaping hard taffy into lacy birds, fish, and animals; two 8-year-olds playing Ping-Pong on a makeshift table; a row of umbrella-covered men fixing shoes on leg-powered sewing machines; a formal festive midnight parade of the armed forces; and a tourist hotel with a penthouse discotheque and computer games.

Overnight boat rides offer a good introduction to sardine-style river travel. If maintenance of sanity is a higher priority than intimacy with China, an upper-class ticket is a worthwhile splurge.

Those who try to do too much spend most of their time on trains. China is enormous—larger than the United States including Alaska. You can ride for eight days (1,500 miles) on the train from Beijing to Urumqi in arid Xinjiang Province immersed in chitchat with awed Chinese. They'll plant themselves on your bunk and query with eager eyes about your life while sharing glimpses of their own. Locals drape their face cloths on a rail above the windows (to keep out the coal ashes) and produce large-lidded cups for their jasmine tea. Attendants pour boiled water, sweep and wash the floor, and arrange the face cloths to hang uniformly from the bars. You scramble from your bunk as the too-efficient attendant starts to make your bed at 6:00 a.m.

Accommodations, while still limited, are far better than when China first opened its doors to tourism in 1978. Usually travelers must stay in government-approved hotels, guest houses, or hostels. Prices range from $1 for a dorm bed to $175 for a luxury hotel room. You'll sleep comfortably in hotels for $15 a room and in guest houses for $5 to $10.

China: So Much Country, So Little Time

At one time or another, Confucius must have said, "Man who tries to see all of China quite silly." To call China vast is like calling God smart. Unless you fly, transportation is slow and exasperating. Choose a region and focus. Assume you'll return. Here are our favorite places in China.

Kunming, in southwest China, is actually a likable city, an exception to the dreary Chinese norm. In the old town, wrinkled bearded men smoke pipes and play cards in open-fronted teahouses. Traditional two-story wooden buildings pull you into China's past. But short skirts and sporty designer labeled shirts pull you back.

Explore on foot or rented bike. The northwest part of town is the most interesting. Start out early in the morning at Green Lake Park as the young and old loosen up with Tai Chi. Grandmas and grandpas whack balls at croquet wickets and shuffle cards. Amusement parks whirl, giggle, and spin. On Sundays, the whole city appears to walk their children, watch sword swallowers, and show off their latest Shanghai fashion.

Just to the north of the park you'll find countless old buildings, the zoo, and lots of good street restaurants. Join the pilgrims at the thousand-year-old Yuangtong Temple. South of Green Lake, the Kunming Provincial Museum offers a collection of crafts, weavings, and traditional folk costumes.

Kunming is known for its tasty southwest China specialties: the hot and spicy Sichuan food and Yunnan Province's steamed chicken and noodle soup dishes. Try the street stalls. Or go with a group of fellow travelers to a nice restaurant and order a number of dishes. Just point at what others are eating and looks good. For a breakfast of real coffee and baked goods, head to the Vietnamese Coffee House on the side street of Baoshan Jie near the intersection of Zhengyi Lu and Jinbi Lu. Later, work off your coffee jitters at the local disco where men dance with men and women with women.

Shilin (the Stone Forest) is near Kunming and worth a visit (except on Sunday when it's packed by the locals). Five- to thirty-meter-high spires of rock create several "forests," providing visitors with interesting walks around, under, and through the rocks. Many of the limestone spires have eroded into shapes that conjure up such names as the Five Elders, Moon-Gazing Rhino, and others too interesting to mention here.

Spend the crowded hours wandering paths that lead into the countryside where you can find interesting rock formations without the tourists. Visit the most popular areas in the late afternoon when the tour buses are heading back to Kunming. Walk to the nearby Sani minority villages. These colorful people will hustle to completely outfit you in their local handicrafts. Bargain hard. At night, the Shilin Hotel offers a good song and dance show by the Sani.

To get to the Stone Forest, catch a minibus tour from the train station, or ride two hours on the crack-of-dawn public bus. Kunming's thieves and pick-pockets target tourists around the train station, on buses, and in the tourist areas. Get even with a back pocket full of wet noodles.

Xishuangbana, bordering Myanmar (Burma) and Laos, is a region of jungle-covered low mountains and valleys with the Mekong River as its centerpiece. This is the home of the Dai, Yi, Miao, and an assortment of other colorful ethnic groups.

For maximum scenery from Kunming, take the three-day bus ride up and down mountain roads, past terraced hillsides, lush green forests, and waterfalls. Speedier travelers fly to Jinghong.

Jinghong is just your basic town, but it's a short walk to the Dai villages nearby. You'll probably be invited into one of their large wooden and bamboo houses on stilts for tea and fruit, or to puff the magic bamboo pipe. The local mix of tobacco and marijuana brings on visions of Mao (they say).

To go out farther, take a public bus or boat or arrange a van at the hotel. Menghun, about a three-hour drive southwest of Jinghong, is well worth a visit. On Sunday, hill tribes come to town for one of the largest markets in the area. Other possibilities include a boat ride down the Mekong, backpacking into the hills, and overnight stays in remote villages.

Dali is the Kathmandu of China. Travelers come for the atmosphere of the old town as well as to share tips and stories over tea at small cafés. They also come to trek to monasteries and villages in the mountains.

This town of whitewashed houses is laid out in a square with some of its original walls and gates still standing. The traditionally clad Bai people add to the atmosphere. Time your visit for Sunday when the weekly market has the town teeming. Nestled between a large lake and the mountains, the scene is as picturesque as it is discovered . . . very.

If you don't mind all the other travelers, Dali is great. The "Three Pagodas" complex on the hill behind the town is worth a visit. You can stay overnight at a Buddhist monastery on Chickenfoot mountain, twelve miles away. Bike rental shops, popular for good reason, have maps of the area. Take a ferry or hire a boat to one of the lakeside villages.

Most get to Dali by overnight bus from Kunming. While they miss the pleasant drive past rice fields and forests, the night bus has the advantage of sleeping bunks, no smoking, and no spitting (rare in China). Lone women risk unwelcomed advances at night.

Lijiang rewards those who push northward from Dali. It sits in a valley under rugged 16,000-foot-high glaciated peaks. Much of the town is drab, but the old part is an interesting maze of canals and narrow cobblestone streets with stone and wooden buildings in the tradition of the Naxi people.

China crowned by a pagoda in Lijiang

The Naxi are a proud group who have preserved their traditional culture, including their own style of music and dance. Catch the top 70s band. The ninety-year-old conductor gives a talk in English about Naxi music before the guys in the orchestra, all over 70, play. See them soon!

Rent a bike and explore the valley. Visit Dr. Ho's clinic in Baisha, six miles north of Lijiang. Over tea, he'll tell you stories of all those he saved through Chinese medicine. From Baisha, go another three miles up the hill to the Yufeng Si monastery for grand mountain and valley views.

Around and beyond Lijiang are countless areas to backpack and explore. Though the friendly Naxi let you stay in their villages, be prepared to camp out.

It's a fifteen-hour bus ride from Kunming to Lijiang. Consider a stop in Dali and continue another six hours. For other travel options and more specifics, read *Southwest China Off the Beaten Track* (by K. Mark Stevens and George E. Wehrfritz, published by Passport Books).

Emei Shan (Mt. Emei), one of China's sacred pilgrimages, is on the train line between Kunming and Chengdu. Join vacationing Chinese families, older pilgrims, and a few Western travelers on the trek up the 10,000-foot mountain. Along the way, monkeys demand cookies for safe passage.

From Bob's journal: "A large monkey blocked the trail ahead. He bared his sharp teeth as his hairy gang of ten watched nearby. The large Chinese group approached. Their leader pointed at the monkeys and rattled off something in Chinese. We joined the end of their party and, like the rest, held out open hands. Walking forward, the party chanted 'Mayo' (I have nothing). The head monkey hissed unhappily. The leader of the Chinese group picked up a big stick and charged. The monkey scampered. We passed."

A rice paddy ramble into the mountains of Guilin

The summit is a day's hike each way. You can eat and sleep at trailside Buddhist temples. Wimps and speed-demons go by minibus to within ninety minutes of the top. If you hit it right, you'll witness Buddha's Aura from the summit. Rainbowlike rings sometimes appear in the afternoon when the sun strikes the mist below. In days past, the devout threw themselves off the cliff into the Aura. In days present, people gawk and wait. But nobody jumps.

Don't miss the Dafu (Grand Buddha) rising 210 feet above the river in the nearby town of Leshan. Carved from the cliff almost 1,300 years ago, this spiritual giant has a toe the length of a sailboat. Riverboat tours offer the best look.

Guilin (pronounced Guay-lin), in the southeast, is an area immortalized by generations of Chinese painters. The Li River snakes through mist-covered craggy hills, offering some of this world's most picturesque countryside. The weather has molded the limestone peaks into bizarre shapes, affectionately named Elephant Trunk, Folded Brocade, Old Man, and so on.

Travelers hang out downriver from Guilin in Yangshou. With many small cafés serving Western food, it's not traditional China. But it's smaller, less expensive, friendlier, and cleaner than Guilin. In Yangshou, hike on nearby mountain trails, rent bikes for excursions in the countryside, and catch up on the latest China travel gossip. Take the awesome three-hour boat ride up the river (toward Guilin, opposite the tour crowds). Then get off and return or carry on by bus. Yangshou is easily reached by a two-hour bus ride from Guilin. Guilin town itself is worth a half-day excursion on bike.

The **Silk Road**, in the northwest, is a fascinating trip in itself. The train heads west from Lanzhou into the vast Gobi Desert and the town of Jaiyuguan. From the fort marking the end of the Great Wall, the bleak barren land extends into the horizon. Countless TV antennas stick up like swords fighting the bleakness from the town's tiny houses.

Ancient Buddhist paintings of the Mogao Caves draw many travelers to the oasis of Dunhuang. Visit the caves on your own rather than on the too-short and too-structured tour. Hike the dunes at the edge of town in search of the mystery lake.

Farther west at slow-paced and friendly Turpan, the Uygurs, a Central Asian people, built underground channels from the Taishan mountains to water their fields and trees. Turpan is the second-lowest spot in the world and the hottest spot in China. Thick mud-walled houses keep you cool as summer temperatures soar to well over a hundred degrees. At the guest house in town, spend evenings with a cold beer under a vine-covered trellis listening to local musicians. Before or after the midday heat, hop a donkey cart for the ancient and deserted cities of Gaochang and Jiaohe at the edge of the oasis.

One of the last stops on the train west is Urumqi. This industrial city isn't worth a visit, but nearby Tianchi (Heavenly Lake) is. A three-hour bus ride takes you from the arid wasteland to China's Aspen. Travelers come here to hike in the mountains and in the summer, to stay in the yurts of the Kazakhs who bring their animals to graze.

From Urumqi, a new train line heads west across the border of what was the Soviet Union to Alma Alta. Some head south to Kashgar and onward into Pakistan.

Tibet is a worthy goal and a major hassle. China opens and closes the doors to Tibet depending on the political mood. Even when officially closed to individuals, a few sneak in. In some cases, those not on a tour have been asked to leave on arrival at the airport (some "temporarily" join a group on their flight and get by). Others coming overland by bus from Golmud in the north have gotten in. Once in Tibet, you may be restricted to certain areas.

Tibet, particularly Lhasa, has changed drastically since the first Chinese invasion in 1950. To contain dissent, China transplanted its people into Tibet. Today, Tibet has more Chinese than Tibetans. The narrow streets of old Lhasa have been widened for patrolling army vehicles. Drab buildings replace much of the old. Yet there is still good reason to visit.

In Lhasa, you see devout Tibetan pilgrims from all parts of the country. They circle the Jokhang Temple and throw themselves on the ground before it. They visit the Potala, the former home of their spiritual leader, the Dalai Lama. The nearby Sera Monastery and Drepung Monastery are still active and intact. Most of the other monasteries throughout the region were destroyed during the Cultural Revolution.

Leave Lhasa through rugged dry landscape west to the smaller town of Gyantze with its monastery and old fort. Team up with other travelers to charter a jeep for the drive to the Nepal border and views of Mt. Everest. The farther away, the friendlier the Tibetan faces. For the independent traveler, a useful guide is _Tibet—A Travel Survival Kit_, published by Lonely Planet. For more on Tibetan culture, see our Back Door on Dharamsala, where the Dalai Lama waits in exile.

HONG KONG

27. Hong Kong and Its Island Escape

Hong Kong is a shopper's delight. Landing planes clatter with the chatter of excited bargain hunters. But even those not born to shop find Hong Kong worth experiencing. After sampling its big-cityness, we head for its outer islands. Hong Kong can be a comfortable and needed pause between wearing Third World experiences.

On a recent trip, Rick stopped for a couple of days. Armed only with a budget Asia guidebook, some tourist brochures, and optimistic confidence that Hong Kong was easy to manage, he made his visit a study in touristic efficiency:

"After clearing customs, I took advantage of the airport's energetic tourist information office, picking up a map, lists of sights, accommodations, and tours, and some quick advice. To save time, I grabbed a taxi to the downtown hotel district. To save money, I invited two bewildered-looking tourists to join me. My US$9 cab ride became a $3 ride, and the three of us shared ideas and plans.

"It was noon, and I wanted to tour the New Territories that afternoon. Before finding a room, I stepped into a large expensive hotel and booked a seat on the 1:30 tour. There always seem to be more tours than tourists, and large hotels are happy to sell you a seat on just the tour you're looking for.

"My guidebook recommended several budget hotels and guest houses. Determined to dive headfirst into this culture, I chose a guest house—double the culture for half the price. A seething honeycomb of Chinese-style guest houses called Chungking Mansions offer plenty of cheap sleeps right in downtown Kowloon. I had my choice of meager rooms for $15. A reservation here makes as much sense as calling ahead for a Big Mac. Look like a tourist, and hotel runners will make finding a room too easy.

"The Crown Colony of Hong Kong is made of four parts: Kowloon city, a mainland peninsula that faces Asia's Manhattan; Hong Kong Island, a ten-minute ferry ride or three-minute subway trip across the harbor; the outer islands, wooded and underpopulated, linked to the metropolitan center by ferry; and the New Territories (370 square miles), which stretch north from Kowloon.

Hong Kong, Asia's Manhattan

"My three-hour bus tour gave me a good look at the New Territories. Shacks and paddies ornament the countryside. Bold skyscrapers rip through this pastoral scene like gleaming stiletto blades casting an oppressive shadow on the silent Hakka villagers. Back in Kowloon, where skyscrapers fit and peasants don't, I walked the streets past countless shops and commerce-hardened shopkeepers. Street peddlers unload counterfeit watches before the police drive them off. At night, large markets line side streets with stacks of designer shirts and pants. Block after block of ultra-modern palaces of consumption beg for attention."

Catching the famous Star Ferry to Hong Kong Island costs only a dime and is as easy as catching an elevator. The ride was nearly as fast.

The north end of Hong Kong Island is a forest of skyscrapers—each one guarding its riches, jealously reminding Hong Kong's homeless squatters that they have no business in this lofty world. This is Hong Kong's business center. During the day, office people merge with shoppers at lunch. Colorful double-decker buses, trolleys, and taxis clog the streets. Tourists head up to "The Peak" in the tram to glimpse the islands, skyscrapers, and millions below.

The best tourist strategy is to open your eyes wide and wander. Pop into that small restaurant, point to something on the menu, and see what comes. Browse in the shop with the window display of crushed deer antlers, dried snake, and bottled bear gall bladders.

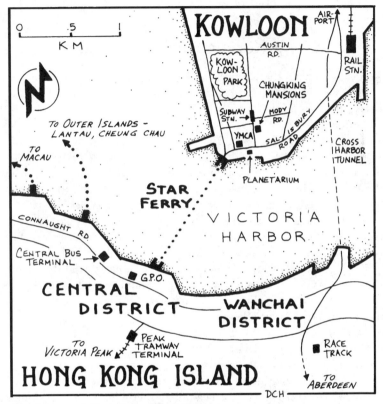

Kowloon and Downtown Hong Kong

Hong Kong isn't noted for its nightlife. There are remnants of the sleazy Wanchai bar district (famous in World War II and Korean War days as the "World of Suzie Wong"), where topless waitresses hang like rags over dull beers and conversation sizzles like bacon on a cold griddle. Nearby you'll find impromptu outdoor restaurants feeding the crowd out for an evening stroll and businessmen working past their wife's bedtime.

The floating restaurants of Aberdeen are a cheap and easy bus ride (#70 from the Central District, 20 minutes) south on Hong Kong Island. Aberdeen was once a floating city of houseboats. But they're disappearing as new high-rises bully the city's waterfront. Soon all houseboat people will be resettled on dry land. The remaining scene of junk boat builders, luxury yachts, pleasure crafts, and fishing boats is still worth a visit. Eat at one of the huge floating restaurants. At night they're lit up like Christmas trees. They have their own free boat service.

See Hong Kong prior to 1997 to experience it before it reverts back to China.

Hong Kong's Outlying Islands

To get away from the Hong Kong hustle, head for the less-populated islands. Ferries leave from several piers, an easy walk west of the Star Ferry, in the Central District.

Lantau Island, while the largest island in the colony, has only 20,000 people. (Hong Kong Island, half the size, has over a million.) Lantau's rugged interior is crisscrossed by 40 miles of hiking trails. It has several fine beaches (uncrowded on weekdays). Take bus #2 from the ferry terminal at Mui Wo for a scenic ride to Po Lin Monastery on the high Ngong Ping plateau. Swim at Cheung Sha Beach on the way. From the beach, the bus winds up through green undeveloped countryside to the monastery. At Po Lin (tel. 985-5669), a dorm bed complete with three vegetarian meals and mosquito coils costs about $25.

For a good dose of traditional Chinese rural life, stay at the slightly run-down, family-run "Jun Gay" inn (a few minutes walk from the bus stand at Po Lin, $10 rooms). Although the inn will cook meals, the monastery's restaurant is better.

During the day, Po Lin is busy with tours coming to see the world's tallest outdoor bronze Buddha. The giant rises 200 feet above a nearby hilltop. In the late afternoon, when the tour buses leave and tranquillity returns, wander around the monastery. Avoid the midday crowds by hiking the trails to Lantau Peak or to the hilltops for views out to sea. Visit the Lantau Tea Gardens, a ten-minute walk from Po Lin. Take a thirty-minute walk past several monasteries and nunneries to the monastery of Po Lam with good sea views. Continuing one hour past Po Lam through pleasant countryside, you'll reach the small town of Tung Chung on the north shore where infrequent buses return hikers to the ferry.

From Bob's journal: "I was lucky to be welcomed at Po Lam. Master Seung Yi said that because of past trouble with foreigners, only Po Lin monastery still accepted tourists. Eager not to become 'past trouble,' I joined the monks and nuns in the meditation hall that evening. A bright ring of a bell signaled the start of the chanting. At the next ring, all rose from their mats. We walked in a silent procession around the enshrined Buddha.

"Early the next morning, after chanting and breakfast with the monks and nuns, I went to thank Seung Yi and offer a donation.

Refusing, he handed me an envelope filled with a generous amount of money. A monk explained this was for my journey as a traveler.

"Reluctantly, I walked up the misty path. The quiet was broken only by a few brightly colored birds darting from tree to tree and the pant of the temple dog who guided me up the path. I offered him a piece of bread, but like his master, he refused."

The nearby fishing town of Tai O offers another look at old Hong Kong. An elderly Chinese woman will pull you across to this island town in her rope-drawn sampan. Tin houses rise above the creek on their stilts. Early each morning fisherman display their catch on Market Street. Enjoy a cup of tea on the town square surrounded by the time-worn faces of old Hong Kong and the twinkling playful eyes of the new. On the edge of town, the tiny Hau Wong Temple has reminded 300 years of travelers of how Merquis Yeung "rendered meritorious service to the boy emperor of the falling Sung dynasty."

Come to Tai O quickly. Waves of change lap at its walls as the city folks build vacation villas and a new Hong Kong international airport will soon shake this sleepy island awake.

JAPAN

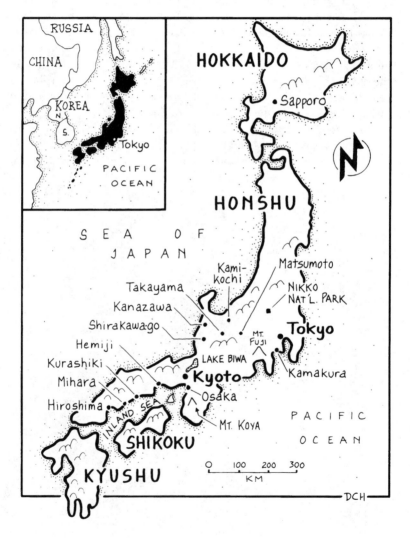

28. Kyoto and Tapping the Essence of Japan

A shaven-headed monk steps soundlessly through a Zen garden of rounded stones and landscaped white sand. An ivory-faced geisha clad in a colorful kimono sits on a tatami floor and plucks doleful notes from a stringed koto. A wizened artisan spins a ball of clay on his potter's wheel, as he begins to sculpt a masterpiece that—like each of the thousands he's created—will for that moment be the single work to which he dedicates his life. Another artisan turns the handle of the pachinko (pinball) machine, sending the metal balls toward a hopeful win and a box of bean paste candies.

No visitor can hope to grasp the essence of traditional Japan without a visit to Kyoto. This ancient city of a million, capital of the island nation from the eighth through the twelfth century and residence of the emperor until 1868, is the epitome of Japan.

Located 300 miles southwest of Tokyo and about 30 miles from Osaka, Kyoto was the only major Japanese city spared the World War II bombings. Though the body of Japan may have been shattered by the war, its heart and soul were left intact. Kyoto is a pincushion of attractions: over 400 Shinto shrines and 1,600 Buddhist temples, dozens of religiously landscaped gardens, imperial residences, and fine museums. Artisans' districts, the old geisha quarter, and outstanding bargains in textiles, antiques, and traditional arts and crafts make Kyoto a hit with travelers from around the world.

Before you start your tour of Kyoto, visit the Tourist Information Center. (The TIC is on the street level of the Kyoto Tower Building, across from the Kyoto train station.) The staff has a wealth of information on everything going on in Kyoto. They can set you up with a Japanese student: you get a tour guide, he gets to practice his English. The TIC can also arrange a visit with a Japanese family (not an overnight stay). Check with them about short introductory workshops on wood block printing and other crafts. Pick up a free copy of the *Travel Guide* put out by the city of Kyoto for more on current happenings. Also get the *Kansai Time Out* and the *Kyoto Journal*. These magazines are edited by foreign residents and have hot tips for things to do. The *Kansai Time Out* includes everything from coverage of the twenty best noodle shops in Kyoto to classified ads such as "Japanese female (20) is looking for a native English speaker for language exchange and friendship. I am a serious person, and I really want friends who enjoy and think a lot of things with me. I am a little shy, but please call me, Fukiko, tel. 123123."

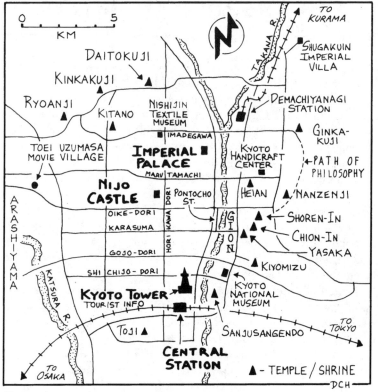

Kyoto

Kyoto has about 2,000 temples. But there's much more. Reserve one day for the once-and-forever emperors. The Imperial Palace was their residence until 1868, when the court was moved to Tokyo to foster closer relations with the West. Its eighteen buildings, simple yet noble, are linked by corridors woven around carefully tended gardens. They yield a picture of what early Kyoto must have been like—compact yet spacious, with Chinese influence far more evident than in modern Japanese architecture. There are tours twice every weekday (apply with your passport well ahead of time at the Imperial Household Agency in the northwest corner of the palace grounds).

A short distance southwest is Nijo Castle, an artistic and architectural masterpiece built in 1603 by the shogun, Ieyasu. (He was the model for the book and TV movie, Shogun.) Intended to be Ieyasu's home whenever he visited Kyoto, the fortresslike construction, with stone walls and moat, indicates the shogun was a powerful guy. Defense was designed in. The floors of linking corridors were made to squeak, warning castle residents of uninvited approaching visitors.

The Heian Shrine, two miles to the east, was built in 1895 to commemorate the founding of Kyoto. Focus on the simplicity of design rather than its gaudy orange colors.

For the best single day of temple-hopping, stroll along the foot of the hills on Kyoto's east side (covered in the TIC's "Walking Tour Courses of Kyoto" publication). This tranquil track beside an old canal is called "The Path of Philosophy" because it was the favorite route of a noted sage. In the spring, petals from cherry blossoms change it to "The Path of Pink."

Start at Ginkakuji, the "Silver Pavilion," on the lower slopes of Mount Daimonji. Built in 1489, this tea-ceremony room is said to be the oldest in Japan. Nearby Nanzenji, the Temple of Enlightenment, founded in 1293, has a magnificent main gate, a thought-provoking white sand Zen garden, and fine seventeenth-century paintings on the sliding screens of the Main Hall.

After a small noodle shop lunch near the Miyako Hotel, continue south on Jingumichi Dori past several more temples. Yasaka Shrine stands on the west side of Maruyama Park, facing the Gion entertainment district. Dedicated to a Shinto god, it's Kyoto's most popular shrine. The Gion Matsuri festival, held here for nine days in mid-July since 876, features worshipers parading through the streets to protect the city from plague.

Chion-in Temple on the east side of Maruyama Park is imposing. The Buddhist founder taught, "Return to ignorance. You can't find the spirit through intellect." Feeling strangely comfortable here, we enjoyed being virtually alone in the immense wooden temple just before closing (with no tour groups).

Climb the hillside east of Gion past pottery and ceramics workshops to the spectacular seventeenth-century Kiyomizu Temple. The view of Kyoto from the Main Hall's dramatic wooden veranda is worth the hike. Pilgrims flock here to stand under a waterfall and pray for safe childbirth and to request just deliverance from their enemies. The principal object of worship is an eleven-faced, thousand-armed Kannon, the goddess of mercy. The icon is considered so sacred that it is shown only three times a century (next showing: 1997).

Farther to the southwest is the Sanjusangendo Temple, stuck in the thirteenth century. Its central icons—a ten-foot wooden image of Kannon and more than a thousand smaller images—were reputedly carved in 1254 by an 82-year-old sculptor, Tankei, and his father. The Kyoto National Museum, across Shichijo Dori (7th Street), has an outstanding collection.

Temple fans can spend a second day touring the shrines on the northwest side of Kyoto. Ryoanji, the Temple of the Peaceful Dragon's famous rock garden, fifteen stones on a bed of raked white sand, is often interpreted as the essence of Zen.

For more worldly pursuits, go shopping. Make your first stop the multistoried Kyoto Handicraft Center, north of the Heian Shrine on Marutamachi Street (daily 9:30 to 6:00). Whether or not you buy, stop here first for craft demonstrations and to learn the fair prices of a great variety of quality arts and crafts. There's an especially good selection of dolls and fans. For more interesting crafts demonstrations and shopping opportunities, walk ten minutes, just south of the Heian Shrine, to the Kyoto Municipal Museum of Traditional Industry (next to the Municipal Museum of Art, closed Mondays).

Don't miss the weavers' quarter of Nishijin in northwest Kyoto. Visit the Nishijin Textile Museum with its fine display of old kimonos and other silks. Then stroll through this district of little wooden houses. Bargains lurk. If antiques and fine arts excite you, try Shinmonzendori and side streets south of Sanjo Station on Gion's east side. You'll find wood block prints, screens, ceramics, lacquer ware, cloisonné, bronzes, and many other exquisite artworks. "Takai" means "expensive," a handy word here.

For drama, head for Gion Corner. This one-hour show in the Yasaka Kaikan Hall (near the Yasaka Shrine, evenings March through November) gives visitors brief demonstrations of the tea ceremony, koto music, gagaku (ancient court music), bunraku (puppet drama), regional dance, and ikebana (flower arranging).

For a look at Japan's answer to Universal Studios, tune into the Toei Uzumasa Movie Village on the west side of Kyoto (open daily except around Christmas). You'll find seven acres of full-scale sets— feudal Japan complete with movie stars in period costume. The Film Art Hall exhibits Japanese film history. Be careful. Bob was taken captive by the shogun and ended up being used as a foreign extra in a war scene.

For geisha gawking, head up Pontocho street (from Shijo-Keihan train station, walk west on Karasuma street, take an immediate right after crossing the bridge, and walk north). Go at dusk when the small old inns are about to open. Enter at your own risk. This is expensive entertainment.

Apprentice geishas

Kyoto's flea markets offer cheaper thrills. One is at the Toji temple on the 21st of each month. Our favorite is at the Katano temple on the 25th. Come early for the best buys on used silk kimonos (as low as $20), pottery, antiques, and other buys. Bargain. The people-watching and eating is as good as the shopping.

Splurge once to try the traditional Kyoto cuisine (_Kyoto-ryori_) at the Hankazushi restaurant on Kiyamachi Street downtown near Pontocho ($30 lunch, $50 dinner, tel. 256-1341). If you have a student guide through the TIC (and a few yen), you might treat her here. Then you'd have someone to explain the local delicacies. For more reasonably priced fun and fare, head to the popular Kushihachi's (two blocks west of Kitashirakawa Street on Imadegawa Street). You'll get an overwhelming welcome from the cooks as you enter. Go with other travelers, grab an English menu, and order a number of plates of the grilled veggies and meats on skewers. The finale . . . ice cream tempura.

For pleasant hikes in the countryside, head west of Kyoto to Arashiyama. Weekend crowds enjoy a number of trails ranging from easy to difficult. Locals pack the area when autumn leaves explode with color. Even in the most crowded times, the side trails are peaceful. Arashiyama's Nenbutsu-ji temple has individually sculpted heads of Buddha and his 500 disciples covering the hillside. One sports a camera.

Mt. Kurama is great, and getting there—on the small train that winds scenically up the hill north from Kyoto—is half, maybe even two-thirds, the fun. From the temple, there are nice views and a number of hikes to smaller shines in the hills. For a great gift or to scare your neighbors, get a mask of the local folk character, Tengo. He's from a tale like Pinocchio. Look for his long red nose.

On the way back to Kyoto, stop to eat your noodles in the river. Get off where the Kibune and Kurama rivers converge (the first station after leaving Kurama: Kibune-guchi). Hike thirty minutes along the west fork (the Kibune) upstream through a thick forest. You'll find about twenty restaurants with low bridges that let you slurp noodles and slosh your feet at the same time. It's a shady, breezy, brook-babble way to spend a hot summer midday. Some of the restaurants are expensive, but a few offer *hiyashi somen* (cold noodles, a summer specialty) for around $10.

In Kyoto, you can sleep in youth hostels, guest houses, temples, ryokans, minshukus, and love hotels. One traveler hangout is Tani House (tel. 492-5489), with both dorms ($12 beds) and private rooms ($35 doubles). The conveniently located Ishikawa International Dormitory (tel. 771-0566) has private rooms for rent by the day and month ($280 to $480 a month). For a traditional inn, Three Sister's ryokan and their Annex is pleasant and convenient to many sights ($80 doubles, tel. 761-6333, fax 761-6335). Some of the temples (*shukubo*) allow you to stay for a small charge. Some ask attendance at the morning service and possibly some light work. Reservations must be made in advance (in Japanese, the TIC can help). Some of the temples are Daishin-in (tel. 461-5714), Heian-bo (tel. 351-0650), Jorenge-in (tel. 744-2408), and Torin-in (tel. 463-1334).

Funiya Ryokan, a traditional Japanese inn, has a great location, price, and atmosphere. This inn, with a tiny garden and a friendly staff, is located near Ginkakuji temple, close to the Path of the Philosophers ($40 a night or $75 per person with two meals, Kyoto's TIC can call to arrange a stay or try yourself in simple English by calling 075/771-4422). On our last visit, the older woman manager kneeled on the floor and bowed as we left. A few steps out the door we remembered a left article. We opened the door to find the woman still bowing.

Cultural Catch-alls in Kyoto

Kyoto is a great place to dabble in a little bit of everything— from flower arranging to "love hotels." Kyoto is a great base for getting to know the culture, both old and new. This is a different type of travel— staying in one place long enough where faces become familiar and you participate in the culture instead of observing it. It's a little trickier than just seeing the big sights. Here are a few fun ways to become a temporary local in Kyoto.

Kinkakuji, Kyoto's "Golden Pavilion"

Places, dates, teachers, and other information are found in the various English-language publications for Kyoto. *Kansai Time Out* is a monthly that covers what's happening in the Kobe-Kyoto-Osaka area with a classified section listing classes on the local culture. *Kyoto Journal,* a quarterly with an interesting mix of articles, includes a small but useful event calendar and classified section. The Kyoto YWCA's *Resident's Guide to Kyoto* has valuable information not only on living in Kyoto but also on cultural studies, sports, museums, and theaters. You can find these magazines at the Tourist Information Center in Kyoto or in the English-language section of one of the big bookstores such as Maruzen (between Sanjo and Shijo streets on the east side of Kawaramachi Street, third floor). You can also order a copy of the *Resident's Guide* by writing to: Resident's Guide Committee, Kyoto YWCA, Demizu-agaru, Muromachi-dori, Kamikyo-ku, Kyoto 602, Japan.

Live houses are places to hear live music and join in with Japanese university students and young adults. Groups play folk, blues, rock, reggae, and African pop. It's especially fun to hear country western. Saturday nights are for dancing. The monthly *Kyoto Visitor's Guide* (from the TIC) has locations and dates.

Meet both English-speaking Japanese and other foreigners at the Pig and Whistle Pub. This is a hangout for many Americans, British, and others working in Japan. If you visit on Irish night, you'll tap your chopsticks to Jay-san on the fiddle and Kyoko on the penny whistle.

The pub, on the second floor of the Shobi Building, on Sanjo Street, near the Sanjo Keihan train station, is open daily until midnight.

Experience a Japanese disco. Lines of dancers face mirror-covered walls. Don't ask, just jump in. Zen of dancing? Constant self-reflection. The TIC lists current hot spots. Cover charges start at $20.

Love hotels (*Abec Hoteru*) are gaudy, fanciful escapes for lovers, young and old. Since apartments and homes are small, some married as well as not married couples escape here for privacy. If you see a pink and purple castle with turrets, it's a love hotel. These places are outlandish and easy to recognize. The rooms are designed to make your dreams come true: beds created from convertible car bodies, mock beaches, your dentist's chair, and so on. Outside the hotel, prices are posted for an hour or an overnight stay. You'll pay a "see no evil" hand behind a curtain on your way out.

For more traditional cultural experiences, you can do a half-day introductory craft workshop or apprentice for years under a master. Teachers prefer students to study for a year (special visas are available), but the TIC lists plenty of classes and private instruction for shorter periods taught by teachers who speak some English. Another good information source is the *Resident's Guide to Kyoto*.

Ikebana, the Japanese art of flower arranging, expresses the beauty of plants and flowers as well as the beauty of the human heart. For lessons, check in the classified sections of the references above or call Kyoto's Ikenobo Headquarters (075/221-2686, English spoken).

If you have the yen for Zen, Kyoto's your place. It has a number of temples with public meditation open to foreigners. Some offer one-hour sittings, others overnight or longer. Always call in advance (with the translation help of your hotel or the TIC). Arriving late at a meditation class is bad style. For information, contact the Zen Culture Institute at Hanazono University (Zen Bunka Kenkyujo, Hanazono Daigaku-nai, Nishinokyo Tsubunouchi-cho 8-1, Nakagyo-ku, Kyoto 604, tel. 811-5189, Japanese spoken) and see the listing of temples in the *Resident's Guide to Kyoto*. For a longer, deeper Zen experience, stay at the International Zen Center of Japan (Kyoto branch: Kennin-ji temple, $560 a month for meals and lodging, write: Mirokunosato Shinsho-ji Kokusaizendo, Numakuma-cho Numakuma-gun, Hiroshima-ken, Japan 720-04, tel. 0849-88-1305, fax 0849-88-1200).

There are endless cultural possibilities (some only for the committed student): brush painting, calligraphy, tea ceremony, fan making, wood block printing, traditional dancing, martial arts, cooking, Japanese archery, and so on. The YMCA (tel. 231-4388), YWCA (tel. 431-0351), KBS Academy (tel. 441-4161), and Oomoto School of Traditional Japanese Arts (tel. 0797-23-2094) all offer an interesting list of classes.

Minshuku-ing It Around Japan, the Poor Man's Ryokan

A stay in a minshuku plugs a traveler directly into Japan. These family-owned, overnight boardinghouses are budget inns offering the same traditional experience of a more expensive ryokan without the elegant frills. Comparable to English bed and breakfasts, they are especially common in vacation and resort locations.

You become a member of the family, expected to pick your futon off the tatami mat and stow it in the closet each morning. Since minshuku owners are often farming or fishing families, your meals are usually prepared with fresh local ingredients.

From Rick's journal: "Looking for a minshuku, our ceiling was $40 each. We spent more, and now my ceiling is old wood paneling—pure and unfinished. We were immersed in a tatami mat world—slippers off at the sliding rice-paper door and a small quilt-fringed table with a heater underneath. We sat comfortably on chairs that had no legs. The middle-aged Japanese woman shuffled in tea followed by dinner: raw fish, strong pickles, hot sake, Japanese beer, steamed vegetables, and rice. Wearing yukatas (robes), we sat in an open space with only Buddha and flowers in the corner: the less there is, the more purely you perceive.

You're part of the family at a minshuku

"Breakfast was a raw egg broken over a bowl of sticky rice, mixed with business card-sized sheets of dried and crispy nori (seaweed), a small mountain of dried two-inch fish—heads and all, several slices of colorfully dyed fishcake, and plenty of tea. Chopstick dexterity is required as you bundle up a mouthful of rice in your soy-soaked seaweed and pop it into your mouth. Oishi! (Delicious!)"

Here are some tips for going properly local in a minshuku or a ryokan. The same tips apply for a Japanese home.

Take off your shoes before entering a Japanese house. Wear the slippers you'll find near the entry inside. Leave your shoes at the entrance of the minshuku. When you go outside, wear your shoes or borrow the *geta* (traditional Japanese wooden shoes) or sandals that are provided for the guests. (Some minshuku allow shoes in the public areas, and you'll slip on slippers at your guest room.)

In a traditional room, there is a slightly elevated straw matted floor. Park your slippers on the lower level and step, clean and cozy, on the matted floor barefoot or in stockings. The room will be traditionally, simply, and elegantly furnished with a low table, cushion, and mirror stand. A yukata (light cotton kimono) will be set out for you to relax in and wear as a bathrobe or pajamas. In the wintertime, this is supplemented by a heavier gown called a *tanzen*. You can wear both the yukata and tanzen indoors and outdoors. Western shoes look gooney with a yukata and tanzen. The tanzen is worn only over the yukata, which serves as a lining.

Japanese bedding, a covered futon, is laid directly on the soft matted floor. A blanket or light quilt is your cover. A rather hard pillow is provided. The whole works is kept in the built-in cupboard. Your innkeeper prepares and takes up the bedding.

The Japanese bath is used not to wash yourself but to relax in. In the minshuku or public bath, place all your clothes in a basket provided or on the shelf in the changing room. Enter the tub area with only a towel. First wash yourself outside the tub using the faucets or showers along the walls in the bathroom. Use soap only outside the tub. Rinse off all the soap suds by scooping and pouring hot water over your shoulders. Enter the hot water very slowly and settle quickly into a seated position. The more you stir, the hotter it feels. Parboil for about five minutes. You'll emerge on a natural high, with open pores and skin like a cooked lobster. If the temperature really is much too hot for you, ask for cold water. If there are several tubs, the temperatures may vary. If you are in a minshuku and have the tub to yourself, you can turn on the cold water faucet to adjust the water temperature. (Don't do this in a public bath, as others will be entering with you.) Don't make the water lukewarm or drain the tub when you leave.

The usual nightly minshuku charge of about $50 per person includes breakfast and dinner. Home-cooked Japanese food is always superb. It's courteous to reserve early in the day or a day in advance if possible. During peak travel seasons, make reservations as far ahead as possible. If you're traveling alone, you may be put in a room with others during the peak holiday seasons. You can make arrangements through the Japan Minshuku Center in Tokyo (Tokyo Kotsu Kaikan Building, 2-10-1 Yuraku-cho, Chiyoda-ku, Tokyo, tel. 03-216-6556) or in Kyoto (east side of the Hachijo entrance to Kyoto Station, tel. 075-661-5481). You can also get help using the "Japan Travel-Phone" (see the Japan Itinerary Back Door) or from the TIC. An English listing of a limited number of minshukus is available through the Japan tourist offices in both the United States and Japan.

For travel specifics, see the Back Door Survival information under Japan in the Nitty Gritty section.

29. Tokyo— Rebels without a Cause

Imagine a couple of hundred James Dean imitations, their long, wavy black hair slicked back into ducktails, cigarettes rolled up inside T-shirt sleeves.

Imagine several dozen more Sandra Dee look-alikes, ebony ponytails replacing blond, plaid skirts lifted high above bobby sox and tennis shoes.

Imagine these young boppers rockin' and reelin' in colorful, choreographed harmony to everything from Danny and the Juniors to rap and reggae.

This isn't a Broadway stage setting. It's a typical Sunday afternoon in Tokyo's Harajuku district.

"I want to bring the '50s back to life," seventeen-year-old Susumu told me in all seriousness as he dropped a pair of dark glasses over his eyes and lit up a Winston. "That was such a wonderful time."

Susumu, of course, remembers the 1950s well. His "to be" parents were just entering elementary school. But he's seen all the films—*Rebel without a Cause, Beach Blanket Bingo, American Graffiti*. He's listened to all the music, Elvis and Buddy Holly and Leslie Gore. He bought a life-sized poster of James Dean at a shop in Shinjuku. And now, "Don't you think I look like James Dean?"

Susumu and his schoolmates have a dance club, the Blue Suede Shoes. They meet here on Omote-Sando Boulevard every week. They arrive in navy blue school uniforms, having promised their parents they were headed to the library to study. They carry their dance "uniforms" in paper sacks. The girls change in the rest rooms at Harajuku Station, the boys in the bushes on the fringe of the stately grounds of the Meiji Shrine, whose venerated forebears roll over in their graves every week about this time. They emerge in pegged jeans, leather jackets, and saddle shoes. Susumu proudly carries a gargantuan ghetto blaster. He spent a full afternoon, he said, bargaining for this model in Akihabara (where Tokyo's best electronics buys are found). Now the tape player blares out the cassettes that the Blue Suede Shoes have chosen for their routines this week.

"We want all the people to see us dance," said Atsuko, sixteen, tee-heeing through the gap in her front teeth.

Not all the Take-no-ko ("bamboo children") as they're esoterically called, do '50s takeoffs. Some are into the modern disco scene, decked out in flowing Day-Glo satins with beads and medallions. (Tokyo may be the only city in the world with a high-rise disco—eight floors, each a separate club, in Roppongi Towers.)

The mile-long Omote-Sando Boulevard, extending west from Hara-juku Station beside Yoyogi stadium, is blocked off by police barricades

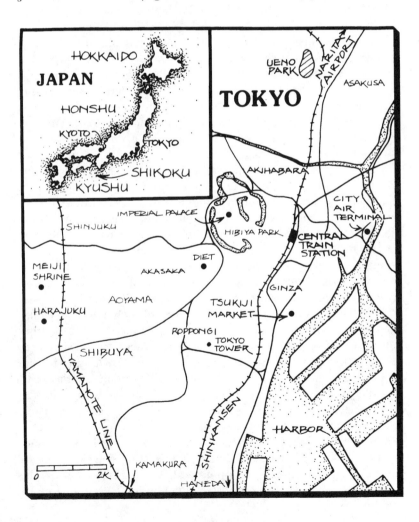

each Sunday for the safety of the exhibitionists. Throngs of people stroll past—bewildered Japanese adults out for a Sunday excursion, admiring fellow teens who wish they had the guts to join in, camera-laden Western tourists whose clothing often looks as outlandish as that of the young Japanese they're photographing.

Of course, Harajuku is only one of Tokyo's attractions. Tokyo should be seen . . . but quickly. Give it a day or two, and head for Japan's more peaceful charms. A subway/train pass makes getting around this mega-city easier and cheaper. With pass in hand, check out these day plans in or near Tokyo:

Plan One: Get off the subway at Hibiya Station and stroll to the outer garden of the Imperial Palace. Visitors are not allowed within the palace walls except on New Year's Day and the Emperor's Birthday (April 29). The National Diet (legislature) building and other government offices are a short walk west of the palace. For lunch, walk back through Hibiya Park to the yakitori stands and noodle shops beneath the Marunouchi train tracks. Spend the afternoon browsing through the Ginza department stores, cities in themselves. Don't miss the fine arts sections and the basement-floor food markets. And get used to hearing "Irrashaimase!" (Welcome!). At night, see what's on at Ginza's Kabukiza Theater.

Plan Two: Take the morning train south to Kamakura, a one-hour trip. This seaside town was the capital of Japan from the twelfth to the fourteenth century. Its famous 42-foot bronze Great Buddha dates from that era, along with a concentration of other religious sites. At the Hase Kannon Temple, see myriad stone images purchased by mothers for aborted babies. The Tokeiji Temple, sometimes called the "divorce temple," was a former convent and refuge for battered wives. On your return to Tokyo, entertain yourself in a pachinko parlor (Japanese-style pinball) or find a conversation in a *kissaten* (coffee shop).

Plan Three: Awaken early and take the Hibiya line to Tsukiji Station and the boisterous and colorful Central Fish Market. An amazing variety of seafood is unloaded and sold here. Then catch the subway to Ueno Park, a Japanese Smithsonian of attractions. You can visit the national zoo, national science museum, two important art museums, and the great Tokyo National Museum. With 86,000 exhibits, it's the best display of Japanese art and history anywhere. Lunch in the park, then walk or take the Ginza subway line to nearby Asakusa (pronounced a-sak-sa), the former geisha quarter. Asakusa Kannon Temple is at the end of a long, narrow street lined with souvenir shops. If the sumo wrestlers are in town (ask locally), take a short walk to the Kuramae Kokugiken for a completely different form of evening sports entertainment.

Plan Four: Make a day trip to Nikko, Japan's finest complex of temples magnificently set among mountain lakes and waterfalls. Toshogu Shrine is considered an architectural masterpiece. Take the quicker but more expensive limited express from Tokyo Ueno Station or the 2.5-hour local (Tobu Line) train ride from Asakusa Harajuku, with a transfer in Utsunomiya. From Nikko Station, catch a local bus to the shrine complex.

Plan Five: Spend Sunday at Harajuku (JR line to Harajuku Station or the Chiyoda subway line to Meiji-jingu-mae). Make a morning pilgrimage to the fine Meiji Shrine, with its treasure house and gardens dedicated to the nineteenth-century emperor who brought Japan out of the dark ages. After an afternoon of people-watching in Harajuku, head for the entertainment world of Akasaka, Roppongi, or Shinjuku. This is where the Tokyo youth scene thrives after dark.

The international crowd living in Tokyo parties in the Roppongi district. The wild and weird appear at the Deja Vue. Everyone who thinks they're someone (rock and movie stars) and those wanting to see them show up at the Lexington Queen. For Japanese '50's dancing, head to the Lollipop disco. Maggie's Revenge is a more relaxing spot, an Austirlian pub with live ballad and folk music. To meet international people in their 30s and 40s, linger around the Charleston. Regular bars and pubs generally have no cover, but disco charges are expensive ($25 to $40), although the price usually includes a complete buffet dinner and several drinks.

Sumo wrestlers—sake to me

For up-to-date happenings in the city, pick up the *Tokyo Journal* (in a bookstore's English-language section), *Tokyo City Life*, a free weekly newspaper (at hotels), or one of the daily English-language newspapers such as the *Japan Times*.

You may chance on an experience such as Diane, one of our Back Door travelers, had:

"We hit the Brazilian Club on Saturday night for some live music. No one had partners, you just got up and danced to the Latin beat. A Rio man living in Tokyo danced with me most of the evening. I was doing moves I didn't know I could do. When the club closed for the night, the owner bowed and thanked me saying, 'Beautifulu, beautifulu dancer come back,' then handed me 10,000 yen ($80). I had a great time and still came out 5,000 yen ahead for the evening."

30. Fourteen Days in Japan—Two Plans

For many, Japan is enjoyable and affordable for about two weeks. Here are two good two-week plans designed to show you the real Japan. This means alternating between city and countryside, staying in minshukus and with families, and diving into the culture.

Use the big city Tourist Information Centers (TICs) for information and help in arranging lodging and transportation. They man the "Japan Travel-Phone" help line daily from 9:00 a.m. to 5:00 p.m. They give excellent travel advice and act as on-the-spot interpreters—just pass the phone back and forth. (In Tokyo, tel. 502-1461; in Kyoto, tel. 371-5649; toll-free outside of Tokyo and Kyoto, tel. 0120-222800 for information on eastern Japan, 0120-444800 for western Japan. Travel-Phone doesn't work on the red public phones.)

While the Japan Rail Pass can be a good bet, the sample itineraries listed here don't call for enough travel to justify the cost of a rail pass.

Especially in Japan, your lodging greatly affects your experience. We get intimate with Japan by staying in traditional Japanese inns (ryokans), minshukus, youth hostels, and with families. Cable radio comes only with the more expensive hotels— 440 channels. At night, you can tune into the sleep channel: a woman counting sheep. In the morning, tune into the wake-up channel: birds chirping and roosters crowing. When necessary, tune into the alibi channel: sounds of bowling, Pachinko (pinball machines), and street noises—used by husbands amiss for background when calling home late at night.

Itinerary #1: Mountains, Towns and Villages

Days 1-2   Fly into Tokyo's Narita Airport. See Tokyo.
Day 3   Take the train to Matsumoto to visit one of Japan's finest castles, Matsumoto-jo (jo means castle). Its black slate walls rise from its moat with a backdrop of mountains.

Days 4-6	From Matsumoto, go by train and then bus to Kamikochi in the Japan Alps for the great hiking (good conditions from May through October, crowded in July and August). Backpack or stay in the inns and huts along the trails.
Days 7-8	Bus to nearby Norikura-Onsen (hot springs) to soak away the aches and pains of hiking. Then go on some of the more level hikes in this area.
Days 9-10	Bus to Takayama from Shim-Shimashima near Kamikochi. In Takayama, a small pleasant city near the mountains, you can tour a number of fine old merchants' mansions and some interesting old sake warehouses. Spend the early morning at the canalside market and walk or bike around the old area of town. Stay at the Sosuke minshuku or the youth hostel in the temple on the hillside.
Days 11-12	Bus to Shirakawa-go. Surrounded by mountain peaks and good walks, our favorite Japanese village has fifty large traditional thatched-roof houses. Several are minishukus.
Days 13-14	Return to Tokyo. Go out for a Roppongi night on the town (see Harajuku Back Door) and side-trip to nearby Nikko, or Kamakura.

Itinerary #2: Tradition, History, Sea Coast Villages

Day 1	Fly into Osaka. Bus to Kyoto.
Days 2-4	Visit the temples and back streets of Kyoto (see the Back Doors on Kyoto and Culture in Kyoto).
Day 5	Side trip to the temples in Nara.
Days 6-7	Take the train from Kyoto to Koya-san (Mt. Koya). This mountaintop retreat features a constant flow of pilgrims making the rounds of the 121 Buddhist temples to honor the dead and travelers enjoying an escape from the summer heat and humidity of the lowlands. To best experience Mt. Koya, stay overnight in one of the temples and get up early with the monks for chanting and meditation. The temples ask $60 to $80 per person a night, including two meals. Don't miss the large cemetery at the edge of town. From Kyoto, Mt. Koya is 3.5 hours by train and then a cable car ride.

Day 8	Ride the train west from Osaka to Hemiji to visit Japan's most impressive castle. Head farther west by train to Kurashiki. Its interesting canalside old town is a short walk from the station. Stay in one of the minshukus or ryokans by the canal and roam the back streets after dark.
Days 9-10	Ride the train to nearby Mihara to catch the slow, cheap ferry to Ikuguchi-Shima, an island in Japan's Inland Sea. In the small seaside town, stay at a ryokan, a minshuku, or the hillside youth hostel. Rent a bike at the ferry dock and explore. A three-hour pedal can take you over a bridge and around the next island past fishermen digging sea worms for their night's fishing, workers in the orange groves, and a peaceful remote village.
Day 11	Ferry, then train to Hiroshima to visit the Atomic Bomb Peace Memorial Park. The museum and its documentary movie are a must. If you are a Servas member (see Host Families in chap. 3), stay with a Japanese family.
Day 12	Take the ferry from Hiroshima to Miyajima Island nearby. Walk the trails in the mountain park to see the monkeys and deer. There's a full range of lodging on the island including a youth hostel.
Days 13-14	Train back to Kyoto (or Tokyo). Use your last two days to enjoy Japanese life. Side-trip to Mt. Kurama, north of Kyoto. Take a workshop on wood block printing (check with the TIC). See a performance of Bunraku (puppet theater) or Kabuki (musical drama). Visit the Handicraft Center. Go to a disco. Sign up with the TIC to visit a Japanese family.

Nitty Gritty, Country by Country

Countries follow the same sequence as Back Door section.

Asia Through the Back Door is designed as an introduction to Asian travel, not as a country- or region-specific guide to navigate by. The 30 Back Doors are a sampler of travel adventures written to take a little of the hit-and-miss out of your trip by sharing with you our favorite slices of Asia.

To unclutter the Back Doors and to help us keep this book easy to update and therefore more reliable, we've swept all the "nitty gritty, country by country" material into this almanac section. You'll find a nitty gritty section here for each country covered in the Back Doors. While we don't want our readers navigating solely by this guidebook, we do think of this section as a handy supplement to the country-specific guidebook we hope you'll travel with. Here we've collected any of our special thoughts on itineraries, transportation, eating, sleeping, and so on. This section rips out for easy packing and doubles as a handy mosquito swatter.

Indonesia

Best time to go: On the equator, it's always hot and humid. For much of the country, the wet season is from November to March or April, and the dry from May to October. However, from east Java going west, the seasons are ill-defined, and in the far west on Sumatra, there's no dry season. To the east, on Bali and Lombok, the dry season is the best, but the wet is fine for traveling.

Festivals: See the Appendix.

Visa: Visa not required for up to two-month stay. Onward/return ticket required. Visa extensions may be possible. Embassy: 2020 Massachusetts Ave. N.W., Washington, D.C. 20036 (tel. 202/775-5200).

Tourist information: Write the Indonesia Tourist Promotion Office at 3457 Wilshire Blvd., Los Angeles, CA 90010 (tel. 213/387-8309).

Language: Indonesian, a modern language designed for simplicity, is one of the easiest Asian languages. Take the time to learn at least a few words. In touristed areas, English is spoken by many.

Health: Eat only cooked food and drink treated water. Read chapter 7 concerning immunizations and malaria.

Transportation

Indonesia by plane: Flying between islands is cheap and saves lots of time. There are several equally thrilling domestic airlines. Some offer discounts if tickets are purchased in conjunction with an international flight.

Indonesia by train: There is an extensive rail network on the island of Java and three separate lines in Sumatra's south (Palembang), west (Padang), and north (Medan). Indonesian trains aren't plush but generally are quite satisfactory. Second class is comfortable; third class is cattle car. Train travel is very cheap.

The main trunk line on Java runs from Jakarta through Yogyakarta to Surabaya. The air-conditioned Bima night express goes from Jakarta to Yogyakarta in ten hours. It's another six hours to Surabaya. Second-class cabins have three berths. Palatable meals are served aboard. From Surabaya, connect to Banyuwangi at the east end of Java, where ferries shuttle to Bali.

Trains fill up quickly in Indonesia. Book ahead. Expect inefficiency. The station master probably won't know exactly when your train will leave and may not open the ticket window until several dozen people are jostling for position. Try to reserve a seat on a train originating from your station; those passing through are, inevitably, already full. If you have problems getting a ticket, check with the station master. Bribes help. Some stations have special ticket windows for foreigners. Pay a small commission for a travel agency to get a ticket for you in advance. Try third-class for a crowded but unforgettable experience.

Indonesia by bus: Buses go everywhere. Reservations are rarely needed. We prefer train for long distances but take a bus when we can't get a booking. Many roads are quite rough.

Indonesia by boat: Ferries go between islands, some small and shaky, some quite nice. Some travelers go together to hire a small boat to move about an island or between.

Accommodations: The inexpensive losmen, Indonesia's $2 a night guest houses, are generally spartan, with a bed, a table, and little else. The bath, _mandi_, is a water tank with a bucket; the toilet facilities are paperless squat-and-drop pits. But many are also family homes that offer wonderful food and a live cultural classroom. More expensive losmen have more comfortable rooms with higher quality pit toilets and baths. Hotels in all price ranges are also available.

Eating: Standard fare at most low-priced Indonesian restaurants is *nasi goreng* (fried rice) or *mee goreng* (fried noodles). Either is a meal in itself, cooked with meat and vegetables and topped with a fried egg. Another favorite is *gado gado*, a hot vegetable salad with spicy peanut dressing. You'll find the expensive *rijstafel* ("rice table") only at major big-city hotels. Famous in Holland, it is a Dutch colonial feast designed for colonial palates.

Cultural do's and don'ts: Many of the customs are the same as in other Southeast Asia countries, see those and chapter 12. Some customs peculiar to Indonesia: People will invite you stay with them—a great experience, but tiring. You'll be shown off to all the relatives. Indonesians think it's strange to want to be alone, so expect constant company. Many festivals and cultural events, such as puppet shows, last all night. If you go with locals, it's more difficult to cut out. (The local coffee is very strong.) As in Malaysia, the main religion is Islam, so women should dress conservatively, especially in the rural areas.

Guidebooks: Bill Dalton's *Indonesia Handbook* (Moon Publications) has long been the independent traveler's bible to Indonesia. Lonely Planet's *Indonesia: A Travel Survival Kit* is also good and full of detail. Both publishing companies offer guides to some of the individual islands.

Thailand

Best time to go: Late October to February is the best. Then the weather is a bit cooler, although in the 80s, and dry. In February, the temperature goes up and peaks in the mid-90s in late April. The monsoons come June through September, keeping it quite warm (average in the low 90s) and humid. A short blast of rain comes about once a day, the rest of the day overcast or clear. This is okay for traveling but not ideal for trekking.

Festivals: See the Appendix.

Visa: A 15-day transit visa, not extendable, is given free at the border. The official but rarely enforced rule is that those who enter must have an air or surface ticket out of Thailand. For longer periods, apply for a one- to three-month visa outside Thailand. If you plan to leave and return (such as a visit to Burma), get a multiple entry visa. If you get the three-month nonimmigrant visa (for business purposes), complete a tax form (from immigration in Bangkok) on leaving to avoid a $30 fine at the airport. For a visa application form write to the Embassy of Thailand, 2300 Kalorma Rd., Washington, D.C. 20008 (tel. 202/483-7200), or to one of the consulates, such as at 801 N. La Brea Ave., Los

Angeles, CA 90038 (tel. 213/937-1894).

Language: Due to tourism, English is widely understood (except in remote spots).

Health: Eat only cooked food and drink treated water. (Though some travelers drink the water in Bangkok and have no problems, we don't.) Read chapter 7 concerning immunizations and malaria. By taking precautions, most travelers have no problems. Assume prostitutes have AIDS.

Tourist information: The Tourism Authority of Thailand staff are friendly and offer many helpful pamphlets. The Bangkok office is at 4 Rajadamnern Nok Ave., tel. 662/282-1143. For information before you leave, write to the Tourism Authority of Thailand, 3440 Wilshire Boulevard, #1101, Los Angeles, CA 90010 (tel. 213/382-2353); or to 5 World Trade Center, Suite 2449, New York, NY 10048 (tel. 212/432-0433).

Transportation
Arrival at the airport: The tourist information booth in the arrival lounge at Bangkok's Don Muang International Airport has maps of Bangkok and Thailand and a variety of brochures. The Thai Hotel Association booth arranges reservations for the more expensive hotels. For the cheaper ones, use your guidebook and a pay phone.

For cheaper taxis, ignore those who approach you and walk to the exit doors on the left of the arrival lounge. The taxi counter there will arrange a ride to Bangkok, about $10. For buses and the cheapest taxis, walk about five minutes to the highway in front of the airport.

Thailand by plane: Domestic flights are reasonably priced. Consider a fast and easy flight one way and a more interesting rail or bus return trip.

Thailand by rail: Although buses will get you there more quickly, trains are more comfortable and safer. They're also cheap, frequent, and punctual.

First class has air-conditioned cars with reclining seats and compartments with sleeping berths. Second class offers seats and sleeping cars with overhead fans or air-conditioning (surcharge). Third class is crowded and spartan, with hard seats. Okay for shorter trips, but we go second class with a berth for long ones.

There are three types of trains. Ordinary trains stop at every town. Rapid trains have fewer stops and get you there about twice as fast. Express trains are a bit faster yet. There are surcharges of a dollar or two on international express (going to Malaysia), express, and rapid trains. Try to book three to five days in advance.

Thailand by bus: Bus is the fastest but not safest way of travel. Normally cool-headed and sane, Thais placed behind the steering wheel of a bus undergo a dramatic change. Sit toward the middle or rear of the bus. Reservations are rarely necessary. Go directly to the station, or book with a travel agency.

Buses are comfortable with a few pains. Private companies offer air-conditioning (usually too cold; take a light jacket or sweater), reclining seats (often short on legroom), and videos. A hostess serves snacks and soft drinks. On overnight trips you even stop for a snack at 2:00 a.m. (whether you want one or not). Public buses don't have reclining seats, but you'll be with the locals instead of tourists. And you won't get frostbite.

The Thai government encourages tourists not to accept food, drinks, or sweets from strangers. Some people have been drugged and robbed on the buses (usually the luxury ones).

In Bangkok, there are air-conditioned buses in addition to the regular ones. Get a city map for the routes. Be careful of pickpockets.

Thailand by taxi: In Bangkok, we use the river taxis when possible to avoid the pollution and congestion in the streets. Regularly scheduled boats go up and down the city's canals (*klongs*) and river. An express boat operates along the Chao Phya River between 6:00 a.m. and 6:00 p.m. Get the Bangkok map which shows the stops. Fares are just pennies.

Taxis are often air-conditioned and have no meters. Ask a local about the fares, then bargain. Anywhere in Bangkok shouldn't be more than $5 or $6. Don't use a major hotel as a landmark to direct a driver. The Sheraton and Hilton have their own special "zones."

Three-wheeled tuktuks, named for the noise they make, dart through gaps between buses, trucks, and taxis. Being open air, you get all the smells, noise, and sights you need to actually experience a Hollywood chase scene. Tuktuks are half the price and double the thrills of a taxi. Bargain hard.

Except around the tourist areas, you won't find many taxi or tuktuk drivers that speak English. Have someone at your hotel write down your destination in Thai. Make sure you have a card for your hotel in Thai for the return. Either learn the Thai numbers or use your fingers to bargain.

Thailand by car: After seeing the traffic in Bangkok, most wouldn't think of renting a car. However, outside the city traffic is reasonable and the roads are fairly good most places. Direction signs are in English along the major routes. The local rental agencies are cheaper than the international ones, with less reliable cars.

Motorcycles can be rented most places tourists go outside of Bangkok. If you haven't ridden before, don't start now. Biking is good for exploring certain areas of the country but not Bangkok. In most tourist areas, one-speed bikes and, in some cases, mountain bikes are avoid the wild truck and bus drivers on the major routes.

Biking around the islands such as Ko Samui, you'll find hills but light traffic and beautiful scenery. We enjoyed local biking in Pai (see the Back Door), Chiang Mai, Ko Samui, and along the Mekong River (see the Back Door).

Accommodations: Thailand offers a variety of good lodging, from inexpensive beach bungalows to what has been judged the best hotel in the world. Even the cheap places are usually clean, so you can hardly go wrong.

If you want to blow $200 in one night in Bangkok, there's probably no place as grand as the Oriental Hotel. Or just stop by for an expensive beer, and use the other $195 to cover your three-week holiday on the beach. The **YMCA** and **YWCA** have nice, moderately priced, air-conditioned rooms in Bangkok, starting around $30 to $50. The Swan Hotel, just behind the Oriental, is well worth its moderate price.

We stay at the numerous inexpensive small hotels, guest houses, youth hostels, and beach bungalows. The cheapest places run about $2 for a dorm room and from about $3 for a single (more in Bangkok). These are basic rooms with a bed, mosquito net, overhead fan, single light, and shared bathroom. Add plumbing and furniture and the price goes up. Even so, you can get a comfortable room with a bath for around $10 (more in Bangkok). We enjoy staying at guest houses in Bangkok behind the National Library (see the Bangkok Back Door).

Eating: Thai food is tasty heat, at least if you eat it the way the Thais do. In the U.S., Thai restaurants will ask you how hot you want it, between one and ten. In Thailand, it's often ten, and no one asks. However, restaurants in tourist areas tone down the food. Rice puts out the fire.

Food is good everywhere, even the 10-bhat (50-cent) meals at the small roadside stalls. Ingredients are fresh and nicely spiced. Some of our favorites are _tom yam kung_ (shrimp soup with lemon grass), _tom kha kai_ (chicken soup with coconut milk and lemon grass), _phud thai_ (noodles with vegetables and peanuts sprinkled on top), _gaeng gy nam prik_ (chicken curry with red chiles), _preo waan pla_ (whole sweet-and-sour fish), _kow neo_ (sticky rice), and _kluay buad chee_ (bananas in sweet coconut milk).

In general, dishes are inexpensive, less than a dollar. In the tourist areas, many restaurants have English menus and serve both Western and Thai food. At the small food stalls, a variety of noodles, vegetables, and meats are displayed. Point to the ingredients you want. Take a risk. Your mouth only lives once.

The blended fruit drinks are wonderful. Singha is a good Thai beer. Mekong whiskey will bring back memories of the old days in Thailand, even if you missed them.

Cultural do's and don'ts: Here are some points not covered in chapter 12.

Buddhist monks should be treated with the utmost respect. To help with their celibacy, they aren't allowed to touch or be touched by a woman. Women travelers should not sit directly next to a monk on a bus or train. The back seats of buses are unofficially reserved for monks.

The **king** is highly respected. There is no criticism of royalty, but you can join the Thais who aren't happy with their government.

Anger will get you nowhere. Thais will turn you right off. If you're frustrated over a visa extension, plane flight, or whatever, it's best to blow off some steam before you go in to talk about the problem.

The *wai* is how Thais greet each other, hands together as if praying and a slight bow. The way this greeting is performed is based on social status. To avoid embarrassment, it's best if travelers only wai individuals of definite high status, such as monks and the king (if you're so lucky).

Guidebooks: Lonely Planet Publication's *Thailand: A Travel Survival Kit* offers practical advice and information for the budget traveler. Both Moon Publication's *Southeast Asia Handbook* and Lonely Planet's *Southeast Asia on a Shoestring* have helpful sections on Thailand for the individual traveler.

Pai—Trekking in North Thailand Back Door Survival

Getting there: First go to Chiang Mai from Bangkok by plane, train, or bus. Catch a bus to Pai from the Chiang Mai Arcade Bus Station. Buses leave hourly for the four-hour trip.

When to go: Best late October to February when it's dry and cooler. Ideal late October through November when the forests are still lush from the monsoons. Worst May through September or mid-October when monsoons mean mud and leaches on the trail.

Where to stay: Cheaper guest houses in Pai start at $3. **Charlie's Guest House**, between the bank and the morning market, is clean, friendly, and has a nice garden. **Pai River Lodge**, across from the high school and near the river, has thatched huts on stilts with good views. **Pai Mountain Lodge**, four miles to the west of town, near a waterfall and interesting villages, has clean rooms with nice views (have a motorcycle drive you from town).

Where to find a trekking guide in Pai: A number of trekking companies work out of Pai's guest houses. All have had good reports, but things can change. "Trekker's for Life," run by Sith Zathu with two other guides (Dech and Pen), was good. They operate out of Pai Home Style Restaurant and Charlie's Guest House, speak English, and know the languages of the local hill tribes.

Other trekking areas: Stop at Air Guest House, one hour east of Pai on the main road to Chiang Mai. Air is friendly, speaks English, and leads treks in the area. Areas near the towns of Phayao and Nan to the northeast of Chiang Mai are reported to be good and not too touristed. If you do go on a trek from Chiang Mai, Youth's Tours (associated with the Chiang Mai Youth Hostel, tel: 248604) is a trekking company with a good reputation.

Odd sightseeing ducks: For a cave experience, head to Sappong, two hours from Pai by bus toward Mae Hong Son. At Sappong, walk four miles on a dirt road or pay $1 for a motorcycle ride to the Cave Lodge. Nearby is the Tham Lod Cave. A Thai called Slowly guides you along a river through a cave with prehistoric coffins. Most spectacular are the half million fork-tailed swifts and bats that swarm through the cave exit at dusk. Further on the main road toward Mae Hong Son are the more interesting Tham Nam Lang Caves (six miles long with many waterfalls). Nearby is Nam Khong Wilderness Lodge. Bus to Narm Khong. A sign past the Nam Khong bridge (going toward Mae Hong Son) points the way.

Guidebooks and maps: John Davies' _The Trekker's Guide to the Hill Tribes of Northern Thailand_ (Footloose Books of Salisbury, England) is an excellent resource. For a 1:50,000 area map, check the larger bookstores in Chiang Mai for the _Map of Chiang Mai & Northern Part._

A Swig of Mekong Back Door Survival

Getting there: For Chiangkhan, take one of the daily buses from Bangkok to Loei, a ten hour trip. Then a one-hour bus or songthaew (truck with rear seats) ride to Chiangkhan. For Nongkhai, buses and trains leave daily from Bangkok, about 12 hours. Best is by second-class sleeper on the overnight train.

When to go: November through February is best when dry and cooler. December and January temperatures are the coldest in Thailand, freezing at night, and April and May are the hottest, above 100 degrees.

Where to stay: In Chiangkhan, **Nong Sam Guest House** is pleasant. From the main road through town, head down Soi (street) 12 toward the river, and turn right at the end. Rob, the owner, also has bungalows out of town along the river (inquire at the main guest house). Nongkhai has a wide range of guest houses and hotels. In addition to Niyana's Guest House (mentioned in the Back Door, tel. 041/412-164) is the **Mut-Mee Guest House**, pleasant and on the river. **Sawatdee Guest House**, on Meechai Road near Soi Sri Kunmuang, is clean. Guest houses are $3 and up for a single.

A Beach for Every Dream—Back Door Survival

Getting there: Bangkok travel agency buses will take you direct to the beach or the nearest port, and link up with a ferryboat to the island. The fierce competition between agencies keeps prices low. Both regular air-conditioned and VIP class ($5 extra) have reclining seats. Apparently, VIPs have longer legs. Fares include the ferry. Here are some travel times and one-way prices for air-conditioned buses from Bangkok to: Ko Samui (12 hours, $10), Ko Phangan (12 hours, $10), Ko Phuket (14 hours, $14), Ko Phi Phi (14 hours, $14), Krabi (14 hours, $13), Ko Samet (4 hours, $6), Ko Chang (5 hours, $9). For Ko Tao, go to the mainland port for Ko Samui for a boat, or take one that leaves from Ko Samui several times a week.

We prefer the train for comfort and safety. A Bangkok travel agency will arrange a combination of train, bus, and boat. If we can't book a sleeping berth, we go by bus. Planes fly daily to Ko Phuket and Ko Samui. You can also fly to Surat Thani in the south and go by bus and boat to Ko Samui, Ko Phangan, or Ko Tao.

When to go: The weather varies depending on the coast. Monsoons bring rain to the west coast islands in the fall and to the east coast in the winter. However, it usually rains only once a day in the afternoon or evening.

Where to stay: Lodging varies with the beach and island. Some places have primitive bungalows, others range to nice hotels. Thatched huts on stilts with thin-mattressed bamboo beds start at $3. Toilets and showers are separate. Rooms with a shower, toilet, fan, and nice bed cost $8 and up.

Malaysia

Best time to go: Located so close to the equator, Malaysia is hot and humid year-round. The east coast is best during its drier season, October through February. The west coast is rainy from September through December. As elsewhere in Asia, the monsoons bring brief downpours, with the rest of the day dry. In the highlands of the interior, it's cooler (bring a sweater).

Festivals: See the Appendix.

Visa: Visas are not required for tourism up to three months. Embassy: 2401 Massachusetts Ave. N.W., Washington, D.C. 20008 (tel. 202/328-2700).

Language: Malay is a simple language to learn and essentially the same as Indonesian, so helpful throughout the region. English is widely spoken, especially on the west coast.

Health: Health standards are quite high compared to other countries in the region. Most travelers drink the water in major cities and towns but avoid it in out-of-the-way areas. Malaria is a low risk on the peninsula (not true on Sarawak or Sabah), but get up-to-date advice on this and on immunizations before you go.

Tourist information: In the U.S. check with the Malaysian Tourist Information Center, 818 W. 7th St. #804, Los Angeles, CA 90017 (tel. 213/689-9702).

Transportation
Malaysia by train: Malaysian trains are cheap, clean, and on time. You'll know your class by your seat cover. In deluxe (first class) they're upholstered, in _eksikutif_ ("executive," second class) they're padded leather, in _ekonomi_ (third class) they're cushioned plastic. _Ekspres_ (express) trains are fastest. The local rail pass (sold at the major stations) is rarely worthwhile. Even though Malaysian buses are inexpensive, comfortable, and air-conditioned, we do Malaysia mostly by train.
  Malaysia by taxi: Unique to Malaysia are the long-distance taxis. Although about twice the bus fare, a taxi (_teksi_) is a comfortable and convenient alternative. Go to the taxi stand and state your destination. As soon as a few others are going your way, the taxi will leave (or charter it for yourself). If going to the next major city, the wait will be short.

Accommodations: Malaysia offers hostels, beach bungalows, guest houses, and hotels. Guest houses start at $8 for a single, and dorm rooms are cheaper. Hotels range from $8 to sky high. For a cheap, clean, spartan room in an area with fine atmosphere, head to the Chinese section of any city.

Eating: Because of the variety of ethnic groups in Malaysia, you can sample many types of food, usually prepared nicely. There's Indian (our favorite), Chinese (everywhere), Malay, Indonesian, some Japanese, and plenty of Kentucky Fried, McDonald's, and other Western and Asian fast foods. Try the wonderful local fruits and the _laksa_, a spicy chowder of seafood and noodles in coconut milk. Watch cooks spin and stretch dough to make _roti telur_, a thin, pastry-type pancake, with an egg cooked inside.

Cultural do's and don'ts: The country is predominantly Muslim. In the very traditional east coast women should dress conservatively, and both sexes should be careful not to offend the locals by public displays of affection or drinking. Bathing suits can be worn on the beach but not in town.

Guidebooks: Lonely Planet's _Malaysia, Singapore, and Brunei: A Travel Survival Kit_ is good for the independent traveler. _Southeast Asia Handbook_ by Carl Parkes (Moon) and _Southeast Asia on a Shoestring_ by Tony

Wheeler (Lonely Planet) have useful but briefer sections on Malaysian travel.

Cameron Highlands—Back Door Survival

Getting there: Take a bus from any Malaysian city to Tapah (south of Ipoh). From here, take a regular bus for two hours to Tanah Rata (or a minibus from Restoran Caspian, No. 9, Main Road). Some travel agencies have direct tour buses to the Cameron Highlands for a bit more than the regular bus fare (e.g., $10 from Penang Island). The train also connects some cities to a stop outside Tapah.

When to go: Though the coastal weather is always hot, it's cooler in the 4,500-foot altitude of the Highlands. It's wet from October to January. Better February through September. During the tourist-free wet season, the misty mountains and jungles are particularly mysterious.

What to bring: For the cool nights and possible rain, bring a rain jacket and a sweater. For walking, bring sneakers, shorts, and light cotton pants. Also take a water bottle, flashlight, and a basic first-aid kit.

Where to stay: There's something for every budget. Our favorite is the **Seah Meng Hotel** (#39 on the main road through Tanah Rata, very clean rooms, friendly owner, $8 singles without bath, $13 doubles with bath, tel. 05\941618, call ahead). **Bala's Holiday Chalet** offers a quiet spot with nice views of the hills (walk 20 minutes up the main road from Tanah Rata toward the golf course, or taxi, $5 dorm beds, $10 doubles, tel. 05/941660).

Where to eat: For Indian food, try the **Kuman Restoran** or the **Thanam** on the main road in Tanah Rata. Try the **Excellent Food Centre's** oat porridge with bananas and strong Malay coffee for breakfast. The **Yong Oi Kim Cafe,** warmly run by a mute Chinese couple, has good food. For chocolate and carrot cakes, hike up the hill behind the Seah Meng Hotel to the **Rich Bake Cake House**.

Odd sightseeing ducks: Visit one of the tea plantations in the area such as **Boh** (call 05/996032 for hours), **Blue Valley Tea**, or **Sungei Palas**. The **Butterfly Garden,** six miles north of Tanah Rata, has more than 300 varieties of butterflies (tel. 05/941364). Hotels and shops in Tanah Rata have sloppy but helpful area maps.

Marang—Back Door Survival

Getting there: The nearest city is Kuala Trengganu, 20 km to the north. From northwest Malaysia (Butterworth/Penang), bus to Kota Baharu on the east coast. Then bus or taxi 3.5 hours south to Marang. From the southwest (Kuala Lumpur) or Singapore, bus to Kuantan on the east coast. Then bus or taxi 3 hours north to Marang. Express buses don't stop at the Marang bus station, so tell the driver "Marang." He'll let you off along the main road, a few minutes walk. Or take the express bus to Kuala Trengganu, and a local bus or taxi to Marang. Avoid the wet season.

What to wear: Women should wear clothes that cover their shoulders and knees (and everything in between). Have a cotton dress tailored quickly and inexpensively from this area's beautiful batik cloth. While many Muslim women cover their heads, this is not expected of Western women. Men should wear a shirt in town.

Where to stay: The **Island View Guest House**, a ten-minute walk from town on the road that parallels the beach, offers self-cooking facilities, free coffee and tea, and an entertaining monkey (cheap but the A-frames are stuffy). On a small hill just down the road sits the newer **Marang Guest House** with good sea views, $3 dorm beds, and rooms with bath for $8. More deluxe hotels are in Kuala Trengganu, 20 minutes away by bus or taxi.

Odd sightseeing ducks: For the budget traveler culture (sunbathing, eating, and dancing), go to **Cherating**, an hour to the south. Many inexpensive bungalows and restaurants are along the beach. Close to the main road is the popular **Mak Long Teh's Bungalows** and the nearby **Maznah's Bungalows,** whose friendly owners serve excellent communal meals. Bus to Kemamin, then take a local bus nine miles south to Cherating.

Perhentian Island—Back Door Survival

Getting there: Coming from the Northwest of Malaysia (Butterworth/Penang), take the bus to Kota Baharu on the east coast. From Thailand, take a bus or train to Kota Baharu. Then take a bus or a taxi ($4 for a shared taxi) for the one-hour ride south to port of Kuala Besut.

Coming from the south of Malaysia or Singapore, take a bus toward Kuantan on the east coast and then north to Jertih (one hour south of Kota Baharu). Then catch a bus or a taxi ($2 for a shared taxi) for the nine miles to Kuala Besut.

Arrive in Kuala Besut by late afternoon to catch the last boat. Have the taxi drop you off at the boat jetty or walk one minute from the bus station. If no one asks to take you to the islands, you'll find the boat operators hanging out at the bus station. Fishing boats take one hour, $10 one way. If you're the only one going to Perhentian Kecil, you may have to go to Perhentian Besar first and then to Kecil.

When to go: If you risk the timing and go just before or after the wet months, there will be fewer travelers. For no travelers, go during the wet season (you may get stuck on the islands during storms).

What to wear: Women can wear swimming suits at the beach; however, wear clothes covering shoulders and knees in the village. Well-worn snorkeling gear is available for rent.

Where to stay: Both islands have a number of inexpensive bungalows with small restaurants. On Perhentian Besar, on the west end of the main beach, the **Cocohut Bungalows** charge $8 for a small basic A-frame with a bed and mosquito net. Toilets are outhouses with a pleasant view of the jungle overhead. For a bath, draw a bucket from the well. At east end of the beach are some pleasant bungalows with verandas. Most of the bungalows here have generators for light. Going deluxe, there is a resort two miles north of the main beach.

On Perhentian Kecil, there are a few bungalows on the small beaches around the island. **D'Lagoon Chalet** at the northeast tip is very quiet (basic $6 thatched bungalows, $3 dorm beds, $4 to pitch your tent). The day before you leave for Kuala Besut, arrange for a boat with your bungalow host.

Myanmar (formerly Burma)

Getting there: No overland travel is allowed in or out of Myanmar. You must fly into Yangon (formerly Rangoon). Myanmar Airlines is cheaper but riskier. We fly Thai.

Best time to go: Same as Thailand (see above).

Festivals: See the Appendix.

Visa: Visa required, valid for 14 days. Currently must sign on a package tour (see Myanmar Back Door). Onward ticket required. Embassy: 2300 S St., N.W., Washington, D.C. 20008 (tel. 202/332-9044).

Health: Same as in the previous section on Thailand, except AIDS not a major problem, yet.

Tourist information: The government-run Myanmar Travel and Tours makes all long-distance transportation reservations. Generally travelers must also coordinate lodging with them. Main office: 77-91 Sule Pagoda Rd., Box 559, Yangon (Rangoon), Myanmar (tel. 78376). U.S. Office: 2514 University Dr., Durham, NC 27707 (tel. 919/493-7500).

Transportation
Myanmar by plane: Domestic flights will save you time. Book through the Myanmar Travel Office. Often flights show as fully booked but aren't. If you go to the airport, you'll probably get on.

Myanmar by train: There are over 2,600 miles of tracks with express trains, mail trains, and local trains. Most of the lines are off-limits to tourists, however, because Myanmar would rather not mix the tourist mentality with rebel activities in its outlying states. The 400-mile, 12- to 14-hour Rangoon-Mandalay run is the country's most reliable, and the only trip you'll probably want to take.

Buy tickets from the quota available for foreigners in Yangon or Mandalay from Myanmar Travel. Foreigners aren't allowed to buy tickets at the Rangoon or Mandalay stations. Upper class has upholstered, adjustable seats; lower-class seats, one-third the price, are wooden. Except for the daytime Yangon-Mandalay express, trains don't have diners, so buy food from vendors along the way or bring your own.

Myanmar by jeep or truck: Some travelers hire jeeps or small trucks with drivers for their entire trip. This is convenient but exhausting since roads are poor. Go long distances by train or plane, and hire a jeep or truck locally.

Cultural do's and don'ts: As in Thailand, temper gets you nowhere; patience is important with people. The head is considered the spiritual part of the body, so don't pat kids there. Go barefoot into the temples and most homes.

Guidebooks: Lonely Planet's _Burma: A Travel Survival Kit_ is the best for travelers on their own. _Southeast Asia Handbook_ by Carl Parkes (Moon Publications) has a good section on Myanmar.

India

Best time to go: Traveling is best from November through early February. The north is sunny, in the 70s and low 80s during the day, and cool enough for a sweater and windbreaker in the evening. In the mountains, it's cool to cold, with some snow. In the south, it's dry and in the 80s.

From February, the temperature rises until it's uncomfortably hot in the south by March, in the north by April, and over 100 degrees by May. The monsoon season from June until as late as early October cools things down to the 90s. This means one or two downpours a day, and dry the rest of the day.

The best time for hiking in the Indian Himalayas is from May to October. Trails and lower passes are usually snow-free by May, although late spring snows are possible. The higher mountain ranges protect Kashmir and Ladakh from the worst of the monsoons (although downpours still hit). From the end of September through October, it's usually sunny and cool to warm—ideal for hiking. For more detail, see _Trekking in the Indian Himalaya_ by Gary Weare, Lonely Planet Publications.

Festivals: See the Appendix.

Visa: One- to six-month visas (depending on the political situation) are available. If you plan to leave and return, request a multiple-entry visa.

Onward/return ticket (not usually checked) and proof of financial capability is required (traveler's checks or cash). Request application from: Embassy of India, 2536 Massachusetts Ave., N.W., Washington, D.C. 20008 (tel. 202/939-9839), or from one of the consulates, such as at 540 Arguello Blvd., San Francisco, CA 94118 (tel. 415/668-0662).

Darjeeling and Sikkim require special permits. It takes one day at the Foreigner's Registration Office in a major Indian city such as Delhi or Calcutta. You can also apply through the embassy or consulate in the U.S. Permits are short but extendable. The special permits required for visits to the states of Assam and Meghalaya are more difficult to obtain. Bhutan is currently restricted to group travel.

Money: The black market pays up to 15% more for U.S. cash. Large bills ($50 and $100) get the highest rates. When changing money, get an officially stamped **currency exchange form**. You must show these when buying a plane ticket with rupees (enough dollars exchanged to cover the flight) and to change money back when you leave (officially, Indian currency can't be taken in or out of the India).

Changing money in a bank takes up to an hour, so exchange enough to last. While 100 Rs notes reduce bulk, ask for a supply of 10 Rs to 50 Rs notes; many small shops don't have change. Don't accept soiled or torn notes, since Indians won't accept them from you (exchange them at a bank). Upper-end hotels exchange any tourist's money faster than banks and often at bank rates. Since some rural banks have been stung and won't handle a certain type of check, carry plenty of cash or two types of traveler's checks.

Use credit cards at the more expensive hotels and restaurants and for cash advances (some banks have a $200 per day limit). The American Express office can give you more (see chapter 4). Wiring money from the U.S.A. can take weeks.

Language: India has two dominant languages, English and Hindi. Most educated Indians speak English as they travel through their country. It's the big-city language of business and the national language of travel.

Health: Health concerns keep many out of India. While you should take the proper precautions, the worst that happens to most is an upset stomach and diarrhea. Expect a little diarrhea. India is well worth it. The best prevention for illness is to take India slowly. Reread our health chapter for pointers on food, water, immunizations, and so on.

Tourist information: Write to the Government of India Tourist Information Office at 3550 Wilshire Blvd., Suite 204, Los Angeles, CA 90010 (tel. 213/380-8855), or 30 Rockefeller Plaza, North Mezzanine, Suite 15, New York, NY 10112 (tel. 212/586-4901).

Transportation

Arrival at the airport: Most people arrive at the Delhi airport. The tourist office runs a downtown shuttle bus. If you opt for a taxi, bargain hard.

India by plane: Reserve domestic flights early. Many routes are solidly booked. Consider the special domestic ticket passes that allow a number of stops around India.

Some Indian agents discount international tickets. You must purchase all plane tickets in India with either traveler's checks, foreign currency, or officially exchanged rupees (noted on a currency exchange form). The discount system in India is different. The agent charges you the full amount and then gives a refund. Your currency form will note you paid the full amount, so you can't exchange the refund into dollars when you leave India. Therefore, leave enough time to spend the refund, or buy gifts.

India by rail: India has the fourth-largest railway system on Earth— 38,000 miles of track carrying nine million passengers every day. Mix these statistics into a society that is essentially ungovernable but loves bureaucracy and you're halfway to understanding Indian trains.

Trains are the most practical way to travel around India and the best mode of transport for travelers interested in absorbing Indian culture.

Avoid local passenger trains and second-class unreserved seating. "Mail" and "express" trains are fairly direct in their routing, stopping only at larger cities. Local trains make every stop.

Unreserved means squeezing onto a corner of a wooden seat or squatting on a filthy portion of floor next to the gag-a-maggot toilet. As soon as you know where you want to go, get a reserved seat ticket. This is possible up to six months in advance in the U.S. through an agent specializing in Asian travel.

Indian trains offer second-class reserved seating, first-class recliners, and first-class air-conditioned (on a limited number of routes). Also second-class and first-class sleepers for overnight runs. In first class, these are private compartments. In second class, two-tiered (padded) or three-tiered (hard wood) racks fold down. We usually go second-class reserved and occasionally first-class when we want a break from India. Again, book well in advance.

Indian trains run on three different widths of track. Broad-gauge track trains are faster, more spacious and comfortable.

The Indrail Pass is a great investment for extended rail travel in India. Like the Eurailpass and Japan Rail Pass, it allows unlimited travel through the Indian rail system for the period of validity. The pass can be purchased from a good travel agent before you leave the United States, or in India (in U.S. dollars) from the main railway stations or Tourist Guide offices in New Delhi, Calcutta, Bombay, or Madras. 1993 prices are:

Indrail Pass

	2nd class	1st class	air-conditioned
7 days	$70	$135	$270
15 days	$80	$165	$330
21 days	$90	$200	$400
30 days	$110	$250	$500
60 days	$165	$360	$720
90 days	$210	$480	$960

Second-class rail travel in India is cheap—about $1 per 100 miles on long journeys—and gruelling. The 850-mile trip from Calcutta to New Delhi, for example, takes 30 hours. You can break any long trip with one-day stopovers every 100 miles without buying a new ticket.

Solely on a price basis, the Indrail Pass is not a great investment. (It's a better deal for first-class travelers than for second class.) However, the Indrail Pass does give you privileged status, and in India, that's worth a lot. Which brings us to "quotas."

There is no simple system of allotting seat reservations. There are separate quotas for tourists, station masters' friends, and other VIPs. But by showing the Indrail Pass to the proper senior authority at a train station, seat reservations and sleepers might be discovered where there were none before.

Some booking tricks: Use the tourist booking offices (for foreigners only) at the main train stations of large cities like New Delhi and Bombay. They can usually get you a reserved berth within a day. Women have special privileges. There is supposed to be a separate line for women to get tickets at the station. Usually there's just a mob of men. You can form your own line by walking or pushing to the front (purchase tickets for friends). It's usually easier to get tickets for the ladies' car on the train a good place to meet Indian women. The disadvantage is that it's filled with cute but noisy small kids.

Other tricks are to pay someone at your hotel 10 rupees or so to get the ticket for you, or go directly to the station master's office (there is a sign in English on the platform) and ask for the tourist quota ticket. Offer baksheesh if needed. If all else fails, give a few rupees to a train porter to guide you onto a reserved car. Ask for a seat when the train ticket inspector comes around (baksheesh of 10 or more rupees often required). If you have to ride unreserved, hire a porter to push through the crowds and find a seat.

At railway newsstands, buy *Trains at a Glance*, which gives timetables for faster trains on major routes. The *Indian Bradshaw* (75 cents) lists every train run in the country. Be aware that delays are likely, especially during floods of monsoon season.

Someone will take your order for food in the reserved cars. People come on board to sell food at each stop. At longer stops, you can purchase food from the carts on the platforms. Most stations also have a restaurant. Tea (chai) is always available.

India by bus: Buses are easier to book but less comfortable than trains for long distances. Public buses are noisy and crowded. The private companies reserve seats on their "deluxe" buses certainly not Greyhounds. These often blare nonstop Hindi videos; bring earplugs. Between police checkpoints, you can ride the roof for good views, fresh air, and to escape the noise. As with the trains, women have a separate ticket line, so go straight to the window.

Other forms of Indian transport: Taxis have meters, but drivers won't use them. Ask a local the going rate and bargain. You can hire chauffeur-driven cars. Check with the Tourist Office to see what the going rate is. Bicycle shops and some hotels rent one-speed bikes for less than 50 cents a day. Some tour India on bikes—be prepared for rough rides, buses and trucks, and curious crowds. Quality motorcycles and scooters are available (a joint venture with Japan). Rentals are hard to find. Some travel super cheap by buying and then reselling their motorscooters. Hitchhikers find that there aren't many private cars, and trucks often expect money. Still, in the countryside there's a spirit of volunteerism, and vehicles with space will often pick you up.

Accommodations: Where you sleep can shape your Indian travel experience. Plush Western hotels are designed to insulate you from Indian culture. They succeed. While we prefer to go local, sleeping in middle- or upper-range local-style places, Western hotels offer a handy and affordable alternative to a nut-house if you've had it with the intensity of India.

Western hotels, including international chains, guarantee a plush room, air-conditioning, a pool, Western toilet, isolation from others, and a feeling of being back in America. The rates, while cheaper than comparable hotels in the U.S., can still run about $100 and up. Check with your travel agent for package deal.

Indian luxury hotels are sometimes comparable in plushness to the Western chains. There are many new ones, but some of the older give you a taste of the Raj days. Splurge for one of the old Raj palaces converted to a hotel, or just have tea in the garden under the palms. Any Western tourist can feel comfortable wandering into one of these places even if you're not a paying guest. Check with the tourist offices for information on these.

Inexpensive hotels and guest houses are everywhere and start at $2 a night. The cheapest places offer a bed, a single naked light, an overhead fan, and a bathroom down the hall. For more, you get stuffed chairs, a better bed, and air-conditioning. Often they're family-run and have a common gathering places such as a garden or small restaurant. Attached baths are often smelly and damp. The local tourist office can advise you on government-run clean and reasonable tourist bungalows. And many train stations offer retiring rooms as a service to anyone with a ticket or rail pass.

Rest houses are run by the government for the bureaucrats. They generally require written permission (although many rent rooms to Westerners who just show up). We enjoyed several good nights in a series of forest rest houses in the mountains of Himalchal Pradesh. The local tourist information office sent us to the Public Works Department who operated them. Public Works wrote a letter of permission. We hiked into the villages, showed the letter, and someone appeared to open the rest house.

Ashrams are communities centered around a religion, a belief, or a mission—such as to help the needy. Many allow you to stay from a few days to months. You must follow their rules (such as no alcohol), and they may ask you to join in certain activities such as meditation or yoga. Some ashrams pressure you to join their sect or adopt a belief; others don't. A stay can be a good break from travel and a chance to help others or learn something. Some require advance permission. Most ask for a (usually small) donation or payment.

Temples sometimes offer lodging and food. Sikh temples, particularly in India's Punjab region, give free accommodation and vegetarian meals to travelers. Due to India's struggle with extremist Sikhs, temple stays in the Punjab can be risky these days. Buddhist temples sometimes have lodging. One interesting place for this is in Bodhgaya, in the state of Bihar, where the Buddha was enlightened.

Eating: India's staple is *dhal* (lentil curry) with *chapatis* (unleavened bread) or rice. There is also a wonderful and hot variety of meat or vegetable curries. In the major cities you can also find Chinese, Western, and "fast" foods.

We find that eating vegetarian is the safest way in India. Meat can be more dangerous than vegetables (refrigerators are still rare in India). To break your Western stomach in, progress from Western-type foods slowly into the curries.

North India offers a mix of meat and vegetable dishes. Its *tandoori* meat dishes are marinated and baked in a clay oven. Don't miss its wonderful variety of breads such as *nan* and *paratha*.

Your tongue will remember **South India** for its hot and spicy vegetarian dishes. Cool the curry by eating yogurt (dahi or *curd*). Order a *thali* for a variety of curries with rice. The waiter will circulate and continue to fill your large banana leaf plate. Also try the *dosas*, thin pancakes with savory sauces.

Throughout India try a *lassi,* a wonderful yogurt drink, sometimes mixed with fruit. While we avoid fresh milk, the milk for yogurt is first heated to kill the bacteria. Chai (tea), the national drink, is usually boiled with milk and sugar. Learn to say *chini nahan* (no sugar) if you need to. India has numerous super sweet soft drinks, bottled water, and beer. Indians love sweets. Try *barfi*, a small fudgelike bar made from boiled milk, sometimes with nuts, fruit, or chocolate.

Cultural do's and don'ts: The essential requirements for travel in India are patience, tact, and sense of humor. Any Western visitor will get as much attention as PeeWee Herman in a theater. To get even more, ignore the following advice:

Dress conservatively. Neither men nor women should wear shorts or tank tops. Women should cover shoulders and knees. Consider wearing what the locals do. For women, the beautiful tunic and pants outfit, called *salwar kameez*, is comfortable and cheap. In small Muslim towns, women should wear a scarf. Although many Indian men wear Western clothing in the cities, for comfort, we wear the more traditional. The light cotton tunic, *kurta*, is worn over loose-fitting pajama pants inexpensive and great in the heat. Remove your shoes before you enter a home or a temple. Sandals are handy.

Relating to Indians: An Indian man would not normally speak to an unknown Indian woman, and vice versa. Indian men, however, will speak to foreign women. Whatever your sex, you'll find that the man across from you on the train will talk to you, while a woman probably won't. Indians have plenty of questions, so you'll have to read or feign a nap when you've had enough.

On the streets in tourist areas, especially in Kashmir, shopkeepers are unrelenting. Just ignore them. There's no need to "no thank you" everyone. Better yet, joke or do something to really throw them. Tell them you're interested in an elephant hair carpet. If a merchant continues to badger, tell him to go, using a firm voice and face. Don't be aggressive, just assertive.

People may approach in friendship, then want something. In India, business and friendship may mix, but the Western traveler often feels like a commodity. If approached on the street, it's for business. However, on trains or buses, people are normally sincere. To meet people and not merchants, join activities that Indians are involved in. Many Indians travel India. Sign up on a bus tour of the city through the local tourist office (rather than at the big Western hotel). Going to the Taj Mahal, you'll sit next to a family from Madras. They'll probably invite you to visit. Do. Stay at an ashram in Rishikesh. You'll work and meditate with Indians. Go hiking in Darjeeling. You'll meet Indians from Calcutta along the trail. Join SERVAS, which allows you to stay with host families throughout India (see chapter 3).

Eat with your right hand. Indians use their left hand rather than toilet paper. Some restaurants will offer you a fork and spoon. Try your hand. It's strange and awkward at first, but sensual. Tear off pieces of the chapati or nan (unleavened bread) and use it to scoop up the curries. Otherwise stir in a bit of rice with the curry and scoop it up with your fingers.

Toilets are as described in chapter 3. If your bus stops at a village without public toilets, men should follow the men and women follow the women. Sometimes, because you don't fit into the caste system, you may be waved to the outskirts of the village.

Baksheesh (bribes) are sometimes the only way to get something done. Often it's expected. Ten or fifteen rupees to the train conductor may get you a sleeping berth on a "full car." Beggars are everywhere. Hindus build merit by giving to beggars. While we give a few coins to some, it makes more sense to support an effective international development and relief organization at home.

Recommended reading: *India File* by Trevor Fishlock (John Murray Publishers or Rupa and Co.) provides a candid look into Indian society (available in India). *An Area of Darkness* by V.S. Naipul (Penguin Books), is a perceptive and critical look at India today. Also try his second book, *India—A Wounded Civilization*. *Midnight's Children* by Salman Rushdie is an interesting fictional account of the partition of India. *Freedom at Midnight* by Dominique Lapierre and Larry Collins offers a good look at the partition. *The Wonder That Was India* by A.L. Basham is a good Indian history.

Guidebooks: *India—A Travel Survival Kit* by Lonely Planet Publications is the Bible for budget travel in India. *India and Nepal* by Klaus Wolfe (Hildebrand's Travel Guide) is compact and has a sensitive approach to travel in India. *Trekking in the Indian Himalaya* by Gary Weare (Loney Planet Publications) is helpful for trekking. Phrase books are cheaper there but better here.

Varanasi—Back Door Survival
Recommended reading: Edward Rice's *The Ganges: A Personal Encounter* offers good background reading on the cultural and spiritual importance of the Ganges and Varanasi. The **Motilal Benarsidass Bookstore** in the Chowk area of Varanasi has a great selection on Indian religion, philosophy, medicine, art, and music. Books printed in India are very reasonable, and stores will ship them home for you.

Khuri—Back Door Survival
Getting there: First go to Jaisalmer, 30 miles northeast of Khuri, in the state of Rajasthan. Get a permit there for Khuri, easily obtained in four hours. The local bus to Khuri runs twice a day and takes two hours.

Kashmir—Back Door Survival
Getting there: The overland trip is tedious but worthwhile. Try Delhi-Jammu by train, then a scenic bus to Srinagar (10 hours). Upon arrival

(or earlier), book a Srinagar-Delhi return flight (70 minutes, daily).

Getting around: Transportation in Kashmir is part of the fun. Take the long, graceful shikara boats ($2 an hour with helmsman, or rent one of your own for a day). Rent a bicycle to circle the lake.

Where to stay: On a houseboat! Boats on Dal Lake are closer to the action. For peace and quiet, settle on the lovely Nagin Lake. Boats are carefully regulated and classified. You can spend from $5 to $40 per night. Reservations are never necessary. Hire a shikara and shop around. You'll probably take most of your meals on your houseboat. If you fancy something special, ask for it—well in advance.

Odd sightseeing ducks: Take a full-day shikara tour of the lake. Visit the romantic **Shalimar Gardens** of Moghul fame late, so you can stay for the sound and light show. If you're interested in the life-styles of the rich and famous, drop by the ritzy **Oberoi Palace Hotel** (once the maharajah's palace) for an elegant lunch, tea, or buffet dinner. Definitely take the 30-mile trip up to Gulmarg, a hill station at over 8,000 feet elevation, then rent ponies and climb even higher to Khillanmarg.

Sri Lanka

Getting there: No direct flight from the U.S., so go through London/ Middle East or Hong Kong/Bangkok/Singapore. From India, it's cheapest to fly from Trivandrum. Ferries from India to the north of Sri Lanka have been suspended because of the fighting.

Best time to go: Lying close to the equator, it's hot all year. Best is September to January when it's a bit cooler. March to May is very hot and dry. There are two monsoons. From May to August, it rains on the south and west coast and in the central hills (the main touristed areas, since the fighting is in the north and east). From October to January, rains come to the north and east. Monsoons mean a morning or evening downpour and partly cloudy to cloudy the rest of the day. It's still hot, and the ocean is rough. In the hills, it's warm during the day and can be cool at night.

Festivals: See the Appendix.

Visa: Tourist visa not required for stay up to one month. Onward/return ticket and visa for next destination required. Apply at Embassy: 2148 Wyoming Ave. N.W., Washington, D.C. 20008, tel. 202/483-4025.

Language: Sinhala is the official language, but English is spoken almost everywhere a traveler would go.

Health: The same precautions apply as in India, though conditions are generally better. Eat cooked food and drink treated water. Check with your doctor for immunizations and malarial preventions.

Tourist information: Write to the Embassy address above.

Transportation

Sri Lanka by train: First-class seating is offered only on overnight trains, on the service from Colombo to Kandy, and through the tea plantations of the Hill Country to Badulla. Seating is in an air-conditioned coach, observation saloon, or sleeper compartment. Most trains have only second- or third-class seating. Second class is comfortable with padded seats, while third class comes with wooden seats and crowds (especially on days of pilgrimage).

The most popular trip is the $1 three-hour run from Colombo to Kandy. There are eight first-come, first-served departures a day from Colombo. The 6:55 a.m. and 3:35 p.m. intercity express train, which covers the distance in two hours for the same price and guarantees a seat, is usually booked well in advance.

For travel from Sri Lanka to India, a train leaves Colombo daily for Talaimannar pier. But the ferry runs only three times a week between Talaimannar and Rameswaram, India, and not at all during the dangerous winter monsoon season. All tickets for train and ferry must be purchased in Colombo.

What to eat: Curry! Every one is different—not just a turmeric-and-cumin affair. Curried cashews, curried jackfruit, curried *brinjal* (eggplant), curried boar—they're a hot and spicy treat, served in a tray of rice. Cut the flames by drinking *thambali* (coconut water). *Curd* (buffalo milk yogurt) and *treacle* (molasses) is a favored dessert. *Hoppers* (like pancakes topped with curry sauce) are a popular breakfast specialty.

Nepal

Getting there: International flights arrive in Kathmandu. Many budget travelers enter overland from India through Sunauli or Birganj on the Nepalese border, each about ten hours by bus from Kathmandu. It is possible to fly to Gorakhpur in India and catch a ride north, sneaking in through the border town of Butwal, overnighting in Tansen and catching the all-day bus ride north to Pokara in west Nepal.

Best time to go: From October to April is ideal, dry and not too hot. The monsoon hits from June through September. The heavy but brief rainstorms won't stop you from traveling, but the clouds kill most of your mountain views. See the Trekking Survival that follows for more specifics.

Festivals: See the Appendix.

Visa: Transit visas for visits of 15 days and less are available at the airport for $10. Extendable up to three months in Kathmandu, if you've officially cashed $20 for each day you plan to extend. Since it's hard to spend $20 a day, get a visa before you go for longer stays. Send for an application from the Nepalese Embassy: 2131 Leroy Place N.W., Washington, D.C. 20008 (tel. 202/667-4550).

Black market: For traveler's checks and U.S. dollars you'll get about 15% more on the street ($50 notes and up, best). Remember Nepalese rupees can't be exchanged outside Nepal.

Language: As in India, English is the second language. Nepalis greatly appreciate your efforts in learning a few of their phrases.

Health: Plan on a little diarrhea in Nepal. It comes in adjusting to the new food, bacteria, and from the water-borne parasite, giardia. Consult chapter 7 for information on preventions and remedies, as well as for immunization advice. If (when) you get sick, the Nepal International Clinic and the CEWIC in Kathmandu have foreign-trained and English-speaking doctors.

Tourist information: The Nepalese Embassy (listed above) will send information. In Nepal check with the government tourist office in Kathmandu on Ganga Path near Durbar Square.

Transportation
Arrival at the airport: For the short trip into Kathmandu from the airport, go by the bus which meets each flight, or buy a fixed-rate ticket near the terminal exit for a taxi.

   Nepal by plane: Save time but add expense by flying into some of the small airfields around the country. The small fleet of prop planes are often booked up well in advance, especially during the height of the tourist season in October and November. The same goes for those flying to Lukla (a flight that saves many days on the trek to Everest base camp). Try to reserve your seat before you leave the U.S.

   Nepal by bus: You'll be traveling by bus, since Nepal has only 31 miles of train tracks. Take the public bus for short distances, and the more comfortable private buses for long ones you'll get a reserved seat as wide as the average Nepali. Even the private buses are poor by Western standards. Travel agencies operate comfortable but cramped minibus service. Reserve early, especially during peak tourist season. The roads in Nepal are poor and, in the mountains, blocked on and off by slides. Expect delays. Ride the roof for awesome views and fresh air. (Dress warm in the mountains, and duck for low branches.)

Other modes of Nepali transport: With three or four people, a taxi is reasonable for long distances and allows you to stop where and when you want. Check with the tourist office for the going rate and negotiate with a driver. A Kathmandu travel agency can arrange one for a commission. We routinely employ Kathmandu's bicycle rickshaws. The slow ride is great for people- watching. Ask the locals the going rate, then negotiate. You can rent cheaper model mountain bikes and one-speeds in the tourist areas of Kathmandu. Both are fine around the valley.

Accommodations
In the city competition among the smaller hotels and guest houses keeps prices low for decent rooms. Most aren't heated but have hot water. In December and early January, you may want to splurge for a heated room. Or stay at an older thick-walled guest house. Kathmandu has more expensive hotels with both heat and air-conditioning, fancy restaurants, and the works. While we don't sleep there, we enjoy hanging out at the **Hotel Yak and Yeti.** Drop in for a great cultural evening of folk dancing, or sip a cup of tea in the large garden; savor a hot drink in front of the fireplace at their **Chimney Restaurant.**
  In the countryside, the more touristed towns have a range of lodging. Pokara has a good variety of lakeside hotels. And Dhulikhel (see its Back Door) has both inexpensive and moderately priced hotels. Along the trails, there are simple rooms or dorms in family-run lodges or people's homes. Buildings are simply built of rock and wood. Rooms are spartan with wood or cloth-covered dirt floors, thin-mattressed beds with wool covers, and kerosene lamps or bare bulbs. Toilets are outhouses or a bush at the edge of the village. Bathing is in the stream or sometimes water can be heated (good if solar; using wood further depletes the forests). Places lack in comfort, but abound in smiles.

Eating: **In the countryside,** you'll get to know the national dish *daal bhaat. Bhaat* is boiled rice, and *daal* is a lentil soup. Often, curried vegetables are served as a side dish. This combination is a complete diet. However, you can always bring vitamins.
  On the more popular treks, such as from Pokara, menus are literally as big as the food stalls. The locals throw together their own version of tacos, pizza, apple pie, and yak steak and eggs. On the less-traveled trails, the fare is daal bhaat, potatoes, and maybe porridge or eggs. Areas with Tibetans have *momos*, dumplings with a meat or vegetable center, Tibetan bread, unleavened fried dough, and *tsampa*, roasted barley flour the locals eat plain, mixed with water, or cooked as a porridge. Tea shops along the trails serve sweet biscuits and *chiyaa*, tea boiled with water, milk, and sugar. *Chang*, home-brewed beer, is a mountain favorite.

Kathmandu has a tremendous variety of restaurants. Though not always authentic, the food is usually good and inexpensive. Try cinnamon rolls for breakfast, burritos for lunch, and vegetarian lasagna for supper. Many restaurants serve tempting fresh salads. Even though the greens are washed in "treated water," we refrain. After supper, go for cheesecake and an espresso. Read about our favorite places in the Kathmandu Back Door Survival section that follows. Kathmandu's famous pie shops dish out apple, cream, and lemon pies and cakes that come with transit visas. Locally made cheese and breads are tasty.

Bottled water, soft drinks, and beer are everywhere in the city. The local beer is good, but the hard liquors are harsh, except the homemade _raksi_ (which inspires frequent late-night rickshaw drag races).

Cultural do's and don'ts: See the cultural do's and don'ts in the India section for dress, eating, shoes.

Begging isn't as bad as in India, except from children, especially on the trails. Kids beg for candy, rupees, pens, and anything else a previous foreigner handed out. We feel encouraging begging among children encourages a loss of their self-respect and traditional values.

Leftovers are sometimes offered by travelers to Nepalese children in their lodges. Although this is a charitable act, someone's leftovers are considered polluted by the Nepalese (traditional wisdom). If you want to help, don't take more than you'll eat. Trash or leftovers shouldn't be thrown into your host's fire. The household fire is treated as a special spot.

Getting away: A unique way to leave is through Tibet, although of late (because of the political situation in Tibet) you can only go on an organized tour. Check with a Kathmandu travel agency such as Nepal Travels (tel. 412899) or Yeti Travels (tel. 221234). If you're allowed to travel independently, get a Chinese visa in Kathmandu and hope the road isn't closed by the landslides.

Recommended reading: _The Snow Leopard_ by Peter Matthiessen (Viking) is a descriptive and sensitive look into the land and the spirit of Nepal. _Video Night in Kathmandu_ by Pico Iyer (Alfred A. Knopf) is a different perspective on the old tale of East meets West (only one chapter is specifically on Kathmandu).

Guidebooks: _Nepal Handbook_ by Kerry Moran (Moon Publications) is a well- organized and useful general guidebook. Lonely Planet Publications' _Nepal: A Travel Survival Kit_ is also very helpful. See the Trekking Survival section that follows for more.

Kathmandu—Back Door Survival
Where to stay: There's an abundance of good places, but here are a few for starters.

Thamel area: The **Imperial Guest House** (tel. 229339), in back of the supermarket on Tri Devi Marg, is fairly quiet, quite clean, and has a rooftop garden. The rooms are cold in the winter. Doubles with bath about $12. The **Mustang Holiday Inn** next door is nice but more expensive. Doubles start at $20. Nearby is the **Yeti Cottage and Rainbow Restaurant**. Rooms are basic but Nepalese style with thick walls and small windows, thus warmer in the winter ($5 doubles). **Hotel Shakti** (tel. 410121) is down a quiet back lane in the northeast part of Thamel, a medium-sized hotel of good value with a friendly staff and $10 rooms with bath.

Durbar Square area: The cozy **Kathmandu Lodge** has basic $5 rooms with baths and a friendly staff. Their small restaurant is a good place to meet others.

Paknajol area (NW of Thamel): The **Glacier Dome Guest House** is quiet, clean, and offers good views ($8 doubles). The **Chalet Guest House** has a garden with views of the mountains ($16 doubles with a bath).

Between Thamel and Swayambhunath Temple: Hotel Vajra (tel. 271545) sits across the river in the quiet west of Kathmandu. Although more expensive, it has a traditional Nepalese flair, with an art gallery, library, and nice views.

Where to eat: In the Thamel area, **KC's Restaurant** has great Western-type meals. The "Rosti" breakfast of eggs, toast, jam, and fried potatoes will beat the best diner at home. Try their $3 "sizzling" steak. The nearby **Utse Restaurant** serves a variety of cheap Chinese and Tibetan food. A four-minute walk north of the Kathmandu Guest House is **Nirmala Vegetarian Restaurant**; it serves a variety of vegetarian dishes such as lasagna and pizza. South of Thamel in the Chhetrapati area, **Narayan's Restaurant** has good Mexican and Italian dishes, fresh baked bread, and espresso.

In the central area, near the Yak and Yeti Hotel, try **Mike's Breakfast** (Mike is a former American Peace Corps volunteer). Try the huevos rancheros or pancakes; coffee comes with free refills.

Trekking—Back Door Survival
When to go: October and November are the best times for trekking, with clear dry weather. At lower elevations, temperatures range from the 80s during the day to the 40s at night. Above 10,000 feet, it's in the 70s and below freezing at night.

December and January are the coldest months. At lower elevations, days are in the 60s and freezing at night. Above 10,000 feet, the temperatures are more than 10 degrees lower. In very high areas, such as the Annapurna Sanctuary (13,000 to 14,000 feet), temperatures can go well below zero. It's usually dry and clear, with occasional rain or snow. Snow may close some of the high passes.

From February, trekking improves as the weather warms; flowers bloom by April. Late spring dust can cause haze. May to mid-June are hot and hazy with daytime temperatures in the 90s in the low valleys, and very warm up to 8,000 to 9,000 feet. At much higher elevations, the temperature can still drop below freezing at night. Mid-June through September brings the monsoon with its leeches and muddy trails.

Trekking permits: Go to the Central Immigration Office on Tri Devi Marg, the main road going past the Royal Palace as it enters the Thamel area. Bring an official bank exchange receipt showing you've changed $20 for each day you plan to trek and two passport-size photos. Expect a long line.

To save time and money, go through a Kathmandu trekking company. For a fee, they'll arrange the permit without the $20 per day requirement. On an independent trek of 20 days you'd spend about $100 but would have to exchange $400. Since you can only change 15% of the $300 back when you leave, you'd have to buy a few carpets to get rid of the rest.

Trekking gear: Take a sleeping bag, preferably light down. Even in trail-side lodges, it gets cold when the fire dies. A sleeping pad (Therm-a-Rests are good) is handy, though most lodges have mattresses. We find external frame packs carry heavy loads better. Staying in lodges, you won't need a stove or a tent. If you bring a stove, a filter is helpful since the kerosene is not pure. Other important items: water bottle, water purification system (chemical or filter), compass, flashlight, dark sunglasses with UV protection, matches, and a sewing kit. In your first-aid kit include medication for giardia, an anti-diarrheal, aspirin for strains and sprains, "moleskin" to cover blisters, sun block, and sunscreen for your lips.

Light cotton clothes, including shorts, are needed for the lower elevations, and wool shirt, pants, and sweater for the higher. Foreign women often wear shorts trekking, but a skirt is a cool and more culturally acceptable alternative. A large poncho for the rain is better than a rain jacket cooler while walking, and it covers your pack. A down jacket is helpful in winter and anytime at altitudes above 10,000 feet. Other items include mittens, light windbreaker, cotton hat with brim, a wool hat, and long underwear. Use the layer technique. Start with a long underwear top. As it gets colder add a wool shirt, next a sweater, then a windbreaker. And finally a down jacket.

Lightweight hiking boots are good, although on some trails, running shoes will do if you're carrying a light pack. Other items: thongs or sandals for after trekking on warm days, several pairs of wool/polypropylene socks.

Recommended reading: The British mountaineer Chris Bonnington writes about several of his expeditions in *Annapurna South Face* and *Everest the Hard Way*. Learn about the different mountain ethnic groups in Dor Bahadur Bista's *People of Nepal* (available in Kathmandu bookstores).

Guidebooks and maps: Stephen Bezruchka's *A Guide to Trekking in Nepal* is an excellent resource for treks throughout Nepal. This doctor also offers good health advice and includes a section on altitude sickness. Lonely Planet Publications' *Trekking in the Nepal Himalaya* by Stan Armington is good. Kathmandu bookstores carry these (new and used), as well as trekking maps (also available at the Tourist Information Office). The series of maps produced in Nepal covers all the major treks. Although not always accurate, they get you there. More detailed and expensive foreign-produced maps are available in Kathmandu. Erwin Schneider's 1:50,000 series is good.

Dhulikhel—Back Door Survival

Getting there: Buses leave from Ratna Park in Kathmandu every half hour between 6 a.m. and 6 p.m. The 90-minute ride costs less than 50 cents. A taxi costs $12 or more. Or bike the 20 miles along the paved road over a pass, down to Banepa, and then up again.

Where to stay: As you walk into town off the main highway, turn right on the main street to reach the **Dhulikhel Lodge** (they plan to move to a different building; check with the Kathmandu booking office for their Hotel Himalayan Horizon, tel. 2-25092), $2 without bath. There are also some smaller family-run lodges at the east end of town past the football field. The **Himalayan Horizon Hotel**, a half mile out on the road to Kathmandu, is a fairly new and comfortable hotel with good Himalayan views, a garden, and a good restaurant. Singles/doubles with bath are about $35/$45. Contact the booking office number above. A few miles past Dhulikel on the highway is the **Dhulikhel Mountain Resort** (tel. 2-20031) with comfortable $50 rooms and good views.

China

Getting there: Most people fly to Hong Kong and then go to nearby Guangzhou (Canton)—5 hours by train, overnight boat (our favorite), or hovercraft. The cruise ship to Shanghai is a fun alternative. Flights to cities in China are cheaper from Guangzhou than from Hong Kong.

Best time to go: In such a vast country, the world's third largest, the weather varies by the region. In general, spring and fall are the best times. The summer is either hot and dry (northwest and Tibet) or hot and rainy. The winters are cold most places, with the south (Hainan Island and Xishuangbanna in Yunnan province) more mild.

Festivals: See the Appendix.

Visa: Visas are required. In the U.S., apply with the Embassy: 2300 Connecticut Ave., N.W., Washington, D.C. 20008, tel. 202/328-2517, or with a consulate such as at 1450 Laguna St., San Francisco, CA 94115, tel. 415/563-4857. Up to six-month visas granted. Visas are easily obtained in 24 hours in Hong Kong through most travel agencies.

Money: For travelers, the exchange system in China is unique. You'll use two types of currency: renminbi (RMB, "people's money,") and foreign exchange certificates (FEC, tourist money). FEC must be used for most major purchases, including long-distance transportation and Western-style hotels. Change your dollars into FEC at banks usually located in large hotels. Keep the exchange receipts so you can convert FEC back to dollars when you leave (renminbi can't be converted). The black market rate for FEC is often 25% higher than the official rate. Exchange some FEC for RMB to pay for meals, gifts, buses, and so on. Some locals will buy train tickets for you at a discount if you pay them in FEC.

With more capitalism has come more theft. Watch out for pickpockets and bag grabbers, especially around train and bus stations. Use a money belt.

Language: Mandarin Chinese is the official language; Cantonese is spoken in the south. It's popular to learn English, so you'll usually find someone to talk with any place you go. Bring a phrase book.

Health: Follow the precautions discussed in the health chapter for food and water. Check with a doctor or travel clinic on immunizations and malaria prevention. The most common traveler health problems are colds and bronchitis. It can be cold and wet; few places besides large hotels have central heating.

Tourist information: In the U.S., write to the China National Tourist Office, 60 E. 42nd St., Lincoln Bldg., Suite 3126, New York, NY 10165 (tel. 212/867-0271), or 333 W. Broadway, Rm. 201, Los Angeles, CA 91204 (tel. 818/545-7505).

Transportation
China by plane: Domestic airfare costs nearly what you'd pay to fly around the U.S.A. The Civil Aviation Administration of China (CAAC) is famous for its poor service and safety record. Though you can book with CITS or CTS, it will be quicker through a CAAC office. Recently, some smaller internal airlines have started up, so compare prices.

China by train: Remember, China is huge, slightly larger than the United States including Alaska. It's a 34-hour 1,450-mile ride from Guangzhou (Canton) to Beijing (Peking). Chinese trains are reasonably clean and comfortable. You can buy tea and food en route; hot water is provided in berths. Trains do not, however, provide drinking water, toilet paper, or soap. BYO.

You can ride either "hard" or "soft" class and regular or express train. "Hard seat" means third class, noisy, packed, and horrible. "Hard sleeper" is akin to second class: survivable with assigned seats and open compartments with fold-down hard bunks for sleeping. Pillows, sheets, and blankets are provided. "Soft seat" means a reclining seat in first class. "Soft sleeper" is a closed compartment with four berths. Relative luxury, for twice the price of "hard sleeper." The seats convert into soft sleeping berths for overnight travel.

Chinese trains charge foreigners 75% more than local Chinese for the same ticket. While you can sometimes get a ticket for local prices, you're wise to go by the rules. Instead of offering student or youth discounts, China has a system of shrimp specials. If you're under one meter (about 33 inches) you travel free, and if you're under 1.3 meters (about 43 inches) you travel for quarter fare.

Reserve your seat at least three days in advance with a China Travel Service (CTS) or China International Travel Service (CITS) office attached to a major hotel.

Trains leave Beijing twice weekly for Ulan Bator, Mongolia, where connections can be made to the Trans-Siberian Railway across Russia. The Beijing-Moscow journey is 4,888 miles and takes five full days . . . and then some. A newly opened line heads west from Urumqi (in the northwest) into the central Asia regions of the former USSR.

While you'll manage on the crowded buses for short trips, the trains are more comfortable. You can go down most major rivers by boat, a memorable highlight of many Chinese trips.

Accommodations: Most likely you'll be required to stay in a government-regulated establishment. These range from small hostels and guest houses to large international-class hotels. There are many basic and cheap places where foreigners aren't allowed. Dorms are often available at hotels. Ask, since they won't necessarily mention it. Dorm beds are around $5, and hotel rooms start at $15 most places.

Eating: The easiest way to get what you want is to point at what someone else is eating, or go in the kitchen and look in the pot. Around touristed areas, some places will have English menus. **Cantonese** cuisine, from southeastern China near Guangzhou and Hong Kong, is known for its subtle, delicate flavors and great variety of natural ingredients, largely seafood, vegetables, and noodles. Give the snake restaurants a try; we liked sweet and sour black snake. In Guangzhou, some of the restaurants look like pet stores, and it's all on the menu. **Peking** cuisine is a hearty blend of Mongol and Manchu influences; sample the syrupy skin of Peking duck wrapped in wheat crepe with scallions. **Shanghai** favorites include sauteed eel boiled in garlic and soy sauce and drunken chicken, marinated in rice wine and served cold with coriander leaves. **Szechuan** food has a reputation as the spiciest—red chiles are a prime ingredient. Try Kung Pao chicken (diced fowl sauteed in garlic, soy sauce, and chilies) and hot-and-sour soup (wild mushrooms, bamboo shoots, and other forest vegetables in a rich broth). **Hunan** cuisine is spicy like the Szechuan but a bit lighter.

For good food, ask someone in your hotel for recommendations. Some of the smaller inexpensive restaurants offer poor to okay meals. Western-style fast-food places springing up around the country serve quick noodles and burgers. Restaurants continue to get better as capitalism grows and more locals eat out.

Cultural do's and don'ts: Anger gets you nowhere quick with the Chinese bureaucracy. It's easy to get frustrated when dealing with the inefficient CITS, CTS, and other agencies in arranging transportation, and so on. Practice patience. Scream in the street.

Guidebooks: Lonely Planet's *China: A Travel Survival Kit* has been the independent traveler's bible, though it's not always accurate. *Southwest China Off the Beaten Track* by Mark Stevens and George Wehrfritz (Passport Books) is great, full of travel specifics for that region. Lonely Planet's *Tibet: A Travel Survival Kit* is also has a good regional guide. Pick up a China map in both English and Chinese characters at a bookstore in Hong Kong.

Hong Kong

Best time to go: The fall is best, when it's mild to cool and not as humid. It's chilly from mid-December through early February. March and April are good times to visit. It gets hot and humid by May. The summer is hot and rainy.

Festivals: See the Appendix.

Visa: Tourist visas are not required for stays up to one month with onward/return transport. Embassy: 3100 Massachusetts Ave. N.W., Washington, D.C. 20002 (tel. 202/462-1340).

Money: Banking here is modern and efficient, and most businesses eagerly accept plastic money and American currency.

Language: Cantonese is the major language; English is widely spoken.

Health: High health standards. No need to worry about food and water. No immunizations required.

Tourist information: Write to the Hong Kong Tourist Association, 333 N. Michigan Ave., Suite 2400, Chicago, IL 60601 (tel. 312/782-3872).

Transportation: Taxis, buses, and a fine new subway system will get you around reasonably. As always, insist on the metered rate when you use a cab. Avoid riding a cab from island to peninsula or vice versa, because you'll be charged the taxi's fare back to its home base. The Star ferry will take you from Kowloon to Hong Kong Island for just pennies, or take the underwater subway. Ferries connect Hong Kong Island's Central District with the outer islands and Macau.

Accommodations: While modern hotels are expensive, there are plenty of budget alternatives. The **Chungking Mansions**, at 44 Nathan Road in Kowloon, is infamous among budget travelers. Described by some as a high-rise "rabbit warren," the Mansions has elevators labeled A to E, each with its own small hotels, guest houses, dormitories, and hostels. It's absolutely essential to shop around to find the best price. "A" block has the more expensive places. The end elevators are somewhat cheaper. Many places have cooking facilities, but there are plenty of cheap eating places scattered around the floors as well. Tiny singles start at $17 and dorm beds at $7. The **Traveler's Hostel** on the 16th floor of A Block is a well-known hangout for travelers going to China.

On spacious Lantau Island, the **Po Lin Monastery** has a dorm for $25 a night, including three vegetarian meals. The Trappist fathers have a monastery on tiny Peng Chau Island, in route to Lantau, where you can stay in the dorm. There are also hostels and guest houses on the outer islands.

Eating: Eating seems to be second only to shopping in Hong Kong. There are plenty of fine Cantonese restaurants. In the Chungking Mansions are several good and inexpensive Indian and Pakistani restaurants.

Odd sightseeing ducks: For a wonderful contrast to the Hong Kong hustle, take the hydrofoil (75 minutes) to Macau, a slow-paced Portuguese colony.

Guidebooks: Lonely Planet's *Hong Kong, Macau & Canton: A Travel Survival Kit* is a useful book for the budget traveler. The Hong Kong Tourist Association offices have excellent and free pamphlets.

Japan

Best time to go: The southern islands, such as Okinawa, are tropically hot in the summer months and mild in the winter. Tokyo and the main island of Honshu have more seasonal variation, with hot humid summers and cold winters. The northern island of Hokkaido has cold winters and warm, but short, summers.

Visit Honshu from mid-October to mid-November for pleasant sunny days and beautiful fall leaves (typhoons often hit from September through early October). The spring is unsettled but fragrant . . . cherry blossom time.

Summer is hot and humid along the coast of Honshu and islands to the south but more pleasant in the mountains. From around mid-June to early July, it rains nearly every day. Although uncomfortable in the cities, there are many interesting festivals then, and the countryside is lush and green.

Winter has almost no tourist crowds and no central heating. Avoid travel in crowded festival times: New Year's (about Dec. 27-Jan. 4), Golden Week (first week of May), the Obon festival (mid-August). Hostels are packed during school holidays (late March through early April, and late July through August).

Visa: None required for Americans or Canadians for up to 90 days with an onward or return ticket. You can receive another 90 days only if you leave and return. Get visas for longer stays from the Japanese Embassy, 2520 Massachusetts Ave., N.W., Washington, D.C. 20008, tel. 202/939-6700.

Cost of travel: If you stay in youth hostels, eat cheaply, and travel by subway, bus, and train, plan on $50 to $70 a day. Figure $70 to $90 a day if you stay in inns rather than hostels. Hotels bump it way up. With a mix of youth hostels and inns, Sushi bars and McDonald's, and an occasional taxi, we do fine on about $70 a day. Credit cards are good at big hotels, in expensive restaurants, and for cash advances.

Language: You can survive on English, but the locals will love it if you try some "Nihongo." Bring along a Japanese/English phrase book.

Health: No shots are required to enter Japan, and, unlike the rest of Asia, we drink the water, eat what we like, and never suffer from diarrhea.

Tourist information: Use the helpful Tourist Information Centers (TIC). The staffs are well informed on any aspect of travel, from festivals to ferry schedules. They are helpful over the telephone. **Tokyo:** Kotani Building 6-6, Yurakucho 1-chome Chiyoda-ku, tel. (03) 502-

1461. **Kyoto:** 1st floor, Kyoto Tower Building, Higashi-Shiokojicho, Shimogyo-ku, tel. (075) 371-5649. **Narita Airport**: Airport Terminal Building, tel. (0476) 32-8711. Service hours 9 a.m. to 5 p.m. (9 a.m. to 8 p.m. at Narita) weekdays, 9 a.m.to noon on Saturdays. Closed Sundays and national holidays.

TIC runs the Japan Travel-Phone, which offers toll-free travel information and help in talking with locals from anywhere in Japan. Offices in Tokyo (tel. 502-1461), Kyoto (tel. 371-5649); for information on eastern Japan, tel. 0120-222800; for information on western Japan, tel. 0120-444800. Service hours 9 a.m. to 5 p.m., every day (not possible on red phones).

In the **U.S.** write to the Japan National Tourist Organization, 45 Rockefeller Plaza, 630 Fifth Ave., New York, NY 10111 (tel. 212/757-5640), or 624 South Grand Ave., Los Angeles, CA 90017 (tel. 213/623-1952).

Transportation

Arrival at the airport: Arrange onward travel at airport's Tourist Information Center (TIC). Most international flights come into Narita, Tokyo's International Airport (42 miles west of Tokyo). Save the $200 taxi fare by taking a bus to the Tokyo City Air Terminal (about 1.5 miles from the main Tokyo train station). Take a subway, bus, or a much cheaper taxi from there to your destination. An express train goes from the airport into Tokyo (covered by Japan Rail Pass). From the Osaka Airport, take a bus to a hotel or train station in Osaka, Kyoto, or Kobe. Fares are reasonable (airport to Kyoto, $10).

Japan by rail: Trains are streamlined and efficient to a fault. Hostesses and vendors sell everything from hot tea to sushi in the passenger cars. A strong-armed, white-gloved conductor will cram you into the rail car like a sardine if you venture into a big-city commuter train system during rush hour. That said, it's generally a pleasure to ride the train in Japan.

Japanese Railways (JR), the largest of the lines, has five services, from slowest to fastest: local train (Futsu), ordinary express (Kyuko), limited express (Tokkyu), rapid train (Kaisoku), and super express (the Shinkansen or "Bullet Train"). No smoking except on the Shinkansen and the Tokkyu, which have a no smoking car.

Seats on the Shinkansen, which stops at major cities, are both reserved and unreserved. First class (the Green Car) is an unnecessary expense. Local runs are unreserved seating and unlimited stops.

The Shinkansen covers the 730 miles from Tokyo to Fukuoka, on the southern island of Kyushu, in just under seven hours. And with the new tunnel connecting the islands of Honshu and Hokkaido, you can now ride the bullet train to Sapporo on Hokkaido. Trains leave every five to ten minutes and are utterly precise. Stations are announced in Japanese and English a couple of minutes prior to arrival; be standing at the door ready to disembark or you won't make it out of your seat before the train departs again.

Directional signs, both on the platform and on the exterior of the train, are written in English as well as Japanese. And locals are helpful. Have the ticket agent write out the platform number and other information in English.

Your baggage should fit in the airline-sized overhead racks (sometimes there's additional storage area near the entrance). Most stations have cloakrooms to check your bags ($1 per piece per day, up to 15 days) or coin lockers ($1 to $3, depending on size, for up to 3 days).

For extensive train travel, the Japan Rail Pass is the best way to go. Similar to the Eurailpass, the Japan Rail Pass offers foreign tourists unlimited travel on JR trains, buses, and ferries. Buy the pass "exchange order" before you get to Japan from your travel agent or from Japan Airlines. Exchange this order for your pass at the JR Information Office in Narita Airport or at one of twelve JR offices in Japan, including Tokyo and Kyoto.

Japan Rail passes, 1993	7 day	14 day	21 day
Ordinary (2nd cl) Pass	$224	$356	$455
Green (1st cl) Pass	$298	$483	$628

Second-class cars are fine, so first class (Green Pass) is an unnecessary expense. Passes must be validated within three months. They are irreplaceable if lost or stolen and, after validated, nonrefundable. The price varies according to the yen-dollar exchange rate.

A ticket on the Shinkansen from Tokyo to Kyoto return costs as much as a seven-day Ordinary Rail Pass. So the pass is worth it for many. Also, with the unlimited pass, ticket costs won't impede your travel plans, and you'll never stand in line. However, the pass isn't worth it for all. Determine the cost of ordinary tickets for your expected journeys and compare. If your travel agent can't help, get one who knows Asia.

With the pass, just step on an unreserved car, and when the uniformed conductor comes, flash your pass (and your passport, too, if requested). Reservations (free) are smart during the peak travel season. Simply present the pass to a JR Travel Service Center or Green Window (_Midori-no-mado-guchi_) counter at any JR station. Sleeper berths cost extra.

Validate your pass thoughtfully. A 14-day pass can usually cover a 19-day trip if you plan carefully. Many people start their pass on arrival in Tokyo to cover the $10 day trip to Kamakura and the $20 day trip to Nikko. They spend three additional days in Tokyo, not using their pass. They could have spent the $30 to delay the validation of their pass by five days and, as a result, squeezed a longer trip into a shorter and cheaper pass.

Japan by subway: Most big cities have fast and easy subways. Each stop is announced and there are signs in Kanji (Japanese) and in Romanji (English). Look for discount all-day passes, and so on. We make life in the subways easier by buying the lowest fare ticket at the machine. When exiting, we put the ticket in the turnstile, the buzzer sounds and a man appears to collect the extra we owe.

Japan by bus: Highways being overcrowded, long-distance bus service is limited. But Japan's comfortable intercity buses cost about half what you'll pay for train tickets. Many long-distance buses avoid traffic by going early in the morning or late at night. The popular nonstop Tokyo-Kyoto bus (midnight to 8 a.m.) costs half the Shinkansen fare and saves a night's lodging. Make reservations at the Green Window of the Japan Railway station or at the Japan Travel Bureau Office.

Within the city, subways are faster and easier than buses. Bus signs are only in Japanese, and drivers rarely speak English. Each tourist information office has route information. On some buses you enter at the rear and take a ticket from the machine. The tickets show the zone where you boarded. A display sign at the front changes to show how much your zone pays at each stop. As you exit, put the correct amount into the coin machine next to the driver. Some machines have a slot to make change. On other buses, you pay a flat fare as you enter the front.

Japan by taxi: Although more expensive, taxis cut through the hassles of finding a place. Just give them the address and sit back. For short distances, you won't go bust. Prices vary from place to place, but fares are approximately Y450 ($3) for the first 2 km (1.2 miles) and Y80 for each additional 370 meters (quarter mile). Train stations have taxi stands; elsewhere, stick out your arm to stop a taxi. Since most drivers don't speak English, keep your directions simple, such as "Miyako Hotel." Ask a local person to write your destination in Japanese. Always carry your hotel's card, your ticket to an easy taxi ride home. Addresses are often difficult to find in Japan. Be patient.

Japan by ferry: A pleasant and cheaper alternative to land travel is the ferry. Classes go from a large open room with tatami mats to private cabins. Ferries range from small passenger ferries to large ocean-going vessels with a variety of facilities. Since the longer journeys are overnight, you also save the cost of lodging. Check with the Tourist Information Center for schedules and rates.

Japan by bicycle: The least-traveled rural roads are in the mountainous interior. However, there are some nice, fairly flat rides along the coast, such as from Kanazawa north, then around the Noto-hanto peninsula on the west coast of Honshu. Your bike should be bagged when you take it on a train. To meet other cyclists, stay at one of a small number of cycling inns. For more information write to Japan

Cycling Association, Tokyo Cycling Association, c/o Maeda Industry Co Ltd., 3-8-1 Ueno, Taito-ku, Tokyo, tel. 833-3967 /8 /9.

You can often rent bikes near large train stations, at some tourist destinations, or at bicycle shops. Consider buying a used bike at a shop (unless you're over 5'9").

Japan by hitchhiking: It's almost too easy. Few Japanese hitchhike, so you'll be a curious standout on the road. Japanese are too polite to leave you standing long. Hitchhiking is safe for men and reasonably so for women who stick with private cars (truck drivers have fewer traditional scruples). Write the Kanji (Japanese characters) for your destination on a sign. Use the characters for "homen," meaning area. You're more likely to get a ride to "Tokyo area," than to "Tokyo." You'll do best from the edge of town. Wait at toll entrances since hitchhiking is not allowed on the expressways. Look pleadingly at oncoming drivers to induce guilt, which works well in Japan.

Japan by rental car: Rental cars are widely available for a reasonable charge (around $35 a day for a small car with no mileage charge). Check with the Tourist Information Center to find the best deal. Roads are usually narrow and crowded, and gas is more than double the U.S. price. Go long distance by train and then rent a car for travel in the rural areas. For a little more, you can rent a small van. These are great for camping.

Accommodations: The foreign and domestic offices of the Japan National Tourist Office, as well as the Tourist Information Centers (TIC) in Japan, are great sources of information for all kinds of accommodations.

Western hotels range in quality from internationally famous luxury hotels to simple but clean. They offer familiar services and facilities. You'll hardly know you've left home.

Ryokan, Japan's traditional inns are the place to experience the local culture and customs. A traditional Japanese breakfast and dinner are usually included in the cost. (You may get a Western-style breakfast option.) Your room is a living room by day, a dining room at mealtime, and a bedroom at night. You'll enjoy the traditional hot bath in the evening. Study the "cultural do's and don'ts" discussed in the Kyoto Back Door.

Ryokan are available in all sizes and prices, from $50 to $250 a night per person. Pick a small inn for a more intimate experience. Small groups save money by sharing a single room.

Of 90,000 ryokan around Japan, only 1,500 are government registered, and only 2,300 are members of the Japan Ryokan Association. Membership lists (available from the Japan National Tourist Organization) and the English "Ryokan Guide" are good starting places to find a ryokan—but only starting places. Check with the tourist information offices. At small train stations with no tourist offices, ask someone at the ticket window. Ask someone to write the two characters for ryokan on a piece of paper, then look for those characters on likely looking signs. Shop around, especially near train stations.

Minshuku are family-owned, overnight boardinghouses. They are a budget traveler's ryokan, offering the same traditional Japanese experience with a little less style and elegance. Comparable to Britain's bed and breakfasts, they are especially common in vacation and resort locations. See the Kyoto Back Door for more information.

Youth hostels are the cheapest accommodations in Japan. Hostels are plentiful and beautifully located in the mountains, along the coast, as well as in the cities. Their biggest drawback is a lack of privacy and flexibility. It's "lights out" at 10 p.m., and you must be out during the day. However, they're good places to meet young Japanese travelers. The Youth Hostel Association has an English listing of a limited number of hostels, available in the U.S. and in Japan (at the TIC and YH offices). The complete Japanese listing is easy to decipher since it uses international symbols, has maps, and the phone numbers are in Arabic numerals. A hostel bed costs about $15 a night. Dinner and breakfast are extra.

Shukubo are temple lodgings offering a unique view into another side of Japan. They offer minshuku-style simplicity and vegetarian meals. Ask to join their 30-minute meditation (*zazen*) in the morning. Some ask you to help with a few chores. Others just provide a room. Find shukubo by checking at the tourist office or with the local temple. Costs range from a voluntary donation to a fixed charge of up to $60 per person, including two meals.

In Kyoto, try the Ken-ninji Temple (in Higashiyama-ku) and the Shokokuji Temple (in Kamigyo-ku). The impressive Enryakuji Temple, atop Mount Hiei east of the city, sometimes takes overnighters. Mt. Koya, a day's trip from Kyoto or Osaka, is a mountaintop of temples.

Business hotels are no-frills Western-style hotels that cater mainly to businessmen. They offer small rooms with a bath and TV. Some are just a cubbyhole big enough to crawl into and sleep. These are usually found around train stations and cost about $40.

Home stays: Join SERVAS in the U.S. before you leave. They will provide a booklet of English-speaking hosts in Japan who open their houses to you for free. This is to meet Japanese and not to just get free lodging. See the section on host families in chapter 3.

Camping: Campgrounds are few compared to the U.S. There are some near popular beaches or in the mountains. You can camp for free off the road in rural areas if it's not obviously on private property. In some of the parks, tents can be rented.

Love hotels: Up to about 11 p.m., Japanese having affairs, unmarried couples, or partners living in a single bedroom apartment with three kids use these. After hours, budget travelers can use these rooms for just plain old sleeping, at very cheap rates. Plan on checking out early. Rooms are uniquely decorated. Look for the gaudiest building around and that's a love hotel.

Eating: You can eat well and inexpensively in Japan. You just need to know which places to avoid. The average meal in the average restaurant costs no more than here.

Most restaurants have wax models of food in the window with price tags. Prices are in Arabic numerals and sometimes in Japanese (carry a Japanese phrase book). In tourist areas, some places have English menus. Otherwise, show the waitress the wax model of what you want. For a full meal, point to the tray with rice, miso soup, salad, and a main dish of meat, poultry, or fish. The set is called a _teishoku_, average price 1,000 to 1,200 yen ($10). A good, easy-to-carry resource book is _Eating Cheap in Japan_ by Kimiko Nagasawa.

Types of restaurants: A _soba-ya_ serves noodles, thick or thin, hot or cold, in soup or in a bowl by themselves. A _sushi-ya_ specializes in raw fish, sliced or rolled in seasoned rice, served on seaweed. A _yakitori-ya_ makes skewered grilled chicken—often at a street stand. An _oden-ya_ offers fish, tofu (bean curd), eggs, and vegetables boiled together in a large pot of fish bouillon. An _okonomi-yaki-ya_ features a sort of egg foo yung—a thick, spicy pancake containing vegetables and meat (our favorite is _ika_, squid). It's recognized by the grill on every table. At _roba-ta-yaki-ya_ sit at the counter and point at the fish and vegetables behind the glass screen; prices are posted on the walls (get a Japanese friend to translate). A _chuka-ryori-ya_ is literally a "Chinese food place," with good food at low prices. A _kissaten_, coffee shop, often has spaghetti and other light Western-style meals. A _shokudo_, or "mixed restaurant," has a bit of everything. Famous table-cooked dishes like _sukiyaki_ and _shabu-shabu_ are beyond the budget of most Back Door travelers. Japan has good domestic beers (Kirin, Asahi, Sapporo, and Suntory) and excellent rice wine (_sake_), best served hot in winter and cold in summer.

For the best local specialties at low prices, eat at your ryokan or minshuku; often their room rate includes two meals. Some coffee shops (_kissaten_) provide a free or inexpensive Western-style breakfast with coffee ($3-$4) before 11 a.m. A wax display shows a cup next to toast and eggs. Just point to this. (One cup of coffee rents space to talk with friends all day or read the paper, worth it in crowded Japan). Noodle shops are everywhere and excellent value, $5 for a big bowl with vegetables, meat, or fish. All-you-can-eat lunch specials are reasonably priced at the Shakey's and Pizza Hut chains. Colonel Sanders and Ronald McDonald are everywhere. Order in Japanese: "**big-u mac-u and shake-u.**"

Essential taste bud vocabulary: *Tempura* is deep-fried seafood and vegetables usually with a dipping sauce. *Sukiyaki* is thinly sliced beef and vegetable cooked in a special broth. *Sushi* is various kinds of seafood (often raw) served on top of small rice patties. *Donburi* is a bowl of rice with chicken or meat, a nutritious and cheap meal. *Shabu-shabu* is a brass pot placed in the center of the table with ingredients similar to *sukiyaki* brought on a tray. Place the sliced meat and vegetables in boiling water to cook. *Kare raisu* is, as it sounds, white rice with a curried gravy on it. This is inexpensive and easy to pronounce. *Tonkatsu* is pork cutlet served with rice.

Cultural do's and don'ts: Learn to use chopsticks before going to Japan. Pick up the bowl of miso soup and sip it without using a spoon. If with friends, let them pour your beer or sake (and pour theirs for them). If you've had enough to drink, let your glass sit full or someone will top it off.

Tipping is not expected. Don't pour soy sauce over white rice, unless you're eating in a Chinese-style restaurant. We still remember the shock of the waitress as we soiled the rice with soy on our first visit to Japan.

Recommended reading: *The Japanese Mind: The Goliath Explained* by Robert C. Christopher provides a good introduction to all things Japanese, from politics to diplomacy to everyday life. *The Chrysanthemum and the Sword* by Ruth Benedict examines the Japanese psyche. *The Japanese: Change and Continuity* by Edwin O. Reischauer discusses Japanese society, culture, business, and government. His *Japan: The Story of a Nation* provides its history.

Guidebooks: *Japan: A Travel Survival Kit* by Ian McQueen (Lonely Planet) and *Japan Handbook* by Bisignani (Moon Publications) are excellent resources, with a lot of specifics such as budget lodging and getting to where you want to go. *Japan Solo* by Eiji Kanno and Constance O'Keefe is well organized, although not for budget travelers. *Japan Made Easy* by Boye De Mente (Passport Books) offers practical advice on the essentials of traveling in Japan.

Kyoto—Back Door Survival

Getting around: Pick up a route map from the Tourist Information Center (Kyoto Tower) for bus and subway routes. Purchase a one-day pass for unlimited bus or subway rides within the city. Buses run from 6:30 a.m. to 10 p.m., subways from 5:30 a.m. to 11:30 p.m.

Where to stay: See the Kyoto Back Door.

Cultural events: The Tourist Information Center has a list of what's happening. A Kabuki performance at the Minami-za Theater offers a traditional music-drama, fine costumes, and often great samurai battle scenes. Kabuki lasts up to five hours, but they let tourists out early. Ask at the office for a English summary of the action.

Noh is a very slow-moving drama. We prefer Bunraku (the puppet theater). Each large puppet is moved by at least two puppeteers dressed in black. Music and a chorus accompanies it. The National Bunraku Theatre is in Osaka.

See apprentice geisha dance April 1-20 at Gion's Kobu Kaburenjo Theater, and polished geisha May 1-24 and October 15-November 7 at the Pontocho Kaburenjo Theater.

Appendix

Country Statistics

Country	Sq. Miles	Pop. (in millions)	% Literacy	Tel. Code	Currency, #/US$ (Jan. 1993)	
China	3,718,780	1,100	76	86	Renminbi	4.7
Hong Kong	412	6	77	852	dollar	7.8
India	1,237,000	830	38	91	rupee	29
Indonesia	741,000	185	67	62	rupiah	2060
Japan	146,000	125	99	81	yen	124
S. Korea	38,000	43	88	82	won	787
Malaysia	127,000	18	58	60	ringgit	2.6
Myanmar (Burma)	261,000	42	67	95	Kyat	5.3
Nepal	57,000	18	21	977	rupee	47
Philippines	116,000	60	83	63	peso	25
Singapore	240	2.6	83	65	dollar	1.6
Sri Lanka	25,000	17	86	94	rupee	46
Taiwan	13,900	20	90	886	dollar	25
Thailand	200,000	55	88	66	baht	25

Country	Primary Language	Primary Ethnic Groups	Primary Religions
China	Chinese dialects	93% Han Chinese	Confucian, Taoist, Buddhist
Hong Kong	Chinese, English	95% Chinese	Buddhist, Taoist, Christian (10%)
India	English, Hindi	72% Indo-Aryan	83% Hindu, 25% Dravidian
Indonesia	Indonesian	45% Javanese	87% Muslim
Japan	Japanese	99% Japanese	Shinto, Buddhist
S. Korea	Korean	Korean	Confucian
Malaysia	Malay	65% Malay 20% Chinese	Muslim, Buddhist
Myanmar (Burma)	Burmese	68% Burman	85% Buddhist
Nepal	Nepali	Newar, Indian	90% Hindu
Philippines	English	Pilipin, Tagalog	83% Roman Catholic
Singapore	Chinese, English	76% Chinese 15% Malay	Taoist, Buddhist, Muslim, Christian
Sri Lanka	English,	4% Sinhalese	70% Buddhist Sinhala, Tamil
Taiwan	Chinese	84% Taiwanese	Buddhist, Confucian
Thailand	Thai	84% Thai	98% Buddhist

Capitals: Population in Millions

Rangoon	2.5	Kuala Lumpur	0.9
Beijing	5.8	Kathmandu	0.236
Victoria	1.1	Manila	1.6
New Delhi	0.28	Singapore	2.6
Jakarta	6.5	Colombo	0.59
Tokyo	8.3	Taipei	2.5
Seoul	9.6	Bangkok	5.1

Asian Weather
1st line, avg. daily temp.; 2nd line, avg. precipitation inches/month.

	J	F	M	A	M	J	J	A	S	O	N	D
CHINA												
Beijing	23	29	41	57	68	76	79	76	68	54	38	27
	.2	.2	.3	.6	1.3	3	9.8	5.7	2.3	.7	.3	.1
Shanghai	38	39	46	56	65	73	80	80	73	63	52	41
	1.9	2.3	3.3	3.6	3.7	7.1	5.8	5.7	5.0	2.9	2.0	1.4
HONG KONG	60	60	65	71	78	81	83	82	81	76	70	63
JAPAN												
Tokyo	39	40	46	56	64	70	78	80	74	63	53	44
	1.8	2.9	4.1	5.2	5.2	7.0	5.9	6.0	8.4	8.7	4.0	2.6
Kyoto	38	39	44	54	63	71	79	81	74	62	52	43
	2.2	2.9	4.5	6.0	6.3	10.0	9.0	6.5	7.8	5.2	3.4	2.2
Sapporo	22	23	30	42	52	61	69	72	63	51	39	27
	4.4	3.3	2.6	2.6	2.3	2.6	3.9	4.2	5.7	4.4	4.4	4.1
KOREA												
Seoul	23	29	38	51	16	69	76	78	68	56	43	30
	.7	.8	2.2	2.7	3.4	6.6	14.1	8.8	5.6	1.9	1.4	1.3
COMMONWEALTH OF INDEPENDENT STATES (former USSR)												
Khabarovsk	-10	1	16	37	52	62	68	67	65	40	17	-3
	.2	.2	.3	.9	2.6	3.9	5.1	4.9	1.9	1.3	.6	.3
MYANMAR (Burma)												
Rangoon	79	81	84	87	85	82	81	81	82	83	82	80
	.2	.2	.3	1.6	12.0	18.0	21.4	19.9	15.2	6.9	2.8	.4
Pagan	71	75	82	87	87	83	82	82	82	81	76	71
	.0	.0	.2	.6	2.9	3.5	1.8	3.5	5.1	4.0	1.4	.3
NEPAL												
Kathmandu	49	54	60	67	72	75	75	75	74	67	59	51
	.6	1.6	.9	2.3	4.8	9.7	14.7	13.6	6.1	1.5	.3	.4
SRI LANKA												
Colombo	79	80	81	82	82	81	81	81	81	80	79	79
	3.5	3.8	4.6	10.2	13.9	8.3	5.5	4.9	6.0	13.9	12.8	6.9
Kandy	74	75	77	79	78	76	85	76	75	75	75	74
	4.7	3.3	4.7	7.4	7.5	7.3	6.1	5.6	4.8	10.2	9.8	8.3
BANGLADESH												
Dhaka	65	69	78	85	85	84	83	83	83	81	74	67
	.3	1.2	2.4	5.2	9.7	13.3	12.7	13.2	9.5	4.7	.8	.2

	J	F	M	A	M	J	J	A	S	O	N	D
INDIA												
Bombay	76	77	80	84	86	84	81	81	81	83	82	78
	.1	.0	.0	.1	.6	20.5	27.9	17.3	11.7	3.5	.8	.1
Calcutta	68	73	82	87	88	87	84	84	85	82	75	69
	.5	.9	1.1	1.7	4.8	10.2	11.8	12.0	11.4	6.3	1.4	.1
New Delhi	58	62	73	83	92	94	88	86	85	79	68	60
	1.0	.9	.7	.3	.3	2.6	8.3	6.8	5.9	1.2	.0	.2
Madras	76	78	82	87	91	90	87	86	85	83	78	76
	.9	.3	.6	1.0	2.0	2.1	3.3	4.9	4.0	10.5	12.2	5.5
Srinagar	34	38	47	56	64	71	76	75	69	57	46	38
	2.9	2.8	4.1	3.1	2.5	1.4	2.4	2.5	1.3	1.1	.7	1.4
INDONESIA												
Jakarta	78	78	79	80	80	79	79	79	80	80	79	79
	12.1	12.3	7.8	5.2	4.0	3.4	2.3	1.6	2.7	4.4	5.4	8.3
Denpasar	80	80	80	80	79	78	78	78	79	81	82	81
	13.1	9.6	8.1	3.6	3.2	2.8	2.2	2.0	1.4	4.4	6.2	11.7
Medan	77	78	79	79	80	79	79	79	78	78	77	77
	5.7	3.3	4.2	5.2	6.8	5.2	5.2	6.8	8.4	10.5	9.4	8.5
MALAYSIA												
Penanag	81	82	83	83	82	82	82	81	81	81	81	81
	3.7	3.5	5.7	7.9	10.9	7.3	7.7	11.0	15.1	16.6	11.5	5.3
Kota Bahru	77	78	80	81	81	81	80	80	79	79	78	77
	8.9	4.8	6.0	4.2	4.9	5.8	5.6	6.4	8.1	11.8	24.5	24.5
PHILIPPINES												
Manila	78	80	83	85	85	83	80	79	79	80	79	78
	.9	.5	.7	1.3	5.2	10.2	17.3	16.9	14.2	7.7	5.8	2.6
SINGAPORE	78	79	80	81	81	80	80	79	79	79	79	79
	10.1	6.9	7.7	7.5	6.9	6.9	6.8	7.8	7.1	8.3	10.1	10.3
THAILAND												
Bangkok	81	83	85	88	85	83	82	82	81	80	79	79
	.3	.8	1.4	2.3	7.9	6.4	6.4	7.0	12.2	8.2	2.6	.2

Selected Festivals and Holidays

China
Full moon of February-March: **Spring Festival**, a three-day celebration over the traditional Chinese New Year.

June 1: **Children's Day**

October 1: **National Day** observes the 1949 founding of the People's Republic.

Hong Kong
Full moon of January-February (1st day of 1st lunar month): Honkers go bonkers on **Chinese New Year** with noise, light, and bright red colors designed to drive away the demon of winter.

Late April (23rd day of 3rd lunar month): **Festival of Tin Hau**. This colorful festival, dedicated to the mother goddess of the sea, is most important to the colony's 70,000 boat people.

Early May (8th day of 4th lunar month): The **Bun Festival** on Cheung Chau Island placates spirits with an offering of buns. It climaxes with a bizarre race, almost like an adult Easter egg hunt, to see who can accumulate the most buns by climbing the 80-foot bamboo towers on which they're offered.

India

January 26: **Republic Day**, commemorating India's establishment as a republic in 1950. The most spectacular event is a military parade in New Delhi, the capital.

February 22: **Maha Shivaratri**, a day of fasting, chanting, and temple processions dedicated to Shiva. Varanasi has a wonderful parade in the Chowk area.

February-March: **Holi**, bonfires and festive water fighting throughout the Hindu world.

September-October: **Dussehra** is a major 10-day festival celebrating Rama's legendary victory over the demon king, Rawana. The _Ramayana_ is continually reenacted, huge images are burned, and some cities have parades and fireworks.

October-November: **Diwali** (also Deepavali) is a happy Hindu holiday in which oil lamps light the night to lead Rama home from exile. Day One of this five-day festival is the start of the Indian business year.

Indonesia

Because 90% of Indonesians are "officially" Muslim, the country follows the 354-day Islamic calendar. Thus the festival calendar slides back 11 or 12 days each year. Obtain a current events listing from the Indonesian Tourist Promotion Office.

Ramadan, the ninth month of the Islamic calendar, is a time of fasting. The devout are expected to abstain from food, alcohol, tobacco, and sex from sunrise to sunset. It's an awkward time to be a traveler in Indonesia in strict Muslim areas. (Bali and some other islands are predominantly Hindu or Christian.)

Lebaran or Hari Raya Puasa, called Id-ul'Fitr in Arabic, celebrates the end of Ramadan with religious songs and processions and the exchange of gifts. Most Muslims spend the day visiting friends and relatives and gorging themselves on food.

Nyepi, the Balinese new year, is a national holiday observed the day after the new moon of the ninth month of the Balinese (not the Islamic) calendar. Hindus consider it a day of retreat and spiritual purification. The other most important Balinese holiday is **Galungan**, a day of feasting, dancing, and gamelan music 210 days after Nyepi.

The following holidays go by the solar calendar and do not change from year to year:

April 21: **Kartini Day** is a national holiday in memory of Raden Ajeng Kartini, a turn-of-the-century women's emancipator. Women are not expected to work on this day; they traditionally turn out in colorful regional costume.

August 17: **Proklamasi Kemerdekaan**, or Independence Day, is observed with ceremonies throughout the country.

Japan

January 1: **Ganjitsu**, or New Year's Day, is observed with gift-giving and visits to Shinto shrines.

Early February: **Yuki Matsuri**, Sapporo's Snow Festival, is famous for the huge number of elaborate snow sculptures in downtown parks.

May 5: **Kodomo-no Hi**, Children's Day, urges parents to respect their children and children to show gratitude to their parents. Tubular carp are traditionally flown from poles to honor male children: this holiday previously was Boys Day. This and other national holidays comprise Golden Week, during which little or no work is done in Japan.

July 13-15: **O-Bon**, the Feast of Lanterns, is a Buddhist rite celebrated all over the country. Lanterns are lit for the souls of the deceased, who are believed to come back to Earth during this period. In Kyoto, huge Japanese characters are set ablaze on the surrounding hillside.

July 16-17: **Gion Matsuri** in Kyoto has been celebrated since the ninth century, when it was staged to beseech the gods to end a plague—which they did. Colorful morning and afternoon processions are among the most famous in Japan.

August 6: The **Peace Festival** in Hiroshima has been held since 1947 to comfort the souls of those killed in the 1945 bombing and to pray for permanent world peace.

October 22: **Jidai Matsuri**, Kyoto's Festival of the Eras, commemorates the city's founding in 794. Those who take part in the main parade dress according to the different periods of Kyoto history.

Malaysia

May through September: **Giant turtle season** on the east coast of peninsular Malaysia, mainly on Rantau Abang, where rare leatherback turtles lay their eggs.

June-July: **Kite-flying** and **bird-singing** competitions are important adult recreations, especially in the more traditional east coast states of Kelantan and Trengganu.

June 29: Portuguese and Eurasian Catholics of Malacca celebrate the **Festa de San Pedro** with colorful boat parades and feasting.

Traditional Muslim holidays (see Indonesia), Hindu festivals and holidays (see India and Nepal), and Chinese festivities (see China and Hong Kong) are celebrated throughout Malaysia by those religious groups. Malays, who comprise roughly half the country's population, are Muslim, more vigorously on the peninsular east coast.

Myanmar (Burma)

Full moon of January-February: **Htamane**, the harvest festival, is a time of great feasting.

Full moon of March-April: **Thingyan, Burmese New Year**. A three- or four-day "water throwing" festival, this is Burma's biggest bash.

Full moon of April-May: **Buddha's birthday.**

Full moon of August-September. **Boat racing festivals** are held all over Burma. The best are among the leg-rowers of Inle Lake.

Full moon of December-January: Local temple festivals are excuses for merry-making, often with dramatic performances, magic arts, and boat and pony races. Among the best are the festivals at Ananda Temple in Pagan and the Shwedagon Pagoda in Rangoon (sometimes held in February-March).

Nepal

February: **Tibetan New Year** is celebrated at the Bodhnath stupa with lamaistic processions and the burning of oil lamps. **Holi**, held throughout the Hindu world, is a mischievous occasion marked by the throwing of colored powder and water.

Mid-April: **Nepalese New Year** celebration. Hill people throng to Kathmandu for ritual baths, the honoring of their dead, and a ceremonial tug-of-war followed by a citywide parade.

June: The Sherpa religious festival of **Mani Rimbu** is held at Namche Bazar, near the foot of Mount Everest. It lasts three days. Monks perform masked dramas and dances at the Thame monastery. Six months later, ceremonies are repeated at the Thyangboche monastery.

August: **Gaijatra**, the festival of cows, is an eight-day carnival held in the main city squares to honor those who have died during the past year with dancing, music, and colorful costumes.

September: The eight-day **Indrajatra** festival honors the god of rain with the like of torch-lit elephant dancing, heavy beer drinking, and a procession dedicated to the Kumari, Kathmandu's "living goddess."

October: **Dasain (Durga Puja)** marks the triumph of good over evil and celebrates fertility with ten days of ritual seed planting, kite contests, military parades, and animal sacrifices. On the last day, the king and queen personally greet all visitors to the royal palace.

Late October or early November: **Tihar (Diwali or Deepavali)**, the five-day Festival of Lights, is held. Crows, dogs, cows, and bulls are honored on the first four days, respectively, and lights greet Lakshmi, the goddess of wealth, when she visits every home on the third evening.

Sri Lanka

January (one week concluding on full moon): **Duruthu Perahera**, Kelaniya Temple, near Colombo. The mythical first visit of the Buddha to Sri Lanka is celebrated with great pomp and ceremony.

April 13 or 14: **Avurudu**, the Sinhalese and Tamil New Year, is tied to astrology rather than Buddhism or Hinduism. After preparatory house-cleaning and body purification (with fasting and prayer), families light fires and cook the year's first meal at the exact time the sun enters the constellation Aries. The exchange of money and betel, and the anointing of family members with oil, are traditional practices.

May (full moon and following day): **Wesak** is the most sacred of all Buddhist holidays, honoring the Buddha's birth, enlightenment, and passing to Nirvana. Temple pilgrimages, homemade paper lanterns, and displays depicting chapters of the Buddha's life are seen everywhere.

July and/or August: The **Kataragama** Festival in the southeast of the island features not only two weeks of fire-walking and other Hindu acts of self-mortification but also Buddhist, Muslim, and Christian worship, vows, and alms-giving. The three-day **Vel Festival** in Colombo immediately follows the Kataragama Festival with pageantry and colorful processions honoring the trident of the Hindu god Skanda.

July–August: Some say Kandy's **Esala Perhala**, 12 days concluding on the full moon of August, is Asia's single greatest festival. Honoring the sacred tooth relic of the Buddha, symbol of Sri Lankan sovereignty, it involves 11 nights of parading— each procession more spectacular than the previous one—and a final day parade following a water-cutting ritual. Dozens of brilliantly decorated elephants are the stars of the show, along with various costumed dancers and musicians.

Thailand

January 1: **New Year's Day**. Though there are observances throughout the country, the best are at the three-day **Winter Fair** in Chiang Mai.

February (full moon): **Maha Puja** is an important Buddhist holiday, highlighted by the release of caged birds at temples.

April 13-15: During **Songkran**, the classical New Year, Thais throw water on Buddha images—and happily drench anyone else who happens to be around. There are also parades, boat races, and folk dances.

Mid to late May (full moon): **Viksakha Puja (Wesak)**, the day on which Buddhists observe the birth, enlightenment, and passing to Nirvana of the Buddha.

Early November: The annual **Elephant Roundup** at Surin, in northeast Thailand, sees hundreds of trained elephants and their mahouts putting on a spectacular presentation for the benefit of tourists.

November (full moon): **Loy Krathong** is a nighttime spectacle in which Thais sail small lotus-shaped boats, carrying candles and incense sticks, down rivers and canals to honor the water spirits and carry away their sins. It's especially colorful in Chiang Mai.

December 5: The **King's Birthday**, a national holiday, is celebrated with flags and portraits lining the streets of the cities, especially around the Grand Palace.

Send Us a Postcard

It's our goal to make this book the most helpful introduction to independent Asian travel around. Any suggestions, criticisms, or feedback from you would really be appreciated. Write to us at Europe Through the Back Door, Box 2009, Edmonds, WA 98020, tel. 206/771-8303. Traveling computer buffs may want to tap into our free travel information bulletin board system (BBS: 206/771-1902, 1200 to 2400, 8/N/1). Thanks and happy travels.

All Authors' Royalties from This Book Go to Support Third World Development Organizations

Our travels have given us both a global perspective and an appreciation of our own country. This "global perspective," our most prized souvenir, shines an unflattering light on American consumerism.

The economic canyon that separates our world from the undeveloped world grows bigger every year. Our travels have painted the other half in vivid human faces. With these in mind, we are happy to contribute all of the royalties we make from the sale of this book to Bread for the World, Oxfam, and other organizations working to help the poorest parts of our world develop and become self-sufficient. For specifics, write to us at Europe Through the Back Door, Box 2009, Edmonds, WA 98020.

A New Enlightenment Through Travel?

Thomas Jefferson said, "Travel makes you wiser but less happy." We think he was right. And "less happy" is a good thing. It's the growing pains of a broadening perspective, a tearing off of the hometown blinders, reality shock. It exposes you to new ways of thinking and to people who live by different, "self-evident" truths. We've shared with you a whole book of our love of travel. Now allow us to share some thoughts on how travel has given us new ways of thinking.

On any trip, the biggest culture shock can occur when you return home. America is a land of unprecedented material wealth. Only 4 percent of the world's population, we gobble up over 25 percent of the global economic pie. We've built a wall of money around our borders, insulating ourselves from world problems. We can't see that our rampant pursuit of material wealth, both as individuals and as a society, has global repercussions: long-term damage to the Earth, impoverishment of weaker nations, and military aggression to maintain our disproportionate standard of living. Only by traveling can we see ourselves as others see us.

For us (Rick and Bob), travel has brought a new perspective. Like the astronauts, we've seen a planet with no boundaries. It's a tender green, blue, and white organism that will live or die as a unit. We're just two of six billion equally precious people. And by traveling we've seen humankind as a body that somehow must tell its fat cells to cool it, because nearly half of the body is starving and the whole thing is threatened.

Returning home, we've found that you can continue the mind-expanding aspect of travel by pursuing new ideas. Expose yourself to some radical thinking. *Small Is Beautiful* and *Fate of the Earth*-type books, *The Nation* magazine, and the newsletters of small peace and justice groups are just a few sources that have opened our eyes and made us think globally.

A new enlightenment is needed. Just as the French Enlightenment led us into the modern age of science and democracy, a new enlightenment must teach us the necessity of realistic and sustainable affluence, global understanding, peaceful coexistence, and controlling nature by obeying her.

We hope that your travels give you a fun and relaxing vacation or adventure—and also that they'll make you an active patriot of the planet.

Bob and Rick

About the Authors

Bob Effertz (on right) has spent part of almost every year since 1977 in Asia. He enjoys sharing his travel experiences and motivating others to seek their own by teaching Asian travel classes at the University of Washington's Experimental College. Since he'd rather drum than write, this book took lots of self discipline—at times reminding him of his West Point days. While "free as the breeze" is easy on top of a Nepali bus, Bob's ongoing challenge is maintaining that freedom in his work as a school psychologist.

Rick Steves (on left) has gained notoriety as a guru of alternative European travel. Since 1980 he has led Back Door tours of Europe and written 14 travel guidebooks. His classic *Europe Through the Back Door* started a cult of people who insist on washing their socks in sinks and taking showers "down the hall" even when not traveling. Rick also publishes the (free, quarterly) *Back Door Travel Newsletter*, writes a weekly newspaper column, writes and hosts a national PBS travel series called "Travels in Europe," and lectures throughout the U.S. After five trips through Asia purely for the joy of travel, the idea for this book was born. A native of Seattle, Rick and his wife are now learning about traveling with two kids.

Index

Rick Steves' BACK DOOR CATALOG

All items are field tested, discount priced (prices include tax and shipping),
completely guaranteed, and highly recommended for the Asian traveler.

Convertible Back Door Bag $70

At 9"x22"x14" our specially designed, sturdy bag is
maximum carry-on-the-plane size (fits under the seat) and
your key to footloose and fancy-free Asian travel. Made of
rugged water resistant cordura nylon, it converts easily
from a smart looking suitcase to a handy rucksack. It has
padded hide-away shoulder straps, top and side handles,
and a detachable shoulder strap (for use as a suitcase).
Lockable perimeter zippers allow easy access to the roomy
2,700 cubic inch central compartment. Two large outside
compartments are perfect for frequently used items. A nylon stuff bag is also
included. Over 40,000 Back Door travelers have used these bags around the
world. Available in black, grey, navy blue and teal green.

Moneybelt $8

Absolutely required throughout Asia. Our sturdy
nylon, ultra-light, under-the-pants pouch is just big
enough to carry your essentials (passport, airline tickets, travelers checks,
and so on) comfortably. Rick won't travel without one -- neither should you.
Comes in neutral beige, with a nylon zipper. One size fits all.

Sleep Sack $20

A must for the budget traveler in Asia, our lightweight (less than 1 lb.) 100%
cotton sleep sack puts a cozy barrier between you and potentially buggy
bedding. It measures a generous 35"x86" and comes with a built-in pillow
pocket, velcro flap closure, and its own space-saving stuff bag.

Compact Toiletries Kit $20

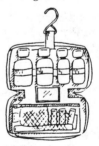

The perfect bag for your toiletries. Zips open to reveal:
2 compartments (one in quick-dry mesh); 5 elastic-
held squeeze bottles (for your favorite shampoo, creme
rinse, soap, bug juice, etc.); 3 pill bottles; a toothbrush
case; 3 moistened towelettes; a handy velcro-fastened
mirror; and a big hook for hanging in the open position. All this in a sturdy nylon that measures just
9"x4½"x2". Comes in hard-to-leave-behind red.

Free Travel Newsletter/Catalog

Although our emphasis is on Europe, you'll find lots of travel tips and
accessories that will make your Asian travels more rewarding, too.
Call us for a free 64-page issue.

All orders will be processed within 2 weeks. Prices good through 1993 (maybe
longer), and include tax and shipping. Rush orders add $10. Sorry, no credit cards.
Send checks to: **Europe Through the Back Door, 109 Fourth Ave. N**
PO Box 2009, Edmonds, WA 98020   ❖   *Phone: (206)771-8303*

Other Books from John Muir Publications

Asia Through the Back Door, 4th ed., 400 pp. $16.95 (available 7/93)

Belize: A Natural Destination, 336 pp. $16.95

Costa Rica: A Natural Destination, 2nd ed., 310 pp. $16.95

Elderhostels: The Students' Choice, 2nd ed., 304 pp. $15.95

Environmental Vacations: Volunteer Projects to Save the Planet, 2nd ed., 248 pp. $16.95

Europe 101: History & Art for the Traveler, 4th ed., 350 pp. $15.95

Europe Through the Back Door, 11th ed., 432 pp. $17.95

Europe Through the Back Door Phrase Book: French, 160 pp. $4.95

Europe Through the Back Door Phrase Book: German, 160 pp. $4.95

Europe Through the Back Door Phrase Book: Italian, 168 pp. $4.95

Europe Through the Back Door Phrase Book: Spanish & Portuguese, 288 pp. $4.95

A Foreign Visitor's Guide to America, 224 pp. $12.95

Great Cities of Eastern Europe, 256 pp. $16.95

Guatemala: A Natural Destination, 336 pp. $16.95

Indian America: A Traveler's Companion, 4th ed., 448 pp. $17.95 (available 7/93)

Interior Furnishings Southwest, 256 pp. $19.95

Mona Winks: Self-Guided Tours of Europe's Top Museums, 2nd ed., 448 pp. $16.95

Opera! The Guide to Western Europe's Great Houses, 296 pp. $18.95

Paintbrushes and Pistols: How the Taos Artists Sold the West, 288 pp. $17.95

The People's Guide to Mexico, 9th ed., 608 pp. $18.95

Ranch Vacations: The Complete Guide to Guest and Resort, Fly-Fishing, and Cross-Country Skiing Ranches, 2nd ed., 396 pp. $18.95

The Shopper's Guide to Art and Crafts in the Hawaiian Islands, 272 pp. $13.95

The Shopper's Guide to Mexico, 224 pp. $9.95

Understanding Europeans, 272 pp. $14.95

Undiscovered Islands of the Caribbean, 3rd ed., 288 pp. $14.95

Undiscovered Islands of the Mediterranean, 2nd ed., 224 pp. $13.95

Undiscovered Islands of the U.S. and Canadian West Coast, 288 pp. $12.95

Unique Colorado, 112 pp. $10.95 (available 6/93)

Unique Florida, 112 pp. $10.95 (available 7/93)

Unique New Mexico, 112 pp. $10.95 (available 6/93)

A Viewer's Guide to Art: A Glossary of Gods, People, and Creatures, 144 pp. $10.95

The Visitor's Guide to the Birds of the Eastern National Parks: United States and Canada, 410 pp. $15.95

2 to 22 Days Series
Each title offers 22 flexible daily itineraries useful for planning vacations of any length. Aside from valuable general information, included are "must see" attractions *and* hidden "jewels."

2 to 22 Days in the American Southwest, 1993 ed., 176 pp. $10.95

2 to 22 Days in Asia, 1993 ed., 176 pp. $9.95

2 to 22 Days in Australia, 1993 ed., 192 pp. $9.95

2 to 22 Days in California, 1993 ed., 192 pp. $9.95

2 to 22 Days in Europe, 1993 ed., 288 pp. $13.95

2 to 22 Days in Florida, 1993 ed., 192 pp. $10.95

2 to 22 Days in France, 1993 ed., 192 pp. $10.95

2 to 22 Days in Germany, Austria, & Switzerland, 1993 ed., 224 pp. $10.95

2 to 22 Days in Great Britain, 1993 ed., 192 pp. $10.95

2 to 22 Days Around the Great Lakes, 1993 ed., 192 pp. $10.95

2 to 22 Days in Hawaii, 1993 ed., 192 pp. $9.95

2 to 22 Days in Italy, 208 pp. $10.95

2 to 22 Days in New England, 1993 ed., 192 pp. $10.95

2 to 22 Days in New Zealand, 1993 ed., 192 pp. $9.95

2 to 22 Days in Norway, Sweden, & Denmark, 1993 ed., 192 pp. $10.95

2 to 22 Days in the Pacific Northwest, 1993 ed., 192 pp. $10.95

2 to 22 Days in the Rockies, 1993 ed., 192 pp. $10.95

2 to 22 Days in Spain & Portugal, 192 pp. $10.95

2 to 22 Days in Texas, 1993 ed., 192 pp. $9.95

2 to 22 Days in Thailand, 1993 ed., 180 pp. $9.95

22 Days (or More) Around the World, 1993 ed., 264 pp. $12.95

Automotive Titles
How to Keep Your VW Alive, 15th ed., 464 pp. $21.95
How to Keep Your Subaru Alive 480 pp. $21.95
How to Keep Your Toyota Pickup Alive 392 pp. $21.95

How to Keep Your Datsun/
Nissan Alive 544 pp. $21.95
The Greaseless Guide to
Car Care Confidence,
224 pp. $14.95
Off-Road Emergency Repair
& Survival, 160 pp. $9.95

TITLES FOR YOUNG READERS AGES 8 AND UP

**"Kidding Around" Travel
Guides for Young Readers**
All the "Kidding Around"
Travel guides are 64 pages
and $9.95 paper, except for
Kidding Around Spain and
**Kidding Around the
National Parks of the South-
west**, which are 108 pages
and $12.95 paper.

Kidding Around Atlanta
Kidding Around Boston,
2nd ed.
Kidding Around Chicago,
2nd ed.
Kidding Around the Hawaiian
Islands
Kidding Around London
Kidding Around Los
Angeles
Kidding Around the
National Parks of the
Southwest
Kidding Around New York
City, 2nd ed.
Kidding Around Paris
Kidding Around Philadelphia
Kidding Around San Diego
Kidding Around San
Francisco
Kidding Around Santa Fe
Kidding Around Seattle
Kidding Around Spain
Kidding Around Washing-
ton, D.C., 2nd ed.

**"Extremely Weird" Series
for Young Readers.** Written
by Sarah Lovett, each is 48
pages and $9.95 paper.
Extremely Weird Bats
Extremely Weird Birds
**Extremely Weird
Endangered
Species**
Extremely Weird Fishes
Extremely Weird Frogs
Extremely Weird Insects
Extremely Weird Mammals
(available 8/93)
**Extremely Weird Micro
Monsters** (available 8/93)
Extremely Weird Primates
Extremely Weird Reptiles
**Extremely Weird Sea
Creatures**
Extremely Weird Snakes
(available 8/93)
Extremely Weird Spiders

**"Masters of Motion" Series
for Young Readers.** Each
title is 48 pages and $9.95
paper.
**How to Drive an Indy Race
Car**
How to Fly a 747
**How to Fly the Space
Shuttle**

**"X-ray Vision" Series for
Young Readers.** Each title is
48 pages and $9.95 paper.
**Looking Inside Cartoon Ani-
mation**
**Looking Inside Sports Aer-
odynamics**
Looking Inside the Brain
**Looking Inside Sunken
Treasure**
**Looking Inside Telescopes
and the Night Sky**

Multicultural Titles for Young Readers
Native Artists of North America, 48 pp. $14.95 hardcover
The Indian Way: Learning to Communicate with Mother Earth, 114 pp. $9.95
The Kids' Environment Book: What's Awry and Why, 192 pp. $13.95
Kids Explore America's African-American Heritage, 112 pp. $8.95
Kids Explore America's Hispanic Heritage, 112 pp. $7.95

Environmental Titles for Young Readers
Rads, Ergs, and Cheeseburgers: The Kids' Guide to Energy and the Environment, 108 pp. $12.95
Habitats: Where the Wild Things Live, 48 pp. $9.95
The Kids' Environment Book: What's Awry and Why, 192 pp. $13.95

Ordering Information
Please check your local bookstore for our books, or call 1-800-888-7504 to order direct from us. All orders are shipped via UPS; see chart below to calculate your shipping charge to U.S. destinations. **No P.O. Boxes please; we must have a street address to ensure delivery.** If the book you request is not available, we will hold your check until we can ship it. Foreign orders will be shipped surface rate unless otherwise requested; please enclose $3.00 for the first item and $1.00 for each additional item.

For U.S. Orders

Totaling	Add
Up to $15.00	$4.25
$15.01 to $45.00	$5.25
$45.01 to $75.00	$6.25
$75.01 or more	$7.25

Methods of Payment
Check, money order, American Express, MasterCard, or Visa. We cannot be responsible for cash sent through the mail. For credit card orders, include your card number, expiration date, and your signature, or call (800) 888-7504. American Express card orders can be shipped only to billing address of cardholder. Sorry, no C.O.D.'s. Residents of sunny New Mexico, add 6.125% tax to total.

Address all orders and inquiries to:
John Muir Publications
P.O. Box 613
Santa Fe, NM 87504
(505) 982-4078
(800) 888-7504